"PROBABLY THE MOST FRIGHTENING BOOK I'VE EVER ENCOUNTERED. . . . *HUNTING HUMANS* MAY BE ONE OF THE MOST IMPORTANT BOOKS WRITTEN IN THE LAST 25 YEARS." —*Calgary Sun*

"I'm not good-looking. I'm not educated, but I was able to put something over on high-class people. . . . They was all college kids and I never had anything in my life, but I outsmarted them."
Albert DeSalvo, "The Boston Strangler"

"It was only hostile aggression. . . ."
David Berkowitz, the "Son of Sam" killer

"What's one less person on the face of the earth, anyway?"
Ted Bundy, convicted of killing two Florida co-eds, suspected of killing at least forty other young women

"How could I be particular about the people I had to kill?"
Charles Starkweather, the Nebraska killer

"SCATHING . . . RIVETING . . . AN IMPORTANT AND TIMELY BOOK." —*MacLean's* magazine

"*HUNTING HUMANS* . . . WORKS BECAUSE OF ITS RICH ANALYSIS. . . . ELLIOTT LEYTON SPARES NO DETAIL WHILE PROVING FACT STRANGER THAN FICTION."
—*Psychology Today*

**Winner, 1986 *Crime Writers of Canada* Award
A Canadian National Bestseller**

ELLIOTT LEYTON is an anthropologist at Memorial University of Newfoundland, Canada, and is the author of two previous books.

HUNTING HUMANS

INSIDE THE MINDS OF MASS MURDERERS

Previously published as *Compulsive Killers*

ELLIOTT LEYTON

POCKET BOOKS

New York   London   Toronto   Sydney   Tokyo

Previously published as *Compulsive Killers*

POCKET BOOKS, a division of Simon & Schuster Inc.
1230 Avenue of the Americas, New York, N.Y. 10020

Copyright © 1986 by Elliott Leyton
Cover photos copyright © 1988 Wide World Photos

Published by arrangement with New York University Press

ISBN: 0-671-65961-8

First Pocket Books printing September 1988

10 9 8 7 6 5 4 3 2 1

POCKET and colophon are trademarks of
Simon & Schuster Inc.

Printed in the U.S.A.

FOR THOSE WHO TAUGHT ME HOW TO LIVE
. . . *especially Sam Feinstein, Morley Clary, Bonnie Leyton, Jack Clary, Barry Naimark, Jim Clary, Stuart Philpott, and Marilyn Clary*

FOR THOSE WHO TAUGHT ME HOW TO THINK
. . . *especially Rex Clark, Judith Adler, George Story, and Elliot Liebow*

AND IN MEMORY OF MY BELOVED LATE AUNT
Tillie Feinstein, who talked with me late into the dry prairie night

Contents

Contents

HUNTING HUMANS

1.
THE MODERN MULTIPLE MURDERER

"For murder, though it have no tongue, will speak
With most miraculous organ."

HAMLET

Are multiple murderers merely "insane"? Can such bizarre
behavior be dismissed as simple psychiatric or genetic
freakishness? There is an ancient chord in our civilization
which insists that such terrible acts be interpreted in terms
of possession by evil spirits, or witchcraft (an explanation
which reverberates today in the press's frequent, and inaccurate, speculation that occultism is a motive for these
crimes); and a more modern variation of this theme similarly dismisses the acts with notions of possession by "mental
disease." It would be most comforting if we could continue
to accept such explanations, for they satisfyingly banish
guilt beyond our responsibility; yet to do so would beg the
question—why does modern America produce proportion-
ately so many more of these "freaks" than any other
industrial nation? Moreover, if the killers are merely insane, why do they in fact so rarely display the cluster of
readily identifiable clinical symptoms (including disorders
of thought and affect) which psychiatrists agree mark mental illness? In one important sense, of course, any person

1

who murders another human being has abandoned all reason and sanity; yet such a position is essentially *moral,* and does not help us in an objective attempt to understand the cause and meaning of such a phenomenon.

I first embarked upon this journey into the souls of modern multiple murderers because I was unable to understand the profound personal fulfillment they seemed to derive from their killings. Now, after four years of total immersion in the killers' diaries, confessions, psychiatric interviews, statements to the press, videotapes, and photographs, I see their motives as so obvious and their gratifications as so intense that I can only marvel at how *few* of them walk the streets of America. Nevertheless, their numbers do continue to grow at a disturbing rate: until the 1960s, they were anomalies who appeared perhaps once a decade; but by the 1980s, one was spawned virtually each month. Today, according to unofficial U.S. Justice Department estimates, there may be as many as one hundred multiple murderers killing in America, stealing the lives of thousands. The uncomfortable conclusion reached in this book is that there will undoubtedly be many more before this epoch in our social history draws to a close. They may still be statistically rare, but I shall try to show that they are no freaks: rather, they can only be fully understood as representing the logical extension of many of the central themes in their culture—of worldly ambition, of success and failure, and of manly avenging violence. Although they take several forms—the serial killer whose murders provide both revenge and a lifelong *celebrity career;* and the mass killer, who no longer wishes to live, and whose murders constitute his *suicide note*— they can only be accurately and objectively perceived as prime embodiment of their civilization, not twisted derangement.

The mid-1980s were years of unprecedented growth, experimentation, and innovation among multiple murderers, years in which all previous "records" were broken and sacrosanct social barriers were pierced. In 1984 alone, a fortyish drifter named *Henry Lee Lucas* delivered his confessions in which he claimed to have tortured and murdered hundreds of women, a number far in excess of any previous claimant's.* Lucas lived with his fifteen-year-old common-law wife in a trailer parked in The House of Prayer For All People campground, a former chicken farm operated as a Pentecostal retreat in a small town in Texas. His eight-year killing spree was terminated only when he murdered an elderly local woman who had befriended him, which provoked his close scrutiny by the local police. Jailed on little more than suspicion, he passed a note to a deputy, claiming that "I have done something terrible, and I want to talk to sheriff." It was only then that inquisitive police began the lengthy interrogations and checking of his claims. Lucas outlined his story to a largely disbelieving audience, spinning an unrivaled tale of rape, torture, dismemberment, and murder, while conceding only that "I know it ain't normal for a person to go out and kill a girl just to have sex with her."

The thirteenth child of a prostitute mother, Lucas began his career in 1960 when, at the age of twenty-three, he stabbed his mother to death in her bed. He spent the following fifteen years in prisons and mental hospitals in Michigan, without obtaining any relief from his homicidal "needs." "I have been to the Ionia State Hospital for the Criminally Insane in Michigan," he told a Texas judge. "I have been to a mental hospital in Princeton, West Virginia. And I tell them my problems, and they don't want to do nothing about it, but there is a hundred, oh, about a hundred women out there that says different." Despite his protestations, he claims, he was released: "I told them before I ever left prison that I was going to commit crimes, told them the type of crimes I was going to commit, and they wouldn't believe it. They said I was going regardless of whether I liked it or not. And the day I got out of jail is the day I started killing." He says he killed two women that day.[1]

"I was death on women," he told a television reporter in his disconcertingly genial manner. "I didn't feel they need to exist. I hated them, and I wanted to destroy every one I could find. I was doing a good job of it. I've got [killed] 360

---

* Lucas continually revised his claims, undoubtedly in order to insult the authorities and to keep his name in the public eye.

people, I've got 36 states, in three different countries. My victims never knew what was going to happen to them. I've had shootings, knifings, strangulations, beatings, and I've participated in actual crucifixions of humans. All across the country, there's people just like me, who set out to destroy human life." For eight years he crisscrossed the continent, looking for women alone and defenseless—hitchhikers, runaways, women whose cars had broken down on lonely roads. He explained his behavior in intellectual constructs borrowed from his culture, which is to say in terms of his childhood. "That's the way I grew up when I was a child—watching my mom have sexual acts. She wouldn't go into different rooms, she'd make sure I was in the room before she started anything, and she would do it deliberately to make me watch her, you know. I got so I hated it. I'd even leave the house and go out and hide in the woods and wouldn't even go home. And when I'd go home, I'd get beat for not coming home. I don't blame mom for what she done, I don't blame her for that. It's the idea of the way she done it. I don't think any child out there should be brought up in that type of environment. In the past, I've hated it. It's just inside hate, and I can't get away from it." What Lucas says *seems* to explain it all: yet he killed his mother first, when he was only twenty-three, and that should have finished her. Why did he have to spend decades in exorcising her ghost by killing "her" over and over again? His explanation seems most imperfect.[2]

If Lucas claimed the modern record for serial murder (killings spread over time), 1984 was also the year in which the mass-murder record (killings in one explosive burst) was broken in America. It was then that *James Oliver Huberty* burst into a McDonald's restaurant in San Ysidro, California, and began to kill. Before the afternoon was out, during the course of an eighty-two-minute siege, he fired some 245 shots at terrified and dying restaurant customers and at passersby, killing twenty-one and wounding nineteen more, before a police bullet struck him in the chest and killed him. Unlike Lucas, Huberty was no homeless and uneducated drifter. It is true that he did come from a broken home, and that his only friend during his lonely childhood had been his dog; but such minor anguish has been the lot of millions.

His mother, who abandoned her son and his only sister when they were very young, could only say that "I knew he needed help."[3]

The adult Huberty was married and had two daughters. Reportedly, he was a graduate in sociology from a small Quaker college in Ohio, and he owned his own home; which is to say that he possessed some of the exterior hallmarks of the stable family man. Nevertheless, he lost his job as a welder when the plant closed (and he never practiced embalming, for which he had received a license in 1965 from the Pittsburgh Institute of Mortuary Science). According to one news magazine, many of his friends thought he was a communist when he blamed the capitalist system for the closure of his plant. However, his wife said: "If anything, he was a Nazi." Huberty decided to move west and start a new life, but he lost a great deal of money on the sale of his home. Then, inexplicably, he moved to the Mexican border town of Tijuana where, unable to speak the language and feeling (according to his wife) "hopeless, lost and rejected," his hatred of Hispanics began to grow. He then moved back to the U.S., settling in San Ysidro within sight of a McDonald's restaurant much frequented by young Hispanics. He found work as a security guard, but was laid off within a few weeks.[4]

In what seems to have been a last attempt to salvage what remained of his life, he tried to obtain an appointment at a mental health clinic, but was unable to obtain one. The day of the killings, he visited the San Diego Zoo with his family. Staring at the caged animals, perhaps feeling not unlike them, Huberty told his wife, "Society's had their chance!" He drove his family to their home and announcing that "I'm going hunting . . . hunting humans," he armed himself and drove to the nearby McDonald's in his battered Mercury.

The reaction of the state following the massacre was almost as tragic and misguided as the event itself. If television coverage can be taken as meaningful (and it is surely *the* prime cultural disseminator in modern America), the state and its agencies intervened only to express bewilderment regarding the killer's motive, and to offer the services of therapists who would help victims (present and future) to "adjust" to the shock of such tragedies. The state thus moved to avoid the question: are such killings truly inevitable? Why did Huberty choose to kill and die among the predominantly Hispanic customers of that restaurant? Was there in fact any connection between his precipitous decline in the social hierarchy and his assault on the bottom dwellers, the struggling Hispanics who moved too freely in "his" white, middle-class restaurant? Was there deep social meaning to this act, or only bizarre psychopathology? As I write this, scientists were despatched to find answers to the Huberty case. Typically, however, they were instructed to look in the wrong direction, and told to dissect his brain to search for mysterious "lesions" among its folds, rather than analyzing the social content of his acts.

If Lucas and Huberty raised the murderous ante of lives destroyed and minds and bodies maimed, *Christopher Wilder* raised the social ante, for he was the first to prey exclusively on upper-middle and upper-class targets other than the "usual" university women. Wilder's case is especially fascinating, although it must remain an enigma since he was killed during his capture and he left nothing behind to explain himself—except his murders. Yet, he was no enraged lumpen proletarian like Lucas, taking out his rage upon the class that suppressed him; nor was he a dispossessed petit bourgeois like Huberty, protesting his disenfranchisement. Born to reputedly wealthy Australian parents, Wilder emigrated to the United States in 1970 and established his own successful contracting business. He owned Florida real estate worth at least a half million dollars, skied in chic resorts, raced cars, and kept a luxury home—according to all reports. Yet there are many suggestive contradictions in his life. His business partner has disputed the authenticity of his wealth, claiming that Wilder's diamond rings were fakes, his Porsche seventeen years old, and his home a "junk-heap" that he repaired with the construction company's left-over materials. His partner insisted that Wilder was "just an easy-going quiet guy who watches a lot of TV because he has nothing else to do." As the contradictions multiplied during the investigation, Wilder was found to be an animal lover: this rapist torturer and murderer had made donations to Save The Whales and the Seal Rescue Fund. Moreover, he always braked when turtles crossed the road. Nevertheless, after an international career in sexual assault (for which he went virtually unpunished) this easy-going watcher of television, this lover of whales, seals, and turtles, abducted eleven beautiful and elegant women, only three of whom survived the ordeal. Using a standard ruse, he approached young women, some of whom were aspiring models, and offered them careers in modeling. If they refused to accompany him "for photographs," he would forcibly abduct them and subject them to electric shocks and other tortures before killing them. Not unlike Theodore Bundy, whom we examine in great detail later on in this book, Wilder began his cross-country rampage shortly after a beautiful young woman, a teacher of mentally disturbed children and herself a member of an established Florida family, refused his offer of marriage. The authorities were bewildered by the entire case, but a racing partner of Wilder's put the critical question when he insisted there was no logic to Wilder's sex crimes: "If you want to act out a pornographic scene, you just go out and hire a bunch of hookers. He had no reason to subject himself to this." Precisely. Why should Wilder indulge in such life-destroying activities when, if his motivation was only sexual, he could have safely reproduced it on a commercial basis? This book is an attempt to answer that inelegant question in full, and to follow its ramifications wherever they might lead us. We must study them well, for there will be many more such killers in what remains of this century—and it should be clearly understood that their intent is to steal our daughters and sons, and to snuff out their lives.[5]

How can we begin to explain these modern multiple murderers who, whether in a campaign lasting many months or in one that can be measured in hours, launch pre-meditated assaults upon a single social category? The killers appear to defy the social laws by themselves coming from the middle and lower classes. Perhaps they are victims —as psychiatry and the courts argue so vociferously—of obscure mental disorders? Perhaps they are, but if so, why should there be so many more victims of this particular type of mental disease in the 1970s and 1980s than ever before in human experience? Is there something in our modern toilet-training practices, or some strange change in our biochemistry, which is producing so much of this disorder? Perhaps not, for the whole notion of mental disease as latterly defined by psychiatry (which teaches that mental illness is a disease much like, say, tuberculosis) becomes quite untenable when subjected to the anthropological, cross-cultural evidence. The apparently immutable mental diseases of "schizophrenia," "manic-depression," and so on, often disappear or take quite different forms in other cultures. Thus a troubled person's leave-taking from conventional reality (which we call "psychosis") takes a form that his or her culture prescribes. For example, in Ojibwa traditional culture—which taught that persons could be possessed by spirits and that the possessed ones would have an uncontrollable desire for human flesh—madness took the form of Windigo Psychosis. Believing what they were "taught," the victims would kill humans, often their own families, and devour their flesh. Similarly, in that pressure cooker that was Eskimo life, the madness took a special northern form known as Arctic Hysteria, in which the victim would rip off his or her clothes and, insensible to danger, race out onto the ice floes.

In his splendid but little-known study of a schizophrenic, *Oscar,* Peter J. Wilson concluded that madness is the individual's response to the obliteration of his identity by others. "The only recourse available to those who are so overwhelmed is to banish such tyranny from their lives—to a hospital, an asylum, any ship of fools." Thus madness is both a creative, self-protecting act, and a program of the culture, for South American "primitives," the *Yanomamo,* do not experience Arctic Hysteria and Americans do not encounter Windigo Psychosis. In our own society, an increasing number of people kill for the pleasure it appears to give them. Are they mad, or are they acting out some analogous social message? The lesson here is that the psychiatric analogy is a false one: madness is not like cancer or any other physical ailment. Rather, it is a culturally programmed dialogue. It should not therefore be surprising that no matter how hard our psychiatrists search, they are unable to discover much mental disease among our captured multiple murderers (except in the nature of their acts). Therein lies the special horror, for the killers are as "normal" as you or me, yet they kill without mercy, and they kill to make a statement.[6]

If they cannot be dismissed as biological or psychological freaks, neither can they be regarded as mere manifestations of America's astonishingly high homicide rate (the highest in the western industrial world, and by a huge margin*). The evidence for this assertion is clear: a rise or fall in the overall homicide rate is not necessarily related in any way to a rise or fall in the multiple-murder rate. Indeed, in the early 1980s, when the ever-rising U.S. homicide rate finally began to abate, the multiple-murder rate continued its meteoric rise.** In Canada, where the overall homicide rate has been curiously stable for years, the multiple-murder rate seems similarly stable (if periodically and artificially inflated by the presence of foreign killers—a tradition that began with Winnipeg landlady-killer Earle Nelson in the 1920s and continues into the present: with claims by Henry Lucas that he was killing in Canada, with attempts by Christopher Wilder to escape to Canada, with Ted Bundy's occasional visits to Vancouver, and with the recent capture of alleged torturer and serial killer Charles Ng in Calgary). More interestingly, nations such as Britain or Germany, which have very low homicide rates, appear to have high multiple-murder rates; while nations such as Switzerland have low overall homicide and multiple-murder rates. The point should be clear: these are different and almost unrelated phenomena. The multiple murderer, who sacrifices his own life to make an art form out of killing strangers, is qualitatively a very different man from the slum husband

---

* Mexico is often cited for having a much higher homicide rate, but it is a Third World nation, not a western industrial society.

** Statistics are utterly unreliable, and often completely unavailable, for multiple murder, and we are forced to gather evidence where and when we can. Even that is weakened by the number of killers who are never captured, whose many crimes lie buried in wilderness groves and suburban yards. Even the renowned FBI Uniform Crime Reports are dependent on the whims of many tiny police jurisdictions, who may file their reports as they choose.

who, driven beyond endurance by poverty and humiliation, beats his wife or neighbor to death in some drunken brawl. A sophisticated quantitative debate currently rages in social science over whether the ultimate cause of homicide lies in absolute poverty, relative inequality, or in regional subculture; but clearly all three embrace their share of the truth, for *all* deprivation (be it absolute or relative) provokes frustration, and culture is ever the programmed maze instructing individuals how best to display their emotions. In any case, the multiple murderer is quite a different person: most often on the margins of the upper-working or lower-middle classes, he is usually a profoundly conservative figure who comes to feel excluded from the class he so devoutly wishes to join. In an extended campaign of vengeance, he murders people unknown to him, but who represent to him (in their behavior, their appearance, or their location) the class that has rejected him.

With varying degrees of explicitness, multiple murderers see themselves as soldiers: small wonder then that they feel neither remorse for their victims, nor regret for launching their bloody crusades. Moreover, the public treats them as major celebrities. No one ever became famous by beating his wife to death in an alley; but virtually all our multiple murderers achieve true and lasting fame. They are the subjects of articles and books, radio and television shows— for the remainder of their lives—and they thus attain an immortality denied the unenterprising common man. During their trials, they will almost certainly be surrounded by admiring women who press their affections upon the killer, radiating toward him little but admiration and love. Sometimes, as with Theodore Bundy, a reverent member of the public will marry the multiple murderer during his trial— and even conceive his child during his incarceration. He will be besieged with letters and communications from special-interest groups who will see in him some weighty philosophical point or an opportunity to test their theories of rehabilitation. The Son of Sam was not so very wrong when he thought the public was urging him on during his killing spree, for the media chronicled his every deed in a state of mounting excitement. Should any potential killer fail to grasp the cultural message that this is a certain route to celebrity and fulfillment, a popular song of the mid-1980s spells it out:

> Once that you've decided on a killing
> First you make a stone of your heart
> And if you find that your hands are still willing
> You can turn a murder into art
>
> Well if you have a taste for this experience
> You're flushed with your very first success
> Then you must try a twosome or a threesome
> Before your conscience bothers you much less
>
> Then you can join the ranks of the illustrious
> In history's great dark Hall of Fame
> All our greatest killers were industrious
> At least the ones that we all know by name.*

Murder for Profit

It is not my intention in this book to study all forms of multiple murder. A paucity of data made it impossible for me to examine the "Tylenol" murders, the many recent hospital murders, the plunging of automobiles onto crowded sidewalks, or even the common homosexual multiple murderers (for they rarely leave any confessions behind them**): one can only speculate that they might be similar to those studied here. Additionally, I rule out of our province those who kill for profit, like Charles Sobhra who was implicated in 1978 in the murder and robbery of dozens of tourists in Asian resorts. This multiple murder for profit is merely one form of making a living, one in which the murder is incidental to the goal. Those who practice this "profession" would undoubtedly follow another if they

---

* From one of the best-selling albums of the mid-1980s, *Synchronicity*, by the Police, A & M Records of Canada, © copyright 1983, Magnetic Publishing Co.

** This absence of rich data on homosexual multiple murderers (who kill males) has left some readers, especially feminists, with the mistaken impression that modern multiple murder is a misogynistic war on women. I can only repeat that multiple murderers who are homosexual (and they seem to form the same porportion of the population of murderers as they do of non-murderers) choose male victims, suggesting non-misogynistic motive.

were offered more money. We are concerned only with those who appear to kill *for its own sake,* those for whom killing alone is the apparent goal.

Neither are we studying the professional state-employed torturers and murderers who are essentially bureaucrats, wreaking havoc on their fellows on behalf of the rulers of modern governments. They are far more effective in killing than those we study here, for these bureaucratic killers are *apparatchiks,* killing with the latest technology as part of their career strategies and, primarily (or even entirely) for career advancement. Transfer them with a solid promotion to the Board of Weights & Measures and they might be just as happy, although some would miss the shuddering of their victims. These joyless bureaucratic killers find their perfect embodiment in Adolf Eichmann, the efficient ruler of the Nazi death camps, but his emulators have appeared everywhere in the second half of this century. Modern death squads pursue their terror on behalf of ruling elites, and sometimes do so with the enthusiastic assistance of the general population, but they are not the individual entrepreneurs pursuing their private goals who are the object of our study.

Perhaps the most successful government-sponsored mass-murder programs since the Second World War have been in Indonesia, where right-wing Islamic fundamentalists annihilated the political left; and in Cambodia, where left-wing revolutionaries destroyed virtually everyone. In Indonesia, where a conservative estimate puts the murdered at half a million, an Islamic government's decision to eliminate the opposition communist party (PKI) began in 1965 with mass executions by government troops, and then spread to a general slaughter of all party members and their families. Amnesty International's *Political Killings By Governments* records in its dry prose how in many regions "local army commanders loaded lorries with captured PKI members— their names checked off against hastily prepared lists—and drove them to isolated spots nearby for execution, usually by bullet or knife." Elsewhere in Indonesia, however, "most people were executed with long sugar-cane knives and sickles [and] the slaughter often assumed a ritualistic and ceremonial character. In several places the killers held feasts with their bound victims present. After the meal each guest was invited to decapitate a prisoner."[7]

In Cambodia, the slaughter was conceived by the communist government as a means of stopping any potential counter-revolutionary activity. Only high-ranking officers were killed until early 1975, but death was soon extended to any merely *suspected* of resistance to the new regime. One Khmer Rouge soldier, who tired of the killing, testified: "In 1975, we were made to change policy: the victory of the revolution had been too quick. If the population was not wiped out immediately, the revolution would be in danger because the republican forces, the forces of Sihanouk, the capitalist forces would unite against it. It was therefore necessary to eliminate all these forces and to spare only those of the Communist Party of Kampuchea. It was necessary to eliminate not only the officers but also the common soldiers as well as their wives and children. This was also based on revolutionary experience. In the past, Sihanouk had killed revolutionaries, but their wives, children and relatives had united against him and had joined us. That must not be repeated against us now. At the beginning of 1976, however, the families of common soldiers were also killed. One day at Choeung Prey, I cried for a whole day on seeing women and children killed. I could no longer raise my arms [to kill]. Comrade Saruoeun said to me: 'Get on with it.' I said: 'How can I? Who can kill women and children?' Three days later I was arrested." But these wretched creatures with their extermination camps, all prisoners of their own systems and of the empires that manipulate them, are not the stuff of this book.[8]

For Its Own Sake

The men of whom I write seek neither profit nor bureaucratic advancement. On the contrary, they are what the Germans call the practitioners of *lustmord,* joy-murderers who act quite independently, killing simply because of the personal satisfaction they seem to derive from the act. However, I shall try to show that their killings are far more than mere pleasure: that they are a kind of sub-political and conservative protest which nets the killer a substantial social profit of revenge, celebrity, identity, and sexual relief. They conceive of the killings as a kind of mission, task, or crusade—sometimes only dimly perceived (as with DeSalvo and Berkowitz), and sometimes expressed with great clarity (as with Essex, Panzram, and Starkweather). In either case it is the same phenomenon, a kind of primitive rebellion against the social order which has become an increasingly fashionable form of social art. If the murders can only be understood as a personalized social protest, it must be emphasized that these killers are no radicals: they have enthusiastically embraced the established order only to discover that it offers them no place they can endure. Their rebellion is a protest against their perceived exclusion from society, not an attempt to alter it as befits a revolutionary. This fundamentally rebellious, not revolutionary, nature of their protest is undoubtedly why so few government and police resources are allocated to the capture of these killers (compared, say, to the huge police apparatus that monitors political dissidents), for they pose no threat to the established order—neither in their ideology nor in their acts. Thus, in this book, we discuss Huberty the "Nazi"; Essex the racist; Kemper of the Junior Chamber of Commerce; Bundy the Young Republican; Panzram the nihilist; Nilsen the professionally perfect person; Berkowitz the avenger; DeSalvo the social climber; and Starkweather who slaughtered the aristocratic inhabitants of a mansion. These were no more "blows for the people" than they were the acting out of some dreaded mental disease. To the contrary, they were the natural revenge of those who had looked upon their own lives and pronounced them unlivable, and then made the decision to exact a fearful revenge, for which they were willing to sacrifice their lives.

The killings are thus also a form of *suicide note* (literally so with most mass murderers, who expect to die before the day or week is out; metaphorically so for most serial murderers, who sacrifice the remainder of their lives to the "cause"), in which the killer states clearly which social category has excluded him. Our task is to learn to read the note, to pore over the killings and the speeches of the killers, searching for meaning. We must not be content with superficial explanations which focus merely on personal and short-term satisfactions, however compelling they may appear to be, for they avoid coming to terms with the ultimate cause of these abominations. This warning is necessary, for even society's most perceptive spokesmen can fall into this error—as when the astute Judge Ronald George, who presided over the Hillside Strangler trials, confused cause with reward when he concluded that "Angelo Buono and Kenneth Bianchi terrorized this city for several months, haunting the community like the ultimate in evil spirits as they abducted children and young women, torturing, raping and sodomizing them, and finally depriving their families and friends of them forever . . . and all for what? The momentary sadistic thrill of enjoying a brief perverted sexual satisfaction, and venting their hatred of women." While this book must *not* be taken as a plea for the serious consideration of the killers' "philosophies," it does argue that if we are to understand the forces that create them, we must look beyond their vile pleasures to the source of their deformation.[9]

The Settling of Accounts

> "There comes a point when the only way you can make a statement is to pick up a gun."
>
> SARA JANE MOORE[10]

I thus intend to argue the case that these killers are not alien creatures with deranged minds, but alienated men with a disinterest in continuing the dull lives in which they feel entrapped. Reared in a civilization which legitimizes violence as a response to frustration, provided by the mass media and violent pornography with both the advertising proclaiming the "joy" of sadism and the instruction manual outlining correct procedures, they grasp the "manly" identity of pirate and avenger. If they no longer wish to live, they will stage a mass killing whose climax is their execution; but should they wish to live, and to achieve notoriety—even celebrity—they will prepare their careers in serial murder.

In doing so, they settle old scores in a manner which often yields a double dividend of sexual pleasure and defiance of the authorities. The killings are a kind of vituperative monologue with the social order—sometimes *literally* so, as when the macabre British homosexual serial murderer, *Dennis Nilsen,* stood in front of the corpses of the young men he had killed and tied to chairs in his apartment, and lectured at them for hours, apparently on subjects as diverse as civil service regulations and modern social issues. More often, however, the killers' message is whispered too low for the human ear to comprehend unassisted, or it is expressed in garbled riddles. What did Nilsen mean when he wrote to the investigating officers after his arrest that, "The evil was short-lived and it cannot live or breathe for long inside the conscience"? The evil was nothing of the kind, for he would have continued to kill indefinitely had he not been unmasked. "I have slain my own dragon," wrote this killer of sixteen defenseless young men, but he offered no further explanation when asked what form the dragon took, or precisely why he killed. "I don't know," he told police. "I've been trying to work it out. I'm not a headshrinker but everyone keeps walking out on me [a reference to the fact that his friends invariably abandoned him]. There might be a lot of individual reasons. Being a professionally perfect person I hate the establishment. I am under great pressure. I drink to relieve the pressure." Is this mere madness, or some garbled message delivered in an indecipherable code by this professionally perfect person?[11]

Perhaps the most disturbing (yet the most vital) act the killers perpetrate is when, after their apprehension, they so often indulge in the cheapest kind of moralizing—lecturing society, or even the families of their victims. The records of the trial of the fifteenth-century pedophile torture-murderer, *Baron Gilles de Rais,* document the manner in which he instructed the parents of those he had murdered on how best to raise their surviving children. And Nilsen insisted that, "It was my morality and sense of justice which revealed all," when it was nothing of the kind. As I write, the Canadian child-murderer *Clifford Olson* sits in prison and composes philosophical essays, and sends letters to professors of sociology: "I have always enjoyed sociology myself," he writes, "as its [sic] a science of human society. In the last 18 months I have been doing some extenive [sic] writings on a vast amount of my own personal reflections on my own views on many subjects which I believe in myself. . . . Some of my topicts [sic] and papers I have completed . . . are as follows. (1) immortality: (2) good and evil: (3) beauty: (4) emotion: (5) love: (6) logic: (7) happiness: (8) family: (9) knowledge: (10) art: these have all been completed." We do ourselves a great disservice if we simply dismiss this for the pretentious prattle it is—the same disservice that a mediocre general does his army if he ignores the thinking of his enemy (for whom he has too much contempt)—for we ensure the killers' triumph if we do not struggle to understand their motives and goals. If we are to excise this abomination from the universe, we must listen studiously to what they say, despite their insufferability. Some of the killers speak a form of truth.[12]

Who are these modern American multiple murderers? They refuse to meet our expectations. I have already stated that very few of them are "mad," or delusionary in any observable way. They are usually white and male, and from the solid working class or lower-middle class. Most important, in their thoughts and behavior, they are among the most *class conscious* people in America, obsessed with every nuance of status, class, and power. This "sensitivity" expresses itself variously among different types of multiple murderers. Among serial murderers, their truncated sense of self and identity (a reflection of the fact that the vast majority of them are adopted, or illegitimate, or have spent a major portion of their childhoods or adolescences in institutions such as orphanages or juvenile homes) pushes them toward finding their identity and their personal fulfillment in the killings, and all their ambitions in the international celebrity that most often attends their capture. This contrasts strikingly with mass murderers like Essex and Huberty and Starkweather, who are much more likely to come from relatively solid familial situations but find themselves unable to maintain their social position: the gap between their expectations and their realities is so wide that they can only vent their rage upon the hated group in one brief suicidal purple explosion. Huberty felt himself too annulled to yearn for the public spotlight that so bedazzled Berkowitz. Yet both serial and mass murderers are overwhelmed with a profound sense of alienation and frustration stemming from their feelings that no matter how fierce their ambitions may be (and they are, most often, among the most ambitious of men), no matter what they might do, they could not achieve the place in society to which they aspired. They aim high, these multiple murderers: they have not, like Durkheim's contented man, accepted their station in life. Sometimes, as with Bundy and perhaps Wilder, they *do* achieve the position they covet, but their uncertain social origins and their upward social mobility render them unable to feel at ease with themselves while sitting on this lofty throne. In such a milieu, a sense of personal mission begins to incubate.[13]

Typically, their victims are drawn from a single social type or category. Usually this takes the form of those who are members (or who appear to be) of a specific social class, most often one or two narrow social bands above the killer. Typically too, unless their sexuality is undeveloped (as was Berkowitz's) or overwhelmed by their urgent anger (as with Essex and Huberty), they select members of that social class whom they find beautiful, adding the joy of sex to their adventure. Sex is not the prime motivator, but it is vital to the enterprise: a delicious by-product, or extra dividend, to their adventure. Despite the facts that neither Essex nor Berkowitz touched their victims, or that Starkweather made only a few fumbling attempts to do so, we should not dismiss the sexual component of the sprees, but merely emphasize its *secondary* position to the "Prime Mission," which is to wreak vengeance upon the established order. Thus the Boston Strangler was "putting things over on high class people"; Starkweather was showing how "dead people are all on the same level"; Kemper was making "a demonstration to the authorities"; Bundy was stealing the most valuable possessions of the established classes, their beautiful and talented young women; and Essex was killing white people who, he had decided, were the "beasts of the earth." In this special sense then, the killers know precisely what they are doing and why they are doing it. If we are to understand them, rather than dismiss them, their acts must be seen as a kind of deformed creativity, not a consequence of some drooling derangement.

Our purpose in this book is to determine the source of this deformation, demonstrating through the intensive examination of illustrative cases* the fundamentally social nature of their creation and the deep social meaning of their acts. Along our path we shall encounter many lies and half-truths—as often from the professionals who must deal with the killers as from the killers themselves—but we shall attempt a dissection with surgical precision. En route, we will occasionally assess the behavior of the social institutions charged with the responsibility for dealing with multiple murderers: here too we shall encounter surprises, for the police, who are commonly regarded as stupid and brutal, often appear in these pages to possess more intelligence and insight into the killers than do the "professionals." Moreover, as the distinguished American psychiatrist Willard Gaylin has freely admitted, "Most of us are aware how trivial, ephemeral, descriptive, and meaningless are psychiatric diagnoses." Sadly, the evidence in this book is that many of his colleagues are not aware of this problem and that they allow themselves to be used, in the crassest imaginable way, by any legal team that hires them.[14]

Caveat

A warning should be issued here. There is a pitfall which entraps researchers and readers alike when venturing into this kind of territory. I refer to the propensity, recently attacked by Willard Gaylin, to become so emotionally involved with the killers as to minimize, or even entirely forget, the evil that these men have done. This selective amnesia takes many forms, but all are pernicious. I do not speak here only of the kind of sycophantic and grotesque

---

* Illustrative of how many killers? One can guess that there have been rather more than one hundred in America since the Second World War, and most of them in the 1970s and 1980s. Perhaps fifty of that one hundred have been captured, and a dozen of them have provided the world with an explanation for their behavior. Six of the latter appear in this book, selected for the fullness of their description and the reliability of their biographers. Still, it is obvious that we can make no claim to be representative in any statistical sense, for such precision would be impossible.

affection that Flora Rheta Schreiber oozes over her informant, the torture-murderer Joseph Kallinger, in her book *The Shoemaker* (a syrup so thick that it inspires the killer to send poems to his biographer). I also refer to the kind of shift of sympathy that warps books even as beautifully crafted as Daniel Keyes' *The Minds of Billy Milligan.* Keyes, so enraptured by his subject, was unable to control his righteous rage at the "rednecks" who interrupted the multiple rapist's "rehabilitation" by shooting at him as he walked along the grounds of the mental hospital. I do not wish to go on record as approving the shooting of mental patients, or anyone else, but author and reader must maintain their perspective, reminding themselves that Milligan was a brutal rapist who destroyed the peace and contentment— and very possibly the sexuality—of many of his victims. Moreover, it is rather likely that the avengers were friends or relatives of the victims (or perhaps the victims themselves). They deserve more sympathy than Billy, and a society that does not understand this provides fertile ground for the sowing of more rapists and murderers.

Willard Gaylin has written with much insight of the process whereby the victims, not the killers, are diminished and denied their humanity in order to put the killer on trial in the best possible light. A similar infection invades the description of the killer and his works, and scholars are no more resistant to this disease than anyone else. If we insist upon the right to understand the dark forces that propel a person into launching a war upon the innocent, we must also assume the responsibility of recognizing the unholiness of his acts, and the tragedies he perpetrates. A cultural system which does otherwise, as does our own, is guilty of much more than misplaced tenderness: it must be charged with encouraging the repetition of such acts. Conversely, a legal system such as ours that consistently makes a mockery of natural justice for violent offenders, releasing them back into society (or not incarcerating them at all) without any sense of wrongdoing, may occasionally benefit from a dash of free-spirited public intervention. To avoid all these problems, I have tried very hard, while seeking to sympathetically understand the motives of the killers, to deglamorize their acts and to humanize their victims. We are all human beings, but the innocent deserve more than the guilty.

An additional problem is that those who argue from ideological positions sometimes find themselves painted into tiny ideological corners. I have never placed too much trust in the judgment of intellectuals, for too often they love their logical systems more than gritty reality. In such a spirit of closed minds and closed systems of thought, gentlepersons of the left sometimes insist that to devise mechanisms for the apprehension and control of the killers is merely to act as agents for the oppressive system that created the killers. Arguing that since the system created them, it has no moral right to punish or control them is as absurd as arguing that a zoologist has no right to destroy some laboratory culture that has turned poisonous. In consistently making such a case, however, the political left parades its moral bankruptcy, for societies that tolerate the commission of these acts (and I believe that ours do) are doomed. The ideologues of the right err just as grievously when, in their fervent attempts to exonerate the ruling class of all blame, they too often act like simple-minded pollyannas, resolutely tending to the bright side and closing their eyes to a causal reality that cannot exonerate society. In arguing, as they so often do, that we should avert our gaze from the darker consequences of the social and economic formations which pattern our lives, they parade their intellectual bankruptcy.

The fact of this very human matter is that, as Willard Gaylin has observed, "in our unconscious we are all killers, rapists, incestual, exhibitionistic, voyeuristic, aggressive, and homicidal." Many of us are programmed still further by our social system to displace our rage upon others: but why do individuals with equally tragic (or far more so) backgrounds choose not to kill? The fundamental act of humanity is to refuse to kill. Our murderers have consciously rejected that humanity. They are not robots programmed by some machine to do exactly what they do: they know precisely what they are doing. For their betrayal of humanity, they deserve no better fate than to be permanently excised from the social order. Their only value is as objects of study.[15]

Part I

THE MODERN SERIAL MURDERER

2.
A DEMONSTRATION TO THE AUTHORITIES

Edmund Emil Kemper III*

> "I had thought of annihilating the entire block that I lived on."
>
> EDMUND KEMPER[1]

Raised by a shrilly belittling university administrator (and her succession of husbands, none of whom could measure up to her fierce social ambitions) who locked him in a cellar and endlessly berated him for his social failures, and incarcerated throughout his adolescence in a mental hospital for sex offenders, he grew up to be a young man who believed in all the conventional values, but lacked the confidence to be anything other than a flagman for the California Department of Highways. His *task* first drifted into his consciousness well before he was ten. He grew fascinated with execution, the means by which the authorities legally punished and eliminated evil-doers. His younger sister remembered that "he would stage his own execution in the form of a childhood 'game' in which he had her lead

---

* The prime sources for this chapter are the detailed confessions of Kemper, reprinted in the references cited; Donald T. Lunde's scholarly *Murder and Madness*; Margaret Cheney's *The Co-Ed Killer*, a model for journalistic accounts; and Donal West's *Sacrifice Unto Me*.

him to a chair, blindfold him, and pull an imaginary lever, after which he would writhe about as if dying in a gas chamber." One Christmas, her grandparents gave her a doll: when she looked for it one day she discovered it decapitated and handless, a mutilation theme that was to recur within the developing mentality of Edmund Emil Kemper III.[2]

Still younger than ten, his task shifted hesitantly to living things. To transform separate life form into his true and exclusive possession, he later explained, he made his first kill. He buried the family cat alive in his yard. When it had suffocated, he brought it into his room and cut off its head, which he stuck on a spindle. His mingled satisfaction and fascination expressed themselves in the prayers he intoned over the head. At about the same time, one of his psychiatrists later reported, he began embroidering fantasies which celebrated the deaths of people—his sisters, mother, and others. "It was mainly his older sister," a court psychiatrist said many years later. "She had friends, got more attention, respect, and affection from the mother. In general, she had the things he didn't have."[3]

First he had feigned killing himself in his ceremonial executions; then he had killed a symbol of a person by mutilating a doll; then he had killed a living thing in order to possess it; and working ever closer to what would be his prime task, his *raison d'être* (but gradually, for he was a cautious man), his thoughts had been filled with killing people. The purpose of the killing was to demand redress for the injustices that he thought had been perpetrated against him. Still a child, his fantasy matured into what would be his life's work. It blended mutilation, murder, possession, justice, and revenge with his own developing sexuality. The psychiatrist Lunde tells us that Kemper began to "sneak out of the house at night and from a distance stare at women walking down the street, fantasizing about his desire to love and be loved by them. Even at this early age, however, he felt that relationships with women would be impossible for him" unless he had killed them. During this period, Kemper confided to his younger sister that he would like to kiss his second-grade teacher. "She taunted him by saying, 'Why don't you go and kiss her,' and was puzzled at his reply: 'If I kiss her I would have to kill her first.'" He was unable to communicate or satisfy his desire: instead, carrying his step-father's bayonet, he stood one night outside his teacher's house, "imagining himself killing her and carrying her off to make love to her."[4]

His presentation of self was already growing so bizarre, with his silences and his stares, that his peers shrank from him. By the time he was thirteen, he was suspected of shooting a neighborhood pet dog. After that, he was excommunicated by the other boys, "being taunted, intimidated, and chased even more than before," once so "threateningly that he fled into a nearby house, where a woman called the police on his behalf." He considered killing men, but fear of male reprisal and the absence of any sexual promise blurred the fantasy enterprise. His execution reveries temporarily abated when one of his several step-fathers treated him with kindness, taking him fishing and hunting; yet there came a time when Kemper, holding an iron bar, stood behind his step-father, ready to spring. "His plan," writes his biographer Margaret Cheney, "after bashing him over the head, was to steal his car and drive to southern California for a reunion with his natural father." However, courage failed him and he ran away instead.[5]

Upon his return, now thirteen, he killed again in order to possess a fickle cat that preferred his sister, this time killing with a more complex ritual. He sliced off the top of the cat's skull with a *machete,* exposing its brain. The convulsing cat showered Kemper with blood while he held one of its forelegs and stabbed it repeatedly with his knife. Terrified that he would be discovered and punished, he buried the cat in his yard and cleaned his room. "Parts of the cat, for reasons that he did not fully understand, he decided to hide in his closet": it would not be the last time that a mammalian head would be his secret trophy and glittering prize, his just revenge and sensual reward. His mother later discovered parts of the cat and confronted Edmund with them. But, as Lunde tells us, "when confronted with accusations of such behavior by his mother or others, Ed would usually deny the charges and blame someone else."[6]

THE KILLING TIME

Now described by his mother as "a real weirdo," Kemper spent a period shuttling between the homes of his mother and his remarried father, and then was sent against his wishes to live with his paternal grandparents on their isolated California ranch. In late summer, now fourteen, he was sitting with his grandmother at her kitchen table as she went over the proofs of her latest children's story. Kemper rose and took his .22 rifle from its rack, telling his grandmother he was going to hunt rabbits. Suddenly, he felt the same anger that had overwhelmed him when he had killed the cats, and this time too its resolution was clear. Without conscious thought, he sighted the rifle on his grandmother's head and fired. Blood spurted from her nose and mouth, and he shot her twice more in the back. Lunde says Kemper stabbed her many times as if to kill her repeatedly, just as he had done in rehearsal with the cats. When his grandfather drove up to the house, Kemper shot and killed him before he had the opportunity to discover his wife's murder.[7]

After a few moments' hesitation, he telephoned his mother and asked her what he should do. When the police arrived, he briefly denied the crimes but then admitted that "I just wondered how it would feel to shoot Grandma." The court psychiatrist reported that during Kemper's brief detention in Juvenile Hall, he had regretted the lost opportunity of undressing his grandmother, " 'but felt that was an unnatural thought and did not want to talk about it.' " Kemper spent the following four years in a maximum security mental hospital, Atascadero, and in 1969 at the age of twenty-one was returned to the care of the California Youth Authority, who paroled Kemper to his mother—against the advice of the psychiatrists.[8]

Now free, there began an interregnum during which he formed and then rehearsed his final plan of action. Kemper had grown to six feet nine inches tall and weighed close to 300 pounds, and this massive person began to go on endless drives in his car. In the years 1970–71, he picked up dozens of pretty young women hitchhikers, developing his "gentle-giant" presentation of self; exploring his ability to deal with the women; talking to them and putting them at their ease; and training for his task. He was not alone, for the same town was incubating Herbert Mullin and John Frazier, two other Santa Cruz mass murderers, whom Kemper would later come to despise for their lack of "legitimacy" and competence. Finally, at the age of twenty-three, he felt he was ready to begin his ultimate adventure. It was to last eleven months, with eight more dead, before he turned himself in to the police.[9]

On May 7, 1972, two eighteen-year-old Fresno State College roommates, Mary Ann Pesce, an expert skier from an affluent California suburb, and Anita Luchessa, the eldest daughter of a farming family, were hitchhiking to visit friends at Stanford University. Standing on a ramp leading to the freeway, they stepped into Kemper's stopped car. Because they did not know the area well, he was able to take them east instead of south, confusing them with what he later called "a few loopy-loops around freeways and bypasses," until he pulled into a quiet rural cul-de-sac. Pesce tried to reason with him, searching for a chord of empathy and, remarkably, finding it: "I was really quite struck by her personality and her looks, and there was just almost a reverence there," Kemper recalled. He handcuffed Pesce to the back seat with great delicacy: "I think once I accidentally—this bothers me too, personally—I brushed, I think with the back of my hand when I was handcuffing her, against one of her breasts, and it embarrassed me. I even said, 'whoops, I'm sorry' or something like that." He locked Luchessa in the trunk.[10]

Returning to Pesce, he drew a plastic bag over her head, and wrapped a bathrobe's rope-tie around her neck; but the rope snapped when he pulled hard on it, and meanwhile Pesce had bitten a hole in the plastic bag, frustrating his efforts. With her back to him, he later recalled, he "poised the blade over her back, trying to decide where her heart was, and struck and hit her in the middle of the back." He continued "thrusting hard," striking her several more times in the back. In her terror, Pesce twisted around and he was able to knife her in the side: then "she turned completely over to see . . . or to get her back away from me, and I

29

stabbed her once in the stomach." At this point, "she turned back over on her stomach, and I continued stabbing." Kemper remembered worrying that the blows were not working. "I felt I was getting nowhere," so "I reached around and grabbed her by the chin and pulled her head back and slashed her throat. . . . She lost consciousness immediately."[11]

Leaving Pesce dead or dying in the back seat, he stepped out of the car and pulled Luchessa from the trunk, stabbing her in a flurry of cuts to the throat, the heart, the eyes, and the forearms: "What surprised me was how many blows she took. They were all heavy blows." Kemper drove back to his home and carried the bodies into his apartment. In privacy, taking Polaroid photographs of his actions, he decapitated Luchessa, disrobed and dissected Pesce, and sexually assaulted various body parts. Later, he drove into the mountains with Pesce's body in a plastic bag, and buried it, disguising the site with techniques he had learned from the Boy Scouts of America. He kept the heads of both women for a time, but then threw them into a ravine. He never forgot Pesce, nor the "reverence" he felt toward her. "Sometimes, afterward," he later told the court, "I visited there . . . to be near her . . . because I loved her and wanted her."[12]

His task was held in abeyance for four months after the killings, and he contented himself with feasting on the Polaroid photographs he had made of his last mission. On September 14, 1972, Kemper was hunting again. He observed fifteen-year-old Aiko Koo hitchhiking at a bus stop, on her way to an advanced dance class in San Francisco. Koo entered his car and was whisked through the usual bewildering array of freeway ramps, until the car pulled into a rural lane invisible from the main road. Kemper taped her mouth, closed her nostrils with his fingers, and began to suffocate her. Koo struggled violently. When her struggling seemed to cease, Kemper removed his hand from her face to find that she was still breathing: "I guess she became conscious enough to where she remembered what was happening, and went back into the extreme panic." Now he would make certain that he stopped her breathing. Her back arched as her lungs fought for air, but she lost consciousness. She was still breathing slightly as he carried her from the car and laid her body on the ground, removed her underclothing, and began intercourse. She started to breathe again, for the last time. "I took the muffler that she had around her neck and . . . choked her for a moment," he recalled. Sexually satisfied, and convinced that she was dead, he put her body in the trunk of the car, stopping at a bar for a few bottles of beer on the way home—after all, "I was hot, tired, and thirsty."[13]

On his way back to the car, he re-opened the trunk to take another look at Koo, "admiring my catch like a fisherman." Satisfied, he drove to his mother's house for a visit; then took Koo's body back to his apartment, decapitated her, and dissected the body. The following day, with Koo's head in the trunk of his car parked in the psychiatrists' lot, two psychiatrists interviewed Kemper and agreed that he was now "safe." They recommended that his juvenile record be sealed to permit him to live a normal adult life. Kemper then buried Koo's head and hands near a religious camp in the mountains.[14]

Four months passed again before his urge re-asserted itself. On January 8, 1973, he picked up hitchhiking Cindy Schall, a student at Cabrillo College who had not yet decided whether to become a schoolteacher or a policewoman. Using his usual stratagems, he whisked her to a secluded side road. Brandishing his new .22 Ruger pistol, he forced her into the trunk. Out of the corner of her eye, Kemper remembered, she saw him raise the gun. He marvelled at the speed with which the bullet struck her skull and took her life: "One second she's animated and next second she's not. Just a noise and absolute, absolute stillness." Together they drove to his mother's house, where he placed her body in a closet and went to bed. When his mother had gone to work at the university (where she held an administrative position) the following morning, he removed Schall from the closet and carried her to his bed, where he made love to her corpse. Afterwards, he placed her in the bathtub and, using his Buck knife and his California Department of Highways axe, dissected her. Washing away all traces of blood, he placed the body parts in plastic bags and took them for a drive along the coast, stopping to throw the bags off a cliff. A few days later, when Schall's body parts were discovered by the police, Kemper still had her head in a box in his closet. Later, he buried her head in his mother's back yard.[15]

Schall had been his first kill he had picked up in his own town. It bolstered his confidence that he would not be unmasked before his mission was completed. With growing assurance, he moved his operations to the campus where his mother worked, and increased the rate of his kills. Less than a month passed before the opportunity presented itself once more. On February 5, 1973, twenty-three-year-old Rosalind Thorpe, a student at Santa Cruz's Merrill College, was hitchhiking on campus. Kemper picked her up and, a little further along the campus drive, yet another hitchhiker, Alice Liu, entered his car and sat in the back seat. With no one visible on the campus's broad road, he turned to his front seat passenger and shot Thorpe just above her left ear: "She had a rather large forehead and I was imagining what her brain looked like inside, and I just wanted to put it right in the middle of that." Liu's response to the explosive assault in front of her was to cover her face in fear. Kemper tried to shoot through her hands, but missed twice. The third shot "hit her just right around the temple area." He shot her several more times. The firing ceased when a car came into view. He drove through the campus's guard station, with Liu gurgling in the back seat. When they had passed the campus and reached the edge of town, "I slowed down very slow, turned her head to the side, and fired point-blank at the top of her head." Pulling over to the side of the road, he was able to put both bodies in the trunk without being seen.[16]

Kemper drove to his mother's home, but he left the bodies in the trunk while he talked with his mother until bedtime. Then he went outside to the car and decapitated both corpses, his knife flashing in the trunk. He stopped to buy cigarettes at a bar and then went to bed at his mother's. When his mother left for work the following morning, he carried Liu's headless body into the house, placed it on the floor and made love to her torso. As "an after-thought" when carrying her torso back to the car, he severed her hands while she lay in the trunk. He then took Thorpe's head into the house and meticulously removed the bullet from it: "I cleaned the blood off both of them in the bathroom . . . so I wouldn't get all bloody." Later, with both bodies in the car, he drove to Alameda to visit a friend, but he was unable to eat dinner that night. He went to a film, bought gas, and dumped the bodies miles from Santa Cruz.[17]

The task was now nearing completion. He would kill no more young university women. For a time he toyed with alternatives, even giving serious consideration to the idea of killing everyone on his block: "I thought of making this a demonstration to the authorities in Santa Cruz—how serious this was, and how bad a foe they had come up against . . . I had thought of annihilating the entire block that I lived on. . . . Not only the block that I lived on but the houses approaching it, which would have included as many as ten or twelve families. And it would be a very slow, a very slow, quiet attack." But it was not essential to his mission, and it came to nothing. It seems that, in entertaining the possibility, he was merely half-consciously delaying what he knew must come next, shirking his responsibilities by pretending to fabricate new ones.[18]

By Easter weekend he could no longer pretend. At 4 a.m., he lay in bed "thinking about it. It's something hard to just up and do," he later admitted. "But I was pretty fixed on that issue because there were a lot of things involved. Someone just standing off to the side, watching, isn't really going to see any kind of sense, or rhyme or reason." But his sense of responsibility and commitment prevailed. "I had done some things, and I felt that I had to carry the full weight of everything that happened. I certainly wanted for my mother a nice, quiet, easy death like I guess everyone wants."[19]

Determined thus to be responsible, and claiming to be kind (one of the few instances where he claims to be moral), he carried a hammer into his mother's bedroom at 5:15 a.m. "She moved around a little bit, and I thought maybe she was waking up. I just waited and she was just laying there. So I approached her right side . . . and I hit her just above the temple on her right side of the head . . . with a very hard blow. . . . Blood started running down her face from the wound, and she was still breathing." With his usual passion for detail, he later described how he had then turned his mother over on her back, held her chin up with his right hand and slashed her throat. While she bled profusely, he decided that "what's good for my victims was good for my mother." He decapitated her, handcuffed her wrists, and put her in the closet. Rumors suggest that he placed his mother's head on the mantel and either threw darts at it, or punched it, or both; but he did cut out her larynx and pushed it down the garbage disposal, and then sexually attacked her headless body.[20]

Even now his mission was not entirely fulfilled. He felt ill and could neither eat nor enjoy his surroundings: "I couldn't stand being around the house anymore." Still in a murderous rage, he drove through town and encountered an acquaintance, Robert, who owed him ten dollars. He could not help "chortling" at what Robert did not know—that he had buried Koo's head behind his chum's house, as a kind of joke. They decided to do some drinking and drove to a liquor store where Robert offered him the ten dollars: "To tell you the truth [that] saved his life, because with his little excuses, I needed to kill somebody at that point, and I think he deserved it more than anybody."[21]

Yet if Robert "deserved" to die in the sense that he had delayed his repayment of Kemper's loan, he was insufficiently central to Kemper's emotional life. Kemper decided that the "someone else" to die would be his mother's friend, Sally Hallet, who had enjoyed the affection and confidence that had been denied him. He telephoned Mrs. Hallet and invited her to a "surprise" dinner with his mother. When she arrived at the house exhausted from her day's work, Mrs. Hallet said, "Let's sit down, I'm dead." "And I kind of took her at her word there," said Kemper, who punched her in the stomach and finally choked her to death. He severed her head and left her body on his bed as a final trophy, but spent that night in his mother's bed.[22]

Now his task had been discharged and his homicidal energy almost spent. He had killed ten people in almost perfect symmetry, by strangulation, stabbing, and shooting: first, two kin (his grandparents); then, six beautiful young women; and concluding with a kinswoman and quasi-kin (his mother and her intimate friend). He had eaten the flesh of two of his victims. According to journalist Don West, "he finally admitted having cut flesh from their legs, freezing it and then cooking it in a macaroni casserole." He ate them, he said, because "I wanted them to be a part of me—and now they are." Later, under police questioning, he would confess many of the details of how he had mutilated his victims—removing their teeth and keeping bits of skin and hair as keepsakes.[23]

Yet having completed his task, he did not know quite what to do. He left a note for the police in his mother's house, assuming they would soon find it.

Appx. 5:15 a.m. Saturday. No need for her to suffer any more at the hands of this horrible "murderous Butcher." It was quick—asleep—the way I wanted it.

Not sloppy and incomplete, gents. Just a "lack of time." I got things to do!!![24]

But he did not know what the "things to do" were. At 10 a.m. on Easter Sunday, he began driving relentlessly east. He drove to Reno, Nevada, where he rented a car and continued racing away from the coast. After eighteen hours, he was pulled over by police in Colorado and given a speeding ticket. He was surprised and then disappointed to realize that an All Points Bulletin had not been put out for him. In fact, the police knew nothing of his activities.

He continued driving east, stuffing himself with No-Doz tablets to maintain the pace. Then, in eastern Colorado, explicitly signaling that he felt his previous behavior to have been rational, he grew afraid of becoming irrational: "I felt I was losing control, and I was afraid that anything could cause me to go off the deep end, and I didn't know what would happen then. I had never been out of control in my life," Kemper said, and this fear moved him to pull over to a public telephone booth. The Santa Cruz police, some of whom were his drinking companions, would not take his confession seriously, and it took several calls and an extended vigil at the telephone booth before Colorado police arrived and arrested him. In his terms, his responsibilities had been discharged with honor: soon he would sleep and eat like a fulfilled man. He would never be out of protective custody again.[25]

THE TALKING TIME

What a remarkable creature was Edmund Emil Kemper III, not only in that his murders combined two usually separate homicidal themes—killing both relatives *and* young women —but also in his personal attributes. He was immense; so much so that his size disqualified him from his dream of joining the police. Yet this was no deranged Frankenstein's monster, for his IQ measured a gifted 136, and his conversation was textured with wit and irony (even if its content was monotonously homicidal, its purpose narrowly to shock). Neither was he delusional like the killers Mullin and Berkowitz claimed to be, building unconventional and therefore "false" worlds. His mind perceived the world clearly and conventionally, and did not fill it with fantasies of demons and spirit forces. We must pay serious attention to Kemper.

It is the jumbled messages given off by the ideological conformity of a Kemper and the pseudo-radicalism of a Charles Manson that creates the public perplexity about multiple murderers. Why do they do the terrible things they do? What kind of an explanation can we expect from this John Wayne–glorifying giant (he grew up worshipping and identifying with the American hero-actor, John Wayne, whom his rival, Mullin, grew up hating*), sporting his bloodstained buckskin jacket, his prized Junior Chamber of Commerce pin (hard-won during his years in Atascadero mental hospital) adorning his lapel and proclaiming his utter conventionality? Can we expect a thoughtful answer from this freak whose childhood was little more than a sustained torrent of verbal abuse from his much-married mother? Fortunately we can, not only because he described

---

* Wayne's grip on the psyches of American multiple murderers is both deep and consistent. See also John Wayne Gacy, the homosexual torturer and multiple murderer.

and justified his acts in such detail, and not only because he was so intelligent, but also because, as Cheney reminds us, although a troubled person may make a "poor autodiagnostician," nevertheless "Kemper with his years of psychoanalysis had greater insight than most."[26]

We cannot, however, expect a *straightforward* answer from him. Perhaps we might have had we not stared for so long into the photographs of his face and been struck by his ill-concealed contempt for everyone and everything around him. He loved to toy with his simple-minded inquisitors, first offering one explanation, then denying it, and bringing forth another; leaving his audience always feeling that he "was holding back the real key to his behavior." He would play with the court psychologists, starting interviews by trying to give *them* the Minnesota Multiphasic Personality Inventory (a test which he had learned and administered to others during his years in the mental hospital). He never, thought his interrogators, told the whole truth; and whenever he was in danger of telling more than he wished, he would simply begin to describe dismemberment in detail, riveting the attention of his interviewers and leading the conversation in other directions.[27]

Moreover, his black humor would continually re-surface, partly to amuse himself, but more it seems to shock his audience. Thus he would satirize both the California dialect and himself, claiming he dreamed of decapitating hitchhikers as a means of "finding out where their heads were at"; or claiming that cutting off the hands of two of his victims had been "an afterthought." He used the standard rules of Hollywood humor to shock a woman reporter for a detective magazine who tried to sound him out on his attitudes to women: "What do you think now when you see a pretty girl walking down the street?" "One side of me says, 'Wow, what an attractive chick, I'd like to talk to her, date her.' The other side of me says, 'I wonder how her head would look on a stick.'" Surely this is playing the game for all that it is worth.[28]

This amused malice also typified his behavior toward his rival and fellow multiple murderer Herbert Mullin, who for a time occupied a cell adjacent to him. Kemper insisted upon calling him "Herbie," a diminutive Mullin hated. When a reporter asked him why he continued to ridicule and torment Mullin, Kemper replied: "Well, he had a habit of singing and bothering people when somebody tried to watch TV. So I threw water on him to shut him up. Then, when he was a good boy, I'd give him peanuts. Herbie liked peanuts. That was effective, because pretty soon he asked permission to sing. That's called behavior modification treatment."[29]

Yet we should not be lulled into thinking Kemper's purpose was mundane, for he felt he was on a kind of crusade, and despised those (like Mullin) who killed without any apparent ideological justification. "He [Mullin] was just a cold-blooded killer . . . killing everybody he saw for no good reason." Kemper laughed when he realized that his audience would not understand his own "good reason," and added: "I guess that's kind of hilarious, my sitting here so self-righteously talking like that, after what I've done." When asked if Mullin was insane, Kemper replied with a mixture of pomposity and self-satire: "Yes, judging from my years in Atascadero, I would say he is mentally ill." We shall see if this is all mere rationalization and persiflage.[30]

If Kemper found the act of contrition unthinkable, he sometimes claimed he found the act of confession disturbing. "This is a bummer. Which is why I get depressed in that damn cell 'cause I realized earlier today after talking to you guys that I . . . make a very strong attempt not to think about any of this stuff, anything related to it, and especially my mother while I'm in that cell, because I just get super depressed. I'm just sitting there, I still haven't slept in four days. I tried two more times back there to sleep, and I'd lay down—and the first thing, I'd start thinking about this last weekend. And I get super torqued-up and I'm wide awake; just absolutely not drowsy. And this is including 1,500 miles of driving almost constantly. And the last nine hundred miles of it was nothing but gas—a bottle of pop once in a while, and a lot of No-Doz."[31]

Unlike the killers Bundy, who tells us nothing, and Panzram, who puts it too succinctly, Kemper talks freely, with mingled embarrassment and delight, despite protestations, reservations, and contradictions. In the end, he leaves us with not one, but five explanations. Taken separately, as they were by his examiners, they seem to contradict one another and cancel each other out. That is why his interrogators complained that he could neither stop complaining nor tell the "whole truth." "We always felt he was holding something back," said one. I think not. The examiners did not see that they were being handed a complete and consistent package, merely delivered in superficially contradictory bundles, and sometimes wrapped in Atascadero's flimsy psychology.[32]

Again and again, Kemper patiently explained that the murder spree was an organized "operation," subject to specific "rules"; and that the murders were formal "executions," for which his childhood games had been mere rehearsals. He repeatedly denied police suggestions that the murders had been "spontaneous urges," and insisted that they had deep meaning. It would, he said, be "kind of hard to go around killing somebody just for the hell of it. . . . It's not a kicks thing, or I would have ceased doing it a long time ago. It was an urge. I wouldn't say it was on the full of the moon or anything, but I noticed that no matter how horrendous the crime had been or how vicious the treatment of the bodies after death . . . still, at that point in my crimes the urge to do it again coming as often as a week or two weeks afterwards—a strong urge, and the longer I let it go the stronger it got, to where I was taking risks to go out and kill people—risks that normally, according to my little rules of operation, I wouldn't take because they could lead to arrest."[33]

He did not plunge cavalierly into such reckless behavior: in fact, he procrastinated for months. At first, he admitted, "I was scared, and kept telling myself I didn't really want to do it. But I was determined. I was very frustrated, because it was like a game to me. Up to that point, it always had been. It was a big adventure, a big thrill. But I never permitted myself to follow through." Once committed, however, his operation was conducted flawlessly, so much so that "if I had kept my mouth shut, I would have gotten away with them I think, forever."[34]

To what intent does he refer when he said that after the tenth kill, "the original purpose was gone"? Which plan had been fulfilled, which force released, to allow him "to burn out the hate and fear"? What had changed so much that now "the need that I had for continuing death was needless and ridiculous. It wasn't serving any physical or real or emotional purpose. It was just a pure waste of time." Our quest requires a detailed explication of his statements.[35]

Sexual Mania

The "natural" or common-sense explanation for Kemper's behavior, much preferred by police, psychiatrists, journalists, and the public, is of course a sexual one; and Kemper himself offered this for our titillation from time to time. After all, it does make a certain sense: he was primarily engaged in killing beautiful young women and sexually assaulting their corpses. Sometimes he even went so far as to claim he was little more than an especially brutal rapist who killed merely to eliminate the only witnesses to his sexual exploits. He explained that he learned this tactic during his adolescence in the mental hospital, when his fellow patients had warned him that too many rapists were identified and caught. Arguing logically from this, he said: "I had decided from my past stay at Atascadero and listening to a lot of stories, that what I thought was my past experience—it seemed to me a lot more efficient not to have someone, unless you're absolutely sure that they weren't going to go to anybody." "I decided to kind of mix the two and have a situation of rape and a murder and no witness and no prosecution." All of this would make sense if he had systematically raped his victims. But he did not. In some cases, he hardly touched them sexually. Perhaps other needs were being satisfied?[36]

To pursue this even further: on the one hand he claimed that rape without murder was "just way too chancy"; but on the other hand he wondered if the murders had been necessary at all, allowing himself to speculate: "Thinking back on it, I really honestly think I could have gotten away with doing exactly what I told them I was going to do, which was rape. I didn't say that word. But one of them asked me, 'What do you want?' And I pointed the gun. I just lifted it up between the two of them, and I told her, 'You know what I want.' "[37]

Yet this overlooks his sexual incapacities. He insisted that he had a "very strong sensual drive, a weird sexual drive that started early, a lot earlier than normal, before I was aware of the phallic responsibilities." His sexual fantasies "were usually around women and rather than just having an orgasm it was having it with a dead woman. That was my fantasy. It would be more along the lines of a not so forceful rape." Still, we search in vain for any clear indication that sexuality was his strongest impulse. In places, he came close to denying his own claim of an all-powerful sexuality. He admitted that he "felt very inadequate sexually and sensually and socially," and that his fantasies of making passionate love to people "became dissatisfying because part of me knew that I couldn't really carry these things out. I couldn't follow through with the male end of the responsibility, so my fantasies became . . . if I killed them, you know, they couldn't reject me as a man. It was more or less making a doll out of a human being . . . and carrying out my fantasies with a doll, a living human doll."[38]

He insisted that he would have preferred to have raped Mary Ann Pesce and Anita Luchessa, his first victims, but "I had full intentions of killing them both. I would love to have raped them. But not having any experience at all in this area . . . this is one of the big problems I had." Yet his murders were always associated with an extraordinary, lace-curtain kind of sexual delicacy. He emphasized that he had attempted "no hanky-panky" with Cynthia Schall before he killed and dissected her; and recalled that he had apologized to Mary Ann when his hand had accidentally brushed against her breast while he was smothering her with a plastic bag: "There was absolutely no contact with improper areas," he insisted absurdly. Is this some sort of insane lower-middle-class sense of "refinement," some lunatic Puritanism that concerns itself with touching "improper areas" while murdering a young woman? Conversely, if he killed his mother to spare her the "embarrassment" of learning that he was a multiple murderer, then why was it necessary for him to sexually and symbolically assault her corpse?[39]

There are too many contradictions here, and the most fundamental one is surely that of his claimed super-sexuality. Despite all his protestations about his powerful sexual drive, he did not appear to be driven to exercise it very often. Moreover, the only act he seems genuinely to have found sexually exciting was decapitation. "I remember there was actually a sexual thrill," he said, for he loved to hear the "pop" when the head was separated from the body. "You hear that little pop and pull their heads off and hold their heads up by the hair. Whipping their heads off, their body sitting there. That'd get me off." Undoubtedly, but in what sense was that a sexual experience?[40]

For Kemper, *death,* not sex, was the ecstasy. Death, not sex, was much closer to the prime goal, for he knew "there was always a disappointment in not achieving a sexual rapport, let's say, with the victim. That's why the sex after death sometimes, because it's through frustration." Thus sex seemed to be a secondary benefit, and this suggestion is made even more explicit in his explanation of why he killed no men (other than his grandfather, who was in the way): "I suppose I could have been doing this with men, but that always posed more of a threat. They weren't nearly as vulnerable. . . . Plus, like in the case where sex is involved, or the thrill of having a woman around, alive and dead, wasn't there with a man." In sum, he "could have" killed men, and to have done so would not have violated his prime purpose; but they were physically less vulnerable and infinitely less exciting. Thus sex was the secondary, not the primary, benefit. If death, not sex, was a more important motive, then why?[41]

Possession

Possession is a second major motivational theme running through Kemper's monologue to the authorities. On the witness stand, he claimed he had killed women for the same reason that, as a child, he had killed cats—"to make it mine." He killed the women because: "Alive, they were distant, not sharing with me. I was trying to establish a relationship, and there was no relationship. . . . When they were being killed, there wasn't anything going on in my mind except that they were going to be mine. . . . That was the only way they could be mine."[42]

Here Kemper was arguing, in a vein commonly found in "primitive" cultures, that certain acts allowed an individual to possess the body and spirit of his victims. "I wanted the girls for myself—as possessions. They were going to be mine; they are mine!" In this spirit too, he ate the flesh of several of his victims: "I wanted them for my own. I wanted them to be a part of me—and now they are."[43]

The process of possession as he described it is to turn something human and animate, which he could neither own nor control, into something material and inanimate (yet of the very stuff of life) which he could control. In his words, "It was more or less making a doll out of a human being." "Taking life away from them, a living human being, and then having possession of everything that used to be theirs. All that would be mine. Everything . . . I was swashbuckling." Precisely. With their torsos in his closet, their heads in his trunk, or their last photographs in his bedroom, he came into possession of their material form and their spirit: swashbuckling, like a pirate ransacking golden galleons. We shall return to this theme.[44]

Trophy Hunting

Kemper offered an additional explanation, often misinterpreted by observers as yet another contradiction, which stressed the exhilaration of this ultimate triumph. "The head trip fantasies were a bit like a trophy. You know, the head is where everything is at, the brain, eyes, mouth. That's the person. I remember being told as a kid, you cut off the head and the body dies. The body is nothing after the head is cut off. . . . [at this point in the confessions, according to West, Kemper paused and chuckled] Well, that's not quite true. With a girl, there's a lot left in the girl's body without a head. Of course, the personality is gone."[45]

Once again, Kemper marshaled his thoughts to sort out what had been his goals. He tried to emphasize that the blood and gore were not central to his enterprise, dismissing it as a deviation that only emerged later. "I had started to really get into gear towards the end there. I was getting what I think is sicker, and it was much more of a need for more of the blood—and the blood got in my way. It wasn't something I desired to see. Blood was an actual pain in the ass." "What I wanted to see was the *death,* and I wanted to see the *triumph,* the exultation over the death. It was like eating, or a narcotic, something that drove me more and more and more," he said. "I just wanted the exultation over the other party. In other words, winning over death. They were dead and I was alive. That was a victory in my case." Moreover, the victory was a double one, for the triumph was not only over the lifeless victim, but also over his own fear—the latter triumph enhanced by his use of the pistol, which "made it much simpler, much easier, much quicker, less of a threat to me personally. I was less afraid to attack."[46]

Mother Rage

A fourth explanatory thread is the notion, obviously heavily influenced by his years of "therapy" in the mental hospital, that the killings were a kind of displacement to safer objects of the rage he felt toward his mother. More than any other, this explanation was seized upon by the psychologically oriented public as the True Version of Events. "Had he killed her [his mother] first, perhaps the others might have been spared," mused Cheney, ignoring the fact that he killed another after his mother. Still, there is plenty of evidence that mother rage was a profound reality in his life, and the theory is not to be dismissed.[47]

Kemper described his troubled childhood with considerable insight. "Very early, my natural parents were always loud and very pushy. As I was growing up, I shied away from loud noises and arguments. My mother was very strong and she wanted a man who was very strong. My father was very big and very loud, but he was very weak and she wanted the opposite. . . . You know, wooing and dating, you're one thing, but after you're married you let it all hang out. She was just too powerful. She would drive them away, attack them verbally, attack their manhood."[48]

Cheney touched on an important point when she observed that Kemper's mother felt her husband's work was menial, and the two often argued over money. In addition, Mrs. Kemper had claimed her husband "never spanked the children and they never had any respect for him. All he ever gave Ed was his medals and war stories." In an earlier letter, she recalled that his father "favored the son and was overprotective. . . . He resented my disciplining the boy at even an early age and sometimes blames the girls for letting him get in trouble." For his part, the father reported alarming maternal practices: "His mother made him at the age of eight years sleep in the cellar of the house for about eight months. He was terrified of this place. There was only one way out. Someone had to move the kitchen table and lift the trapdoor. I put a stop to it and threatened her with the law." Kemper's mother justified this behavior in terms of her reluctance to be "overprotective"—a stance her sister had taken with her own son, and thereupon had produced a homosexual.[49]

Kemper's parents had separated in 1957, and Mrs. Kemper moved with her three children to Helena, Montana, where she found work as a bank secretary. She was divorced from Kemper in 1961, and two months later married a German immigrant. This second husband soon left, and a year later, divorced once more, she married a forty-five-year-old plumber named Turnquist. "I found out," Kemper later recalled, "that she didn't need any protection at all. She used always to tell me how much I reminded her of my father whom she dearly hated, of course." Turnquist was a kindly step-father, taking Kemper on fishing trips and teaching him to hunt; but it was Turnquist whom Kemper had stood behind with an iron bar, planning to knock him unconscious and steal his car in order to visit his natural father. About that time, his mother wrote: "I was deeply worried during the years about the lack of a father relationship, and so I tried everything I could to compensate for that." But, according to Lunde, she interpreted this as *carte blanche* to "punish and ridicule him in order to 'make him a man.'"[50]

After his first incarceration for the murder of his grand-parents, Kemper rapidly internalized the psychological definitions of self dispensed by the staff at Atascadero, a process which revealed itself clearly in his later remarks: "I found out in the hospital that I really killed my grandmother because I wanted to kill my mother." But why then was he still in a murderous rage after killing his mother? Why then go on to kill her friend? "My grandmother was worse than my mother. I had this love-hate complex with my mother that was very hard for me to handle and I was very withdrawn—withdrawn from reality because of it. I couldn't handle the hate, and the love was actually forced upon me, you know. It was a very strong family-tie type love. There was a constant battle inside me that was the major thing of my whole life. I didn't have any social attitude, any social personality at all." This echoes a theme especially common among those who annihilate their own families. At Atascadero, he "learned" that he "really" hated his mother: surely true, but insufficient cause for what was to come.[51]

When he was released from Atascadero, the authorities ignored the psychiatrists' sound advice and "They paroled me right back to mama. Well, my mother and I started right in on horrendous battles, just horrible battles, violent and vicious. I've never been in such a vicious verbal battle with anyone. It would go to fists with a man, but this was my mother and I couldn't stand the thought of my mother and I doing these things. She insisted on it, and just over stupid things." And what were these epic struggles about? They were the classic obsessive concerns of those gripped by status insecurity, by the fear of downward mobility, expressed in fears that their work is too menial, their income too low, their personal styles inappropriate to their class aspirations: "I remember one roof-raiser was over whether I should have my teeth cleaned."[52]

Kemper tried to flee. He took a job with the state's Department of Highways and rented his own apartment. But in early 1972, he broke his arm in a motorcycle accident and began spending more time at his mother's home, recuperating. West recorded that their neighbors knew when Kemper was visiting from the shouts and loud arguments reverberating through the walls, during which Kemper would be "upbraided for lazing about drinking beer and not *making something of himself*. . . . She had been known to reduce Guy [her pet name for Kemper] to tears in front of his friends with her sharp tongue." At the time, Kemper denied that the fights were important, insisting to a neighbor that the vehement quarrels were simply his family's means of expression. Parading his Atascadero psychology, he told the neighbor: "We like to get things out in the open. My mother and I are really very close and we know these fights don't mean anything."[53]

In the meantime, Kemper appeared to struggle for her love, showering her with presents on social occasions such as Easter, on her birthday. But there was nothing that this beer-swilling, ex-mental patient, and flagman for the Department of Highways could possibly do to please this university administrator. When he fled back to his own apartment, she continued to pursue him. "I couldn't stay away from my mother. . . . She would get madder than cat shit, got my phone number, calling me up wanting to come up and visit all the time. The hassle with my mother made me very inadequate around women, because they posed a threat to me. Inside I blew them up very large. You know, the little games women play, I couldn't play, meet their demands, so I backslid. . . . With my Atascadero learning, I kept trying to push her toward where she would be a nice motherly type and quit being such a damned manipulating, controlling vicious beast. She was Mrs. Wonderful on the campus, had everything under control. When she comes home, she lets everything down and she's just a pure bitch, bust her butt being super nice at work and come home at night and be shit."[54]

He occasionally attributed the murders of Rosalind Thorpe and Alice Liu to an argument with his mother. "I was mad that night. My mother and I had a real tiff. I was pissed. I told her I was going to a movie and I jumped up and went straight to the campus, because it was still raining and ideal [hunting weather]. I decided that the first girl I picked up who looked halfway decent, I'm going to blow her brains outs." Most students of Kemper supported this view, painting the killings exclusively as a kind of dialogue with his mother. After he shot Cynthia Schall, West said Kemper "felt pleased with this choice of the long hollow-point slugs, because she had died more quickly and easily than anyone. He had a sudden impulse to go home and tell his mother, so she could know that there were some things he could do right." Yet Kemper himself explained it in subtly different terms, emphasizing broader issues than his disordered relationship with his mother: "The real me was somewhat bolstered at Atascadero to where I wouldn't let anyone push me over the brink any more to just self-destruction. In the case of the girls, it was fantasy coming back. Rather than fight my mother, fight the world, finally I decided, well, screw it. I'm going to play their little game." Exactly, but what was this game of theirs, and in what sense was he playing it?[55]

Kemper told the psychiatrist Lunde of his "recurring fantasies of killing women, his mother in particular"; and he had often considered killing her, entering her bedroom at night, carrying a weapon. But Kemper rationalized the actual murder of his mother as an attempt to spare her embarrassment. "I felt . . . that I was going to be caught pretty soon for the killing of these girls. . . . A long time ago, I had thought about what I was going to do in the event of being caught for the other crimes, and the only choices I saw were just accept it and go to jail, and let my mother carry the load and let the whole thing fall in her hands, like happened the last time with my grandparents, or I could take her life." Kemper rationalized as much as any human being, especially one caught in such a persona-degrading circumstance as he was in, but he rarely did so with such transparent self-serving naivety as here: undoubtedly he did so because nothing else he had done was so unequivocally taboo in his civilization.[56]

When asked why he had taken so long to actually kill his mother, he confessed his fear of her: "I never had the nerve. You would have to understand the gap I had to bridge the way people had been manipulating me." When it was finally done, her killing was more than he could have wished, for it both reduced her in his eyes and released him from her prison. "I had always considered my mother very formidable, very fierce and very foreboding. She had always been a very big influence in my life and whether I hated her or loved her, it was amazing to me how like every other victim of mine had died, how vulnerable, how human she was. It shocked me for quite some time. I'm not sure it still doesn't shock me [but] I felt quite relieved after her death." During his last run, through Colorado, Kemper thought deeply of the biblical symbolism associated with his acts. The Bible had always fascinated him, and the severing of his mother's left hand was "symbolic, I suppose." "I think it is like the left-hand-of-God thing," God's punishing hand, of which the cutting from his mother's body freed him from all retribution.[57]

Revenge

The biblical eye-for-an-eye is the fifth and final explanatory theme running through Kemper's ambiguous confessions—an Old Testament theme that he spelled out in great detail, most convincingly, and then repudiated during his trial. Still, the central emphasis is clear: he wished both to "make a demonstration to the authorities" and to "even up the Accounts Receivable to match the Accounts Payable." But what did he wish to demonstrate to the authorities; and what were the missing payments in the accounts ledger? This phrase "demonstrate to the authorities" is peculiar wording, resonant more of political proclamation than of private act. And a demand for payment is an odd position for Kemper to take: he was no impoverished black proletarian denied forever a place in the social order. To the contrary, with his intelligence and his mother's marginal middle-class membership, he could have easily made good his deficiencies in a junior college, then transferred to university and entered the middle-class world himself. But he did not do so: unlike so many false rebels, his acts confirmed his advertised disdain. He chose instead to wage a complex vendetta as the only means to validate himself and seize control of his own destiny (even if in doing so he transferred the remainder of his life to the state).[58]

What *was* this John Wayne–worshipping laborer's conception of his society? "I consider it a very phony society, a very phony world, where people are too busy copping out to so many things to exist and fit into a group that they had lost sight of their individual aims and goals. I had become completely lost, and very bitter about what I considered these phony values and phony existence, and decided that I was going, not necessarily to weed things out—because I would have ended up killing most of the world if I weeded out—but I was striking out at what was hurting me the worst, which was the area, I guess, deep down, I wanted to fit in the most, and I had never fit in, and that was the in-group." This statement begins with a measure of accuracy and coherence, if expressed in most childish terms, but soon degenerates into a contradictory Atascadero group-therapy form of analysis—where he first claims to reject society (and especially those who abandon their principles in order to "fit in") and then "admits" that all he really wanted was to be a part of it.[59]

We would be foolish to expect consistency in any human being, let alone in a multiple murderer engaged in the enterprise of justifying his existence. Nevertheless, a man of intelligence is talking here about the ultimate purpose of his life, a purpose he embraced so passionately that he sacrificed all else for it. His thoughts deserve careful scrutiny. He edged toward a truth when he discussed his unfulfilled plan of "annihilating" his neighborhood. "Yeah. That was one of my things. I'd feel inadequate there, feel like everybody's catching up with me, and I'm not doing anything. Considering the abilities I did have, in say creating a calm about me where people weren't excited or suspicious or nervous . . . I believed and I still believe that had I wanted to, just as a demonstration—and I thought of making this a demonstration to the authorities in Santa Cruz—how serious this was, and how bad a foe they had come up against."[60]

This "foe" of the authorities wanted more than just to exult in the possession of his trophies, or to punish his mother. "It wasn't just deaths I wanted. It was, like I said, somewhat of a *social statement* in there too." Entirely congruent with this was his discussion of why he did not prey on children, despite their vulnerability. "There are two things against that. One is the most important—that is that children are innocent. Children are unknowing. And I have always been very protective of children for that reason." But of *what* are their elders guilty? He continued: "These girls weren't much more than children, I suppose, but I felt . . . that they were old enough to know better than to do the things they were doing . . . out there hitchhiking, when they had no reason or need to. They were flaunting in my face the fact that they could do any damn thing they wanted, and that society is as screwed up as it is. So that wasn't a prime reason for them being dead. It was just something that would get me a little uptight, the thought of that, them feeling so safe in a society where I didn't feel safe." But of what could a 300-pound, six-foot-nine-inch giant be afraid?[61]

Kemper preyed only on those he felt shared the guilt (either directly in their power over him, or indirectly via their apparent social association with the authorities): the dominant class, and most especially on that class's beautiful and desired young women whose "flaunted" indifference toward him hurt him most. Thus he could say with honesty that "I had some Accounts Payable and I closed my Accounts Receivable, and so I had to balance the accounts." The targets for his "little game" were to be young women who were appropriately upper class, at least in appearance. Hitchhiking was the only mechanism that made such targets vulnerable: "I couldn't entice young, well-to-do smart asses whom I dearly hated into my car to go for a ride any other way." He did not consider himself a meaningless "bubble that burst all over society—I was more organized than that." He knew where to find his victims, and why he was destroying them. "I was swashbuckling, I was destroying only society's finest young girls. I was not interested in the ragged, dirty little hippies, that would have been simple. I could have run up a huge score that way."[62]

This foe of the authorities made his coherent plan, organized his demonstration, and decided to attack. "I was frustrated in my dreams and desires totally. It was sad, really. I didn't blame society for me not being able to be a policeman, but . . ." society seemed so utterly *indifferent* to him. Even when he was returning Liu's torso to the car, "I just wandered right out there with her and put her in the trunk right under the window. That's one thing that amazes me about society. That is, that you can do damn near anything and nobody's gonna say anything or notice." "Rather than fight my mother, fight the world, finally I decided, well, screw it. I'm going to play their little games. They are going to see what they want to see—Ed out working, Ed doing this and that. Meanwhile Ed is deep in deciding how he can get back at society for putting him in this hellhole in the first place."[63]

Within this dweller in hellholes crystallized a new identity, undoubtedly his first agreeable one: the Swashbuckling Avenger. Only through the series of intellectual twists and transformations we have charted could an intellect so conventional that it embodied all the mainstream themes of his civilization—John Wayne and policemen, the Boy Scouts, the National Rifle Association, and the Atascadero branch of the Junior Chamber of Commerce—commit itself to the slaughter of women. He would annihilate a sample of the excluding class, women who kept him in his hellhole literally, as in locking him in a cellar, or by offering him only contempt, disrespect, and bland indifference.

Kemper was too proud to spend his life as a flagman for the Department of Highways, too obsessed with his inadequacies to do anything about them, too rattled by his mother and Atascadero to devote his energy to anything but staying alive. The choice made a certain sense: now, if he picked up women in his car, it would be only for an entirely serious purpose: "It was for possible execution . . . and it would only be if they were young, reasonably good looking, not necessarily well-to-do, but say, of a better class of people than the scroungy, messy, dirty, smelly, hippie types I wasn't at all interested in. I suppose they would have been more convenient, but that wasn't my purpose. *My little social statement was, I was trying to hurt society where it hurt the worst,* and that was by taking its valuable . . . future members of the working society; that was the upper class or the upper-middle class, what I considered to be snobby or snotty brats, or persons that was actually—that ended up later being better equipped to handle a living situation than I was, and be more happily adjusted."[64]

With the commitment sealed, he still yearned to communicate with these snobby, happy brats. During their drive, he tried to establish a kind of relationship with his first victims, Pesce and Luchessa, but his sense of social incompetence so overwhelmed him that "I felt like a big bumblebutt. . . . They were both eighteen at the time, I think, and I was twenty-three, which isn't that much of a gap, but it was just like a million years."[65]

After killing them, he made scrupulous attempts to ensure that they had been suitably upper class (for if they had been otherwise, his protest would have been pointless), especially Mary Ann Pesce, to whom he had been most attracted. He went through her wallet and noted the middle-class college student card and the Bear Valley ski-patrol card. Obtaining her family's address, he drove the hundreds of miles to ensure that it was a "country club district" (for had it not been, his plan would surely have been malfunctioning). Later, he allowed himself to fabricate a close relationship with Pesce: "I was quite struck by her personality, her looks, almost a reverence," but it was a frustrated one, for even "with me in control of the situation there, I still wasn't in control of her and it made me mad."[66]

Ted Bundy consciously eliminated all emotional contact with his prospective victims, speaking to them as little as possible to avoid the development of any inhibiting social bond. Kemper did the opposite and tried to cultivate a relationship—not to make the kill more difficult, but largely to obtain the necessary social information to be sure the girls were of the targeted upper class. "This was something I usually tried—to talk to the girls about, and gently probe about, different things; to find out their life-style, their living conditions, whatever." At first he was not certain that Aiko Koo was from the correct background: "She was very free and prolific in her speech, and I believed from her speech that she came from a home of meager means, that her parents had either divorced or her father had left her at an early age. . . . And there was no family car. The only transportation that she had was a bus to and from where she would go. Her clothing was rather plain and she apparently had taken pains to dress herself . . . as clean-cut as possible." If she was a marginal case, she was available; her *style* was suitably upper class, and Kemper correctly sensed that she came from "an aristocratic type of family" in a state of genteel poverty. Still, it troubled him that Koo had not been a proper choice.[67]

In essence then, this evidence paints Kemper as a swashbuckling pirate who boards the upper-class galleon and carries off its most valuable possessions, its beautiful young women. But in court, under questioning from his own attorney, Kemper denied the entire theory he had constructed so painstakingly during the interrogations. Now he claimed he killed only to possess them (theory two): "When the girls were alive, they were distant and not sharing with me. I was trying to establish a relationship." Is this a legitimate denial, or mere frustration at trying to explain his story so often? Or was it a bored accommodation with his attorney to the kind of sentence they wished to receive? I think it was the latter. It takes no great imagination to sketch in the hurried conversations, during which the virtues of a "crazy" plea (of some psychic need to possess his victims) would be pressed in order to ensure the relative comfort and safety of a mental hospital. A statement of revenge might have ensured only the tender mercies of a prison.[68]

At the close of the trial, the swashbuckling pirate showed his true ideological affinity: he was leading a brief rebellion, not a revolution. The only relationship he established during the trial was with Deputy Sheriff Colomny who was his jailer. "He's more like a father to me than anyone I have ever known. He's like the father I wish I had had," Kemper said at his sentencing. With that, he removed his precious Junior Chamber of Commerce pin from the lapel of his buckskin jacket. Deputy Colomny watched as "Ed looked at it for a long time and tears came to his eyes. Then he handed it to me and said, 'Here, I want you to have it.'" Like so many swashbuckling pirates before him, once his rampage was stopped, he embraced the social order, and counted his booty.[69]

TALES FROM PSYCHIATRY

"I see no psychiatric reason to consider him (Kemper) to be a danger to himself or any other member of society."

KEMPER'S PSYCHIATRIST

Psychiatry's unrivaled access to the court system makes it the heir to the richest data on all criminal behavior. What insights did the psychiatrists construct about Kemper during the many years he was in their care? Kemper first came to their attention after killing his grandparents. The psychiatrists immediately disagreed about him. The court psychiatrist, one of the few mental health professionals ever to understand how dangerous Kemper was, found him to be "psychotic," "confused and unable to function." His notes continued with the observations that Kemper "has paranoid ideation, growing more and more bizarre. It is noteworthy that he is more paranoid toward women, all except his mother, who is the real culprit. He is a psychotic and danger to himself and others. He may well be a very long-term problem," he predicted with eerie prescience. Whether or not the court psychiatrist's "diagnosis" of "psychotic" was accurate, he was to be the last professional whom Kemper could not fool about his threat to the world.[70]

The California Youth Authority social workers and medical staff, responding presumably to Kemper's articulate and duplicitous intelligence, disagreed with the court psychiatrist and found Kemper's thinking to be neither confused, bizarre, nor psychotic. One report stressed that he showed "no flight of ideas, no interference with thought, no expression of delusions or hallucinations, and no evidence of bizarre thinking." Their diagnosis was that while Kemper had poor ego strength and suffered from passivity and a fear of injury by other boys, he merely suffered from "personality trait disturbance, passive-aggressive type." Just before his sixteenth birthday—and despite the nonsexual nature of his killing—Kemper was admitted to Atascadero mental hospital for sex offenders, a "learning experience" in which he would be immersed for five years.[71]

In the mental hospital, Kemper established a relationship with Dr. Vanasek, and began earning his good opinion by working for him, administering psychological tests to patients in the psychology laboratory. "He was a very good worker," Vanasek remembered, "and this is *not* typical of a sociopath. He really took pride in his work." Taking pride in his work, passing through adolescence in a milieu of violent rapists encouraged to broadcast their crimes and fantasies in group "therapy," Kemper internalized both their disordered sexuality and the hopsital's psychological theories—although he seems to have used his psychological knowledge primarily to conceal his own developing ideas, and to dupe his examiners.[72]

Still, his tests revealed the rage that was still boiling inside him. When he was nineteen, the usual Rorschach inkblots provoked from him a response of non-human and violent images—"two bears running into each other"; "alligator's jaws—his mouth is wide open"; "oil fire in the distance, black smoke going up in the air, reflecting in water"; "a trapdoor with a spider at the bottom, sitting down in the hole waiting to snatch an insect." The testing psychologist's conclusions, based on the results of the Rorschach and TAT tests, were that: "Emotionally, Mr. Kemper is somewhat immature and volatile. The prevailing mood is that of moderate depression accompanied by generalized anxiety. There is evidence of a rather substantial amount of latent hostility. . . . He gives the impression of a rather passive, dependent person rather than one who is overtly aggressive. The possibility of explosiveness is certainly evident, however." The collection of his personality traits revealed the following profile: "Intelligent, emotionally unstable, easily upset, shy, suspicious, self-opinionated, artless, apprehensive, noncritical, careless, follows own urges, tense, driven, overwrought, and fretful"—a set of traits which might, one speculates, belong to half the human race. Still, this non-aggressive, "rather passive, dependent person" was soon to be released.[73]

Paroled to his mother over the objections of his psychiatrists, Kemper left Atascadero with a rapidly coalescing vision of what his life task might be. But his bland manner reassured the parole psychiatrist who, months later, released him from parole after the satisfying and intimate interview. The psychiatrist did not look in Kemper's trunk, where lay a victim's head. In an evaluation that may well stand for all time as the least prescient, the psychiatrist wrote: "I see no psychiatric reason to consider him to be a danger to himself or any other member of society. His motorcycle and driving habits would appear to be more of a threat to his own life and health than any threat he is presently to anyone else."[74]

Later, after his murderous task had been completed and he had turned himself in, having made his demonstration to the authorities, Kemper received even closer psychiatric scrutiny. Psychiatric specialist on sexual deviation, Dr. Joel Fort, examined Kemper and concluded that he was a "sex maniac": "The two central themes were an overwhelming sexual curiosity and obsession with sex, to such an extent that, insofar as we use lay language or concepts that have been widely circulated in society, I think he could best be described as a sex maniac, certainly to a greater degree than anyone else I have seen in working with sexual and criminal problems in the past twenty years. The second theme was a tremendous range of hatred, rage, or aggressiveness that stemmed from a series of childhood experiences and subsequent experiences, and that involved or included getting back at a society that he felt wronged him, getting back at his mother and father that he felt had wronged him." But was Kemper's *sexual* obsession really much stronger than any lonely and frustrated virgin? And, in a world replete with wrongs, was he not wronged far less than many, perhaps most?[75]

As any Freudian scholar might do, Fort concentrated with gusto on Kemper's bizarre sexual practices, dwelling on his "oral copulations with several of his victims," and the "violent, extremely exciting acts of penile vaginal intercourse where he rapidly had orgasms and ejaculation," "taking Polaroid photographs of them and of the heads of several after he beheaded them," "then followed in a sort of a declining . . . sense of sexual pleasure by collecting their clothing, keeping some of it for varying periods of time, and collecting objects like books or other paraphernalia that they were carrying with them, and keeping them for varying periods of time, and glancing at them sometimes."[76]

Fort rejected a diagnosis of paranoid schizophrenia, a label that was much in the air after Kemper's capture, on the reasonable grounds that "a paranoid schizophrenic should have marked feelings of unreality, depersonalization —meaning that you lose your sense of identity, and lose the boundaries between yourself and other people in your environment [but why is this a sign of some mental disease, and not a response to his niche in society?], and most of all, has delusions, meaning false beliefs, beliefs that you are being persecuted." Similarly, Fort rejected a paranoid label, since Kemper's mother and grandmother had in fact appeared to reject him and deny him affection. Unfortunately, Fort insisted on merely stigmatizing Kemper with a diagnosis that labels a mere sense of social disengagement: "I would place him in the broader category of personality disorder, specifically antisocial personality, which is no more, and no less, than the old diagnosis of psychopath or sociopath." Fort said the characteristics of those in this mental state include "not operating by any recognized or accepted moral code"; not profiting "from experience in the usual sense, that is, does not modify his behavior to conform to societal standards." Here Fort is simply describing some of the characteristics of any eccentric or nonconformist, not providing any useful insight into the mind of a multiple murderer. A more canny observation was that Kemper had achieved the celebrity status commonly granted multiple murderers in America (ever being asked for his autograph). Fort noted that Kemper "gets a considerable amount of pleasure and satisfaction from his status as a mass killer," but rather than looking for possible meaning in this, he explained it in terms of Kemper's inadequacy—it was all "the recognition that he sometimes desperately sought as a child, the attempt to overcome rejection."[77]

In the most scholarly assessment Kemper was to receive, the psychiatrist and writer Donald Lunde dismissed the applicability of the "criminal chromosome" theory, the profoundly unscientific product of the Harvard Medical School and elsewhere which suggests that "XYY boys are more impulsive that XY boys." Lunde noted that Kemper "fits one proposed description of the XYY—unusually tall, above average intelligence, and unusually violent" (along with a substantial minority of the American male population), but concluded that tests performed at Stanford University's Medical Center revealed that Kemper's chromosomes, like those of all our multiple murderers, were normal. Lunde went on to reject the categories of paranoid schizophrenia, sociopath, and personality disorder, but inserted his own: the "sadistic murderer." "In rare individuals, for reasons that are not well understood, sexual and violent aggressive impulses merge early in the child's development, ultimately finding expression in violent sexual assaults, and in the most extreme cases, sadistic murders or sex murders." Interesting, but we are left wondering *why* some individuals should link sexuality and violence, and why they must kill to be satisfied, and whether that satisfaction is sexual or social.[78]

KEMPER'S TASK

> "I didn't want to kill all the coeds in the world."
>
> EDMUND KEMPER[79]

It is our responsibility, of course, to offer proof of our assertions: that it helps us little to know that "psychotics" or "sadists" may have a desire to humiliate and destroy their victims; that Kemper's rampage is more than the expression of a mental disease or the egomaniacal indulgence of a deranged sexuality; and that his task or mission permitted him to construct a crisp identity and terminate his alienation from society. Where then do we begin to decipher Kemper's code? One logical place is where he ended—with his conscious decision to shut down his "operation" and capitulate to the authorities: it was through this action that Kemper made the point most forcefully that his murder spree had been a task, and that the task had been fulfilled.

His Capitulation

Kemper reasoned, using his knowledge of police techniques garnered through his friendships with many officers, that so long as he followed his carefully considered procedures, he could have continued murdering: "If I had kept my mouth shut, I would have gotten away with them, I think, forever." He knew that the police were trying to capture the killer, but he also knew that "with the tools the police have to work with and with the basic concept that society isn't as cold-blooded and ruthless and backstabbing as I am, they didn't really have [a chance]. I was being rather cunning about the whole thing." This statement alone would surely disqualify any literal application of the "sex maniac" theory, for why should he cease for all time (and he knew that once he confessed, he would be incarcerated for the remainder of his life) an activity he found so necessary and enjoyable (unless he was riddled with guilt and remorse, which he was not)?[80]

A partial explanation might lie in the strain he was feeling. "I was fairly agitated," he said. "I was kidding around a lot and was very nervous. My stomach was killing me. I think I'm developing ulcers because of all this. Not so much now, but I was in a great tension whenever something like that was happening, especially people in the trunk and having to dispose [of their bodies]. I'd get close to the point of panic until it was done." "Shit," he said, "I couldn't keep on going forever . . . I really couldn't have. Emotionally, I couldn't handle it much longer." "Towards the end there, I started feeling the folly of the whole damn thing, and at the point of near exhaustion, near collapse, I just said the hell with it and called it all off. Let's say . . . I wore out of it."

Kemper said of his last run, the frenzied drive away from the coast before he made the decision to capitulate: "It was very late at night. I was exhausted . . . I was past exhaustion. I was just running on pure adrenaline. My body was quivering . . . and my mind was slowly just beginning to unravel." However, this explanation overlooks the fact that if he was under terrible tension before and during a kill, once it was done and the body disposed of, he experienced something verging on euphoria: "I would just completely relax." What was different now? Why would the ecstasy of total relaxation no longer return to him? Could it be because his task was finished, his point made, and he could no longer justify his killings?[81]

A second partial explanation of why Kemper capitulated is contained in his remark that, during his drive to Colorado, he began to feel that for the first time in his life he "was losing control" of himself. "I had never been out of control in my life," he said, a remarkable statement coming from someone we are taught to think of as quintessentially out of control, a rabid mad dog killer. Kemper explained this by distinguishing between mental and physical control: "I had lost control of my body. I had experienced this in the killing of my grandparents when I was fifteen. I just completely lost control of myself. But as far as my mind went, I had realized what was going on and I couldn't stop it. In this case my body was just exhausted and my mind was starting to go. I was hallucinating."[82]

Continuing with this illumination of his perspective, Kemper said: "I finally had a thought. I was trying to think, 'Wow, I have got to stop this because it is getting so far out of hand. I am not going to be responsible for what happens any further' . . . and I didn't like that idea." In other words, he accepted full responsibility for what to us is madness but to him was not—the murder of ten human beings—but he was concerned that he might do something that was not justifiable, to kill without meaning or awareness. "The original purpose was gone. It was starting to weigh kind of heavy. Let's say I started returning to some lucid moments where I—where I started to burn out the hate and fear . . . and the need that I had for continuing death was needless and ridiculous. It wasn't serving any physical or real or emotional purpose. It was just a pure waste of time." To kill without meaning was unacceptable to him; and when he had killed ten times, his quota had been filled. Further killings would have been without purpose, and he did not wish to leave that charge in his wake. If he submitted to the authorities then because he had achieved his objectives, what were those objectives?[83]

Unfinished Business

The most remarkable thing about Kemper's life—like that of many multiple murderers—is how unremarkable it was, at least before he began his homicidal career. It is true that being locked in the cellar by his appalling mother must have been deeply traumatic for him, but many people have experienced similar deprivation and yet still grown to a healthy maturity. It seems to be true that his mother, endlessly and maniacally picking at him, was an impossible woman to live with, for she could not control her status hysteria or her unloading of that insecurity upon her son. But he was not living with her when he began to kill; and even if he had been, a more plausible solution to his dilemma would have been to run away. It is true that his mother was much-married during his childhood, a practice which profoundly disorients a child,* but from all accounts, including his own, his step-fathers seemed exceptionally kind to him. This is not at all the stuff of legend. Indeed, it seems misleading to look only to his family and childhood for the causes of his murderous career since his childhood was, by modern standards, not that appalling.

The reader may feel that in doing so we have closed the doors to understanding, for our civilization is entrapped in the mental custom of explaining the adult *exclusively* in terms of the child. But we have not closed all doors, and Kemper has opened still others. In his confessions, Kemper gave five "theories" to explain his behavior; theories which,

---

* A quite disproportionate number of multiple murderers had mothers who had married three or more times; see Leyton, 1983, for a brief discussion of this matter.

the reader will remember, often contradicted one another—
or seemed to. They were his frustrated sexuality, his need to
possess, his exultant trophy hunting, his rage toward his
mother, and the lust for revenge. If we take him only partly
at his word, and see these not as separate and contradictory
theories, but as insufficiently articulated *elements* of a single
theory, we can then edge closer to the truth—which is that
they were all part of his motive and his profit, all incorpo-
rated in a single plan.

Baldly stated, the question "Why did Kemper kill?" is the
wrong one. The truth is that many humans have in them the
capacity to terminate life (ask any psychiatrist or police
officer)—to eliminate opposition, say, or for sadistic
pleasure—but few choose to do so. Most avoid such an act,
not because they are morally superior, as they so commonly
claim, but because they are imprisoned in a web of responsibilities, commitments, beliefs, and sentiments which would
render murder either an absurd gamble or ridiculous self-
destruction. As inalienable parts of family, community, and
society, most humans either already receive sufficient satisfactions in their lives, or they have been convinced that
further prayer, work, or luck may bring them about. All of
which is to say that most humans have too much to lose; and
unless they are burdened by an ill-considered rashness, they
will not embark on any homicidal venture, let alone a
sustained campaign.

But imagine another man, perfectly sane, but one who has
from his earliest beginnings found himself to be set aside
from all the life that swirls around him; a boy who comes to
feel that he could neither love nor be loved; and whose
identity begins to coalesce around an adolescent fantasy of a
pirate adventurer, or perhaps a cowboy who rights all
exclusionary wrongs. It makes a certain sense that, rejected
by both parents, living with a grandmother he found even
more punitive, and obsessed with his growing violent fantasies (the only way he could retaliate against the constant
assaults on his *persona*), he might explode and kill, and lose
control of his body but not his mind, as Kemper would put
it. Imprisoned then through steamy adolescence in an
all-male institution, he had no opportunity to accidentally

experience a loving sexual relationship (or even to hear of one, given his sex-criminal companions), or to discover that he might be more than he had come to believe. It makes sense that, with an identity so stunted and abridged that he could later confess he had "no personality at all," he might be easy prey for any fantasy which would offer him a measure of identity. Similarly, his incapacity for forming relationships resulted in a personal alienation so complete that there was no one in his life except his raging mother. Here was a man with very little to lose. Hardly surprising then that the mature cowboy/pirate/adventurer might elect to swashbuckle, to form a game plan that would confront all the major issues in his life—and do so with a forcefulness and finality in keeping with the spirit of a true adventurer.*
What were these major issues? His rage at his mother, his frustrated sexuality, and his utter alienation from all humanity.

Putting the flesh of reality to his fantasy through a conscious decision to swashbuckle would deal not only with the ghosts of his childhood, but with the empty promise of his adult life (for he could not bring himself to believe that anything would change—and perhaps he was right). Yet Kemper was no revolutionary, had no desire to transform the social order under the banner of some brave new ideology: on the contrary, he identified with its most conservative symbols. And yet he knew that he could never be a part of life unless he revoked his excommunication through some extravagant act, establishing thereby a social niche for himself and a firm identity: a simple desire, but a necessary one, for only if he has his own borders can a man negotiate with adjacent entities.

Thus Kemper's motive was clear: "I had been frustrated in my dreams and desires totally." A remedy soon

---

* With the special gift of hindsight, it is easy to see that the signs were there much earlier: in his TAT test at the age of nineteen. When shown a photograph of a boy and an older man, he replied: "In this situation we've got a young man who's got problems, and his dad is counseling him. . . . He wanted to follow in his father's footsteps, but then he had a lot of other interests he couldn't really follow if he did take a position in his father's corporation. . . . He decides he really doesn't like that kind of work. It's holding him down, so he sells out and joins the Merchant Marine and goes tearing off around the world."[94]

crystalized in the form of a task: he must make a demonstration to the authorities, confronting the social order with the fact of his excommunication. He would not beg for admission like some sniveling coward: no, like his adventurer, he merely exacted revenge coolly, acting out his "social statement" by "destroying society's finest." Why young women? Partly, it is their vulnerability that makes them so easy to subdue, and, partly, their flamboyant sexuality which he could now exploit; but primarily because they were the front line, as it were, of the class that humiliated him daily through their acts of indifference, their refusal to accept him.

The task of this foe of the authorities is now clear. In performing it, his lowly flagman status would disappear, his identity would fuse and, paradoxically, his alienation cease. As he slipped into the social niche of celebrated multiple murderer, he cured society's indifference to him, and did so while exacting his fearful revenge and indulging all his repressed sexuality. Thus one single all-encompassing task yielded many profits—of revenge, of triumph, and of ecstasy.

Yet Kemper stopped when he had killed six young women: "I didn't want to kill *all* the coeds in the world." Having made his social statement and indulged his sexual fantasies, having created his identity and his niche, it went without saying that his "purpose was gone." Soon it would be time to retire, but not before he had completed the trilogy of communal, sexual, and familial revenge. In killing his mother and her best friend—and doubly violating the most fundamental taboos by doing it with the utmost savagery—this once-alienated man without any identity or sexuality established himself in the world. Not a man to be trifled with is the bearer of such a crisp and powerful masculine identity. He had come to terms with that "total frustration" which all our multiple murderers remedy in their crusades. After his lengthy confessions had staked his claim to greatness for all time, his task was utterly discharged; *now* he could rest and sleep (not while he was confessing, but only when he was finished).

Although we should grieve for his victims and their

bereaved families, we must not grieve for him. If his recent photographs are anything to go by, he sits in his institution a happy man. This should not be any surprise, for he has confronted all the major issues in his life, and resolved them. Kemper has, in his own terms, re-written his personal history, and in the lunacy of destruction, created himself.

3.
OWNING A FEMALE PERSON

Theodore Robert Bundy*

> "What's one less person on the face
> of the earth anyway?"
>
> TED BUNDY[1]

One cannot be precise about how many beautiful young women he killed, for he has never made a full confession. It is generally accepted that he killed at least twenty, and he is suspected of killing close to forty, making him—until the advent of Henry Lee Lucas**—among the most "successful" of all modern multiple murderers. Like Edmund Kemper, he preyed only on the middle class and the desirable. Because he was both handsome and intelligent, the notion became widespread that he was some kind of

---

* Bundy's own comments in letters and transcripts are of some use, and they are recorded in many books written about him. The most revealing is *The Only Living Witness*, by Stephen C. Michaud and Hugh Aynesworth; but I was also helped a great deal by Ann Rule's *The Stranger Beside Me* (which so fascinated me that it brought me to the study of this phenomenon); as well as Steven Winn and David Merrill's *Ted Bundy: The Killer Next Door*; Richard W. Larsen's *Bundy: The Deliberate Stranger*, and Elizabeth Kendall's *The Phantom Prince: My Life With Ted Bundy*.

** See Chapter One.

"enigma," but he was no such thing, although he often spoke cryptically. The mandate here is to show how his killings were all of a piece, and a comprehensible one at that—part of a logical and systematic campaign. We know that he was conceived in what he thought was the terrible shame of illegitimacy, and that he was raised in a lower-middle-class household whose possessions and style he despised. His increasingly frantic desire to rise in the social hierarchy revealed itself during childhood in the humiliation he felt as he and his step-father harvested vegetables for a pittance in the Seattle market gardens; during adolescence in his theft of cars and luxury goods that gave him the upper-middle-class style he so desperately coveted; and during early adulthood in his powerful need for the dual social validation of marriage to a socialite and the status of an attorney. In the final event, he did not feel comfortable in carrying off this impersonation of an upper-middle-class person; but in an important way, his serial killings provided him with his desired union with upper-middle-class women, and launched him in his "career" as an attorney.

His task began to struggle to the surface in 1972. Making love to a casual date, he shoved his forearm against her neck, tightening it until she could not breathe. She shouted at him, but he did not respond. He removed his arm only after he had climaxed and, according to the woman, he seemed to have had no idea what he had been doing. Within a few months of this incident, he began tying up his mistress during their lovemaking, an experiment she terminated after he began to strangle her, as if in a trance. Soon Bundy was stalking a woman who had left a bar to walk along a darkened side-street. He found a piece of two-by-four in an alley and scurried ahead of her, hiding in a spot where he estimated their paths would intersect; but to his disappointment, she turned into her house before she reached him. Overwhelmed with the desire that the experience had kindled in him, he began following other women, finally striking one woman with a wooden club as she fumbled nervously for her keys at the door to her house. She screamed and fell, causing him to panic at the enormity of what he had done, and to run off.[2]

It was not until early January of 1974 that he had both

mastered technique and conquered fear sufficiently to become a more effective assailant. He attacked a young woman asleep in her windowed basement apartment in his own neighborhood, the university district in Seattle, Washington. She was sound asleep when the heavy metal rod crashed into her skull, and unconscious when a medical instrument was thrust roughly into her vagina, causing severe internal injuries. "Mary" was in a coma for months. She recovered, but could remember nothing of the attack.[3]

THE KILLING TIME

He made his first kill a few weeks later. On the night of January 31, 1974, Lynda Ann Healy, a twenty-one-year-old psychology student at the University of Washington, a worker with retarded children, was asleep in the basement apartment of the home she shared with four other young women. He crept into the house, apparently through an unlocked door, knocked Lynda unconscious and gagged her, removed her nightgown and hung it in the closet, re-made the bed to give the impression it had not been slept in, and carried her out of the window. Describing the abduction in the curious "as-if" third-person style he later adopted with his biographers Michaud and Aynesworth, he said: "He'd probably put her in the back seat of the car and cover her with something. . . . Let's say that he decided to drive to a remote location that he just picked out. Once he had arrived at this point where he didn't have a fear of alarming anyone in the neighborhood with shouts or screams or whatever, [he would] untie the woman. . . . He would have the girl undress and then, with that part of himself gratified, he found himself in a position where he realized that he couldn't let the girl go. And at that point he would kill her and leave her body where he'd taken her." It is not clear how long he kept the body before disposing of it in his burial ground in the woods near Seattle, but it is unlikely that it was for long.[4]

It took him six weeks to recover from the fear engendered by the first murder, and to regain the confidence to kill again. On March 12, 1974, he talked nineteen-year-old college student Donna Gail Manson into his car as she walked the short distance from her college dormitory to a jazz concert on the campus of Evergreen State College in Olympia, Washington. Her body was never recovered.

The technique he was developing to abduct intelligent university women was first revealed in a failed attempt he made on yet another college campus, Ellensburg's Central Washington State College. On the evening of April 14, 1974, wearing a cast and splint on his left arm and fumbling with a load of books, he induced a nineteen-year-old college student to help him get his books to his car. He asked her to unlock the door, but she was alert and refused. When he unlocked the door and ordered her to get into the car, she later told police, "I sort of ran away. Kind of fast." Three days later on the same campus, he approached another woman student. This time he had a sling on one arm and a brace on the other, and was dropping his books. She volunteered to help him, but was too wary to bend over and search for the keys he had "dropped" beside the car, and she left him there. Moments later, however, he was luckier. Biology major Susan Rancourt had left her meeting of prospective dormitory counselors and was heading back toward her own room. He intercepted her somewhere along her route, presumably using the same ruse. He cracked her skull with a blunt instrument, then kidnapped, raped, and murdered her, eventually dumping her body beside Lynda Healy on the forested slope. Susan Rancourt was his third kill.[5]

Less than three weeks later, on May 6, 1974, he killed again. Kathy Parks, a major in world religions at Oregon State University in Corvallis, Oregon, was leaving her dormitory to meet friends for coffee in the Student Union Building. He approached her as she walked the short distance, then kidnapped, raped, and murdered her. He had traveled the 260 miles to Corvallis, he suggested to Michaud and Aynesworth, as "an attempt to commit a crime without it being linked to other crimes." He described meeting Kathy, once more in his curious non-culpable third-person: "Let's say she was having a snack in the cafeteria and [he] just sat down next to her and began talking, and representing himself to be a student there, and suggested that they go out somewhere to get a bite to eat or to get a drink. Either he was convincing enough or she was depressed enough to accept his invitation. Of course, once she got in his car, then he had her in a position where he wanted her, and could then assume control over her. . . . Let's say that as he travels further and further away from a populated area, she probably is becoming uncomfortable . . . and, of course, by the time he pulled up and stopped, there would be virtually nothing she could do about it. . . . She would submit to whatever instructions he gave her, out of fear." After the rape, Bundy suggested that Parks was driven to Seattle alive. He drove her to his burying ground, raped her once more, and "at that point he killed [Kathy]. Either in the car or he marched her off the road and killed her in a more secluded location."[6]

He altered his method to make his fifth kill. He picked up twenty-two-year-old Brenda Ball in the early hours of June 1, 1974, in a working-class tavern in Seattle, drove her back to his apartment, and kept her there. As he described it to Michaud and Aynesworth: "He was interested in varying his M.O. [method of operation] in such a way as not to fan the flames of community outrage or the intensity of the police investigation. That is why this girl found herself to be the next victim . . . he picked her up hitchhiking and they got to talking and she had nothing to do. He would ask her if she wanted to go to a party at his place and take her home. . . . The initial sexual encounter would be more or less a voluntary one, but one which did not wholly gratify the full spectrum of desires that he had intended. And so, after the first sexual encounter, gradually his sexual desire builds back up and joins, as it were, these other, unfulfilled desires, this other need to totally possess her. After she'd passed out [from the alcohol], as she lay there somewhere in a state between coma and sleep, he strangled her to death." He kept her body in his apartment for several days, moving her between his bed and the closet: "There wouldn't be any urgency [in disposing of the body] since she was in a place that was private. Ultimately, he'd have to bundle her up in some fashion and take her out to his car when it's late one night." While her body was with him in his apartment, there is evidence that he re-did her make-up and shampooed her hair.[7]

Less than two weeks later, on the night of June 11, 1974, he returned to the University of Washington campus in Seattle to abduct former cheerleader Georgeann Hawkins as she walked the few yards from her boyfriend's dormitory to her own. She would be his sixth known rape and murder. At about the time Georgeann disappeared, other students saw a man in the vicinity wearing a leg cast and using crutches.[8]

He seems to have waited a full month before he struck again, killing two in one day, as if to make up for lost time. On July 14, 1974, a summer Sunday with sunbathers converging on the beach at Lake Sammamish, he used a variation on his earlier ruse and approached a woman with his left arm in a sling. He struck up a casual conversation with her and asked if she would help him with his boat. She agreed to do so and accompanied him to the parking lot, but balked when she saw no boat there. "Where is it?" she asked. "It's at my folks' house," he replied. "It's just up the hill." She was too wary to accompany him, but shortly after, twenty-three-year-old Janice Ott agreed. As Bundy later told his biographers: "He would not be able to drive a great distance without arousing the suspicions of the girls in the car. And so he would seek a secluded space, a secluded area, within a fairly short driving distance of the Lake Sammamish area. Somewhere where there were no cars, no traffic, or whatever. [He'd] be acting a role. Talking about the weather, reinforcing the ruse, just chitchat. He had a house somewhere in the area, and took them there, one girl to the house and came back and got the other one. . . . Once the individual would have her in a spot where he had, you know, security over her, then there would be a minimum amount of conversation which would be, you know, designed to avoid developing some kind of a relationship . . . had he been cautious, he would've probably killed the first individual before leaving to get the second girl. But in this instance, since we've agreed he wasn't acting cautiously, he hadn't killed the first girl when he abducted the second.

. . . He'd follow the same pattern with the second girl as the first. . . . Then the normal self would begin to re-emerge and, realizing the greater danger involved, would suffer panic and begin to think of ways to conceal the acts—or at least his part in them. So he'd kill the two girls, place them in his car, and take them to a secluded area and leave them." In this fashion, both Janice Ott and Denise Naslund were abducted and transformed into his seventh and eighth possessions. When he was finished with them and their bodies, he dumped them at one of his burying grounds, and went out for the evening with his mistress, the pseudonymous "Elizabeth Kendall." He complained of a cold that night, but ate voraciously, consuming several large hamburgers.[9]

Nineteen days later, on August 2, 1974, he abducted Carol Valenzuela, twenty, in downtown Vancouver, Washington. When he was finished with her, he strangled her and dumped her body at another one of his burial grounds near the Oregon border. She was his ninth confirmed kill. The body of his tenth, another young woman, was never identified, but her corpse was found near Valenzuela's.[10]

The people of Washington heaved a collective sigh when there were no further disappearances in September or October; and police began to speculate that the killer might have left the state. They were correct. He had moved to Salt Lake City to enter the University of Utah's Law School. He waited until October 2, 1974, before making his first confirmed Utah kill, taking sixteen-year-old high-school cheerleader Nancy Wilcox. On October 18, 1974, he stole his twelfth, Melissa Smith, the seventeen-year-old daughter of the Chief of Police of Midvale, Utah. He raped and sodomized her, strangled her with one of her own knee-high stockings, and left her nude corpse by the road, her vagina stuffed with dirt and twigs. There is some medical evidence that he kept her captive for as long as a week before killing her, although she was probably unconscious for that period from the heavy blow that fractured her skull.[11]

Three nights later, he took his thirteenth victim, Laura Aime, apparently while she was hitchhiking. It is clear from her autopsy report that he followed his usual pattern with her—breaking Laura's jaw and fracturing her skull with a blunt instrument, then committing anal and vaginal rape before strangling her with her own stocking. Laura Aime also suffered a vaginal puncture wound and her hair appeared to have been freshly shampooed, suggesting that he kept her body for a period after her death, as he had done with Melissa Smith.

On November 8, 1974, he made the critical fumble that would, in due course, end his homicidal career. Posing as a policeman, he talked Carol DaRonch into his car on a pretext; but she had the wit to fight back when he tried to handcuff her. In her frantic struggle, she escaped from his car and took shelter with a couple in another car. He drove off and left her there, but her testimony as the only survivor of a Bundy assault would soon convict him on the charge of kidnapping. For the moment, however, all that lay in the future. That same night, after his aborted attack on Carol DaRonch, he continued his murderous efforts and talked Debra Kent out of a high-school drama concert in Salt Lake City. She was his fourteenth victim.

The ensuing uproar in Utah caused him to become slightly more circumspect in his operations, and he moved his Killing Ground to Colorado, driving endlessly in his beloved Volkswagen—hunting. On January 11, 1975, he stole his fifteenth victim, twenty-three-year-old holidaying nurse Caryn Campbell, as she walked from the lobby to her room in her luxury hotel in Aspen. He killed her in his usual manner, crushing her skull with a blunt instrument. On March 15, 1975, he took his sixteenth victim, young ski instructor Julie Cunningham. Her body was never recovered. On April 6, 1975, he stole twenty-five-year-old Denise Oliverson, as she rode away from her boyfriend's home on her bicycle. Most often after these murders, he would ease his tensions in extended and emotional long-distance calls to his mistress in Seattle, Elizabeth Kendall.[12]

His momentum was broken suddenly in August of 1975 when an alert and intuitive Utah police officer saw Bundy driving uncertainly through a suburb late at night, and pulled the car over for inspection. Inside the Volkswagen, the officer found handcuffs, an ice pick, a pantyhose mask, a ski mask, several lengths of rope, and some torn pieces of white sheet. The police officer impounded the material as evidence, and warned Bundy to expect a warrant against him for the possession of burglary tools, an all-purpose charge that often (as with this case) yields bigger dividends. From now on, Bundy would be always under the scrutiny of the police. If he could still kill with near-impunity, he did so now with great difficulty. He was soon charged with Carol DaRonch's kidnapping and sentenced to the Utah State Prison for a short term. Not long after that, he was transferred to Colorado because the evidence against him was beginning to mount. He was to stand trial for the murder of Caryn Campbell. After two years in jails with abysmal security, a second ingenious escape attempt was successful. He made his way across America, looking for an appropriate university town in which to settle—for it was only in such an academic atmosphere that he could feel comfortable. He considered Columbus and its Ohio State campus, examined the University of Michigan at Ann Arbor, but finally settled on Florida. He took a room in Tallahassee and posed as a graduate student at the city's Florida State University.[13]

He seems to have tried to hold his task in abeyance, for had he been able to resign from it (and from his reckless and constant petty thefts) he might have remained free for the rest of his life since the police were searching for him thousands of miles away. Yet within a few weeks he was hunting humans again. In his penultimate outrage, in the early hours of January 15, 1978, dressed in dark clothing and armed with a log club, he took advantage of a faulty lock on the door of the university's Chi Omega sorority house and ran from room to room, silently attacking the sleeping women. His eighteenth victim was Lisa Levy: he crushed her skull with his club and bit deep into her buttocks as he raped her, and then sodomized her with an aerosol can. He crossed the hall to another room, wielding his club with such force upon his victims that the "room was spattered and smeared with their blood; even the ceiling was dotted with red drops that had sprayed up from their attacker's thrashing club." He was unable to kill the two women in this room, but he broke Karen Chandler's jaw, right arm, and one finger, fractured her skull, the orbit of her right eye and both her cheek bones, and left deep gouges and cuts on her face. He turned at some point to Karen's sleeping roommate, Kathy Kleiner, and broke her jaw with such force that several of her teeth were later found in her blood-soaked bedclothes. Moving to another room, he clubbed and then strangled Margaret Bowman to death: she was his nineteenth confirmed victim. At this point, his energies remarkably unabated, he was interrupted from his carnage, probably by one of the sorority sisters returning late to the house, and he fled. Racing back toward the safety of his room, he stopped outside the apartment of Cheryl Thomas, a twenty-one-year-old student of dance, who was asleep in her bed. Having broken in, he smashed her jaw with several blows from his club, left a pantyhose mask and a large semen stain on her blood-soaked bed, and escaped. Cheryl Thomas did not die, but she lost the hearing in one ear permanently and suffered a partial loss of balance that put paid to her career as a dancer.[14]

With the community and state in an uproar over the Chi Omega attack, Bundy began his confused and meandering last run. Had he simply made for another state, he might never have been captured. But his behavior suggests that he could no longer sustain the task: he roamed in circles through Florida, finding time only for heavy drinking, and his twentieth kill. On February 9, 1978, he talked twelve-year-old Kimberly Leach out of her high-school playground. He kidnapped her, raped her vaginally and anally, and either strangled her or cut her throat (by the time the body was found, it was in too advanced a stage of decomposition to be certain of the cause of death). He dumped her body in an abandoned hogshed after keeping her in his possession for an undetermined length of time. Within a few days, he was behaving so erratically that yet another alert and suspicious police officer pulled his car over, this last time on the night of February 14–15. After a scuffle, he was arrested. He asked the arresting officer to shoot him. He would never be free again.[15]

BUNDY AND PSYCHOLOGY

"I'm a psychologist, and it
really gives me insight."

TED BUNDY[16]

Bundy seems always to have been tortured by what he felt were the dual social stigmas of his illegitimacy and his "common" lower-middle-class upbringing, but he did not become a patient of psychologists and psychiatrists until his criminal acts had deeply embroiled him in the judicial system. Even that contact proved futile, since he used his intelligence to dissemble and obfuscate, hampering all efforts to determine his inner condition. Inevitably for one so uncommunicative, the diagnosis was singularly unenlightening, except insofar as it revealed some of the difficulties experienced by the forensic psychological sciences. Most notable among these are the inability to predict an individual's potential for future violence, or to diagnose a condition, despite being expected to do so by the judicial system.

This occasional inability to perceive the nature of what is sitting in front of them was made apparent by Bundy's happy passage through the Bachelor's degree program in psychology at the University of Washington (before he embarked upon his career in Law). His psychology professors there thought the world of him, one writing at the time that: "He conducts himself more like a young professional than a student. I would place him in the top one per cent of the undergraduates with whom I have interacted." And a second wrote about Bundy in 1972: "It is clear that other students use him as a standard to emulate. . . . His personal characteristics are all of the highest standards. Ted is a mature young man who is very responsible and emotionally stable (but *not* emotionally flat as many students appear— he does get excited or upset appropriately in various situations). . . . I am at a loss to delineate any real weakness he has." During his summer employment at Seattle's Crisis Clinic, charged with the task of counseling individuals who were emotionally troubled, he passed smoothly among the staff, except for only a few who noted his wooden and rigid presentation of self. "Ted," one suspicious colleague told Larsen, "always seemed to respond to the callers with sort of a cold lecture, telling them they should learn to discipline their emotions, to take charge. He didn't seem to have . . . the compassion, the understanding that these people were unable to take control." This woodenness reflected his own uncertain passage through the social order, and it is unclear whether the fact that he was trained in psychology, and was actually practicing a form of it while his homicidal resolve was hardening, constitutes any testimony against the profession.[17]

Indeed, until the eminent forensic psychiatrist Tanay interviewed him in his Florida cell, the only astute attention he had received was from the Seattle psychiatrists who, interviewing *in absentia* the killer they knew only as "Ted," early in the investigation prepared a profile for the police. Journalists Winn and Merrill summarized the profile: "His actions and demeanor tend to categorize him as a sociopath and it is fair to say he is also a sexual psychopath, [a type of person] characterized by certain typical traits, including a lack of emotion and an absence of remorse, yet strangely, such people tend to be extroverts: likable, engaging, often deliciously hedonistic. . . . In short, the experts said, such a person appears perfectly normal. But . . . untroubled by feelings of guilt, a psychopathic killer tends to repeat his act again and again." Yet even this analysis, however astute it may have been, failed to transcend mere categorization: and it was based typically upon the retrospective knowledge of the disordered behavior (the murders), rather than upon any examination of the qualities of a person.[18]

The first professional actually to examine Bundy was Dr. Gary Jorgensen, a clinical psychologist at the University of Utah, whose diagnosis must rank with that of Edmund Kemper's psychiatrist as among the least prescient of all time. Jorgensen was retained by Bundy's lawyer to offer a diagnosis. He spent several hours with Bundy and administered the inevitable battery of psychological tests, including a Rorschach and the Minnesota Multiphasic Personality Inventory. He concluded that Bundy was a "normal person." "Mr. Bundy," he wrote, "is an extremely intelligent young man who is intact psychologically. In many regards he is the typical young Republican that he has been in the past." Jorgensen compounded his error by listing what he saw as Bundy's psychological attributes—"good social presence," "ego strength and good self-concept," "positive self-identity," "highly intellectual, independent, tolerant, responsible." Bundy also seemed to him to have "a normal psychosexual development." It would appear that Jorgensen's constructions were based upon an assumption of Bundy's innocence and an "analysis" of his carefully constructed middle-class mask. Many others were to make the same mistake and pay a much higher price—with their lives. Meanwhile, the only people who had had the wit to suspect Bundy's presentation of self were the much maligned police. As one intuitive deputy put it, shortly after Bundy's arrest for possession of burglary tools: "I don't know. Bundy is the strangest man I've ever met. . . . It's just a gut reaction. This man's into something big."[19]

After Bundy's conviction for the kidnapping of Carol DaRonch, he was given an intensive ninety-day medical examination at Utah State Prison. The medical staff searched for some biological flaw that might explain his violence but, as with all of our multiple murderers, were unable to find one. X-rays of his skull discovered nothing untoward, and a brain scan was negative. Electroencephalograms were "completely unremarkable," and there was "no evidence of organic brain disease" or any form of mental impairment. The psychological tests seemed more revealing, but they were so primarily because the psychologists now *knew* from his conviction that he was capable of violence toward women. Since he had just been convicted for kidnapping, this knowledge now enabled them to "find" some problems. Thus the prison psychiatrist, Dr. Van O. Austin, felt that Bundy "does have some features of the anti-social personality, such as a lack of guilt feelings, callousness, and a very pronounced tendency to compartmentalize and methodically rationalize his behavior. . . . At times he has lived a lonely, somewhat withdrawn, seclusive existence which is consistent with, but not diagnostic of, a schizoid personality."[20]

On the basis of the psychological tests they directed at Bundy, the prison staff contrasted the positive and negative sides of his personality. On the positive side, they thought, were his "high intelligence," "no severely traumatizing influences in childhood or adolescence," "no serious defects in physical development, habits, school adjustment, emotional maturation, or sexual development," "adequate interest in hobbies and recreational pursuits," "average environmental pressures and responsibilities," and "no previous attacks of emotional illness"—observations which reveal rather dramatically how much the tests rely upon the individual's presentation of self and the tester's notion of the immutability of what are essentially middle-class values. On the negative side, the staff complained that "when one attempts to understand Mr. Bundy he becomes evasive," but this insight seemed to be based on their prior knowledge of his kidnapping charge, rather than on any psychological insight—as was their additional remark that Bundy was "somewhat threatened by people unless he feels he can structure the outcome of the relationship."[21]

Finally, what seemed on the surface to be significant may well have been merely characteristics of a large proportion of the human race: for example, the staff's comments on the one "fairly strong conflict . . . evidence in the testing profile, that being the subject's fairly strong dependency on women, yet his need to be independent. Mr. Bundy would like a close relationship with females, but is fearful of being hurt by them. In addition, there were indications of general anger, and more particularly, well-masked anger toward women." Alas, all we really learn from this is that a conviction in court tells us more about a human being than any number of Minnesota Multiphasic Personality Inventories. Perhaps we must speculate that the art of the police officer and the judge is at least as revealing and accurate as that of the psychologist's science. Regardless, the prison psychiatrist concluded on June 7, 1976, that "I do not feel that Mr. Bundy is psychotic. In fact he has a good touch with reality, knows the difference between right and wrong, has no hallucinations or delusions."[22]

Bundy's observation about his observers was at least as insightful. In a letter to his friend Ann Rule, he wrote: ". . . after conducting numerous tests and extensive examinations, [they] have found me normal and are deeply perplexed. Both of us know that none of us is 'normal.' Perhaps what I should say is that they find no explanation to substantiate the verdict or other allegations. No seizures, no psychosis, no dissociative reactions, but in no way, crazy. The working theory is now that I have completely forgotten everything, a theory which is disproved by their own results. 'Very interesting,' they keep mumbling." Presumably he was also unimpressed by the results of his California Life Goals Evaluation Schedules Test which showed, rather unhelpfully, that he had six rather common goals in life: "To have freedom from want. To control the actions of others. To guide others with their consent. To avoid boredom. To be self-fulfilled. To live one's life one's own way."[23]

Yet if the tests produced little but nonsense, his letter to Rule regarding his feelings about his trial while experiencing the psychiatric evaluation was immensely revealing: "I was whistling in the wind," he wrote, "yet in a curious sort of way, I felt a deep sense of fulfillment. I felt relaxed but emphatic; controlled, but sincere and filled with emotion." What manner of man talks about "fulfillment" as his life is draining away in prison? What was there in the judicial and psychological process that "filled" him "with emotion"? These were profoundly significant statements of Bundy's, and we shall return later to their substance.[24]

His last known contact with the professionals was when he stood trial for his life in Tallahassee. There, he was examined by the distinguished psychiatrist, Dr. Emanuel Tanay, who "thought Bundy had an antisocial personality, was characterized by bad judgment, 'thrilled' at the chance of defying authority, and could be dangerous." Tanay himself wrote that Bundy "has an incapacity to recognize the significance of evidence held against him [although] it would be simplistic to characterize this as merely lying inasmuch as he acts as if his perception of the significance of evidence was real. He makes decisions based upon these distorted perceptions of reality. Furthermore, he maintains an attitude and mood consistent with his perception of reality, namely, he is neither concerned nor distressed in an appropriate manner by the charges facing him." Tanay wrote that "transcripts of the many hours of his conversations with police officers constitute a variety of 'confession' [but that] when this is pointed out to him by me, he does not dispute my inference, he merely provides a different explanation." Tanay felt strongly that "this behavior was not, in my opinion, the result of rational reflection and decision making process but a manifestation of the psychiatric illness from which Mr. Bundy suffers." Thus Tanay thought Bundy's refusal to accept the weight of evidence against him was in itself indicative of a mental disease. "It is his view that the case against him is weak or even frivolous. This judgment of Mr. Bundy's is considered to be inaccurate by his defense counsel and, most likely, represents a manifestation of his illness." Tanay concluded with the important insight that "It is my impression that a major factor is his deep-seated need to have a trial, which he views as an opportunity to confront and confound various authority figures." *Precisely.* But why should Bundy have such a deep-seated need? What could he possibly gain from it?[25]

PUBLIC PRONOUNCEMENTS

"I don't feel guilty for anything . . . I feel sorry for people who feel guilt."

TED BUNDY[26]

Bundy never *quite* confessed his murders. Indeed, during his trials in Utah and Colorado, he loudly protested his innocence. In an impassioned letter written at the time to his friend Rule, he wrote: "I want you to know, I want the whole world to know that I am innocent. I have never hurt another human being in my life. God, please believe me." Even then, however, there was often the curious element of dissociation and confusion in his denials, as in the bizarre statement he made before the television cameras in Colorado: "More than ever, I'm convinced of my own innocence." More than ever?[27]

He dropped his fervent claims of innocence after his final capture in Florida, texturing his comments with a kind of scrupulously honest ambiguity. He did not deny the charge of murder, but criticized instead the quality of the state's evidence against him. Throughout this Florida period, whether in exhausting interviews with the police or in intimate letters to his friends, he would maintain this brand of crypticism. When asked by Florida police about his role in the Chi Omega murders, for example, he told them, "The evidence is there. Don't quit digging for it." Similarly, in a letter to a friend he said, "I dreamt of freedom. I had it and lost it through a combination of compulsion and stupidity," an apt judgment on his final murders—yet no admission. He talked vaguely about his "problem," about his "antisocial acts," and told detectives that, "I want to talk to you, but I've built up such a block so that I could never tell." So too, rather than answer an incriminating question, he would say instead, "I don't want to have to lie to you."[28]

When he admitted to police that he preferred Volkswagens because the passenger seat could be removed easily, he elaborated: "Well, I can carry things easier that way."

"You mean you can carry bodies easier that way?" asked a detective.

"Well, let's just say I can carry cargo better that way," Bundy replied.

"That cargo you carried, was it sometimes damaged?"

"Sometimes it was damaged, sometimes it wasn't," Bundy replied. When he felt himself edging too close to making an admission, he would back off: "Laying in bed," he said to police, "I said to myself, 'Shoot, it's going to be easier than the dickens and it would all come out.' Again, I know what you want, but I'm interested in the whole thing, in everything. It's the whole ball of wax, and it's got to be dealt with . . . I'm interested in clearing up everything . . . and in giving answers to questions that would be helpful. . . . [but] What is it I wanted to do? It's not as clear to me now as it was before."[29]

For a time he implied that he was holding back in order to negotiate the most favorable terms for himself. Undoubtedly this is partly true, but since he maintained that position long after he had received three death sentences, it is legitimate to conclude that more was involved than mere haggling. Still, he haggled. "My attorney's position," he said, "is that all the state and you all want to do, besides solve these cases, is to execute me. And that would be the logical result of anything you were attempting to get from me, if indeed that's what you wanted. There's no doubt in their minds, given the laws of the State of Florida, that's what would happen if the guilty party were captured. They advocate a different point of view: going right down the line and eventually securing my freedom. I like these kinds of situations because it allows me to take—well, it doesn't allow me really anything. Now if I had my choice—and I don't necessarily—but if I sit back and think about how I would like the thing to resolve itself, everybody satisfied by getting all the answers to all the questions they want to ask, then after that was all over, I would like to be back in Washington State, because that's where my mother is, that's where my family is, and that's where I'm from. . . . It's just being home, back where I was raised, being close to my family." "I know it sounds rather complex," he continued, "but it just seems to work for me now. Okay, Ted Bundy wants something out of this and maybe that's not right and maybe he doesn't deserve it—and in a way that's true. But still I've got to take care of my own survival. Ted Bundy wants to survive, too. I have many responsibilities, as I've told you before, to my parents—and that's part of it. The second part is getting out of the limelight as quickly as possible without all these horrendous trials. . . . And getting close, back close to my parents, and giving the knowledge and peace of mind that can be returned to people who don't know what happened . . . to their loved ones." Here Bundy is posing, in an incredibly unconvincing way, as a kind of dispossessed homebody, devoted to little but his parents, and whose prime concern is to give "peace" to the parents of his victims. Why such a pose? I think it obvious that at the time he could not overcome his stagefright for what would be his greatest performance, the Florida murder trials. Time and rest would heal his anxiety.[30]

For the time being, he could merely claim to police that "I'm trying to avoid infuriating you, believe me. I don't mean to be saying this is the way it's going to be, because I can't do that. There's one thing I know for sure: that I've got the answers here and they're for me to give. I want to get to the point where it would be the best all around, not excluding me. I still place a value on myself." Yet when detectives begged him to tell them where his last victim's body was hidden, he seemed overwhelmed with embarrassment: "But I'm the most cold-hearted son of a bitch you'll ever meet." Again, the detective asked, "Ted, if you will tell me where the body is. . . ." Bundy replied: "I can't do that to you, because the sight is too horrible to look at." Recovering quickly, he reminded the detectives that "I've got the answers, and the answers are mine to give."[31]

He continued this charade long after his convictions, even with his literary interrogators, Michaud and Aynesworth, speaking only in "as-ifs" and in the third person, and bridling if the queries came too close to indicting him: "I'm not going into that," he told Michaud. "This is already too thinly disguised. I've gone further now than I wanted to." He insisted that he was a victim of a malicious judicial system and the media, trapped by what was entirely circumstantial evidence and a venal, incompetent press. But his *definition* of innocence was not whether he had in fact committed the murders, but whether the state had marshaled sufficient evidence against him: "I am not convinced, in any objective sense, of the strength of the state's case," he said in court in Miami. He embraced sheer legalism with a passion that is rarely encountered, and this puzzling quality demands explanation.[32]

Biographies

"I've always felt somehow lost in my life."

TED BUNDY[33]

The apparent paradoxes that litter Bundy's life have engaged the imaginations of the many who knew him and who have written about him: the Crisis Center counselor who raped women . . . the potential Governor of the State who was driven by secret urges to kill . . . the law student who threw away his life rather than accept the reality of his own incompetence as an attorney. Bundy did not fit the shape that the public requires from its multiple murderers. Yet there were many Bundys. In one of the ironies which dot this case, the daughter of the police chief who would pursue him, worked with him and found him "the kind of guy a girl my age would look at and just say wow! Sort of Kennedylike." "He was a champion of causes," she recalled. "He was concerned about the situation of the blacks, of all minorities. And the poor. He was unhappy with the injustices of society, and he wanted to do something about them." On the other hand, a widowed pastry cook found his friendship and his dedicated rhetoric a mixed blessing: "He was always borrowing money from me," she told Bundy's biographer Larsen, and not always paying it back. A young woman who dated him glimpsed his contradictions. Although they were close friends, Bundy would not visit her parents in their middle-class home: "It was funny," she commented, "Ted was always so self-confident, so sure of himself, but I got the feeling that he felt terribly inferior at times."[34]

Many loved him, including his mother, who seemed to have doted on her love-child, seeing him perhaps as the family's potential for re-entry into the respectable middle class. Louise Bundy did what she could for all her children. She told Winn and Merrill: "They had the best we could give them on a middle-class income. The most we could give them was lots of love. . . . Many a night we stayed up well past midnight. He'd have a big test coming up the next day, and I'd go through with him and ask the questions . . . I've always had a very special relationship with all my children. . . . But Ted being my oldest, and you might say my pride and joy, our relationship was very special. We talked a great deal together." Admiring women and a loving family? There seemed to be little unusual in his background: certainly it defied all assumptions of an abused childhood, and revealed nothing to suggest the growth of such a disordered creature.[35]

The Official Autobiography: Bundy the Young Republican

Like many public men and women's best efforts, Bundy's autobiography presented himself as he wished to be seen; and this performance was unwavering in its studied banality, at least until his capture in Florida. If an undistinguished career in school was followed by an equally undistinguished career at university, he was able to reminisce about his boyhood in pleasant, if ambiguous, terms: "I haven't blocked out the past. I wouldn't trade the person I am, or what I've done—or the people I've known—for anything. So I do think about it. And at times it's a rather mellow trip to lay back and remember." At university, he avoided the fraternity/sorority life with even greater zeal than he avoided studying, claiming that he "wasn't interested in the social politicking, the emphasis on clothes and parties. It was shallow and superficial."[36]

If his own commitment to scholarship was similarly superficial, he seemed to have thrived in the university atmosphere. "People are great anyway, but college students are beautiful people. Good-looking people. Healthy people. Exciting people." In particular, he loved the life of the university district—the district where the killings began—and the special feeling it gave him: "I love the district. I have never become so attached to any other place that I lived. I never felt so totally a part of the eco-system." Indeed, and therein lay the problem.[37]

He spent the late 1960s putting together his image as a confident and upper-middle-class young Republican. His social adeptness grew, as did that air-of-a-Kennedy about him. He was admired by many men and women (although many also distrusted his facade, which struck them as bumbling and artificial). He even won a commendation from the Seattle police for chasing a purse snatcher and returning the purse to its rightful owner. In 1970, he saved a young girl from drowning. What stopped this guardian of the moral order from continuing this trajectory? Ideologically, he was conservative in the extreme. His applications to the law schools are models of the dedicated young establishmentarian—"a believer in the system," as his Republican Party employer called him. He wished to be a lawyer, he wrote one law school, "to arbitrate questions between individuals and institutions; to search for the facts; and ultimately, to provide for the orderly resolution of conflict and the avoidance of 'violence'—these activities have attracted me to a program of legal study. I see the legal profession engaged in a quest for order."[38]

How remarkable that this future multiple murderer would be so concerned with "order," with the "resolution of conflict," and with the "avoidance of violence." How odd that this rebel-to-be should be so committed to change in government through legislative, not revolutionary, change. "His stance made him something of a loner," wrote his friend Rule, "among the work-study students working at the Crisis Clinic. They were semihippies . . . and he was a conservative Republican." Moreover, he was infuriated by the student riots. "On more than one occasion, he had tried to block the demonstrations, waving a club and telling the rioters to go home. He believed there was a better way to do it, but his own anger was, strangely, as intense as those he tried to stop." He argued with Rule at the time that his conservatism was really a progressive stratagem: "Anarchy isn't going to solve anything," she remembered him saying. "You just end up scattering your forces and getting your head broken."[39]

Even after he was arrested, he stuck to his version of his autobiography. "When I first came under attack by the legal system," he wrote, "I was twenty-eight, a bachelor, a law student, engaged to be married, and enjoying the brightest period of my life. I had come to terms with many things

. . . and one thing I had come to terms with long ago was the circumstances of my birth," a reference to his illegitimacy. He insisted that there was nothing abnormal about him or his life, and continued to describe himself as a kind of quintessential middle-class young man with excellent prospects, concerned only with discovering himself and his place in society. "I am still too young to look upon my life as History," he wrote to a Seattle magazine. "I am at a stage in life, an egocentric stage, where it matters only that I understand what I am and not what others may think of me."[40]

The Revised Autobiography: Bundy the "Entity"

After his capture in Florida, his autobiography was extensively, if hesitantly, "rewritten." It revealed a glimpse of what lay underneath the Young Republican. "In an even, professorial tone," Michaud and Aynesworth recalled, "he began to speak of themes in modern society—violence, the treatment of women, the disintegration of the home, anonymity, stress. Finally, he turned from the sociological to the specific, and began describing the killer. Within 'this individual,' he explained, there dwelt a being—Ted sometimes called it 'an entity,' 'the disordered self,' or 'the malignant being.' The story of 'the entity's' birth came slowly, chronologically, a consistent tale of gathering psychopathy that nurtured itself on the negative energy around it. Protected by his use of the third person, he forged ahead in detail to explain how thoughts about sex in general came to concentrate on sexual violence, how pornography shaped and directed the 'entity,' how the illness inside him drew him toward ever-increasing shows of violence, and how the killer managed to mask his disordered self from his unsuspecting friends. He took pains in his explanations lest I develop overly simplistic ideas. . . . The killer was not a schizophrenic, Bundy iterated and reiterated. 'It is truly more sophisticated than that,' he cautioned. Ted called it 'a hybrid situation,' a psychopathology in which the 'entity' is both in and of the killer, not some alien presence but a purely destructive power that grew from within."[41]

Bundy's third-person self-analysis was studded with the

psychological euphemisms so characteristic of psychology graduates—"inappropriate acting out" for murder, and "satisfying that part of himself" for rape. Yet his thoughts on the internal struggle he experienced seemed real enough: "This person was constantly attempting to be objective and to determine whether or not any of his psychopathological tendencies were being exposed. He was constantly assessing that probability and trying to keep a sense of proportion within himself. Not just for a surface kind of demonstration, but also in the hopes of keeping on an even keel, rationally, normally. Not isolating himself too much from the mainstream. Not simply to preserve conditions under which the malignant part of him could survive, but also sometimes to overcome those desires."[42]

He frequently reminded Michaud and Aynesworth that the gratification he sought lay in the possession of the victim, not in the violence or in the sex. But what bothered his interrogators most was their important insight that there were "elements of will, *conscious will,* taking part in the creation of this entity, as if Ted had wanted to become a killer." *Precisely:* this was no uncontrollable compulsion. Bundy made a decision, a solemn commitment, and then reaped the whirlwind. Tracing the growth of his linkage of sexuality with violence, Bundy recalled: "This condition is not immediately seen by the individual or identified as a serious problem. It sort of manifests itself in an interest concerning sexual behavior, sexual images. It might simply be an attraction such as *Playboy,* or a host of other normal, healthy sexual stimuli that are found in the environment. But this interest, for some unknown reason, becomes geared towards matters of a sexual nature that involve violence. I cannot emphasize enough the gradual development of this. It is not short-term." Bundy thus argued for a kind of sexual origin for the killings, suggesting that he began to focus on "pornography as a vicarious way of experiencing what his peers were experiencing in reality. Then he got sucked into the more sinister doctrines that are implicit in pornography —the use, abuse, the possession of women as objects." Sucked in?[43]

Then, Bundy continued, came the fantasies in which "this person" began to see himself as an actor. "He was walking down the street one evening and just totally by chance looked up into the window of a house and saw a woman undressing. He began, with increasing regularity, to canvass, as it were, the community he lived in. He peeped in windows and watched women undress or whatever could be seen during the evening. He approached it almost like a project, throwing himself into it, literally, for years. . . . He gained, at times, a great amount of gratification from it. And became increasingly adept at it, as anyone becomes adept at anything they do over and over again."[44]

Bundy thought his interrogators might "make a little more sense out of much of this if you take into account the effect of alcohol. It's important. It's very important as a trigger. When this person drank a good deal, his inhibitions were significantly diminished." One evening he found himself trailing a woman with the intention of attacking her: "The revelation of the experience and the frenzied desire that seized him really seemed to usher in a new dimension to that part of him that was obsessed with violence and women and sexual activity—a composite kind of thing not terribly well defined but more well defined as time went on. This particular incident spurred him on succeeding events to hunt this neighborhood, searching." Finally, he struck one woman, as recounted earlier, and fled in panic. "What he had done terrified him," Bundy surmised, "purely terrified him. Full of remorse and remonstrating with himself for the suicidal nature of the activity, the ugliness of it all, he quickly sobered up. He was horrified by the recognition that he had the capacity to do such a thing. He was fearful, terribly fearful, that for some reason or another he might be apprehended. But slowly, the pressures, tensions, dissatisfactions which, in the very early stages, fueled this thing had an effect. Yet it was more self-sustaining and didn't need as much tension or as much disharmony externally as it did before. It sort of reached a point where this condition would generate its own needs, and wouldn't need that reservoir of tension or stress that it seemed to thrive on before."[45]

He learned to conquer his fear. "The next time, it took him only three months to get over it," said Bundy. "What happened was this entity inside him was not capable of being controlled any longer, at least not for any considerable period of time. It began to try to justify itself, to create rationalizations for what it was doing. Perhaps to satisfy the rational, normal part of the individual. One element that came into play was anger, hostility. But I don't think that was an overriding emotion when he would go out hunting, or however you want to describe it. On most occasions it was a high degree of anticipation, of excitement, or arousal. It was an adventuristic kind of thing."[46]

Bundy insisted that he "received no pleasure from harming or causing pain to the person he attacked. He received absolutely no gratification. He did everything possible within reason—considering the unreasonableness of the situation—not to torture these individuals, at least not physically. The fantasy that accompanies and generates the anticipation that precedes the crime is always more stimulating than the immediate aftermath of the crime itself. He should have recognized that what really fascinated him was the hunt, the adventure of searching out his victims. And, to a degree, possessing them physically as one would a potted plant, a painting, or a Porsche. Owning, as it were, this individual."[47]

The particular victims he selected would be images of "the idealized woman," he said, which for him meant the upper-middle-class woman: because he wished to maintain them as images, and not develop relationships, he avoided talking to them. "They wouldn't be stereotypes necessarily. But they would be reasonable facsimiles to women as a class. A class not of women, per se, but a class that has almost been created through the mythology of women and how they are used as objects." He selected a particular woman if the opportunity was there and if he found her handsome; but even that beauty was *socially* defined—"The person's criteria would be based upon those standards of attractiveness accepted by his peer group." When the female object had been spotted and captured, he "would not want to engage in a great deal of serious conversation" with her: "once the individual would have her in a spot where he had, you know, security over her, then there would be a minimum amount of conversation which would be, you know, designed to avoid developing some kind of relationship."[48]

After his arrest and escape from the Colorado jail, he made his way across the country and experienced an immense sense of fulfillment and peace, when other fugitives might have felt only fear of apprehension. Within days of arriving in Florida, however, that special feeling disappeared. "All of a sudden, I just felt smaller and smaller and smaller. And more insecure too. And more alone. Bit by bit by bit. I felt something drain out of me. I felt it slip away from me like in the old movies where you see the ghost lift out of the body lying on the ground. And by the time I got off the bus in Tallahassee, things just didn't seem right. From the time I first set foot on Tennessee Street, I kept saying to myself, 'I gotta leave here.'" Just as his sense of self disappeared, so did his resolution to steer clear of the law. But why? What made him feel so lifeless again, and so small?[49]

Michaud and Aynesworth, and many others, thought all this was clear evidence of "an unconscious need to return to confinement," but I think not. In fact, his task was incomplete. Within five weeks he would kill the women in Chi Omega's sorority house. He would never discuss these murders, but he did once boast to Aynesworth that "I'm the only one that can do it. The only one." Similarly, he was boasting to his rooming-house fellows within hours of the massacre. Neither was this a form of self-destruction in the psychiatric sense, for his task was now completed: once he accepted that, in the state of mental and physical exhaustion that followed his murder of Kimberly Leach, he would be free to find a measure of personal happiness in incarceration, to develop his own philosophy, and to revel in the fame that was now his. "There is no true answer," he concluded during his final trial, "only controversy." The statement reflected his constant delight in mystifying his audience.[50]

THE DEMYSTIFICATION OF TED BUNDY

Theodore Robert Bundy was no "enigma": he spoke to us only in lies and riddles because such obfuscation and insult were central to his task. Even then, long after the trials, when he consented to read us chapter and verse, he elected to do so only in that third-person style to further tantalize and antagonize us and, perhaps, not foreswear the possibility of a stay of execution. To understand the man, we need merely examine two of his personal qualities—his relentless snobbery, and his uncivil behavior toward the authorities—and the two central events in his personal history: his illegitimacy, and his inability to love the woman he wanted to love.

Bundy the Snob

"Personalized stationery is one of
the small but truly necessary
luxuries of life."

TED BUNDY[51]

"Even the little Teddy was deeply class-conscious," observed Michaud and Aynesworth. Younger than ten, when Edmund Kemper was burying alive the family cat, Bundy was already "humiliated" to be seen in his step-father's "common" Rambler automobiles. Indeed, the only relative who did not inspire disdain in him was a cultivated uncle who taught music at Tacoma's College of Puget Sound. The uncle's professorial home, with its gleaming grand piano, emitted for him an aura of substance and middle-class refinement. He daydreamed of being adopted by Roy Rogers and Dale Evans, a common enough fantasy among eight-year-olds, to be sure, but with him the prime motive was to have his own pony and to be rich, and so escape from what the precociously ambitious Ted Bundy seemed to feel so profoundly beneath him. So intense was this premature materialism that, according to his mother, the little Teddy would always pull her to the most expensive sections of clothing stores.[52]

The snobbery of the adult Bundy was so extreme as to suggest an exceptional degree of status anxiety, however smoothly it might have been articulated in his daily performances. How many awaiting trial for murder would concern themselves with the bourgeois niceties of personalized stationery, or trouble to comment so affectedly on its worth? How many would retain a food and wine snobbery in prison, writing to a friend: "Yet, whatever supernatural force guides our destinies . . . I must believe this invisible hand will pour more chilled Chablis for us in less treacherous, more tranquil times to come." Certainly, he used his snobbery to impress others. His rather simple mistress, Elizabeth Kendall, wrote disarmingly of the breathless manner in which she watched him select a wine from France for their first meal together, at a time when she confessed she "was impressed by any wine that had a cork in the bottle." Later, in a darker time, when urged to recall terrible things about ghastly murders he had committed, he said instead to his interrogators: "How do you describe the taste of *bouillabaisse?* Some remember clams, others mullet." These were carefully assembled and exquisitely constructed snobberies, quite out of character for a lower-middle-class Tacoma upbringing—as was his loathing for everything he thought (and he used the word) "common." Again, why was his psyche so colonialized that he felt it essential to affect an "English," or at least a mid-Atlantic, accent?[53]

The status anxiety seemed particularly intense in his relationships with women. Was it a youthful prank, or a symptom of a deep sense of status deprivation, that drove him to the bother of borrowing a friend's best china and silver for a dinner he orchestrated for a girlfriend—and dressing for that dinner in a waiter's jacket and satin-striped trousers? What made it impossible for him, despite many invitations, to visit the home of an early girlfriend from the middle class? "He didn't feel that he fit in with . . . my 'class,'" she later recalled. "I guess that's the only way to describe it. He wouldn't come to my parents' home because he said he just didn't fit in." Most important of all, when he did ultimately fall in love so deeply—with a California socialite, long-haired and graceful like his victims, who was a fellow student at the University of Washington—why, after years of ardently pursuing her, did he coldly reject her the moment she accepted his proposal of marriage? "I just wanted to prove to myself," he later wrote, "that I could have married her." But is this not an extravagant means of proof? "She moved like something out of *Vogue*," Bundy continued, "and anything she wore looked like a million dollars. I, on the other hand, possessed the innocence of a missionary, the worldliness of a farm boy . . . She and I had about as much in common as Sears and Roebuck has with Saks."[54]

There can be no doubt that he was obsessed with what he called his "social deficits." It was this profound feeling of social inferiority and personal worthlessness that made him turn away from his university's fraternity and sorority life—an otherwise appropriate niche for a person of his pretensions—and rendered hollow his claim that he spurned them because the Greek Row life was "shallow and superficial." It was inevitable that by his first year in college, as he later told a psychiatrist, he would be obsessed with a "longing for the beautiful coed," and a frustrating fore-knowledge that "I didn't have the skill or social acumen to cope with it." Perhaps it now becomes more apparent why he ultimately captured and killed sorority girls, or their "idealized models," for it was an obvious way in which his class-scarred soul could conceive of their possession.[55]

Bundy the snob immersed himself in *classless* material possessions and activities. The only car he loved was the Volkswagen Bug, an automobile remarkable for little other than its classless image (so unlike those detested lower-middle-class Ramblers of his step-father). In these classless vehicles, he transported the idealized sorority girls to their deaths, thus transforming the desired possessions into owned objects. Similarly, he was only comfortable in university districts—universities, where talent and style supposedly overwhelm social origins, where a shared student style obliterates differential "breeding." That undoubtedly accounted for the worshipful manner in which he always considered university districts and their inhabitants: "College students are beautiful people. Good looking people. Healthy people. Exciting people." He confirmed this by spending not only his salad days in Seattle's university district, but by considering only other university districts as possible places to live, even when he was on the run from the law. He consciously embraced politics because, through them, one could rise regardless of one's social origins; and this too was clearly what accounted for his interest in the law. Even his sport—skiing—while class conscious enough, permitted this enterprising thief to equip himself for it with a few deft shoplifting tours. Through the classlessness of the universities, the political game, and the ski slopes, he tried his best to jostle among the right sort.[56]

Bundy the Rebel

Bundy reached first for an establishment image. The Young Republican was described by his colleagues as "a believer in the system," and it was this "believer" who attacked the student protestors with words and club. But when it became apparent to him that his psyche could not make the transition from Tacoma bungalows to California socialites, when he abandoned the closest thing to love he ever experienced, he radically altered his ideological stance, and became Bundy the rebel. This metamorphosis is evident in every confrontation he would now have with the authorities—a rebellion that was usually misinterpreted by observers as a kind of psychotic self-destructiveness. From the moment of his first arrest in Utah, he treated the police with a dangerous contempt more consistent with a radical than a Republican: "I thought I had a bunch of klutzes who were going to fuck me around," he said of his interrogating officers. He first offered them a bogus alibi, which fell apart after the merest scrutiny, and essentially complained that his interrogation gave him no room to *perform:* "I thought there might be some time for song and dance. I didn't even get much dance in." Subsequently, as Michaud and Aynesworth noted, "By his actions, Ted invited the detective to pursue him, apparently expecting to tease and humiliate the opposition." Why should he chart such a treacherous course for himself? In this rebellious spirit, Bundy would photograph police who were stalking him, leave them notes, or playfully confront them: these were not the actions of a confident middle-class person faced with a serious charge. Later, a psychiatrist wrote that "in a certain sense, Mr. Bundy is a producer of a play which attempts to show that various authority figures can be manipulated," which is most insightful, but he concluded that "Mr. Bundy does not have the capacity to recognize that the price for this 'thriller' might be his own life." Surely he is in error about Bundy's "capacity": the true rebel is contemptuous of both his life and the consequences of his performance, not incapable of perceiving them.[57]

It was while awaiting trial in Utah that he first began to taunt the press. "I was trying to project an image," he said of his dealings with the media. "I was feeling proud of myself. That's when I started to be pleased about fucking with the press. From then on, it was a lot of fun." Bundy the rebel was finding his feet. Out on bail in Seattle, he strutted about with law books, commenting loudly and sarcastically on the remarkable opportunity he had been given to participate in the legal system. At his trial in Utah, when the prosecutor asked him why he carried a crowbar in his Volkswagen, he replied with an air of mocking civility, "Well, it's a useful tool. What can I say, Dave?" And when the prosecutor asked him to estimate how many miles he could expect from a tank of gasoline in his Volkswagen, he merely responded: "Oh, I'm not really thinking about it, Dave. I thought you made your own conclusion. I'm not here to do mathematical problems." These were not the words of someone who was trying to fight his own conviction: rather, he was trying to fight something quite different. But what?[58]

For the Utah trial he had waived his right to a jury; but this had provided him with an insufficiently appreciative audience for his performance as rebel. For his trials in Florida, he would steel himself to play before a jury and, through the television and press coverage, to the entire nation. He described the FBI as himself, calling them "Fornicators, Bastards and Imposters"; issued "Statements to the Media" in which he compared his position to that of the Soviet dissidents; and fought constantly with his attorneys, frequently firing them. Always, he would paint himself as the persecuted rebel, flamboyantly carrying a copy of *The Gulag Archipelago*. He was, he said, unjustifiably attacked by a malicious judicial system; he was the dissenting intellectual paying the price of his independence. It was a bizarre posture, perhaps, but no one can deny that he lived it.[59]

Bundy the Bastard

Theodore Robert Bundy was born on November 24, 1946, in the Elizabeth Lund home for Unwed Mothers in Burlington, Vermont, the result of a brief liaison between his twenty-two-year-old mother and a man she described as "a sailor," although there were hints that this sailor came from a monied family. Had Louise Bundy been truly proletarian, the event might have been brushed off as one of no significance, but she was not: she was from a deeply religious lower-middle-class Philadelphia family, and she was made to feel her "shame." Too many knew the story of Ted's paternity in Philadelphia, so at the age of four, son and mother moved to Tacoma, Washington, where the secretary Louise soon met the army cook Johnnie Bundy. They were married on May 19, 1951, when Ted was not yet five. This provoked a corollary shame in Ted, for they were not wealthy. So much was this the case that Ted and his step-father would spend hours laboring in the fields of the market gardens near Tacoma to supplement their slender income, sweating and bending for a few dollars a day while the cars of the wealthy wafted past. This would mean little to someone whose sense of self was secure, but a great deal to someone cracking under the weight of the hierarchy.

Perhaps the ultimate responsibility of the social order is to implant in each individual his or her sense of identity. Few have had such a fearful absence of a crisp identity as Ted Bundy. The man was forever disguising himself, and not just to avoid capture. He wore a false moustache when working for the Republican Party, studied the arts of make-up in theater school, frequently altered his hair or his weight to change his appearance dramatically, and used false casts and false facial hair as basic props in his theft of the idealized women. Yet he did this not in some deranged or delusional semi-consciousness, for he was very much aware that much of his life was "a Walter Mitty kind of thing." "I'm disguised as an attorney today," he told the judge in Florida, revealing more about his inner self than he was prone to do.[60]

The social strain of illegitimacy, infinitely more intense in the 1950s than it is today, sunk deep into Bundy's soul. He felt intensely that this illegitimacy deprived him of a past and that, as Winn and Merrill remarked, "without a past it was impossible to have a 'meaningful relationship.'" In his public and "Republican" statement, he would always claim to have risen above any anxiety on this matter: "One thing I had come to terms with long ago was the circumstances of my birth." Yet in any personal relationships he had, he always took pains to emphasize the agony his illegitimacy caused him. A childhood friend recalled the day Bundy told him he was illegitimate: "I think I said I thought it was no big deal. But he said something to the effect that for him it made a big difference. This was important to him. It wasn't just something to be swept under the rug. When I made light of his situation he said, 'Well, it's not you that's a bastard.' He was bitter when he said it." As an adult, in a conversation with his friend Rule, she remembered him saying words to the effect that: "You know, I only found out who I really am a year or so ago. I mean, I always knew, but I had to prove it to myself . . . I'm illegitimate. When I was born, my mother couldn't say that I was her baby."[61]

Bundy has given contradictory accounts of how he discovered his illegitimacy, and of whether his mother admitted her relationship to him (sometimes he claimed she said she was his sister); but the revelation seemed to bring his social development to an abrupt halt. "In Junior High everything was fine," he later recalled, "but I got to High School and I didn't make any progress. I felt alienated from my old friends. They just seemed to move on and I didn't. I don't know why and I don't know if there's an explanation. Maybe it's something that was programmed by some kind of genetic thing. In my early schooling, it seemed like there was no problem in learning what the appropriate social behaviors were. It just seemed like I hit a wall in High School. I didn't think anything was wrong, necessarily. I wasn't sure what was wrong and what was right. All I knew was that I felt a bit different." This new alienated and confused Bundy was not popular with his schoolmates, and he had only one date during high school. He felt comfortable only in the social niches—the classroom and the ski slopes—which offered avenues for social mobility. "I spoke up in class. It's a formalized setting and the ground rules are fairly strict. Your performance is measured by different rules than what happens when everybody's peeling off into little cliques down the hallway."

Thus the social order literally deprived him of his identity and acted upon him as a kind of disordering and unbalancing hallucinogen. He tried to fight back by constructing his own identity, but inevitably it was an artificial and alienating process—what Michaud and Aynesworth described as being "like an alien life form acquiring appropriate behavior through mimicry and artifice." "I didn't know what made things tick," Bundy said. "I didn't know what made people want to be friends. I didn't know what made people attractive to one another. I didn't know what underlay social interactions." Society would pay dearly for its malfunction.[62]

Bundy the Lover

Bundy as lover was Bundy as failure. Indeed, his off-and-on affair with the only woman he has convincingly claimed to have loved, functions as source, symbol, and metaphor for his meteoric passage through the social hierarchy. He made his bid for social advancement at the university: driving the classless car and living in the classless university district, he eschewed the fraternity social life which, with its intense class consciousness, by definition declassed him—"I didn't feel socially adept enough. I didn't feel I knew how to function with those people. I felt terribly uncomfortable." Instead, he set about fabricating a middle-class identity, the fullest expression of which was his love for the California socialite. He courted her in the second year of university and then followed her to California for the summer, enrolling in a summer university program. Soon he found himself falling behind the other students: "I found myself thinking about standards of success that I just didn't seem to be living up to," referring ambiguously to both his courses and his lover. Sensing inadequacy and a "loser," the socialite dropped him; and what remained of 1967 was "absolutely the pits for me—the lowest time ever." He returned to Seattle for the following academic year, but was barely able to attend class and finally withdrew from school. Utterly demoralized, he traveled across the country, searching for his roots among his eastern relatives. He returned to Seattle for the ultimate trauma to his fragile ego, to find himself proletarianized, working as a busboy in a hotel dining-room and as a night stocker in a Safeway store. "I absorbed all this uncertainty and all this confusion about why I was doing what I was doing, wondering where I was going, all by myself . . . I'm not the kind of person who socialized a lot, there was no way to let off steam." Soon he was letting off steam and descending into the lumpen proletariat by becoming a thief and shoplifting everything he wanted—stealing, among many other things, a television set, his clothing, a stereo, art, home furnishings, even a large ornamental tree.[63]

As he touched bottom, his fortunes suddenly improved. A casual encounter with an acquaintance led to his employment with a black politician contending for the Republican nomination for Lieutenant Governor. "I just pitched right in. Oh boy! Here we go again. I hadn't had a social life for some time. It just felt good to belong again, to instantly be part of something. . . . The reason I loved politics was because here was something that allowed me to use my talents and assertiveness. You know, the guy who'd raise his hand in class and speak up. And the social life came with it. You were accepted. You went out to dinner with people. They invited you to dinner. I didn't have the money or the tennis-club membership or whatever it takes to really have the inside track. So politics were perfect. You can move among the various strata of society. You can talk to people to whom otherwise you'd have no access."[64]

His candidate lost, and he formed a relationship with Elizabeth Kendall, the daughter of a prosperous Utah professional. By this time, however, he was avidly reading violent pornography and peeping into women's windows. Moreover, the mounting rage inside him converted into deep cyclical depressions: "It wasn't dictated by the cycle of the moon, or anything else," he told Michaud and

Aynesworth. "Not mood swings, just changes. It's goddamn hard for me to describe it. All I wanted to do was just lay around, just consume huge volumes of time without doing a thing." Still, he had not given up yet. He returned to the University of Washington in the summer of 1970 and completed his degree in psychology in 1972 while working part-time for a medical supply company and the Seattle Crisis Clinic. His applications to several law schools were rejected. By now he was fantasizing in earnest, scouting his future killing grounds in endless drives through the countryside, studying the terrain.[65]

What remained of 1972 and 1973 would be the years of decision for him: he would start to kill in January of 1974. Meanwhile, however, his star continued to rise. The election of 1972 enabled him to re-enter the political system, and he worked as a volunteer for the incumbent Republican Governor. After the election, a strong letter of support from the re-elected Governor gained Bundy admission to the University of Utah's College of Law for the fall of 1973. He waited, busying himself with government contracts and positions. Persuaded by a colleague that Washington's University of Puget Sound would be a more appropriate school for someone wanting a career in the state, he enrolled there, telling the Utah Faculty that he had been injured in an automobile accident.

Now, flushed with success, he revived his moribund affair with the California socialite. He flew to San Francisco to see her, this time as a man of some substance, his Young Republican image complete. He seemed different to her now, more desirable, no longer a loser, her "erstwhile wishy-washy beau transformed into a Man of Action." They met frequently and by Christmas of 1973, she thought they were engaged to be married. For his part, however, he had already abandoned his plan to rise with her in the hierarchy: either he had rehearsed his lines so often that they had become ashes in his mouth, or he felt unable to maintain the facade of Royal Consort. In either case, it was this crisis that foreclosed his conventional career. Neither did he like what he saw when he went to class at his new law school: an anonymous office building in downtown Tacoma, and not the ivied campus he had expected. According to Michaud and Aynesworth, "the perceived taint of attending a *déclassé* law school was every bit as demeaning to him in his mid-twenties as Johnnie and Louise's boxy Ramblers were to him as a child." He seemed to have made no effort to do well at school and quickly began to fail. Clearly, the hour of decision had come: he decided to commit himself to another career. He never contacted his "loved one" again, and when she called him a month later in a rage, to terminate the engagement, he had already begun to kill. "Why the hell haven't you written or called," Bundy remembered her shouting at him. "Well, far out, you know," he thought he told her through his alcoholic haze, relieved merely to be rid of her and the unshoulderable burden of aspirations she represented.[66]

Having failed at *social* mobility, through either a brilliant career or a fashionable marriage, he turned his attention to another kind of mobility. "Another factor that is almost indispensable to this kind of behavior," he said later in his discussion of the killings, "is the mobility of contemporary American life. Living in a large center of population and living with lots of people, you can get used to dealing with strangers. It's the anonymity factor." Having made the fateful commitment of the remainder of his life, he would now deal exclusively with strangers.[67]

THE THIEF IN THE NIGHT

"I want to master life and death."

TED BUNDY[68]

Why did Bundy kill? He has told us much, but has done so in his own fashion, which is to say that he contradicted himself ten times over. Sometimes he blamed it all on a bad seed, a warp in his genetic structure. At other times, he blamed the prevailing anomic culture of strangers, which permits or even encourages the dehumanization of others. Alternatively, he claimed he killed as a matter of judicial convenience, eliminating the problem of having a witness to his rape: "self-protection," he said, "required that the girl be killed." He also claimed he raped and murdered for the sheer sexual pleasure it gave the "entity" within him; but he also said he did it in order to possess a female person. At times he stated that the tensions and stresses in his life generated the murderous rage; while at other times he claimed the need to kill was self-generating and self-sustaining, a kind of force that existed on its own. Yet after a nonviolent sexual encounter with a young woman hitchhiker, he considered killing her, only to find that "the justifications were not there." What justifications?[69]

Whom he killed at least is clear. He murdered only one type of person, over and over again—the young, beautiful, long-haired and upper-middle-class (at least in appearance) "idealized woman." *When* did he begin to kill? He did so when he formed the opinion that he was incapable of sustaining the rise in the social hierarchy he so devoutly desired. Finally, there is a studied sameness as to *how* he killed. He would entice the otherwise unenticeable through a ruse, most commonly in a feigned need for help (a broken arm or leg). Through stealth or force he would get them in his car and there gain "control" over them, either by handcuffing them or by crushing their skulls with a heavy instrument. Then he would spirit them away to a private place and abuse them sexually for as long as he felt secure. Sometimes his victims were conscious and terrified, but more often they were battered unconscious—and sometimes they were dead. If he felt uncommonly safe, he might keep them (dead or alive) for days, pausing even to adjust their make-up or shampoo their hair. When he was finished with them, if they were not already dead, he would strangle them and dump their bodies in a burial ground. If it were not for bird hunters combing the thickets, many of the bodies might never have been found: many more, it seems certain, remain undiscovered.

Initially then, it seems clear that his task took a purely homicidal form—to avenge himself, in a sexually satisfying way, on the segment of society that had excluded him (by humiliating him to the point where he could not even accept their acceptance of him).

Yet the task underwent a metamorphosis, and his struggle with the authorities became the culmination of the task—and how appropriate, for were the authorities not the controllers of the society that had invalidated him? He first tested this during the events surrounding his trial in Utah. There, his bizarre posturing with the police and the court gave him immense satisfaction. Transferred to the Colorado prisons, he devoted his days to comprehending the metamorphosis: as he wrote to his mistress, "It is time to rethink this awful experience because the stimulus of standing alone in the face of great odds is not satisfying anymore. It is time to reevaluate the value of living without being alive . . . I want to look around me now. I want to master life and death." He had much to rethink, for it was only a few months earlier, during his trial in Utah, that he had "felt a deep sense of fulfillment. I felt relaxed but emphatic; controlled, but sincere and filled with emotion. It didn't matter who was listening, although I desired each word to strike the Judge as forcefully as possible. Briefly, all too briefly, I was myself again, amongst free people, using all the skill I could muster, fighting the only way I know how: with words and logic. And all too briefly, I was testing the dream of being an attorney." Now it all came together. Carrying copies of the works of Aleksandr Solzhenitsyn, and flirting with Mormonism (he said he thought he was "like the brothers of Amulek, being persecuted for our beliefs"), he found his ultimate *persona:* the persecuted dissident, publicly struggling for his belief in freedom. The trials now became the vehicle for the expression of his task—to confound the authorities and, in doing so, become their equal.[70]

His escape from prison gave him the opportunity to resign from his task, but it was absurd to even think of doing that, for the killing and the escaping and the defending had now become the essence of his life and being. Hence his choice of the sorority house and his final murder of the little girl: having understood that he was incapable of abandoning his task, he completed it in a manner designed to be the most shocking possible, giving substance to French scholars Peter and Favret's proposition that "only to those who are excluded from the social nexus comes the idea of raising the question about the limits of human nature."[71]

Yet these murders exhausted him. Instead of escaping, he drifted erratically through Florida until he was captured by the police in Pensacola. Within hours, he was in the hospital emergency room, with ample opportunity to escape, but he did not seize upon it. He claimed not to understand why: "I just can't seem to get up on my own two feet and go for it"—but he must have known that to escape would merely have delayed the discharge of his most awesome responsibility, the trial. During his formal interrogation shortly thereafter, he saw the event theatrically and clearly as a task now almost complete: "They made their solemn commitment to me. We all sat around the room, and the tension mounted. I thought it was really quite dramatic. Maybe I overstate the event, but to me it was the end of the road, you know, right there." He made his confession to a priest, possibly a full one (we can never know). The violence was over.[72]

He struggled to give a confession to the interrogating police, but seemed unable to do so. "I can't talk about it. I'd be a fool . . . I tried to help you understand me . . . I tried to help you understand me a little bit more." When the police suggested that he was merely afraid to confess, he replied: "I'm not afraid to die." Then an insightful detective added, "You're afraid you're going to go before your story gets told." "Sure," replied Ted. "That's right," said the detective, "and Ted Bundy will have lived for nothing." It was at that time that Bundy told his jailer: "I realize I will never function in society again. I don't want to escape, but if I get the chance, I will. I want you to be professional enough to see that I never get the chance."[73]

In the trial that was to come, in the blaze of lights from daily national television coverage, he consummated his dream of becoming an attorney. Throughout the trial, he gave the impression to all that being his own attorney was the fullest expression of his life. As he put it: "The state prosecutor, with all his skill and training . . . a guy with a year and a half of law school can let the air out of his tires."[74]

An Adieu

His Republican employer had called him "a believer in the system," and so he was. He opposed all radical causes until he realized he was annulled himself—pronounced by himself unable to climb the hierarchy. Only then did he embark upon his radical crimes, crimes possible only for those so disenfranchised that they can reverse all social values and thereby act as gods. His world had spun apart twice; first, when he had discovered his illegitimacy and thereby lost his identity and purpose, and second, when he had discovered his inability to live with the creature he had fabricated in order to win the socialite. Many others before him had endured such humiliations, but had gone on to re-construct their lives in a spirit of defiance, or of humility. But Bundy could not take that course. He wanted revenge "for what the system has done to me"; and just as the impoverished materialist Bundy had become a common thief, so the socially annulled climber resolved to steal the ultimate object. Killing those who were at once the object of his desire, the symbol of his annullment, and the now closed avenue for his escape, became the purpose of his existence.[75]

Once he had glimpsed his attainable future as "common," he could not endure it. It was necessary for him to seize control of events and to immortalize himself and his achievements in the process, catapulting himself onto the nation's center stage. He would not accept a verdict of insanity, even though that might have saved his life, for to have done so would have invalidated his rebellion, just as the bastardy verdict had invalidated his person. There was thus a rational reason why he appeared to behave irrationally in court: what Tanay and the other observers thought was the manifestation of Bundy's mental disease—his "inability" to recognize the weight of the evidence against him—was in fact a reflection of his alternate purpose. His innocence or guilt were irrelevant to his purpose, which was simply to confront and confound the authorities by attacking the quality of their case, thus fulfilling his "dream" of becoming an attorney. Ultimately, through the cleverness of his apparently insane maneuverings ("insane" because they denied him life), he was declared sane. Thus society acted against itself to legitimize his deeds. The earlier, young Republican Bundy had, according to his biographers Winn and Merrill, "a visionary personal cast" to his political ideology. "Ted Bundy wanted to do something about America." And so he had. Alas, however, like all our multiple murderers, he had punished the innocent—which is to say he reaped ten thousandfold the original crime of society.[76]

Today, only the families of his victims remain to mourn, for like all our murderers, he feels no remorse. Still awaiting execution in a Florida prison, he studies "Oriental philosophy—Buddhism, Taoism, and spiritual-physical traditions of the East," and finds them "much in tune with the way I have become. I find that the pressures on me have actually permitted me to enter into a period of growth," he told his biographers. No matter how we try to exact revenge, we cannot, for his serene face reveals his fulfillment and contentment: "Anybody matures, I'm sure," he said recently, "no matter where they are. But so many times in these past couple of years I felt like I was looking down from a mountain and seeing so many things I never saw before. I feel much more confident about myself. It's really marvelous! I feel not powerful, but in control of things." Such serenity was little wonder, for the man had mastered life and death.[77]

4.
PUTTING SOMETHING OVER ON HIGH-CLASS PEOPLE

Albert DeSalvo*

"I didn't mean to hurt nobody, I
never wanted to hurt nobody."

ALBERT DESALVO[1]

More widely known as the "Boston Strangler," Albert
DeSalvo is one of the least understood of all modern
multiple murderers. He is also one of the best publicized.
He was the subject of a film and many books following his
deadly rampage through the city of Boston. The murders
seemed to be the work of a frenzied madman: he usually
strangled his victims with their own stockings in their own
apartments. It was widely believed that he was simply a
"psychotic" with a maniacal sexual deviation—and there
was certainly no doubt that he had a formidable sexual
drive, for it demanded release five or six times each day.
This construction worker's career in sexual assault began
first with molestation and then rape. He would pose as a

---

* DeSalvo's confessions are extensive and are available in a number of publications. The most reliable study of the man is Gerold Frank's *The Boston Strangler*, but
I also found much of use in George W. Rae's *Confessions of the Boston Strangler*, and
some in Harold K. Banks' *The Strangler!* and James A. Brussel's *Casebook of a Crime
Psychiatrist*. Frank's book is both pioneering and scholarly.

scout for a modeling agency, flattering and cajoling (or forcing when necessary) hundreds of women into bed with him.

Then, suddenly, with no apparent conscious preparation, his task surfaced and he began to kill. He murdered thirteen women and then, just as suddenly, the task was completed. He was not an intelligent man, and he only dimly perceived his own motivations—which had to be teased out of him by police and psychiatric interrogators. Yet he was not caught by the police for the stranglings: he only came under suspicion for the murders because of his repeated pleas for help from his mental hospital cell (where he had been detained only for the rapes). As it began to dawn on the judicial and psychiatric authorities that DeSalvo the rapist might in fact be who he claimed to be—the Boston Strangler—they entered into a joint venture aimed at unraveling the motives for the bizarre series of murders. DeSalvo cooperated with the enquiry in every way, but the results were impoverished both by his own bewilderment at what he had done, and by his tendency to revel in his center-stage position in what he called "the biggest story of the century."[2]

In more ways than one, he was right. Raised in intolerable hunger and cold in the Boston slums, his violent and alcoholic father subjected him and his mother to savage beatings (he watched him break his mother's fingers one by one). We can only guess at the humiliation he endured after his father sold him and his sister as slaves to a farmer (an enslavement that lasted for months); but we can posit that his thefts during adolescence were an attempt to recoup his situation. We know that the rigid lower-middle-class German woman he met, adored, and married while serving with the U.S. Army in Europe became the focus of his attempt to enter the world of lower-middle-class gentility. When his beloved utterly rejected his physical, emotional, and status needs, he felt excluded from the social class whose membership he so deeply coveted: thus, as he could rationalize within the context of violent male culture, his war on lower-middle-class women was just revenge. The stage was set for his purple explosion.

THE KILLING TIME

His first attempt to kill was a failure. It was marred by the indecision and self-consciousness of the novice. In early June of 1962, he tried to strangle a Scandinavian woman in her Boston apartment. Her long dark hair had reminded him of his wife's, but the urgency of his task had not yet obliterated his compunctions. He was immensely strong, but she fought him until, he later recalled, "I looked in a mirror in the bedroom and there was me—strangling somebody! 'Oh God, what am I doing? I'm a married man. I'm the father of two children. Oh God, help me!'" Unable to complete the murder, "I got out of there fast. It wasn't like it was me—it was like it was someone else I was watching. I just took off." It took a week for him to pull himself together and steel himself to his mission.[3]

He made his first kill on June 14, 1962. Telling his wife that he was going fishing, he drove into Boston and selected an apartment building that suited his needs. He wandered through the corridors until he knocked on the door of Anna Slesers, a fifty-five-year-old Latvian immigrant. When she answered the knock, he told her that he had been "sent to do some work in your apartment." As she led him to the bathroom to show him the work that in fact had to be done, "I hit her on the head with the lead weight. She bled a lot, terrible," he remembered, ". . . after I put the belt around her neck, I ripped open her robe and I played with her and I pulled her legs apart, like this, and I had intercourse with her."* "Then I look around and I'm angry and I don't know why and I don't really know what I'm looking for, you understand me?" He then "washed up in the bathroom," walked into the living-room and turned off the record player, put on a raincoat that was hanging in a cabinet, and left. He disposed of his bloody clothes by throwing them into the ocean. Slesers' son later discovered her body and called the police: they found her lying on her back, nude under the housecoat which had been spread apart, with the

---

* DeSalvo used the word "intercourse" as a kind of euphemism for any form of sexual activity that resulted in orgasm.

housecoat's cord, DeSalvo's biographer, Gerold Frank noted, "knotted tightly about her neck, its ends turned up so that it might have been a bow, tied little-girl fashion under her chin." Subsequent medical investigation showed no evidence of rape.[4]

Two weeks later, on June 28, 1962, he made his second kill. He knocked on the door of eighty-five-year-old Mary Mullen and told her that "I got to do some work in the apartment." She accepted his imposture as a maintenance man and let him in to the apartment. When her back was turned to him, he remembered: "She was talking nice—and I don't know what happened. All I know is my arm went around her neck. I didn't even squeeze her . . . and she went straight down. I tried to hold her; I didn't want her to fall on the floor. . . . She died in my arms, this woman." He picked up her body and placed it on the couch, correctly assuming the police would think her death was from natural causes. "I didn't touch her. I didn't do anything to her—she went, just like that. She passed out. If I close my eyes, as I do now, it's just like being there. I picked her up and put her on the couch and I left."[5]

Two days later, on June 30, 1962, he killed twice. Selecting an apartment building at random and then an apartment, he knocked on the door of Helen Blake, a sixty-five-year-old retired practical nurse. As it was morning, Blake answered the door in her pajamas. Since she had previously asked the apartment supervisor to do some repairs in her apartment, she welcomed DeSalvo with the comment: "Well, it's about time." As he remembered, "We had some conversation. She was telling me about her niece, a very nice woman, you know, talking about her niece." He suggested they inspect the bedroom to determine if it needed any repairs, and he moved behind her as she pointed to a window that required adjustment. "While she was pointing I grabbed my hand right behind her neck; she was a heavy-set, big breasted woman. She went down right away —she fainted, passed right out." He then "picked her up, took off her pajamas—the buttons popped—I took everything clean off. She was unconscious. I got on top, I had intercourse." He bit into her body, wrapped a brassiere around her neck, and then a nylon stocking over that. Then he went out into the kitchen and began what would become one of his trademarks—a major ransacking of the apartment, for no apparent purpose (nothing, for example, was stolen). He tried to pry open a chest under her bed, but the knife he was using snapped. "I just dropped the handle then and took off. I left her about 10:20 a.m." Her body lay undiscovered for two days until concerned neighbors called the police. They found Blake lying face down on her bed, the tops of her pajamas shoved over her shoulders. Her brassiere had been tied in a bow under her chin. The apartment had been torn apart; bureau drawers had been left open, and the drawer of the living-room's desk "had been placed on the floor, as if the killer had crouched there and carefully examined what it held: letters, stationery, rubber bands, a religious medal, and curiously enough, one of a pair of dice." Medical examination revealed that she had been sexually assaulted, but that sexual intercourse had apparently not taken place.[6]

He spent the next few hours "just riding around," in a kind of daze, "like in the middle of the world," until he turned into the parking lot of a still-fashionable apartment building. He pushed the buzzers until one tenant responded, Nina Nichols, a sixty-eight-year-old retired physiotherapist and widow. She was wary at her door when DeSalvo gave his usual "maintenance man" story, but when he said she could call the building supervisor to check on him, she relented. "I felt funny," DeSalvo recalled. "I just didn't want it to happen. But I went in and I proceeded from one room to another. When we got to the bedroom I looked at the windows . . . she was turned away—that's when it happened. Because I grabbed her and she fell back with me on the bed, on top of me." He wrapped a belt around her neck and tried to strangle her with it, but the belt snapped. Finally, he choked her with one of her own silk stockings. He claimed to have had "intercourse" with her. When he finished, he inserted a wine bottle in her vagina: "For what reason I don't know, I stuck the bottle in her." Then he began his now-customary aimless ransacking of the apartment, not knowing what he was searching for, but sensing that he was not looking for something to steal. "I didn't have in my mind the idea of taking anything."

114

When the telephone rang, he left. Nichols' body was discovered within hours. The apartment looked as if it had been burglarized. Bureau drawers were hanging open and her possessions were strewn about the floor. Nichols lay on the bedroom floor, her legs spread, her housecoat shoved up to her waist. The ends of the stockings which had cut into her flesh and strangled her were "arranged on the floor so they turned up on either side like a grotesque bow," Frank recorded.[7]

He then waited six weeks, until August 19, 1962, before he made his fifth kill. Ida Irga was a seventy-five-year-old widow living quietly in a once-fashionable Boston neighborhood. Following his customary procedure, he randomly pressed the buzzers on her apartment building until someone responded: "When I get to the top of the stairs, she's on the landing, looking down over the iron railing, waiting for me. I told her I was going to do some work in the apartment." She was suspicious, but he allayed her fears by insisting that "If you don't want it done, forget it. I'll just tell them you told me you don't want it done." She relented, and as soon as he stood behind her in the bedroom, his arm went around her neck. "She passed out fast. I saw purplish-dark blood, it came out of her right ear . . . just enough for me to see. I saw it more clearly when I put the pillowcase around her neck, but I strangled her first with my arm, then the pillowcase. I think I had intercourse." When the police entered her apartment two days later, they found Irga lying on her back in a torn nightdress. "Her legs," the police officer wrote, "were spread approximately four to five feet from heel to heel and her feet were propped up on individual chairs and a standard bed pillow, less the cover, was placed under her buttocks," leaving her in what Frank called "this grotesque parody of the obstetrical position." Why did DeSalvo now begin to add extra humiliation to the corpse and extra pain to the families of the victims? Irga had been sexually assaulted and her apartment ransacked, but her valuables had not been stolen.[8]

The following day, August 20, 1962, he killed Jane Sullivan, a sixty-seven-year-old nurse who lived alone. He entered her building in his usual manner and found her in the midst of moving in to her new apartment. She mistook him for one of the movers and led him to the closet to show him something. "That's where it happened," DeSalvo remembered. "I'm behind her . . . I put my right arm around her, we both fell back on the floor. She struggled and struggled, she was so big there was nothing to grip hold of—she finally stopped struggling. It took about a minute and a half." He could not remember if he had raped her. Her body was not found for ten days—ten days of disintegration in the August heat. She was discovered grossly exposed, kneeling face down in the bathtub, her housecoat and girdle shoved above her waist, her underwear around her ankles. She had been strangled with two of her own stockings. The condition of her body made it impossible to determine if she had been raped; but her apartment had been ransacked.[9]

Then the pattern appeared to change abruptly: from now on, he would usually kill young women, and his sexual assaults would be more explicit. On December 5, 1962, he made his seventh successful assault, killing twenty-year-old Sophie Clark, a student at the Carnegie Institute of Medical Technology. He had driven aimlessly until he found a suitable building. He then knocked on the apartment door of one woman, who frightened him away by pretending her husband was in the bedroom. In another wing of the same building, he knocked on Sophie Clark's door: "A Negro girl, really beautiful, with beautiful long hair . . . it was very appealing, the way she was dressed." He first told her he was there to do repair work on the apartment, but then returned to an earlier stratagem. "I gave her fast talk. I told her I'd set her up in modeling, I'd give her from twenty to thirty dollars an hour." He asked her to "turn around, let me see how you're built," and when she did so, "That was it. I grabbed her around the neck with my right arm, she was very tall, because she fell on top of me on the settee, my legs went around her legs—she didn't give me any struggle at all." He had intercourse with her as she lay there unconscious, and when she began to awaken, "To keep her from screaming, I grabbed two nylons out of a drawer. She was the one I had to tie really tight. She started to fight. I made it so tight, I couldn't see it . . . I ripped her clothes off her, ripped off her slip, and put it around her neck, then the stockings. . . . Too deep. . . . Whew! . . . So tight." Curiously, DeSalvo remembered that "afterwards I looked through some magazines there." Clark's roommate discovered her body a few hours later: she was on her back, her bathrobe spread open, a gag in her mouth, her legs spread apart. As always, bureau drawers had been ransacked and their contents thrown about the room. A classical record collection, magazines, and Clark's photograph album had been disturbed, as if someone had leafed through them, searching for something.[10]

He made his eighth kill within a few weeks, stealing the life of a twenty-three-year-old Boston secretary, Patricia Bissette, on December 30. He forced her lock that Sunday morning and found her standing in front of him with a blanket wrapped around her, demanding to know who he was. "I gave her the fast talk," he remembered. "I said I was one of the fellows living upstairs and where was her girl friend?—there were three names on the door, and I named one of them." She responded that they were out, but invited DeSalvo in for a cup of coffee, and put on a Christmas record. "I was looking at her and getting worked up. I went over to her. I was on my knees. . . . She said, 'Take it easy.' I said, 'Nobody's here, nobody can hear you. I can do what I want to you.'" This angered her and she asked him to leave, but as she stood up, she turned her back to him. "Next thing, before she knew it, I had my arm around her neck, she fell back on top of me, and she passed out." He ripped off her pajamas: "I picked her up. I remember seeing her on the floor stripped naked." He raped and strangled her.

Curiously, and reminiscent of Aiko Koo for Edmund Kemper and the salesman for Charles Starkweather, he felt remorse at killing her. "She was so different," he remembered ruefully. "I didn't want to see her like that, naked and . . . She talked to me like a man, she treated me like a man." We will return to this particular case, for when the killer feels ambivalence, he is pointing toward his motive for the murders. Still, it saved none of their lives. Bissette's body was found the following day, lying on her back on the bed, a sheet tucking her in. The medical examiner removed the sheet and found her strangled with her own stockings.

Her pajamas had been pushed up to her shoulders and there was evidence of recent sexual intercourse. Her apartment had been ransacked.[11]

His next attempt occurred six weeks later, on February 18, 1963. He entered the apartment of a twenty-nine-year-old German-born (like his wife) waitress and, when she turned her back to him, he grabbed her under his arm and kicked her to the floor. She fought back, kicking and biting: she bit his finger so hard that he momentarily loosened his hold, and then she screamed. As she remembered it, a workman then appeared at the edge of the roof, and DeSalvo fled. DeSalvo remembered it differently. "She was in the position, she was ready to go, she was good as gone. I had both arms around her from behind—but I couldn't do it. I don't know why. She grabbed my finger in her mouth, she was biting it down to the bone—I had a knife, I could have ripped her open . . . and I didn't . . . I couldn't hit her. I could see her brown hair . . . and when I turned and saw her face, I couldn't put my hand to hit her. I said, 'I'm going to let you go,' and I started to give up, but she still had my finger in her mouth and I was doing everything to get her to open her mouth and she wouldn't. I could of laid, I could of hit her with my fist and knocked her out—I don't know what held me back."[12]

Three weeks later, on March 9, 1963, he was successful once more, beating and stabbing to death sixty-nine-year-old Mary Brown. He entered her building, picked up a piece of pipe lying on the floor, knocked on her door, and told her he had been ordered to paint the kitchen. "As she walked from the kitchen, her back to me, I hit her right on the back of the head with the pipe. She went down. . . . Her things were ripped open, her busts were exposed. I got a sheet from a chair and covered her. I kept hitting her and hitting her. . . This is terrible . . . because her head felt—it felt like it was all gone." He took a fork from the kitchen: "I remember stabbing her in the bust, the right one . . . and leaving it in her. . . . It was bloody. . . . Oh, wasn't it, my God!" The autopsy report concluded that Brown had died from a skull fracture and manual strangulation, and also found evidence of a sexual attack.[13]

His tenth victim was murdered on May 6, 1963. Twenty-three-year-old Beverly Samans was a graduate student in rehabilitation counseling at Boston University. DeSalvo felt great difficulty in describing this murder because he thought it was "shocking" in some way that the others hadn't been. He entered her apartment in his usual way and, brandishing a knife, forced her into the bedroom. She was terrified of getting pregnant and DeSalvo remembered her pleading with him: "Promise me you won't get me pregnant, you won't rape me." He promised her he would not, laid her down on the bed and tied her wrists behind her, placing a gag in her mouth and a blind over her eyes. "Then I was going to have intercourse with her, anyway, and she began talking, 'You promised, you said you wouldn't do it to me, don't, don't, I'll get pregnant.' The words kept coming and coming . . . I can still hear her saying, 'Don't do it—don't do that to me.' . . . She made me feel so unclean, the way she talked to me. . . . No matter what I did, she didn't like it . . . she started to get loud. . . . She kept yelling or trying to yell . . . and I stabbed her. Once I did it once . . . I couldn't stop . . . I reached over, got the knife . . . and I stabbed her in the throat. She kept saying something. I grabbed the knife in my left hand and held the tip of the breast and I went down, two times, hard. . . . She moved, and the next thing you know, blood all over the place . . . I kept hitting her and hitting her with that damn knife . . . I stabbed her two times in the breast, too. I hit her and hit her and hit her. Why? That's what I'm trying to tell you. . . . It was just like my . . . Irmgard [DeSalvo's wife]." Samans' nude body was found two days later, her wrists bound behind her with a sequined silk scarf, a nylon stocking tied around her neck. She had been stabbed twenty-two times.[14]

Something in him seemed to have been temporarily satisfied by Samans' murder, because he waited four months before he killed again. On September 8, 1963, he killed fifty-eight-year-old Evelyn Corbin, a youthful divorcée who worked on an assembly line. He entered her apartment as the maintenance man, but found her wary. "How do I know you're not the Boston Strangler?" he remembered her asking him. He "won her confidence" by volunteering to leave. In the bathroom, he threatened her with the knife and she began to cry, saying, "I can't do anything—I'm under doctor's orders." "I was going to do it to her anyway, but she was all in tears; she said she'd do it the other way." When it was finished and she turned her back to him to replace the pillow, he grabbed her and tied her hands in front. "I got on top of her, sitting on her hands. I put the pillow on top of her face so I couldn't look at her face . . . I strangled her manually. She did try to bounce me off. She couldn't do it, and then she didn't breathe anymore." A neighbor discovered Corbin's body within hours of her death. Her housecoat had been ripped open and pushed up and her legs spread apart. Her underpants had been stuffed into her mouth as a gag, and she had been strangled with her nylon stockings. One stocking was tied in the form of an elaborate bow around the ankle of her left foot. Her apartment appeared to have been searched; bureau drawers were open, a jewelry tray had been set on the floor, and the contents of her purse dumped on a couch.[15]

His task was now nearing its dumb completion, but it was another three months before he killed again. On November 23, 1963, feeling awkward because President Kennedy had just been assassinated (and wondering if a killing was appropriate on this day), he murdered for the twelfth time: twenty-three-year-old Joann Graff, an industrial designer and Sunday School teacher. His usual stratagem brought him into her apartment, but—interestingly—he was appalled by the shabby condition of her rooms. "It was a very cheap apartment with really cheap furniture—even the Salvation Army wouldn't take it. Just like she was living out of a suitcase. The kitchen was terrible, the flooring was very bad." Still, he proceeded despite his qualms about her substance. He threatened her with a knife and forced her into the bedroom. "I put my hand right around her neck and pulled her backwards on the bed, and we fell on the bed, she was on top of me . . . and she passed out . . . I took off her clothes. . . . Her busts were large . . . I know I possibly may have bitten her . . . I just had intercourse with her, and that was it. It was very fast—all over within a matter of probably ten minutes." He remembered strangling her with her own leotards. After he was finished, he left hurriedly and drove home for supper. "I had supper, washed up, played with the kids, watched TV." The medical examiner later determined that she had been strangled with two nylon stockings intertwined with her leotards, tied around her neck in a flamboyant bow. She lay on her bed, her blouse shoved up above her shoulders, her legs spread. There were tooth marks on her left breast, and the apartment had been ransacked. Nothing had been taken.[16]

The thirteenth and final murder took place six weeks later, on January 4, 1964, when he killed nineteen-year-old Mary Sullivan, a nurse's aide who had recently moved to Boston. She answered the door, holding in her hand a knife that she had been using to peel potatoes. She did not think to use her own knife when he threatened her with his. He forced her into the bedroom, where he tied and gagged her: "I got on top of her so she could not be in any position, you know, to reach up and scratch me. . . . She was still alive when I had intercourse with her, she was alive, she allowed me to do it to her." He had intercourse with her with her sweater pulled over her head "so I could not see her face." Then he strangled her, cut the ascot from her wrists and flushed it down the toilet. He carried her body to another bed, removed her sweater and straddled her, masturbating so that the semen struck her face. Then, he admitted, he "done something" with a broom. "I feel I did not insert it, at least I hope I didn't, to hurt her insides. You might say, 'What do you mean, hurt her insides? She's dead anyhow.' But it still—it's—it's to me a vicious thing. . . . Mary Sullivan was the last one. I never did it again. I never killed anyone after that. I only tied them up. I didn't hurt them." Her body was discovered a few hours later by her roommates. The manner in which her body had been left seemed to be the Strangler's ultimate insult. The police report recorded that her body was "on bed in propped position, buttocks on pillow, back against headboard, head on right shoulder, knees up, eyes closed, viscous liquid (seminal?) dripping from mouth to right breast, breast and lower extremities exposed, broomstick handle inserted in vagina, steak knife on bed . . . seminal stains on blanket." A pink scarf had been tied with a huge bow under her chin, and a gaily colored card placed against her left foot. The card read: "HAPPY NEW YEAR."[17]

THE EXPLAINING TIME

> "There is got to be some kind of explanation as to why this has all happen."
>
> ALBERT DESALVO[18]

Despite a childhood poisoned by unspeakable physical abuse—including being sold as a "slave"—he did not begin to kill until he felt his social aspirations, such as they were, had become unreachable. Once incarcerated, he tried to cooperate fully with the authorities and tell them everything he knew about the murders. But since he barely understood his own motives, he could only explain the mechanics of how it had been done, and dwell on the grisly details of violation in the act of destroying a life. Still, although at first he confessed only to bewilderment and mystification at his own behavior, like Kemper, Bundy and Berkowitz, he did ultimately offer a number of alternative explanations. However, unlike Kemper who offered many explanations in order to mystify his audience, DeSalvo did so only because he himself groped half-blind toward a conclusion. But in the end, he did tell us enough.

Why did he confess? When the police had announced on the radio that the Strangler, once caught, would be sent to a mental institution, he had considered turning himself in while he was still killing. But shortly thereafter, he remembered that the governor had hinted that he would press for capital punishment in this case, and DeSalvo had abandoned his thoughts of surrender. He seems to have made the decision to confess when the police telephoned him to come to the station on molesting charges. "I looked at my wife," he remembered. "She was crying, sitting near me and the telephone. I knew she was crying and vomiting all day, ever since the call came that morning. I couldn't see her cry any more. She was crying her eyes out, all red—she said, 'Al, are you in trouble again?' I held my hand over the mouthpiece. 'Don't you worry,' I said. 'I'll take care of it.' . . . I knew I couldn't go on any longer. I told the detective, 'Look, I'm coming down tonight.' I says, 'I'm going to come down now. Tomorrow might be too late. I want to get it all cleared up.' He didn't know what I meant, but I knew. I knew deep down this was the way it must end, I think I knew it from the very beginning."[19]

Yet he did not confess all at once. At first, he denied any involvement in the stranglings, and only hinted to detectives and fellow-prisoners that he might be implicated in much more than simple molestation and rape. He told one detective, whom he especially liked: "If you knew the whole story you wouldn't believe it." But when the detective demanded that he explain himself, he merely replied vaguely, "It'll all come out, Leo. You'll find out." Once incarcerated in Bridgewater State Hospital, he boasted constantly about his sexual assaults, even during group therapy. He ambiguously asked one fellow inmate: "What would happen if a guy was sent up for robbing one bank when there were really thirteen banks robbed?" More overtly, he asked his attorney: "What would you do if someone gave you the biggest story of the century? Bigger than the Brink's robbery. It only happens once in maybe two million times. Like Jack the Ripper. I've been known as the Cat Man—the Green Man—the Phantom Burglar—and now the Boston 'S' Man." When an old friend visited him in the hospital and told him he would get life imprisonment for the rapes, DeSalvo replied, "Eddie, I could get life fifty times and they couldn't pay me back for what I done. My family would have to change their name." Again, he told a fellow inmate awaiting trial for the murder of his young wife: "Hell, what you did was nothing. When you find out what I did—I've killed a couple of girls." A few months later, he told his attorney that he had murdered thirteen women and sexually assaulted nearly 2,000, which in fact seems a likely estimate.[20]

Then he changed his mind about confessing. He had spoken to his wife on the telephone and, according to Frank, she had become hysterical and had threatened to kill herself and the children if he admitted he was the Strangler. The following day, during an interview with a Bridgewater psychologist, DeSalvo refused to submit to a routine test. He did express an interest, however, in what people were thinking "about all the excitement." When the psychologist told him that she did not wish to discuss the stranglings, he replied, "I understand that. Besides, I never confessed to being the Strangler. My name's never been in the papers in connection with those things. [The Strangler] should be studied, not buried."[21]

A few weeks later, his attorney arranged for him to be examined by a California hypnoanalyst, and DeSalvo agreed to undergo this eerie experience. In a deep hypnotic trance, punctuated by shattering screams from DeSalvo whenever he came to the brink of recalling the actual killings, he would speak only of the events leading up to the murders. The hypnoanalyst then left him with a post-hypnotic suggestion that he would write down any dream he had that night. The following day, DeSalvo presented him with a dream that edged closer to a confession, detailing the sexual assault and binding—but not the killing—of one of his victims. Unfortunately, this promising development was derailed when the hypnoanalyst insisted on exploring a Freudian theme in which DeSalvo, in attacking the women, was in reality attacking his own crippled daughter. In a deep hypnotic state, DeSalvo wept and denied it, then cried out, "You're a liar!" as his hands shot out at the hypnotist's throat. The hypnotism sessions went no further. The police, meanwhile, had been frustrated in their search for the Strangler because none of the survivors of his attacks could positively identify him.[22]

It was not until the spring of 1965, with the manhunt for the Strangler now in its third year, that the mental patient Albert DeSalvo confessed to police that he was the Strangler. But this information did not pour out until he had established a relationship of deep trust with an official. He prefaced his confessions with an explanation of why the murders had occurred most often on weekends (a fact the police had always taken as significant): "I could always get out of the house Saturday by telling my wife I had to work," he said. "You got to realize this . . . I just drove in and out of streets and ended up wherever I ended up. I never knew where I was going, I never knew what I was doing—that's why you never nailed me, because you never knew where I was going to strike and I didn't either. So we were both baffled . . . I didn't know so how could you know?" Through the summer and autumn of 1965, in endless sessions, he recited his homicidal *mèmoire,* telling everything to the authorities because he wished to understand himself.[23]

DeSalvo Mystified

The recurring theme in his revelations was his mystification at his own behavior. Like so many multiple murderers, DeSalvo usually spoke of his killings in a distancing third person—a linguistic means of removing oneself from full responsibility—as if the murders had been done by someone else and he had only observed them ("I looked in a mirror in the bedroom and there was me—strangling somebody!"). With DeSalvo, however, the distance seemed to have been created not just to spare himself embarrassment, but to express his bewilderment. Still, he insisted that "I am doing my utmost to give you the clearest picture I can without giving you false details."

He seemed to feel overwhelmed by a kind of compulsion that he could neither control nor understand. When Nina Nichols had let him into her apartment, urging him to be quick because she had to go out, he remembered: "But I already know that she ain't going nowhere after I close that door behind me even though I fight it all the way. It's funny. I didn't want to go in there in the first place. I just didn't want it to happen." Nor could he understand why he searched and ransacked the apartments of his victims. When asked what he was looking for, he could only reply: "I didn't know at that time—probably anything. . . . To be honest with you, I never took anything from that apartment, from any of the apartments . . . I wasn't up there for stealing. . . . That's what I'm trying to find out myself. I done these things, I know, I went through them. . . . Yes—why didn't I take it? That's what I'd like to know, too. I understand she had a diamond, too. Why didn't I take that? . . . I don't think I was actually looking for anything to steal." He did venture the suggestion that "I might have searched to make it look that way that something was being taken," but later admitted that he did not know if that was correct.[24]

When he was asked why he seemed reluctant to discuss certain details of the murders, such as the insertion of bottles into vaginas, his interrogators suggested this reluctance might stem from his lack of understanding. "That's part of it," he agreed. "And because it's so unbelievable to me that it was really done by me. Why I done it I don't really understand, but I know at this moment that to do it—well, I wouldn't . . . I can remember doing those things. As for the reason why I did them, I at this time can give you no answer." Had he been thinking of anything when he killed? "No, I just did it." Still, he always knew what he had to do: at Jane Sullivan's, "as soon as I saw her, I had a quick look at the room. I knew what I was there for. Whatever it came to, that was it." Nor did he understand the symbolic content of his acts. "There was nothing about Anna Slesers to interest any man—why did I do it? She was getting ready for a bath. Why didn't I put her in a tub when I put Mrs. Sullivan in a tub? Just like why did I leave a broom and a bottle? I don't understand it."[25]

He seemed to regret especially the killings of the young women. About Sophie Clark, he said: "There was no need for it to happen." He denied suggestions he had killed her to possess her: "It wasn't the reason for having her. This is where the whole thing is messed up. There was no reason to be there, period. There was no reason for her to die. Nothing was taken away from her, no money, no nothing. How can I explain it to you? I'd sit there, looking to find something, looking through photographs like I was looking for someone." About Patricia Bissette, he said: "She talked to me like a man, she treated me like a man. I don't know why I did it. She did me no harm—and yet I did it. Do you follow me? Why did I do it to her? Why did I do it?" About

126

the Joann Graff murder, during the traumatic days of the Kennedy assassination, he said: "I cried . . . when people started talking about how the President was shot—then, that he was dead. I just stood there and cried. Could the President be killed that day and I went out and still did something? Could I have shot out that way toward Lawrence that day, that afternoon? I heard someone say later it wasn't bad enough the President died but someone had to strangle somebody. . . . That Graff thing—it was so senseless that it makes sense, you know? To me, it's so unrealistic as to why these things occur."[26]

Yet he fully knew that he was doing the killings. "I knew it was me. I didn't want to believe it. It's so difficult to explain to you. I knew it was me who did it, but why I did it and everything else—I don't know why. I was not excited, I didn't think about it; I sat down to dinner and didn't think about it at all." "It was all the same thing, always the same feeling. You was there, these things were going on and the feeling after I got out of that apartment was as if it never happened. I got out and ran downstairs, and you could of said you saw me upstairs and as far as I was concerned, it wasn't me. I can't explain it to you any other way. It's just so unreal . . . I was there, it was done, and yet if you talked to me an hour later, or half hour later, it didn't mean nothing, it just didn't mean nothing." "I'm realizing that these things are true and that these things that I did do, that I have read in books about, that other people do, that I didn't think or realize I would ever do those things." "It's true, God knows it's all true. I wish it wasn't. I don't want to be the person who did these things. There's no rhyme or reason to it. I'm not a man who can hurt anyone—I can't do it. I'm very emotional. I break up at the least thing. I can't hurt anyone and here I'm doing the things I did. . . . Thank God they had no loved ones, no children—all single women. I can be very thankful for that. . . . But, still and all, a life is a life." "It's not a dream anymore—it's true—and all these things happened . . . I have a daughter, and I have a son and a wife, but when my children grow older, I want them to get an understanding of me . . . I never really wanted to hurt anybody. Why didn't I do this before, and why didn't I do it after? What drove me to do these? There's got to be a reason. I don't think I was born like this. Why did I start? Why did I stop?"[27]

The Assignation of Blame

"I think there's a lot more involved in this than just being a rape artist."

ALBERT DESALVO[28]

He seemed genuinely to have been bewildered by the cause of his crimes. Yet as the interviews extended through the summer and autumn, he offered several explanations, even —quite untypically for multiple murderers—at one point blaming himself. The most vehemently expressed blame was directed toward his wife, Irmgard, as if her rejection justified the massacre of innocents. As he wrote to her from the mental institution, "You will admit that if you treated me different like you told me all those years we lost, the love I had been searching for, that we first had when we were married. Yes, Irm I stole them. *But why* What happened when Judy was born and we found out she may never walk. How you cried Al please no more babies. Irm from that day on you changed. All your love went to Judy. You were frigid and cold to me, and you can't denie [sic] this. That's why we were always fighting about sex, because you was afraid to have a baby. Because you thought it would be born abnormal. Irm I even asked doctors what was wrong with our sex life and they all said—until you have another baby, and it is born normal will you then be free to love again. . . . Irm I'm not saying this is all your fault. Because I am the one who did wrong. But I had reason I loved you. After I came out of jail—despite everything I tried to do—you denied me my rights as a husband you constantly told me I had to prove myself and in short you tried to make my life a hell whether you knew it or not." Later, when police asked if he had ever been afraid he would hurt his wife, he continued his theme: "In her own way she was hurting me more than anything. If she'd given me the proper sex I wanted, at least treated me like a person and not degraded me all these times, I wouldn't be going out to find out if I was a man or not. . . . 'I used my sex to hurt you,' she told me. I couldn't understand why she, who I loved, treated me like dirt. She'd say, 'Don't go out at night'—for two, three years, I didn't. I stopped bowling. She once said, 'Don't ever leave me— you're the only one I know in this country.' I did everything for her." "Why didn't I ask for help? I wanted to—and I talked it over with Irmgard, but, as I have said, she did not think it was 'nice' to have to admit things about yourself like that."[29]

To support this proposition that it was his rage against Irmgard that had driven him to kill, he claimed that the reason he had killed Beverly Samans with such savagery— repeatedly driving a knife into her—was because, when she had demanded that they not have intercourse, she had reminded him of his wife. "It was just like my . . . It was Irmgard. I grabbed her [Irmgard] right by the throat, she made me feel so low, as if I was asking for something I shouldn't have, that I wanted something dirty. I wanted to kill her that night! Asking her to make love was asking a dead log to move. It was always 'Do it quick, do it fast, get it over with'—she treated me lower than an animal . . . I loved her so much, yet I hated her. I was burning up. How many nights I would lie next to her, so hot, so wanting to be loved and to love her—and she would not—*She* [Samans] reminded me of her. 'Don't do it, don't do it!' "[30]

This explanation seemed plausible enough, but it contained significant contradictions. First, the two women whom he had released from his assaults were those who—in their ethnicity, their manner of speech, and their physical appearance—most closely resembled his wife. Why did he let them go? As well, if it seemed logical enough that he, both loving and hating his wife, must have displaced his rage upon another to save his frenzied love for his wife, it is also true that many people both love and hate their spouses without feeling driven to launch a sustained campaign of murder. Why then did he not merely find a new and loving wife? Thus we must conclude that DeSalvo's appalling relationship with his wife was neither necessary nor sufficient cause for murder. Few of our multiple murderers were so encumbered, and we must search for commonalities if we are to comprehend this social phenomenon.

A second, and equally plausible, explanation for the generation of DeSalvo's rage was his extraordinary childhood, which reads like some Dickensian nightmare. His memories of this period were independently confirmed by accounts from family friends and social workers. "My father would come home drunk a lot and bring these prostitutes with him right up into the house and strike my mother in front of them and make me ashamed to have him for a father who could do things like that to a good woman like my mother. One of my first memories is him beating my mother. I guess I was less than five years old but I remember it. He knocked her over the couch and they fought and he hurt her hand so bad that I can still hear her screaming with the pain and all us kids screamed with her and the old man went around like a crazy man hitting us until some cop or somebody came and put him in his place, the man who came wasn't big, but it was different with my father when he had to fight with a man, you understand me? We didn't have to do anything to get beaten, just be around when the old man was ready to hand out the beatings. I saw my father knock my mother's teeth out and then break every one of her fingers. I must have been seven. Ma was laid out under the sink—I watched it. He knocked all her teeth out. Pa was a plumber, he smashed me once across the back with a pipe. I just didn't move fast enough. He once sold me and my two sisters for nine dollars, sold us to some farmer in Maine. No one knew what happened to us.* For six months Ma hunted for us and couldn't find us."[31]

"But we would take off over to Eastie, Noddle Island, and hide out under the piers and he would be afraid to come looking for us there because the other kids living there would've helped us kill him just for the couple of bucks they might get off his body. The Eastie piers . . . was a kind of

---

* DeSalvo never elaborated on this period of his life, so we can only speculate on what he and his sisters endured during their captivity.

second home for me and my brothers. You know, that was a dangerous place. They was kids there with no home at all. That was where they lived—under the piers and in the old warehouses and wharves. They was wharf rats, that's what the people called them and they was just like rats—and they was a million real rats there, too, big ones that wasn't afraid of you—those kids, those wharf rats, I saw them roll a drunk one night, landing on him the way the real rats would land on one of their own kind who was sick or hurt all in a big dirty, wiggling pile, ripping and tearing until the thing they were on was dead and eaten to bones. Them kids was small, some of them wasn't more than ten, eleven, but they was a lot of them and they got that drunk down, just like the real rats, and they practically tore him to pieces then dumped his body into the water. Nothing happened to them, bodies was always being fished out of the harbor all beat up and fish-eaten. But I say this to tell you about the kind of vicious kids them wharf rats were and that is where I spent a lot of time when I was a kid—not that I was vicious. I was too shy and scared. I didn't like to fight and didn't think I could and was very much surprised to find out that I could fight pretty good when the time came. That was later."[32]

"Other things I remember about when I was a kid in Chelsea are always being too cold in the winter—the house was heated by a coal fire in the kitchen stove and we never had enough coal because of what we got came from the welfare and sometimes the old man would work out a deal for money with the coal man instead of coal. And I remember never having enough to eat, that is another thing I remember. It wasn't that we were hungry and starving, it was just that we didn't get enough, we could always have used more. Even now I can feel that uncomfortable feeling I used to get when I was a little kid, wanting more food so bad and not being able to get it. They was kids over there ate the plaster off the tenement walls and that is a fact. I think a kid growing up that way always has, down underneath, the need to go for all he can get, no matter how, because he is a person who never quite got enough of a full belly."[33]

"I can't remember a time when I wasn't learning something I'd of been better off not knowing. My father took me down to the five and ten cent stores in Boston, Chelsea, Eastie, and showed me how to cop stuff off the counters. I was five years old when he began teaching me this. . . . Now I look back on all that I could see it getting worse all the time. The stealing got worse. It went from shoplifting to purse snatching and then to B and E [break and enter] and then to robbery. And now, at this late date, I can see that it went from robbery to rape to murder." "All this was before I was twelve because by then I'd had two arrests—one for larceny from the person and the other my first B and E . . . and I was twelve when I was sent to Lyman School for delinquent boys. At Lyman School I really began to learn things." "Now Lyman School is supposed to be a place where bad boys are taught how to be good. That is a laugh, ain't it? That is not the case at Lyman School at all. You can learn just about every form of sexual perversion there. You can learn a lot about how to steal. They is nothing criminal that you can't learn there. . . . When you get out of Lyman School you know how a criminal thinks and you are a boy who knows a lot about sexual perversion."[34]

Paroled from Lyman School, he immediately began breaking and entering on a truly gargantuan scale, for he was an ambitious boy, anxious to better his lot. During this period, his family's lawyer Sheinfeld was his primary support, professionally and personally. "He was a very good man, Mr. Sheinfeld, to me. I do not blame him for anything, only blame myself, and what Mr. Sheinfeld said was true. I was taking awful risks and I was certain to bring disgrace on myself and more misery to my family. But I didn't know. I couldn't see it as clear as some people who have had a better life. Mr. Sheinfeld, although he was a very good man, was the same as the guys from the Probation and Parole Office," observed DeSalvo, displaying a remarkable class consciousness. "He was on the inside of something I'd been on the outside of all my life. Oh, I know that guys who have come from bad homes have made good, it's not that, it's just my own personal reaction to what my bad home was like—and it's this thing, this urge, that I had."[35]

This catalogue of horrors from DeSalvo's childhood—

this child slave sold to a farmer; this witness to fantastic assault upon drunks, and upon his mother; this boy with the frozen body in winter and the burning half-empty belly all through the year—was sufficiently provocative, it would seem, to have spawned a multiple murderer. Yet only the killers Lucas and Panzram shared such squalid childhoods; and one can speculate on many other criminal careers which might seem more appropriate for someone from such a stunted background (for example, a career in *professional* murder). Why then should this background have driven him to kill in such a bizarre fashion, without profit, and at a time in his life when he had finally escaped from his lumpen-proletarian background, when he had "made good" as a devoted husband and father, with a steady job and an admiring employer, a home and car of his own? In his own terms, he had moved inside of something he had been outside of all his life. What manner of revenge could he have been pursuing on his bloody trail?

Yet another element in DeSalvo's assignation of blame was his terrible sexual drive, which received a great deal of attention from his analysts. His remarkable sexual capacity was soon appreciated in his neighborhood, and it rewarded him with "a lot of sex on the side from the girls and queers around the neighborhood. Some of them was amazed at how I could come and then five minutes later come again. The queers loved that and they would pay for it, too, which was all right with me since I needed the dough and there was some relief from the urge that was pushing me to sex all the time, but it really was Woman that I wanted—not any special one, just Woman with what a woman has, not just to come, but to have the breasts and body to play with, to bite and kiss, then to go into . . . I didn't even care so much what She looked like, or how old She was . . . it was Woman and not a pretty woman, or any special woman, but Woman that I wanted, even then." Early on too, his mind began to associate sexuality with breaking and entering, a fact that Freudian psychologists made some use of. "I didn't like rolling drunks. I was a B and E man, mostly. There was something exciting, thrilling, about going into somebody's home . . . I think now, too, that it had something to do with going into bedrooms where women had been sleeping, or were sleeping and there was times when I would get a rail on just standing there outside the bedroom door listening to some woman breathe . . . so you see what urge was all part of this and it was only a matter of time before I would feel strong and tough enough to go into the bedroom when the woman was there and make her let me do what I wanted with her."[36]

In this light, was it possible for him to have forged a marriage more *unsuitable* than that which he forged with his beloved Irmgard? About Irmgard, the repressed and puritanical immigrant, who could not bring herself to relieve his demanding urges, he said: "She was very innocent and scared of sex. I think they taught her to be scared of sex, her family, and she never got over that . . . but, to be honest, I think, too, that she was a cold woman which is really bad for a guy like me who is so much in need of sex all the time, you understand me? I was in love with her . . . and I found myself wanting her after we was married, morning, noon and night I wanted her over and over . . . I would sit there looking at her and wanting her, or I would lie in bed and want her so badly and right after I would have her, I'd want her again . . . she didn't like it . . . I've told you that I need a lot of sex, five or six times a day don't mean much to me . . . I can come back minutes after intercourse . . . the terrible urge never leaves me . . . I used to say to myself: 'What's wrong with me?' "[37]

Even before he confessed to the murders, he had described much of his frenzied sexuality in a letter to his lawyer: "How could I tell my wife I am oversexed and have a drive and urge I cannot control," he wrote. "Even you Mr. Sheinfeld, when you had my case in 1961 in Cambridge involving all them women, you asked me if I got a thrill or feeling when I touched them, and I lyed [sic] to you and said no, because I was ashamed to admit it of my sex drive. But now its [sic] got out of hand . . . I was trying with all my heart to be good but my drive got so bad I found myself relieving myself at least four or five times a day. It was so bad. But when I went out and did what I did that I am in here for it was so strange because it was like I was burning up inside and the feelings I was getting put me like a daze it would be like a dream I would not no [sic] where I was going but I was thinking and seeing a woman in my vision in front of me wondering what kind of body she would have and so on. Sometime before I even got anywhere I found myself sitting in the car while driving, already releaved [sic]. But in five min it came back again. I was all ready again." Indeed, during his non-homicidal assaults, he often ejaculated before he touched his victims: "They even said some of the women that they felt when I got nexted [sic] to them, but they had a feeling that I had just releaved [sic] myself because after that I just tied them up and left without even doing anything to them. Its true I just put my hand on and I was finished. And then realized again what I had done. In almost all the cases the women said more than half I didn't even touched them but tie them up and run whitch [sic] took only 3-5 min—so you see I was so build up by the time I found a woman I just got near her and I was releaved [sic]."[38]

DeSalvo's sexual explanation is a compelling one. Yet he frequently failed to engage in anything resembling sex with his victims. More important, the purely sexual need had already been satisfactorily assuaged by the rapes (if it is possible to think of rape as a sexual act in any sense) and assaults that both preceded and followed the string of murders. There seemed in fact to be no explicitly *sexual* reasons as to why he was driven to kill: at no time did he admit to any particularly sexual response derived from the killing. For once in his life, during his confessions, he tried very hard to be scrupulously honest, and to transcend his lower-middle-class notions of what was "nice" to talk about and what was "shameful." Indeed, at times he was very astute, most especially when describing the murder of Patricia Bissette: "Now I say that I had intercourse with her while she was unconscious, but still alive . . . all the time when I was doing this, I was thinking about how nice she had been to me and it was making me feel bad. She had treated me right and here I was doing this thing to her which she didn't want me to do . . . I am sorry about that one, really sorry, but she shouldn't of asked me to stay and then they was the thing I felt. . . . What I mean by that is that a thing pushes a man . . . *I don't know if I done this for a sex act or for hatred or for what reason.* I think I did this not as a sex act but out of hate for her—not her in particular, but for a woman. I don't think that a sex act is anything to do. It is what everybody does, from the top to the bottom of the world, but that is not what I mean. It is one thing to do it when a woman wants you to do it and another when she don't, you understand me? If women do not want you to do what is right and natural then it is dirty if they don't. You are really an animal if you do it just the same, is what I mean, you see? But all I can say is that when I saw her body the sex act came in. I did not enjoy the sexual relations with this woman. I was thinking too much about that she would not have wanted me to do it. There was no thrill at all." Precisely. His sexuality was an obvious and explicit part of the assault, but it was more an afterthought than a motivating force. Even as afterthought, it frequently yielded little pleasure. Why then did he sustain such dangerous and unrewarding assaults? Why too would he claim to feel hatred for "women" in general when *the only loving people in his entire life had been his mother, his wife, and his beloved crippled daughter?*[39]

A fourth theme running through his lexicon of blame was the notion that he was from time to time overwhelmed by an almost "mental," certainly uncontrollable, compulsion to kill. He explicitly linked this to his behavior as a child when he had tortured cats. "I liked horses, but I didn't like cats. Or maybe it wasn't that I didn't like cats but just that I didn't think of them the way I did of horses. I used to shoot cats . . . with a bow and arrow, put it right through their bellies and sometimes they'd run away with the arrow right through them, yowling, and I don't recall being too upset by that even though I'm an emotional guy and can be upset easily . . . sometimes when I would see them, before the shot, I'd get such a feeling of anger that I think I could've torn those cats apart with my bare hands. I don't understand this, but just then I hated them and they hadn't done nothing to me . . . then sometimes when I see them with the arrow through them, dying, I get mad, too, and none of makes it any sense to me . . . especially since I don't usually hate cats or like them, either, for that matter, you understand me?"[40]

He thought of this compulsion as a kind of mental disorder that would periodically seize hold of him. "I was a very good provider and took very good care of my family. I would like to say that if it was not for my sickness, which had not been given the help it needed to make it better, I was making something out of my life . . . trying to bring out the best in me. . . . It is true that my sickness was always with me. It made me go out and do things I knew was wrong. But it was a very immediate thing and I had to do what I did." This "sickness" developed a kind of inflating pressure inside him screaming for release, he thought. When he was alone with a woman in her apartment, "I was all hot, just like you're going to blow your head off—like pressure right on you, right away—I—I—to explain it or to express it, as soon as I saw the back of her head, right?— everything built up inside of me. Before you know it I had put my arm around her and that was it." "By that time, it had gotten beyond my ability to control. There is nothing I can do about it by that time."[41]

Strangely, however, the "compulsion" to kill disappeared just as suddenly and completely as it had appeared. After the murder of Mary Sullivan—the tying of that most flamboyant bow and the writing of that insulting message HAPPY NEW YEAR—he returned to simple sexual assault. "Mary Sullivan was the last one. I never did it again. I never killed anyone after that. I only tied them up, I didn't hurt them. . . . Once in Cambridge I was in three places in a row after that and I started to cry and I said, 'I'm sorry, I don't know why I'm here,' and I took off." Moreover, he maintained a kind of consistency in his insistence upon a theory of compulsion. Unlike many multiple murderers, who resist the plea of insanity because it would annul their task, DeSalvo (who barely understood the nature of his mission) wanted to be found insane by the courts, for it would have relieved him of any responsibility for his crimes. Moreover, it would hold out to him the possibility that he might be "cured," and even eventually be released.[42]

However, the compulsion "explanation" is given the lie by the calm and pragmatic terms in which he explained the cessation of the homicidal assaults. "My wife was treating me better," he offered, explaining himself now in social and economic terms. "I was building up, you might say, my better self, the better side of me, I was very good at my job, they liked me, I got two raises." He understood the personal deprivations that had generated his hatred, but the inarticulate nature of his rebellion—half-conscious and but dimly perceived—could not justify his behavior to himself. He could only cope with what he had done by claiming that a form of insanity had provoked the works he had wrought.[43]

Our portrait of his confessed motivation remains quite incomplete, however, without an explication of his curious but sustained social critique—a kind of personal and primitive *class war,* to which he frequently alluded. Admitting that he was the infamous Measuring Man, who, on the pretext that he could offer modeling jobs, took women's measurements in their apartments while feeling their sexual parts (few complained until no modeling jobs were offered), he told police: "I want to tell you all about it. I been a poor boy all my life, I come from a bad home, you know all that, why should I kid you? Look, I don't know anything about modeling or cameras . . . I'm not educated and these girls was all college graduates, understand me? *I made fools of them* . . . I made them do what I wanted and accept me and listen to me. That was why I was around measuring them . . . I give it to you—I wanted to build myself up." "They were all college kids," he told the probation officers, "and I never had anything in my life and I outsmarted them. I felt they were better than me because they were college people."[44]

This fascination with the niceties of social class, of the nuances of power and domination, not pure chance, determined the neighborhoods he would select for his assaults and killings. "So I go and at first I'm kidding myself that I'm going to take a shot out toward Swampscott . . . now Swampscott . . . is a fancy place with big houses and lots of them smart and educated broads like I used to fool over around Harvard Square but they grew up and got married and now they got kids—girls—like they used to be and you wonder do these girls go to the bathroom and smell and do they play with themselves—excuse me for being vulgar, but I'm trying to tell you what I thought and what I even think now,* you know they is an expression around Boston: 'She thinks her shit don't stink.' And that means she thinks she's too good for what a woman is made to do—sleep with a man when he wants and needs her and to let him do what he wants with her even if she thinks it ain't nice . . . and anyway I don't go to Swampscott because I don't like the way they make me feel like an animal, those kinds of broads, and that is why I always put something over their faces and eyes so that they can't look at me."[45]

Incarcerated at Bridgewater, but before he had admitted to being the Strangler, he told a psychologist that the Strangler "should be studied, not buried." According to Frank, DeSalvo also insisted that it was only the poor who were punished, that "rich people could do all kinds of sex things and get away with it. They just bought their way out." "I want to say here, too," DeSalvo later said, "about the Measuring Man kick that it give me an idea about how you can talk women into things. When you hear about it, it don't sound like it would work with a kid—all it takes a few sharp questions and a little ordinary sense to see through it, but very few of them did. They was married women who should've known that they didn't have the shapes to be models. But they was flattered, it raised their egos, and they fell for it. Some of them that called the cops did so because they was disappointed that I didn't send anybody [to take photographs] . . . they wanted to know why I hadn't. Mostly, I got a big kick out of those girls around Harvard. I'm not good-looking, I'm not educated, but I was able to put something over on high-class people. I know that they look down on people who come from my background. They think they are better than me. They was all college kids and I never had anything in my life but I outsmarted them. I was supposed to feel that they was better than me because they was college people . . . when I told them they could be models that was like saying the same thing: you are better

---

* Significantly, this is one of the few prejudices he still clung to after his confessions. Undoubtedly it had special importance to him.

than me, you are better than anybody, you can be a model. . . . Anybody with any sense could've found out. They never asked me for proof."[46]

"They was times when I was doing that Measuring Man thing," he admitted in a most provocative fashion, "that *I hated them girls* for being so stupid and I wanted to do something to them . . . something that would make them think, even for a little while . . . that would let them know that I was as good as they was, maybe better and smarter too. Now they was a lot of them girls. I want to say that they was at least five hundred and some of them was so excited by what I was saying that they let me measure them without any clothes on at all. They was some of those girls just needed a little push to get into bed with. All this time, I was still afraid to try to force any of these women. If they said the least thing, I would get out as fast as I could. It wasn't until later that I come to the point of being able to force them. I think I am right in saying that at the time I was the Measuring Man it all could've been stopped. After I got out of the Middlesex County House of Correction [for the Measuring Man offenses] there was no stopping it. That is the way it seems to me."[47]

In a similar vein, DeSalvo remarked to an interrogating attorney, "You are a man, you know what I mean, sure you have been to them high-class colleges and you got all them big excuses, but you have had that thing in your pants too—I think this is one of the troubles, sir, that guys like you, who have played with yourselves, who have looked with real lust on women, some of them far too young, away out of your range of possibility with a great deal of lust are afraid to admit it because somehow it takes you down from the goddamn pedestal on which society places you—but you are only a man." Taking umbrage at the expression on the face of this interrogator, he commented: "Let me say this, sir, to you who sits across the table from me with such a shocked face, just let me say this . . . I ain't got nothing to lose no more, you know, and I couldn't give less of a goddamn for your world which is a nice society for you as long as you have money . . . have you ever thought of what it would be like for your ass if you didn't have dough? . . . I bet you ain't."[48]

His wife's behavior toward him exacerbated his sense of social humiliation, he thought, although it is clear that he provoked this behavior. "If she at least treated me like a person and not degraded me at all these times. . . . My own mother said that I was too good to my wife, doing housework for her, cleaning the floors, that I treat her so good that she don't have no respect for a man who does all those things for her." Nowhere was his social awareness better encapsulated than in his snobbish disappointment when he saw Joann Graff's apartment: "It was a very cheap apartment with really cheap furniture—even the Salvation Army wouldn't take it." What sensibility was being violated here? Why should it matter to him that the homes of his victims be unambiguously middle class in style and furnishings? Earlier, he had told his probation officer, "Boy, it makes me feel powerful when I can make those girls do what I want—make them submit to me. I'm nothing in this life. . . . But I want to be something." When his probation officer had asked him if he wished to be caught, he had replied, "Yeah, I'd be somebody then. I'd get publicity in the papers." And when he ultimately made his full confession, he did so in the defiant rhetoric of a rebel: "If you're going to die for telling the truth, to hell with it. You only live once. What good am I alive? If the rich people live and the poor people die, then I die. There'll be other people coming along." To do what?[49]

Finally, as I have mentioned previously, DeSalvo also blamed himself, although it is by no means clear whether he took this unusual step as a means of castigating himself, or as a way of subtly justifying and glorifying his own role. "For a long time, I've known that I needed help. I done nothing about it. I should have, but I didn't. They was no one to push me to do it. Later, when it was real bad and I was married to Irmgard, it wasn't her fault that she didn't understand that it was help and not hell that I needed. Now I am not blaming Lyman School for the way I am. I'm not blaming anybody but myself. Them psychiatrists say I can blame other things . . . yes, to some extent as you have just said, society . . . but I am not doing that. A man does what he does and he has to take the blame himself. That is how I feel about it . . . I often think about who is to blame and I find that it is myself because I could've done other things. I could've tried to get help. Even when I was older and working and supporting myself and my family I could've done something, but I didn't."[50]

ENCOUNTER WITH PSYCHIATRY

"I went to one (a psychiatrist) in 1961. It was the hardest thing to go look for help. I told him about the drive I had and he told me it's up to me."

ALBERT DESALVO[51]

DeSalvo was exposed to a number of psychiatrists during his life, but he was not able to convince them that his problems were severe until he confessed to the sexual assaults. He was first examined when, at the age of thirteen, he was in the "reform" school. The psychiatrist found that he had an IQ of ninety-three, and wrote: "This boy needs adequate social supervision and redirection of his interests into supervised groups such as the Boy Scouts and the YMCA." He received no further attention until sixteen years later, when he was arrested for his first run of sexual assaults. "That was the first time as an adult I talked with a psychiatrist," DeSalvo remembered. "I come very close to getting some help there, but Bridgewater is not the place to get much help, I can tell you. . . . This psychiatrist said that I needed help, he said that I had a long time disturbance and that he recommended a psychological study . . . he said I had psychopathic tendencies—I know what that means—that I should not just be put in jail. But they didn't help me . . . they sent me to jail. I came out in April, 1962 . . . by then it was too late to save any of those women." DeSalvo had warmed to his Bridgewater psychiatrist: "He was a very understanding man and I think he was right in what he said about me about the psychopathic tendencies—and he agreed with me that I needed help." In fact, the psychiatrist had written with insight about DeSalvo: "The picture is that of a long-disturbed personality with polymorphous perverse inclinations involving fantasies of grandeur and omnipotence," and he had recommended detailed examination to determine "the directions of the psychopathic tendencies." His recommendations were ignored, and DeSalvo served a conventional prison sentence.[52]

After DeSalvo was released from prison, and the "Strangler" was at large, police turned to psychiatry in their search for a profile of the killer. No intellectual tool is as cruel and unfair as hindsight, but one cannot help commenting that the profiles were not always accurate. One psychiatrist suggested that the killer was a "psychotic sex pervert suffering from the most malignant form of schizophrenia" and living in a fantasy world. Another wondered if the Strangler's victims were unconsciously signaling to the killer, through some subtle process of nonverbal communication, a sexual personality that the Strangler was seeking. This psychiatrist went on to speculate that in ransacking the victims' apartments, the killer was searching for a phallic symbol. A third psychiatrist suggested that the Strangler was a man searching for his own sexual potency, and was killing his own mother again and again in an effort to find this potency. As the hunt intensified and the public clamor increased, other and more mystical forms of intellectual enquiry were embraced: a Dutch "psychic detective" was interviewed at length for his perceptions, and an advertising copywriter, who claimed he had extrasensory perception, spoke to the police at length, in a trance.[53]

Prominent Boston psychiatrists formed a committee to examine the killings. They concluded that the murders were probably the work of two men, one of whom killed the older women; and they speculated that the killer(s) of the young women were "unstable members of the homosexual community," while the killer of the older women was a passive heterosexual who had been dominated by his mother, "a sweet, orderly, neat, compulsive, seductive, punitive, overwhelming woman [who] might go about half-exposed in their apartment, but punish him severely for any sexual curiosity." Consequently, they argued, "the boy grew up to feel that women were a fearful mystery. He was inhibited heterosexually but the overwhelming respectability of his background probably kept him from much overt homosexuality." They might have fared better had they concentrated on the social, instead of the sexual, characteristics of the victims, and the killer. Still, at least one of their number was more insightful when called upon to explain why the Strangler had not killed since the murder of Mary Sullivan. On hearing the details of her death, psychiatrist James Brussel commented that "I would not be a bit surprised if you did not hear from this man again. I think he has had it." Brussel had deduced that if the killings were the Strangler's search for potency, he had ended his search and been "cured," judging from the spectacular signs of potency on the body of Mary Sullivan.[54]

When DeSalvo was arrested for sexual assault, the police wondered if he was the Strangler, but rejected the idea because he did not fit the psychiatric profile. As Frank put it, nothing fit: "no consuming rage toward his mother, no Oedipus complex, surely no problems of potency—rather, fear and contempt for his father, and shame for the way his father had treated his mother." In Bridgewater, the psychiatric staff examined DeSalvo and concluded that he suffered from "a sociopathic personality disorder, marked by sexual deviation, with prominent schizoid features and depressive trends," which is to say a "diagnosis" entirely in keeping with their knowledge that he was a rapist and molester. They thought he was a borderline psychotic, but competent to stand trial. When the court ordered DeSalvo returned to Bridgewater for a second evaluation, he began to babble incoherently in his cell: this time, the staff found him psychotic, "potentially suicidal and quite clearly overtly schizophrenic." It would be months before anyone believed his persistent claims that he was the Strangler.[55]

Further disagreement between the psychiatrists was provoked at hearings which were held to determine DeSalvo's competence to stand trial for the sexual assaults. Dr. Robert Mezer testified that DeSalvo suffered from "chronic undifferentiated schizophrenia" which "would make it difficult for him to accept the world of reality as most people know it." Dr. Samuel Tartakoff essentially agreed, but characterized DeSalvo as a "sociopath with dangerous tendencies," "an individual who from early life has shown deviations from what are usually considered normal patterns of behavior, thinking, and emotional reactions." Dr. Ames Robey argued quite differently. He thought DeSalvo was a victim of "schizophrenic reaction, chronic undifferentiated type," and concluded that "My opinion is that I cannot—repeat—cannot consider him competent to stand trial." He had watched DeSalvo in hospital, vacillating "back and forth, sometimes appearing strictly sociopathic; at other times almost like an acute anxiety hysteric; at other times appearing much more obsessive and compulsive; again appearing very close to wild overt psychosis." At times, he thought, "he appeared to be almost very much what we refer to as in a homosexual panic, or sexual panic of some sort." Robey felt that DeSalvo "has a real need, because of his underlying illness, to prove to himself and to others his own importance," although he did not speculate on why DeSalvo should have such an intense need.[56]

AN INTERPRETATION

> "Many people have died for a good cause. I think these people may not have died in vain."
>
> ALBERT DESALVO[57]

What are we to make of this supposed "mother-hater" who loved his mother most tenderly and protectively and was her favorite child; this "raging animal" who killed only women, but worshipped his wife and was devoted to his crippled daughter; this man "in search of his potency" who could leave his semen on bodies and clothes a half dozen times a day and still feel unsatisfied; this "psychotic" who spoke freely and openly to us in a language we could all understand, but who thought that his victims "died for a good cause"? We are tempted, as were Peter and Favret when writing of a nineteenth-century killer, to close such an ugly dossier and remain silent—but if we did so, we would have failed to "discharge our debt to these corpses."[58]

One might have little difficulty in understanding why someone condemned to a life of vile and empty suffering could explode in some fantastical homicidal adventure, marking in a lurid pen his otherwise anonymous passage through time. But DeSalvo, like so many of our multiple murderers, had *escaped* his ugly proletarian origins; he had been freed from "enduring the unlivable, day in and day out." It is true that his childhood was enough to break a lesser man—enduring endless beatings from his father; watching his father break his mother's fingers and dragging prostitutes into the house for his public enjoyment; staring at the abandoned urchins on the docks as they killed a drunk for his wallet; feeling the caresses of pedophilic homosexuals in return for a paltry fee; and, with his sister, being sold into slavery. Yet these assaults upon his body and his spirit did not destroy him.[59]

Even before he had left the world of tenement and school, a fiercely ambitious core within him initiated what must have been for him a dizzying and precipitous rise in the social order. If he hated reform school, his behavior was exemplary in public school: there, he capitalized on what qualities he had, especially his humility. "I never got good marks, but the teachers liked me—I was a kind of teacher's pet, running errands, buying sandwiches for them—so I got by." He would use these same qualities during his years in the army, where he prospered as a spit-and-polish soldier, attentive to rank and rule: "always the sharpest uniform, best-dressed, shoes polished, best-kept vehicles . . . I made Colonel's Orderly twenty-seven times." As a child in a violent world he had lacked the confidence to fight, but in the army he discovered he had special gifts, and for two years he held the title of the U.S. Army's European Middleweight boxing champion.[60]

His marriage to the intensely petite bourgeoise Irmgard both reflected and enhanced his social rise: he worshiped her; and why should he not, for she came from stock of such refinement that "no one in her family ever even saw the inside of a jail." In forging such a cross-class marriage, he had repeated the pattern of his detestable father—a lumpen proletarian of the most violent sort, with convictions for larceny, non-support, assault and battery, breaking and entering, common brawling, wife beating, and assault with a deadly weapon—who had married the homely daughter of a respectable family (whose father was an officer in Boston's Fire Department). Indeed, when DeSalvo's case came to light, it was examined by a Court Justice who remembered her: "I liked his mother," he recalled. "Came from a fine Yankee family." Thus a curious social fact emerges: that DeSalvo was forged in a crucible whose primary activity appeared to be a kind of class war, in which the proletarian husband assaulted the bourgeois wife with unspeakable brutality. DeSalvo was determined not to duplicate this calamity, and while he married "up" to improve his position, he treated his wife with the utmost respect, nay servility. She would insult him in front of his friends, "make me feel like nothing . . . she gave me an inferiority complex," he complained, and she wounded him most deeply when she insulted his family. To make matters impossible, the sexual drives of these partners could rarely have been so mismatched. Soon he would be seducing and assaulting women all over Germany (where he was stationed), although he was never charged with these activities. When he returned to America and left the army, he resumed his pattern of sexual molestation, and eventually was arrested as the Measuring Man in 1961, and was committed to a state hospital for one year.[61]

In the hospital, full of enthusiastic love, and excited to be reunited with his wife, he told the psychiatrist of his slavish relationship: "I can hardly wait to get out so I can be with her and treat her the way a wife should be treated, even if it means washing her feet." But when he was released, her natural caution with a convicted molester seemed to him to be inexplicable and utter rejection, and his world spun, for he concluded that his exclusion from the class he coveted was for all time. "I come out of jail after one year, all alone for one year in one room, and Irmgard tells me, 'I wasted a year of my life.' She puts me on probation. I must learn to control my sex wants, she told me. . . . She would say I was dirty and sickening and called me an animal. I felt less than a man in bed with her." Shortly after his release, he put what he had read in prison ("Detective books—I read a lot of sexy stuff") to the test, and his career in multiple murder was launched. But what had happened to him? Why was it now, in his words, "too late to save any of those women"? His molesting and rape during his years as the Measuring Man might have been enough to relieve his sexual drive and release his still-smoldering anger; but such activities were insufficient to protest his total exclusion from the social niche he desired so slavishly. Many of the women he molested seemed to him to like it—one gave him a hundred dollars and begged him to return, he boasted. Certainly he "realized" that many saw his molestation as admiration, not insult. But now he required an unambiguous method of convincing them and society of his avenging and insulting intent: he would kill, mutilate their bodies, and leave humiliating messages (dumping them in bathtubs, leaving them in obscene positions, scrawling offensive notes, or mocking his victims' middle-class gentility by dressing them in frilly bows). Thus was born his task: as half-conscious and unarticulated as it was, it would serve his need to protest his exclusion, reverse his degradation, and reinstate him as a man.[62]

After he began to kill, the psychiatrists who monitored the case made many false assumptions, based upon their dogma that the unconscious expression of sexuality is the prime force in human behavior. But dogma makes its practitioners contemptuous of facts; and so they did not examine the killings, or ascertain the distinct elements, replete with social symbolism, that were repeated in each murder. The first, the significance of which was ignored by all the commentators, was the striking *social homogeneity* of the lace-curtain neighborhoods he assaulted. DeSalvo would not, the reader will recall, hunt in upper-class Swampscott because its confident and sneering women intimidated him—which is to say they emphasized too much the status barriers he had been unable to climb. Neither did he prey upon the teeming tenements, whose denizens interested him not at all (how could it be otherwise, for they were not the class who excluded him). Rather, his killings were all in bourgeois areas—once fashionable, but often now in genteel decline—which provided him with lower-middle-class targets. They were middle class enough to provoke his retribution, yet not so elevated from him as to render him tongue-tied and incapable of action, disarmed by status anxiety. As with all our multiple murderers, he attacked a very specific social category, a narrow band in a stratified society—the segment that represented all those who oppressed, excluded, and annulled him. Small wonder then that he was outraged and disdainful of Graff's "cheap" apartment, for it threatened to violate his purpose.

A second element in our comprehension of his acts was the means by which he *gained entry* to the apartments of his victims. The method he chose for both the earlier molestations and the later killings was the ruse. At times, it might have been easier (and certainly less risky, for the method he chose courted discovery) for him to have forced his way into the apartments (perhaps slipping a lock?). Yet to do so would have negated the meaning of his assaults, which was to put "something over on high-class people." The ruse, then, was essential to his purpose, which was both to outwit and then humiliate his betters, thus proclaiming his superiority. The public and the professionals paid a great deal of attention to this matter, but only to guess how he was able to gain entrance so easily to these apartments: they did not wonder why, in a world of easily jimmied doors and windows, he did not use force.

A third component to his enterprise was the *sex*, but this has been much misinterpreted. The psychiatrists noted the alteration in his sexual behavior as he progressed through the series of killings. At first, they found no signs at all of semen, only seed spilled upon the floor. Evidence of actual intercourse did not appear until the later murders of young and attractive women. They deduced from this that he had "decided" to stop preying impotently on elderly women because his potency had now grown to the point where he could rape nubile younger ones. But we know that in fact the women were picked entirely at random by the simple expedient of whoever answered a buzzer and opened a door. He raped them if he found them attractive: otherwise, the sheer intoxicating excitement of the violence drove him to ejaculate in his clothing or to masturbate in front of the corpse. It was small wonder that he could do either since his sexual drive was so strong: he sometimes ejaculated involuntarily while performing tasks as mundane as driving to work. What was important about the sex was that he was attacking (like Kemper, Bundy and Berkowitz) an idealized Woman—but not the fresh middle-class university students of these other killers, not women of a certain appearance, but women of a certain class—the solid lower-middle class. The sexual release, when it was there at all, was not a prime motive: rather, it was an extra benefit to his task.

Finally, having selected a lower-middle-class victim, having duped her through a ruse, having killed her and violated the corpse with obscene decoration or arrangement, he turned to the last unvarying element, the *ransacking* of the apartment, searching for he knew not what: "I never took anything. I never wanted anything." At first, the police assumed he hunted for valuables, until they realized he left them all behind. The psychiatrists assumed he searched for some Freudian instrument. What is the reality? "I'm angry and I don't know why and I don't really know what I'm looking for," he had said. He rifled purses, went through bureau and desk drawers, thumbed through magazine and record collections, all in a kind of daze, and angry because he did not know what he was looking for, angry because he had not found it. Pouring through photographic albums and record collections, hunting through accounts in bankbooks, achieving a kind of union with the middle classes by fondling their physical possessions as he had similarly maltreated their bodies, he looked for some key to what he was doing and who he was. He found it, finally, in the apartment of his last victim, and that is why he did not need to kill any more. What he searched for materialized as the Happy New Year card, which enabled him to hurl at society the ultimate insult: thus his task was the insult, his enraged answer to his exclusion, and the insult, expressed in the violation of enforced intimacy and brutal murder, was epitomized in the card. When he placed it upon her foot, he came consciously to know why he had killed, and was thus released from his task—for he had fulfilled its objectives.[63]

His task was now discharged. He had put things over on high-class people, outwitting them and stealing their most precious possessions, their lives, and in the process had gained additional relief for his sexual drive. He had claimed his manhood, and as if in recognition of this, Irmgard now warmed to him once more, and gave him "so much loving." Perhaps too he allowed himself the luxury of half-believing he might fall heir to the life of which he dreamed. But he was soon arrested for the earlier rapes. Moreover, the need to confess was growing, for no one seemed to know what he had done or why. It was necessary for him to let the world know that his victims had died not in vain, but for a good cause. Besides, he had come to believe that Irmgard's love was false: "Our last two months together you made me feel for the first time like a man," he told her. "You gave me love I never dreamed you had to give. But why—only because you had just about everything you dreamed of . . . everything you wanted, house fixed up, all the money coming in." In his utter self-absorption, in his limitless capacity for self-justification, he now felt betrayed: he would repay this "treason" in his volunteered confession to the authorities.[64]

An Adieu

Having fulfilled his need to explain and tell, having come to understand at least a measure of what he had done, he begged for absolution by being declared insane. He was deeply depressed when the courts refused this forgiveness, for he was only a sometime rebel, too timid to take the responsibility for what he had wrought. Like so many rebels before him, the cause had lost all its luster. He tried to make a kind of recompense by reverting to his proletarian self, abasing himself by playing body-servant to the elderly prisoners: "Right now I shave all the old men, I wash them up—I could help these people, give them a better life. Even if I may never be released, I'll be doing something for them . . . I think I have a fairly decent attitude towards this whole thing. I still think I can make a contribution. Many people have died for a good cause. I think these people may not have died in vain." Like many of our multiple murderers, this conservative functionary felt ill at ease in understanding that the good cause on whose behalf he had killed so wantonly had been a form of class war. He may well have been relieved when, less than a decade after his conviction, he was stabbed to death in a prison brawl.[65]

5.
THE DEMONS WERE TURNING ME INTO A SOLDIER

David Richard Berkowitz*

"You are hereby ordered to unleash
your terror upon the people.
'Destroy all good and ruin
people's lives.'"

DAVID BERKOWITZ[1]

This illegitimate, adopted son called himself the Son of Sam
in his many and various taunting *communiqués* to the police
and to his public. His clever manipulation of the press made
him a great celebrity long before he was captured. He is
significant to us not only as an additional illustration of our
theme, but also as one of the few to offer detailed evidence
that he might actually be deranged. In claiming to have been
tormented by howling demons of the night, he appeared to
be "insane," and this gave his public much comfort. Unfor-

---

* Berkowitz's confessions, letters, and prison diary are available in a variety of
published sources. His early pieces tend toward hysteria and fabrication, although
they contain much of interest; but his later confessions have the ring of literal truth
to them. The most scholarly and thoughtful studies of the man are Lawrence
Klausner's *Son of Sam* and David Abrahamsen's "Confessions of Son of Sam." In
addition, I found George Carpozi Jr.'s *Son of Sam* and Charles Willeford's *Off the
Wall* to be of some use.

tunately, there is abundant evidence that his thoughts and behavior were not in any sense directed by demon forces—as he originally claimed—or even uncontrolled; and a close examination of his person forces us to revoke his proffered madman credentials. Because he is both a creature of his time and a special test of the utility of the notion of mental illness, at least in a forensic context, his case demands close scrutiny. What we know is that his sense of social identity was dizzyingly kaleidoscopic—this Jewish convert to evangelical Christianity; this sometime auxiliary police officer with a succession of dead-end jobs; this gun worshipper who refused to carry a gun while serving with the U.S. Army in Korea; this illegitimate child who did not kill until he discovered that his social father was one man, his natural father a second man, and his step-father a third. He could not launch his career as an international celebrity, nor construct a tolerable social identity, until he became the avenging Son of Sam.

THE KILLING TIME

> "I am the demon from the bottomless pit here on earth to create havoc and terror. I am War, I am death. I am destruction!"
>
> DAVID BERKOWITZ[2]

According to his prison diary, the demon he claimed he was and the demons who were to direct him first took shape early in his childhood. "There is no doubt in my mind," he wrote, "that a demon has been living in me since birth. All my life I've been wild, violent, temporal, mean, cruel, sadistic, acting with irrational anger and destructive. When I was a child I often had very real and quite severe nightmares . . . I saw monsters often and I heard them, which often caused me to go screaming hysterically into my parents' room. . . . Now I know that they were real—just like now. I've been tormented all my life by them—never having peace or quite [sic]." During his childhood and adolescence, this demonic behavior took the form of setting fires in empty lots. When he was twenty-one, he began recording the location of his fires: between September of 1974 and December of 1975, he recorded 1488 fires and fire alarms, a handful of which led to serious damage. As his anger built toward its culmination, he shot several neighborhood dogs, and began to send threatening letters to neighbors.[3]

During November of 1975, when he was twenty-two, he made serious preparations for his vendetta. He took a month off from his work as a security guard and locked himself in his small apartment in working-class Yonkers. He nailed blankets over the windows to keep out the daylight, slept on a bare mattress, and left the apartment only to buy the cheap food which, along with masturbation, was his only pleasure. He began to write messages on the living-room walls: "In this hole lives the Wicked King." "Kill for my Master." "I turn children into Killers."[4]

His first attempt to kill ended in failure. On Christmas Eve, 1975, armed with a hunting knife and a feeling that the time had come to act, he left his apartment and drove toward Co-op City, the middle-income high-rise community in which he had lived with his father. Parking his car, he spotted his first victim, and walked toward her with the demon voices, he later claimed, murmuring in his ear. "She has to be sacrificed," they said, as they wished to "drink her blood." He was conscious of his mission's importance: "I had a job to do, and I was doing it." Yet after his hunting knife arched into her back, the results disappointed, even terrified him. "I stabbed her, and she didn't do anything. She just turned and looked at me. It was terrible. She was screaming pitifully and I didn't know what the hell to do. It wasn't like the movies. In the movies you sneak up on someone and they fall down quietly. Dead. It wasn't like that. She was staring at my knife and screaming. She wasn't dying." Panicked by the screams, he broke off the assault and fled. Later, he told a psychiatrist that he had been mystified by the woman's fear: "I wasn't going to rob her, or touch her, or rape her. I just wanted to kill her." The identity of this woman was never discovered: presumably her heavy winter coat absorbed the knife blows.[5]

As he ran past the apartment block in which he had lived with his father, he saw fifteen-year-old Michelle Forman approaching. "I didn't know how to kill," he later told his psychiatrist David Abrahamsen. "I stabbed her; she looked at me. I stabbed her again. It was terrible." His biographer, Lawrence Klausner, recorded that Forman was struck three times in the upper body, then twice in her face, before she fell screaming, blood spurting from her. "I never heard anyone scream like that," Berkowitz remembered. "The way she screamed constantly, I kept stabbing and nothing would happen. She kept fighting harder and screaming more. I didn't know . . . I just ran off." She was taken to the hospital suffering from six stab wounds to the head and body, and a collapsed lung, but she survived the assault. Berkowitz celebrated his first "victory" at a cheap restaurant.[6]

It was six months before the voices urged him to act again, he said. On the evening of July 6, 1976, he put his Charter Arms .44 Special Bulldog pistol in a paper bag and began cruising the streets, waiting for "some kind of signal to use the gun." When he saw a car stopped at an intersection with two girls in the front seat, the voices called to him to "get them!" He followed their car as they pulled into a driveway, but by the time he had parked his own car and moved toward them in the dark, they had disappeared.

Soon after, he quit his job. He spent his days searching for work and his evenings cruising, "looking for a victim, waiting for a signal." He found a position installing air-conditioning in new buildings. Soon his hunt would meet with success.[7]

On the night of July 28, 1976, carrying his pistol once more in a paper bag, with the voices shrieking at him for "blood," he set out to hunt, looking for women to slake the demons' thirst. In the Bronx, he passed a parked Oldsmobile with two young women chatting to each other in the front seat: Donna Lauria was an eighteen-year-old medical technician, and her nineteen-year-old friend Jody Valenti was a student nurse. "I knew I had to get them,"

Berkowitz remembered. "Those were my orders. I never saw them until moments before the shooting." He parked his car around the corner and strode confidently toward the Oldsmobile, determined to make the kill "as a kind of joke." As he reached the car window, he opened fire, emptying five cartridges into the women in the car. The first bullet burst the window and struck Lauria in the neck, while the second bullet hit Valenti in the thigh. Writhing in pain, Valenti fell forward, sounding the horn. "I just started to shoot at the window," Berkowitz recalled. "And I just saw the glass come in. My eyes were transfixed to the glass. Thousands of little pieces—you could see them . . . I emptied the gun and I was still pulling the trigger and it was clicking, but I didn't know it . . . I went straight home and went to bed."[8]

At home, he sank into a deep and untroubled sleep. He awoke with a sense of fulfillment, to discover in the newspaper that he had killed Lauria: "I never thought I killed her; I couldn't believe it. I just fired the gun, you know, at the car, at the windshield. I never knew she was shot." He was, he said, "elated" when he went to work at the taxi company: "I was at work promptly at 6:45 a.m. That day I made out better than usual in both tips and fares." As the killer Edmund Kemper had done with his first victim, Berkowitz imagined himself to be in love with Lauria: at one point, he even claimed that the demons had arranged a form of marriage between him and her spirit.[9]

A few weeks of contentment passed, but by mid-September, the demons were tormenting him again and he began to cruise the streets, hunting. The howling of the demons disturbed his rest on the night of October 23, 1976, and at 1:45 a.m., he stuffed his pistol in his belt and drove into Queens. He pulled up behind a parked Volkswagen owned by Rosemary Keenan, the eighteen-year-old daughter of a city police detective.* Twenty-year-old Carl Denaro, whose shoulder-length hair made it impossible for Berkowitz to tell if he was male or female, was in the

---

* This is another of the peculiar coincidences that litter these cases. Just as Seattle police Swindler's daughter had been a friend of Bundy, so Keenan's father would soon be working on the Berkowitz case.

passenger seat. Berkowitz emptied his .44 into the car. "I was more frightened than they were," said Berkowitz. "Only one bullet struck the young man, and he really wasn't the intended target. I had fired with one hand, and wildly. Boy, did I mess up. But really, I was very nervous." "I stayed a couple of minutes watching," then "I ran to my car and drove off quickly to a White Castle [restaurant]." Denaro had been shot in the back of the head, but he recovered after two months of treatment during which a metal plate was placed in his skull. Keenan was unhurt. Berkowitz studied the tabloids the following day to confirm that he had indeed shot a man.[10]

The evening of November 26, 1976, found him cruising again. He drove aimlessly through the killing ground until just before midnight when he saw Donna DeMasi, sixteen, and Joanne Lomino, eighteen, returning to their homes after an evening at the movies. Donna noticed a figure standing behind a lamp post and said, "Joanne, there's a guy watching us over there. He's kind of scary. Let's walk faster." As they did so, he followed them. Berkowitz recalled: "By the time I was able to get back and hide behind the lamp post, they started to walk. I followed. They saw me and walked faster. By the time I'd crossed the street and got to them, they'd gotten to one of the girl's houses. They knew I was behind them and they tried to get in the door." As the girl fumbled nervously for her house key, "I started across the grass to them. Everything was going right. They were right in front of me. I didn't want to get them frightened, so I began to ask them for directions. All the while I was getting closer. They turned back to the door for an instant, but it stayed locked. Then they turned their heads to me. I had the gun out and pointed it in their direction. Then I shot twice. They both were hit and they fell on either side of the stoop. It was just like it should be. You shot them, and they fell. It was as simple as that." In a state of exultation, he emptied his .44, firing two shots through the front window of the Lomino home and one into the sky. DeMasi had been shot in the neck: the bullet had shattered her collarbone, but she would recover. The bullet which struck Lomino had crushed her spine: she would be a paraplegic.[11]

Berkowitz had now served his apprenticeship in serial murder. He had lacked confidence during the first three shootings: "I realized I was doing something that was not only illegal but also dangerous," he later told Abrahamsen. "I, too, could have been killed or wounded. Perhaps the man in the car would pull out a gun and chase me. I didn't know what would happen. The possibility of an off-duty police officer or a patrol car passing through the vicinity when the shots were fired was also taken into consideration by me. So I guess I had a lot to fear." Now he would comport himself as a professional: calm and entirely controlled, without fear.[12]

Five weeks after the maiming of Lomino and DeMasi, on the night of January 29, 1977, he found once more that he could not sleep. He tucked his .44 in his waistband and began hunting through Queens, his killing ground. Something made him park his car and begin to walk. Just past midnight, he noticed a couple walking toward him. "We just passed each other. We almost touched shoulders," but the voices commanded him, he said, to "get her, get her and kill her." Christine Freund, twenty-six, entered the car of her lover, John Diel, thirty, and they embraced. Berkowitz watched them, and wanted "just to kill her. I wasn't told to kill him. I aimed for her head, you know, quick and efficient. I guess practice makes perfect. I was able to control the gun, physically. After walking up, I stood in front of the window, crouched slightly. I brought the gun up with two hands. I opened fire. Three shots were all I had to use. The glass flew into the car and I hit her. I just wanted to kill her, nothing more. I only used three of the five shells in the gun. There really wasn't any reason to use them all. I knew I had hit her. I had to save my ammunition. After I shot her I began to run. I ran to my car . . . I think I heard the car's horn blowing, and I think I heard the man get out. He began to scream. But by that time I was far away." Diel remembered kissing Freund as the window exploded; and he heard her scream as two bullets struck her right temple and neck. The third bored into the dashboard. He stumbled from the car and tried to flag down passing cars, but none would stop. Someone called the police, and an ambulance took Freund to the hospital, where she died at 4 a.m. Berkowitz said that he had known right away that he had killed Freund because "the voices stopped. I satisfied the demons' lust."[13]

While no evidence yet conclusively linked the different shootings to one another, intuitive police officers were beginning to sense that a single killer was hunting in Queens—in what only seemed to be unrelated incidents. In the meantime, Berkowitz, who had grown bored with construction and security work as well as taxi-driving, scored well on a civil-service examination: in March of 1976, he began work with the post office as a letter sorter at the highest salary he would ever earn, $13,000 per annum.[14]

On March 8, 1977, his day off, he was hunting in Queens once again, walking through the middle-class area of Forest Hills. Virginia Voskerichian, twenty-one, a Russian language major at Barnard College, was walking home from school, carrying her textbooks. When they were barely a step apart, he pulled the pistol from his pocket. "She was pretty, slender, and dressed nicely. Without really looking about, because my eyes were focused directly on her only, I just pulled out my revolver from a plastic bag and I shot her once in the face. I don't know why I chose her. I could hardly make out her facial features in the darkness." Voskerichian tumbled into the bushes that bordered the sidewalk and died instantly. As Berkowitz ran back to his car, he passed the first witness to see him leaving the scene of a murder: "Hi, mister," Berkowitz said to him. Walking toward his car, police in a passing patrol car thought he looked suspicious and pulled over to question him; but as they were about to do so, a call came over their radio reporting that a woman had been shot, and they left the scene. Berkowitz returned to his apartment. The single bullet he had fired had cut through the textbooks Voskerichian had raised in front of her face to protect herself, passed through her upper lip, shattering several of her teeth before crashing through her head and lodging in the skull near the spinal cord. However, police were now able to compare ballistic information on the spent bullets: on March 10, they were able to announce that at least three of the Queens attacks had been by the same man firing the same gun. A warrant was issued, using a vague description from witnesses and survivors.[15]

His awareness that he was on a mission intensified. He was pursuing a "conspiracy of evil": in his early confessions, he claimed the conspiracy was that of the demons. Later, he was silent on the matter. Still, on April Fool's Day, he began to compose a letter to the head of the homicide task force that was hunting him. On April 17, he stuck his pistol inside his waistband and went hunting in Queens: this time he had decided to kill both a man and a woman. Valentina Suriani, eighteen, a student of acting at Lehman College, and Alexander Esau, twenty, a helper on a towtruck, parked their car some time after midnight and began to embrace. At 3 a.m., still hunting, Berkowitz noticed them and parked his car a block away. He walked toward the couple, and fired four times. "It was my best job," he told Abrahamsen, "because it resulted in two deaths. Plus, I left my first carefully concocted note on the scene. My shooting pattern improved greatly due to my fearlessness, which slowly developed, and my two-handed shooting method. Four shots were fired. Three hit the victims out of four fired." He ran back to his car feeling, he said, "flushed with power," and drove past the apartment of Donna Lauria (for whom he felt reverence), stopping only at a cheap restaurant to gorge on hamburgers and chocolate malts. Suriani was already dead, but Esau did not die for another eighteen hours.[16]

He was contented for more than two months, until June 25, 1977, when his mind began to wander again to the girls of Queens. "The demons wanted girls. Sugar and spice and everything nice." He left his apartment at 10 p.m., carrying his .44 in a paper bag, and began cruising through Queens. He parked his car and began to walk until he saw a young couple in a car. "I saw her long hair. I looked about. The street was deserted. I then began to approach the car from the rear, keeping just behind the right rear fender . . . I could see them clearly in the front seat. The window was closed. They weren't looking in my direction. I crouched down to bring myself level with the girl, and I fired." Judy Placido, a recent high-school graduate, and Sal Lupo were talking when "all of a sudden," Placido remembered, "I heard echoing in the car. There wasn't any pain, just ringing in my ears. I look at Sal, and his eyes were open wide, just like his mouth. There were no screams. I don't know why I didn't scream; I'll never know why, I just didn't." Lupo had been hit in the right forearm, Placido in the head, neck and shoulder. After the shooting, Berkowitz was disappointed: "I was angry. I don't see how that girl lived." "The window deflected the bullet. It wouldn't go through the window right. I mean, I tried." He ran back to his car, but he was unafraid, for "the demons were protecting me. I had nothing to fear from the police."[17]

His last kill was in Gravesend Bay, a middle-class section of Brooklyn. Stacy Moskowitz, a twenty-year-old telex-machine operator, and Robert Violante, a twenty-year-old clothing salesman, met in a restaurant on the night of July 30. Berkowitz had begun to stalk one couple in a Corvette, but the car drove off before he could reach it. Violante's Buick pulled into the newly vacated space. "They kissed and embraced," said Berkowitz. "I had an erection. I had my gun out, aimed at the middle of Stacy's head, and fired. One bullet struck her head and another nicked her. I didn't even know she was shot, because she didn't say anything. Nor did she moan. Then I got in my car and drove off." Violante remembered that "I heard like a humming sound. A humming. A vibrating. First I thought I heard glass break. Then a humming. Then I didn't hear Stacy any more. I didn't feel anything, but I saw her fall away from me." Violante had been shot twice in the face and was blinded for life. Moskowitz had been shot once in the head and died thirty-eight hours later. A mile away, Berkowitz, a man at peace with himself, parked his car and bought a newspaper. He sat on a bench in a park: "I sat on it for a long time. I sat there for the rest of the night. When the sun rose, I read the news."[18]

Berkowitz slept late on the morning of August 10. He had failed to carry out a plan to open fire on crowds in the upper-class Hamptons, and now had formed a plan to wreak similar havoc in a nightclub in Riverdale. The duffel bag in the back of his car contained his extra tools: a semi-automatic rifle with four loaded magazines, an Ithaca 12-gauge shotgun, and two .22 rifles. But it was not to be. The police had painstakingly put together the circumstantial evidence linking Berkowitz to the Son of Sam (the final piece being a traffic summons he had received near the site of one of the killings). When they checked his car this time, they discovered his arsenal. At 6 p.m., they surrounded his apartment. At precisely 10 p.m., Berkowitz emerged from the apartment block and began walking toward his car, carrying a triangular-shaped paper bag. As he started the car, the detectives approached him from behind—as he had approached so many parked cars. One detective rapped his gun against the window and shouted, "Freeze, police!" According to the arresting officer, "the guy turned around and smiled at us. He had that stupid smile on his face, like it was all a kid's game." Berkowitz's hand remained clearly visible on the steering wheel. They eased him out of the car and spreadeagled him. "Now that I've got you," the detective asked, "what have I got?"

"You know," Berkowitz replied.

"No, I don't. You tell me."

"I'm Sam," said Berkowitz, smiling.[19]

THE CONFESSIONS

> "And huge drops of lead*
> Poured down upon her head
> Until she was dead
> Yet, the cats still come out
> At night to mate
> And the sparrows still
> Sing in the morning."
>
> DAVID BERKOWITZ[20]

The world already regarded Berkowitz as quite mad; as insane in every possible sense of the word—medically, legally, and morally. The letters he had sent to the press and the police during his killing spree provided what seemed to be strong evidence supporting this belief, as did his behavior in court and in the hospital. Most telling of all seemed to

---

* This poem, written by Berkowitz, was found in his pocket after his capture.

be his prison diary, published in 1981 as an appendix to Klausner's thoughtful book. The *persona* Berkowitz presented to the public, and the documents he produced, were his attempt both to explain and to disguise (perhaps from himself as well as from others) his enterprise's inner meaning. At any rate, he felt that it was difficult for others to understand him.

The Demonology

"Questioned, he told his inquisitors
he had killed at the behest of voices.
'Demons' had made him do it. 'Sam,'
a 6,000-year-old man, had passed on
these instructions to kill—through
his dog."

DAVID ABRAHAMSEN[21]

"People feel a certain eeriness about me," Berkowitz wrote in his nondescript handwriting in his prison diary, "something cold, inhuman, monsterous [sic]. This is the power and personality of the demon's. This is the spell used by 'Them' to turn people away from me and create a situation of isolation, lonliness [sic], and personal frustration, as part of their Master Plan." "I've been tormented all my life by them [the demons]—never having any peace or quite [sic]. In fact, last week I went 'beserk' [sic] because they slapped me in the head and made terrible noises." While his homicidal spree was running its course, his neighbors and their dogs appeared to him as demons. Many nights they screamed at him, for they hid in the walls of his apartment. One night, Berkowitz remembered, "I kicked in the wall. I jumped and kicked. I tried to kick his face in. Nothing happened. It just didn't have any effect. I could hear deep in the wall a lot of sounds. Voices, thousands of them. Screams. Funny sounds. Music. Like drums . . . I tried to do what they said, but they were never satisfied. Sometimes I argued with them, asking why they were making me do these things. But they never answered. They just laughed at me. I wasn't a bad person, but they were making me do bad things. I didn't want to. I did everything they said to do, and still they weren't satisfied." Were these "legitimate" delusions, or the constructions of a not terribly intelligent young man who was trying to divest himself of responsibility for his actions?[22]

Let us return to his prison diary, which opens with calm reflection on his own life and that of others. "When I look at all the prisoners in Kings County Hospital I cannot help but feel sorry for them. Their [sic] like lost souls; many in and out of institutions for all of their lives; little hope, no family, no friends. I think people only want peace and comfort in life but apparently few know how to find it. It seems like the only saviour these patients have is thorazine but they really need Jesus. I never thought my life would turn out like this—what a mess. If it wasn't for my family and their love, and my lawyers and their supportive help I don't believe I would survive this ordeal. Some, I guess, are more fortunate than others. Love and companionship and a closeness to God are all that is necessary to challenge the adversary, Satan (Sam). Yes, the demons are real. I saw them, I felt their presence, and I heard them." But there is no more insanity here than routinely dispensed at any evangelical gathering. The blandness continues: "I only wish they would let me read the newspapers here. Especially when its about me. I feel I just have to know what people are saying about me. The judge (Mr. Starkie) hates me I'm certain. He must think I'm some type of woman hater. But I thought the newspapers had done away with that theory when I was apprehended. If a girl had recently jilted me as the judge suspects then I would like to know who she was myself. Who could this mystery woman be?"

Then without warning, the demons surface. Berkowitz's handwriting shrinks and sprawls as he tries to communicate the "fact" that he is possessed once more. "I am a gladitor [sic] against the forces of darkness! I am come into these circumstances so that I might save many lives. I am willing to die to be at peace, to obtain it. I am willing to go to jail so I might be free. My life must be dedicated to the people on earth. Might it be possible to convince the world about the dark spirit forces that live on earth? I will die for this cause! Oh, death, you are victory."

Again he alters, becoming almost academic in his scholarly self-analysis. "After reading the book *Hostage to the Devil* by Malachi Martin I now have no doubt that I am a person who had been visited by an alien force or being. The evidence is overwhelming. Especially since my life fits in so well with the pattern of a person possessed by an intelligent force. The best evidence is a letter to my father dated long before to [sic] shootings began. This letter stated a devine [sic] mission that I felt was intended for me—one of importance although now that I look back at it the whole mission makes no sense. Page 523 of H. to the D. the last paragraph—'It always alienated them from their surroundings and from those nearest to them.' There were even times after my arrest in which I doubted the reality of the demons, thinking of myself to be a person hallucinating or living a delusion but now, after reading Mr. Martin's work, I am convinced beyond my own self doubt about demons."

He combines a purported sense of social responsibility with his demonology, even drawing up the blueprints for new social institutions to cope with the demons. "Now I must go about to correct the wrongs of Son of Sam although they were good works when you look at them from distorted 'alien' eyes and from an 'evil' intelligence point of view. I need to have more personal freedoms such as keeping a pen in my cell, being able to go out, under guard and mail letters, go to the post office, and have a hotline telephone in my cell that leads directly to Chief of Detectives Keenan's office. I know that if the police set up a 'Demon Task Force' then a tremendous step would be taken. It would be a monumental step in the annals of justice and historical law. Also, society needs to erect a 'Demon Hospital' in which suspected cases of demon possession could be treated and alenniated [sic]. There is no telling how many crimes may have been committed by the possessed or how desperately they too need help."

"The demons have an amazing way of leaving you feeling like an empty vacum [sic]—leaving your life void of many things. However, the unclean spirits will fill the very same void which they so subtly created with evil light (darkness) and evil knowledge. 'The void has been filled' I told Mr. Breslin; however, it was replaced with a dark foul substance that resulted in death and destruction. It is this distorted view that makes everything good look bad and everything evil appear right. So I gave up my personal freedom thinking it bad, only to obtain a type of freedom equivalent to that of a dog on a long chain. I can work but I can't have freedom. I can be loved but I cannot love. I could feel and admire good yet, have no good in me."

"There is, no doubt, a deep hidden array of forces behind the Son of Sam killings. This is not a trial simply to be put into black and white. This trial has far greater significance [sic] and far greater depth than one could imagine. The S.O.S. shootings probe hidden motives and expose spirits and forces that never before surfaced in an open courtroom. Good and Evil, God and Lucifer, yet, while every seat in the courtroom is taken, likewise, every corner space at the ceiling will be taken by those of the spirit world. There is no doubt in my mind that the outcome of this trial would affect all of God's angels and all of Satan's demons . . . I have a fear now that I to [sic] will become a demon or, I may be a demon right now. Sometimes the need to kill becomes so overwhelming that I fear myself. However, I know that this is not me. I'm certain there is someone inside me, an alien presence [sic] whose need to obtain blood and kill is in relation to his rebellion to God. This belief of an alien presence is not an escape of responsibility because I am looking forward to a jail cell as opposed to having an apartment filled with demons. Furthermore, I David Berkowitz, do not wish to kill anymore but live my life in peace and with a positive purpose. I wrestle with the evil one daily and silently. I know that if I were home alone I would be busting up my household possessions or punching myself in the head and arguing with the demons who ran amok in my apartment." But what is there about incarceration that would stop the demons from tormenting him?

"My apartment is what I called it even though I always felt that I didn't own it. I mean I paid the rent but I hated that apartment so much because of the demons that dwelled in it—I was even thinking of setting fire to it. I paid the rent;

I signed the lease, I moved in it seeking quiet and rest only to find noise and terror. No, this isn't my apartment. It was reserved for me in the hopes of trapping me, leaving me near broke and unable to escape from the final foe—'Sam Carr' who is but isn't. Sam, who is dead but alive and who torments the earth. . . . What can I do? How can I make people understand? I am worried and with good reason that I may, one day, evolve into a humanoid or demon in a more complete state. I fear that with the loss of my humaness [sic] I will become like a zombie. As a matter of note, some people thought I was void of emotions when they examined me. This is exactly what happens to those possessed. I want my soul back! I want what was taken from me! I have a right to be human." But who had stolen his soul, and precisely what was taken from him?

The calm tone of the diary then changes abruptly, as if the demon spirit had entered his soul once more. The handwriting alters too: "I am Abaddon the Destroyer. I take the lives of those unwilling to give them up. I obtain their blood for Sam and the demons. . . . There were so many things that I wanted to do, so many places I wanted to visit. However, I couldn't. I had no rights as a person. I just couldn't enjoy myself when I had time off—my mission was all I lived for and I hated it. I hated my life as SON OF SAM. But what could I do? Even when I went to Florida I couldn't even stop to sightsee—I had no peace or rest. You could tell by the way I drove down there non-stop, then to Texas non-stop, that I did in fact, have a supernatural power and a special satanic mission."

"I am the demon from the bottomless pit here on earth to create havoc and terror. I am War, I am death, I am destruction! I know who has whored and pimped. I know who has committed grevous [sic] sins and who has spit on their mother and father. Where is the great one who can cast me away into darkness? Where is his coming? I suppose that he likes me at my temporary place—in David the shit the filth. I am the filth and the come. I am the wretch the filth the vomit! I am he the Son of Sam who fears nothing I destroy! I kill and stomp to pieces the people of earth in the name of that wretched. I am kind I am hell I am death. Meysa [victim Stacy Moskowitz's mother] the whore the harlot shall not escape God's curse her children shall die all three for she whored her body and sold her flesh for a mere penance [sic]. Who is like the great whore the harlot of cum who sells herself. Who is like the Son of Sam, me, a fallen angel who has come to kill and to establish the kingdom of terror and misery—me, Son of Sam the killer who fears neither death nor hell. Who is Stacy who sells her soul for a penis? Let us make war with civilization and destroy and cause terror. . . . No peace comes to earth through the gun of kings. Who is sly and cunning? Who can outwit the president? Son of Sam and legion of us destroy and vomit uncontrollably."

Once again, he returns to his mundane "self"—in his terms, the spirit might temporarily let loose the bonds of possession and allow the "real" David Berkowitz to emerge. "The hours pass by so slowly its [sic] hard to make them pass. I guess I have to take the hours piece by piece and not take the day on a whole. Next to the demons, the worse [sic] thing is boredom. . . . What is death that a person should fear it? Perhaps one really fears having to lose ones [sic] possessions, loved one's [sic] or maybe the person fears having to meet God and be shown all of their sins . . . I miss the freedom of travel—New Patty, Bear Mountain, Ferry Point park. It was a glorious experience to just get in my car and travel."

Berkowitz concludes with a bogus-sounding commitment to society and a modest bleat of self-pity. "I owe society a chance to make myself good and repay them for all the troubles I caused as a result of my illness. Someday, people will see a new David Berkowitz and the end of Son of Sam [indeed, it would only be a matter of months]. Son of Sam can be dead forever if the courts, doctors, and me are willing to work together. I am. I owe my freedom to Jesus Christ the Son of God. 'I and the Father are one,' says Jesus. I have made myself a promise not to remain locked up behind bars forever. I have a debut [sic] to pay to society and one day I will be free to repay it. I must repay society and now that I am a Christian I will work to help other people find true freedom and eternal life. In this hospital I found Jesus Christ and it is Him who I am obligated to. I must tell society about the truth and hope." He closes his diary with sad drawings of his face, next to which he wrote, "I am never happy. Rather I am sad. Very often I cry when alone in my cell. I am very nervous. I never never rest or relax. I am going to have a nervous breakdown. I am possessed! I sleep restlestly [sic]. I feel like screaming. I must be put to death. Demons torment me. I am not going to make it." Buried in a creation halfway between a doodle and a drawing, are two words: "HELP ME."

The Revised Version

"I must slay a woman for revenge purposes to get back on them for all the suffering they caused me."

DAVID BERKOWITZ[23]

In February of 1979, less than a year after he had been sentenced to several hundred years in prison, Berkowitz confirmed his celebrity status by calling a press conference, admitting that his story of Sam Carr, demons, and spirit-possession had been an invention. A few weeks later, he wrote to his former psychiatrist, David Abrahamsen, and confessed that the entire demonic story had been a well-planned, carefully coordinated hoax. "I did know why I pulled the trigger," he now admitted. "It would be a good idea if we talked." In the spring of 1979, Abrahamsen began making trips to Attica prison to visit Berkowitz because the latter had "expressed a desire to have a book written, a book that would deal not only with his crimes but also with his emotions."[24]

Berkowitz said matter-of-factly that he had bought the .44 pistol when he realized how much more difficult it was to kill someone with a knife. And he knew precisely what he intended to do with the pistol when he bought it. "I knew I was going to have to do something with it. I think it was going to be shooting people, you know." He described at some length the elaborate and carefully made plans he developed for the killings. "I used to visit my sister, and when I did, my gun, maps, extra ammunition, and other related paraphernalia were always carefully stored in my car for quick use. I did travel in the vicinity of Glen Oaks Village and Floral Park as well as many other places. Yes, Queens was special to me—very special. This I can't explain. Shooting someone in Queens was an obsession. When I got my bad urges about family, knowing that my gun was so close. . . . I'd just go take a long walk to release any mental tensions I had for the moment. Walking for me has always been very therapeutic." The sheer professionalism that he displayed expressed itself not only in his planning, but also in the wary manner with which he conducted his operations. "I was angry when I did [miss], because I went to so much trouble to succeed and I took such huge risks. I familiarized myself with the streets and possible escape routes from those central areas. Also I managed to learn all the streets by repeated trips into the area. I mean, there were nights in which I traveled all through a certain area but it turned unproductive. Towards the end of my spree I developed a keen perception of police tactics. After a while, I was able to spot an unmarked car regardless of its disguise. Some were taxicabs, some were beat-up old rattletraps, but they were police cars just the same, and I 'made' them. Unmarked police vans were also a frequent sight."[25]

He conceded that he had experienced some ambivalence about the killings, but it had never been enough to stop him. At worst, it had made his earlier performances nervous and amateurish: "There were times I was troubled over my sudden urges after the shootings began," he told Abrahamsen. "I wanted to take a life, yet I wanted to spare a life. I felt I had to kill someone . . . I wanted to and I didn't want to . . . [but] I was determined and in full agreement with myself that I must slay a woman for revenge purposes to get back on them for all the suffering they caused me. Of course you would disagree extensively with my immoral view. I don't blame you. Because I, too, realize that this was a poor excuse for all I've done. However, at the time I sincerely believed that I was justified. I believed that I had every moral right to slay a chosen victim. As gross and perverted as this sounds, it was my belief." Nevertheless, his ambivalence emerged merely as a kind of uncertainty or, as he put it (parroting the perspectives of the court psychiatrists), "I guess that shooting with one hand, which I did unconsciously, was a result of my inner conscience speaking to me, and that secretly I wished I had missed."[26]

More disturbingly, his growing confidence was bolstered by the extraordinary coverage the media were giving his activities—a coverage which, not without insight, he interpreted as a form of encouragement. "At this point [the Freund/Diel shootings] I imagine I didn't care much anymore, for I finally had convinced myself that it was good to do it, necessary to do it, and that the public wanted me to do it. The latter part I believe until this day. I believe that many were rooting for me. This was the point at which the papers began to pick up vibes and information that something big was happening out in the streets. Real big!" Later, in a spirit reminiscent of the reluctance with which a satiated lover contemplates yet another amorous bout, he would say: "Now that I look back on this, none of it makes any sense."[27]

Berkowitz was at pains to underline that he had abandoned his earlier religious ideals and now hated God (and all authority). "I hate God," he told Abrahamsen, "and I don't like him because of all the things he did. I blame him for taking my mother. I hate him for making me, my life. . . . But I think he is a liar. He has disappointed me. I fear God, his power, his ability to kill, hell, a personal terror. God has a grip on me and many others via fear."[28]

Still, he tried to leave us with the impression that his primary rage stemmed from, and was directed toward, his disappointing relationships with women. "When I returned home from the army, I tried to go out with some of the girls in Co-op City. They didn't find me attractive. I began to hate girls. I always hated them." When Abrahamsen tried to explore the symbolism of shooting women in parked cars, Berkowitz first responded with an intense and self-justifying puritanism. "I'm trying to remember if Esau and Suriani were having sex [something that, given his almost photographic recall of the killings, he would surely have no trouble doing]. I know they were embracing, but I can't remember if they had their clothes off or not. If they did have their clothing off, and were engaged in sex, then I would be somewhat justified in killing them. Sex outside of marriage is a heinous sin."[29]

Abrahamsen struggled to link the killings in parked cars to the possibility that Berkowitz was himself conceived in a parked car, in an illicit relationship, and was revenging himself for this reality. It was a suggestion that merely puzzled Berkowitz. "Betty [Betty Falco, his natural mother]," Berkowitz wrote, "never told me that she ever sat in a car or that she was impregnated in a car. But it is true that many unwanted children are brought into this world as a result of careless sexual encounters in automobiles. As for those parked cars, I cannot say what drew me to them. Maybe you could take an educated, professional guess. I'm at a loss to explain the hidden motivations. Maybe it was just a question of opportunity—a chance to catch them off guard and with their pants down, to catch them unawares, so to speak." We will return again to his "hidden motivations."[30]

ENCOUNTER WITH PSYCHIATRY

> "Please dad I need you now. I've reached
> an agreement with the doctors that I am
> not well. I'm sure that you must realize
> that I'm no cold blooded killer. Rather,
> there is a problem with my mind."
>
> DAVID BERKOWITZ[31]

How did the psychiatric authorities interpret Berkowitz's life? Was he a victim of a mental disease and not a cold-blooded killer? Perhaps. The story of the development of Berkowitz's "mental illness" is a controversial and provocative one. According to Abrahamsen, he had been told of his adoption when he was three years old, and from early childhood had fantasized about death. Certainly he was a troublesome child: Abrahamsen wrote that "he was unhappy, lonely, obsessed by rejection and neglect. He became antisocial and destructive. He was caught up in fantasies of self-aggrandizement, but he never developed any genuine self-esteem." Nevertheless, as Klausner noted, Berkowitz passed through the elementary and high-school system without providing grounds for intervention, and he slipped through the army's psychological testing program, such as it was. Similarly, none of his post-army employers found any pathological cues to interdict.[32]

It was only when he began to kill that an amazing variety of experts turned their attention to him, although they knew him only as the Son of Sam. Klausner noted that the Omega homicide task force hunting him consulted biorhythm specialists, exorcists, astrologers, handwriting analysts, numerologists, hypnotists, psychologists, and psychiatrists in their frustrated attempts to find patterns in the killer's behavior. The psychiatrists were sometimes no less eccentric than the exorcists, no more prescient than the astrologers. One psychiatrist told police that paranoid schizophrenics such as the Son of Sam unconsciously killed at locations which invariably formed a triangle, a theory which drew some attention until another psychiatrist pointed out that any three points make a triangle. Similarly, nothing more useful than laughter was obtained from the comment of a German psychiatric consultant who announced to an audience of policemen and psychiatrists: "Gentlemen. Every time he shoots his gun, he's ejaculating!"[33]

In May of 1977, the Police Commissioner released a psychiatric profile which diagnosed the killer *in absentia* as "neurotic, schizophrenic and paranoid," and possibly obsessed with demonic possession. More useful and convincing were the police's own notions about Sam—that he led a double life and did not always appear to be insane. "He's the kind of guy," said Commissioner Tim Dowd, "who probably goes to work every day. Maybe he does something with statistics. An accountant or a clerk. He just kind of melts into the city scene. He doesn't *look* crazy." Still, no one had much to go on: Berkowitz saw to that.[34]

After his arrest, the task of the psychiatrist became the determination of whether Berkowitz was "insane," "to determine if Mr. Berkowitz is suffering from any mental disease or defect that would preclude a trial." As always, the legally relevant issues were whether Berkowitz could understand the nature of the offense with which he was charged; and whether he was able to assist his attorneys in the preparation of his defense. On August 29, the psychiatric team, headed by Dr. Daniel W. Schwartz, director of forensic psychiatry at Downstate Medical Center in Brooklyn, submitted its report, based on a total of eleven hours of interviews with Berkowitz spread over six days. "It is the opinion of each of us," the report concluded, "that the defendant is an incapacitated person, as a result of mental disease or defect, lacks capacity to understand the proceeding against him or to assist in his own defense." Their diagnosis was "paranoia," and their prognosis was "guarded."[35]

It was at this point, when the prosecution felt it needed its own psychiatrist, that the court appointed Dr. David Abrahamsen to conduct an additional examination. Abrahamsen's report denied the incompetence conclusion from the defense psychiatrists, and instead found Berkowitz competent to stand trial and to assist in his own defense. "David feels that his distorted beliefs are of such importance," Abrahamsen added, "that all other topics should be relegated to the sidelines. Thus the defendant's main excuse for committing the crimes is his delusions. . . . It is also noteworthy that the delusions the defendant states he has, seem to be more transitory and situational, rather than constant. They may, in fact, be exaggerated by him." Abrahamsen ably concluded that "while the defendant shows paranoid traits, they do not interfere with his fitness to stand trial."[36]

This provoked intense conflict within the court. The prosecution moved that the state-appointed psychiatrists re-examine Berkowitz, while the defense asked for a new competency hearing. After the re-examination was performed, Schwartz's colleague Weidenbacher reversed his earlier decision and found Berkowitz to be competent, doing so on the peculiar and remarkable non-psychiatric grounds that Berkowitz had become a Christian and was espousing *bona-fide* Baptist doctrines (and presumably could not therefore be insane). However, this time Dr. Schwartz now felt unable to draw a firm conclusion—reflecting, presumably, the intense political pressure within the courtroom. The newly appointed defense psychiatrist, Dr. Martin Lubin, found Berkowitz incompetent. Abrahamsen seemed to be the only one to see Berkowitz and his delusion for what they were: "Your Honor," he told the judge, "the defendant is as normal as anyone else. Maybe a little neurotic." Berkowitz's counsel changed their plea to guilty, and he was sentenced to a total of 365 years in prison.[37]

After the Trial

Abrahamsen was the only psychiatrist to appreciate the element of exaggeration and embroidery implicit in Berkowitz's demonology; strangely, this insight seemed to have drawn the two together. After the trial, when the Son of Sam denounced his demonology, he wrote to Abrahamsen and expressed a desire to have a book written about him "that would deal not only with his crimes but also with his emotions." "To understand the psychological makeup of Berkowitz," Abrahamsen later wrote, "would be a challenge to any psychoanalyst. He was not a mindless, psychotic killer, but rather a complex human being, inexorably driven to destroy himself and others."[38]

However, Abrahamsen's subsequent preliminary analysis focused on psychiatric *clichés* and produced a hodgepodge of unintegrated insights.* The analysis began with a narrow focus on the family: "The circumstances of his upbringing remind us how much we are a product of our formative years. By tracing Berkowitz's feelings, thoughts, and deeds, one can see where tenderness fought rage, where love battled hate, where reality and fantasy lived side by side." He made much of Berkowitz's "desperate search for his biological mother," and suggested even that "to an extent his crimes are the horrifying consequences of his finding her." This paradoxical notion that Berkowitz's warm and

---

* His complete analysis appeared in book form after this book went to press.

loving reception by his natural mother and sister should create a murderer was mediated, for Abrahamsen, through the notion that although he was warmly received by them, their reality overwhelmed him. "Meeting his biological mother, Betty Falco, proved to be the ultimate frustration." Berkowitz had "fantasized a complete family, a blissful reunion. After finding Betty, he learned that his real name was Richard Falco. But then he learned that his mother's former husband, Tony Falco, had left her years before he was born. His real father, she told him, was her lover of years' standing, a married man, Joseph Kleinman, who had died several years earlier. Berkowitz was staggered. Even the name on his birth certificate was a hoax. 'I was an accident, unwanted,' he said. 'My birth . . . was either out of spite or accident.' By the time he learned this," Abrahamsen concluded, "there had been too many psychological traumas. Despair and rage had settled in. His feelings of murderous rage towards women, which he so far had been able to keep in check, were ready to be unleashed." So for Abrahamsen, the discovery of the true shape of his genealogy "was one of the precipitating events that brought into action Berkowitz's murderous, sadistic impulses. No one would deny the unsettling effect this would have upon him, but the notion that this might have provoked many murders of women needs much clarification.[39]

A second and inevitable theme was Berkowitz's warped sexuality, which Abrahamsen saw as a kind of prime cause. "Berkowitz's sexual feelings played a significant role in his mass killings, yet for a long time he minimized, even denied, that sexual emotions had anything to do with his murders." Yet was this denial a function of Berkowitz's disordered sexuality (as Abrahamsen charged), or simply a true denial? The distinction is of fundamental importance. However, most psychiatrists would naturally gloss over it on the assumption that sexuality is the fundamental drive. "During my first interview with him," Abrahamsen continued, "as I questioned him about his relationship with women, he began to talk about the demons who had wanted so much from him." When Abrahamsen asked what it was that the demons had demanded, Berkowitz replied: "The demons wanted my penis." But this was at the time when Berkowitz was still fabricating his demonology—justifying his own activities and trying to save himself from both responsibility and prison—an interpretation that the Freudian Abrahamsen ignored because Berkowitz was expressing a sexual (and therefore true) version of events. "By then he felt he already had said too much, and he absolutely refused to go on. He wasn't ready; he had entered a mine field of explosive feelings, from which he hurriedly retreated." Or, alternatively, his imagination had run out.[40]

A year later, Abrahamsen raised the subject once again: "Now I wanted an answer to a question: Why did he kill? There were several topics Berkowitz and I touched upon for the first time that day in Attica, but one remark in particular struck me. 'I joined the army,' he declared, 'in order to lose my virginity.'" Abrahamsen recalled that Berkowitz had first boasted to him of losing his virginity at sixteen when in reality, "Berkowitz's first sexual experience, as he later admitted, was in Korea when he was about nineteen years old. At Attica he told me that in Korea, if you wanted 'to have oral sex, you went to one town, and if you had to have sex naturally, then you went to a different town. I was most satisfied when I did it to them, when I sucked them.'" This is interesting material, but Abrahamsen deduced from this preference for oral rather than genital sex not only that Berkowitz had a kind of sexual immaturity, but that his immaturity explained his murders. "His preoccupation with oral sexuality to the exclusion of genital intercourse, both in fantasy and reality, suggests his immature sexual development. He preferred petting and fondling to adult genital intercourse." Abrahamsen left aside the possibility that such a preference might be dismissed as merely individual taste rather than pathological flaw. He then deduced that "another sign of Berkowitz's undeveloped sexuality was his use of masturbation as a substitute for sexual intercourse. At the time Berkowitz went into the army, he masturbated compulsively several times a day, every day. Even when he raved against sex as a sin and was actively enrolled in every available church program, he couldn't wait to go back to his room in the barracks and masturbate.

When he masturbated, he always fantasized he had a girl. And, he said, 'When I did it, most often my fantasy involved oral sex between heterosexual couples. . . . I always fantasized about girls. Now I cannot go to sleep unless I masturbate first.'" This might seem to have some significance, unless one realized how frequent masturbation must be in an alien environment where vigorous young men had few opportunities for conventional relationships other than frequent trips to brothels. Still, Abrahamsen concluded, "more and more in his sex life, fantasy had become his reality." But is this not true for a pathetically large proportion of humanity? "While his neurotic shyness induced him to masturbate rather than approach a girl sexually, he never learned that a girl was capable of giving him better and greater pleasure. His sexual fantasies about women were almost constant, but he did little to realize them in real life. He was a loner. In fact, he was afraid. Afraid of being impotent, he blamed women for his own shyness . . . 'I began to hate girls. I always hated them.' Almost every waking moment, he once told me, he found himself fantasizing, and he was greatly troubled by his fantasies. They were almost all either sexual or violent. 'I'm really quite perverted,' he confessed."[41]

Abrahamsen argued that Berkowitz's sexual inadequacy "was rooted in the circumstances of his childhood. He knew from a very early age that he was an adopted child, and lived with the fear of being deprived of basic physical and emotional gratification. Having lost one mother, his biological mother, he feared he might also lose his second, adoptive one. That is, in fact, what happened. Pearl died of cancer when David was fourteen. This loss caused him so much anxiety and grief that it overwhelmed his feelings of love, inhibiting their natural expression." Yet what kind of an explanation is this? Many people suffer the tragedy of the loss of a parent, even an adoptive one, in their childhood, yet it does not render future love impossible. Indeed, one might argue the opposite case just as effectively, that such experiences can make the individual even more dependent upon loving relationships. In either case, it makes no sense to proffer this as an explanation for multiple murder.[42]

A third theme centered on authority, which Abrahamsen explored in terms of Berkowitz's unresolved Oedipal conflict, and in his purported witnessing of the "primal scene." "Berkowitz also associated physical affection with competition and antagonism [and what thinking person does not?]. He told me, 'He [his adoptive father] made me leave the room when they wanted to be alone. I resented it. I felt deprived. It was my father who took me out of the room. I asked him, 'What are you going to do, kiss?' Here we see the classical psychological confrontation of childhood," Abrahamsen argued, "in which the young boy battles the father for the affection of the mother. The beginning of self-determination is the child's way of coming to terms with this struggle, if he is to grow successfully into adolescence. But Berkowitz's ego was not secure enough for him to assimilate and transcend this experience. He could only turn toward his own fantasies to find an outlet for sexual desires." Drawing the thread still further, Abrahamsen linked Berkowitz's hostility toward his father with what he felt toward God. "If Berkowitz's sexuality was affected at this time by this unresolved Oedipal conflict, so also was his attitude toward authority figures. At one point during our initial conversation at Attica, having just discussed sexual matters, he launched into a diatribe against God. . . . His fear of God was the same fear he had of his father when he challenged him for his mother's attention. He had to be his mother's favorite."[43]

Brushing aside the question of how jealousy for the mother might lead to multiple murder, Abrahamsen pursued the primal scene theory without corroborating evidence of any kind. "It is probable," he speculated, "that as a child he had seen his adoptive parents making love and had since repressed that primal scene. In 1977 he was to be a witness to another love scene as he stalked Stacy Moskowitz and Robert Violante . . . in observing the young couples, he felt he participated in the lovemaking, and to an intense degree he was also a voyeur, which he greatly enjoyed. In a twisted way he had become both a voyeur and a participant. He too wanted to partake in the act. When he shot his victims he was transfixed, continuing to pull the trigger as if he were both emotionally and sexually engaged." Unfortunately, the evidence from anthropology makes it clear that the "primal scene" is a cultural invention: there are many societies in which it is normal for the young to watch their parents having intercourse, and that observing this scene provokes nothing more than rude giggles or guffaws. It seems most likely that it was only our repressed Victorians, fascinated and horrified by human sexuality, who could concoct a theory attributing mental disorder to such a glimpse.[44]

When Berkowitz invited Abrahamsen to "take an educated, professional guess" about whether there was a relationship between the killings in parked cars and his own possible conception (which Berkowitz knew nothing about) in a car, Abrahamsen wrote: "My educated guess is that he was indeed trying to 'catch them off guard and with their pants down'—literally. His reunion with Betty Falco was enough to send him off on his murderous expeditions, enough to make him want to catch a woman with her pants down and to punish her—he was that furious and that disappointed with his newfound mother." But Berkowitz was disappointed with the complexity of his conception and his genitors, not with his natural mother, who had smothered him with love![45]

Nevertheless, Abrahamsen was Berkowitz's Boswell, and we must follow him to his conclusions. His position essentially was that this man with a crippled sexuality, this voyeur, this victim of the primal scene and of unresolved Oedipal conflict, took out his rage for his natural mother on his victims. "Within our sexual fantasies themselves, violence often plays a part. In the disturbed (though not necessarily psychotic) mind, however, these feelings literally fuse together, and the person may act accordingly. Such was the case of sexuality and violence in the life of David Berkowitz. Violence took over his sexually colored aggression. He confessed to me that he 'had fantasized about shooting women for a long time.' Although he had nobody in particular in mind, he knew it would be pretty women. He fantasized about shooting women, and he fantasized about having sex with them. His hostile feelings toward women made him sometimes want to 'cause bodily harm, but not while having sex.' But despite this assertion, it is clear from the link he makes between the two that his sexual and murderous fantasies were very much closer to each other than he realized."[46]

But did Berkowitz simply fail to "realize" something, in that special way that psychiatrists so routinely deny their patients any insight into their own conditions? Or was Berkowitz trying to tell Abrahamsen something he could not comprehend? Indeed, Berkowitz explicitly denied everything Abrahamsen had so patiently constructed when he emphasized the *non-sexual* motive behind the killings. After murdering Donna Lauria, "I was literally singing to myself on the way home. . . . The tension, the desire to kill a woman, had built up in me to such explosive proportions that when I finally pulled the trigger, all the pressures, all the tensions, hatred, had just vanished, dissipated, but only for a short time. *I had no sexual feelings. It was only hostile aggression.* I knew when I did it, it was wrong to do it. *I wanted to destroy her because of what she represented. I never knew her personally. I knew what she represented."* What can this remarkable denial mean? Why did Abrahamsen so studiously ignore it? Who and what did his victims represent, and what was the source of this "hostile aggression"? To answer this, we must turn to a social interpretation of his life.[47]

THE METAMORPHOSES OF A SERIAL MURDERER

"I hate rebels but I love revolutionaries."

DAVID BERKOWITZ[48]

The person who was Richard Falco and then David Berkowitz was, like all of us, constructed of many parts, any one of which he might choose to bring to the surface. Unlike many of us, his self-absorption and superficiality enabled him to pass from one social *persona* to another almost without comment, as if they did not contradict each other. If we are to understand him, we cannot pass over each transformation with his facile manner. The man who was to make his life's work the killing of pretty women in Queens shed many skins, as would a snake, before settling on his coherent identity as the Son of Sam.

The Brat

Multiple murderers do not have quite the kind of child-hoods we would expect: only a minority are "abused" in the conventional sense (which is to say reared in the turmoil of sexual or physical assault). They are most often illegitimate, or adopted, or institutionalized in their adolescence, but there is a curious relative absence of the classic vile and unendurable childhood. Certainly there was no evidence whatever of any form of brutality in the dull, lower-middle-class Jewish home in which Berkowitz was raised. Nor did he reveal any maniacal urges in childhood. He merely demonstrated that complex of behaviors which has been recently dignified with the euphemism "hyperactive," which is to say that he was widely regarded as a spoiled and uncontrollable brat. As one neighbor recalled: "His parents had a difficult time with him. Kids would complain that he hit them without reason. [But] his parents were nice and they gave him the kinds of toys any child would cherish. More for sure than any kid in the neighborhood."[49]

He seemed strange to some, but no more so than would any other willful, spoiled little bully. The neighbor whose account has the most convincing ring of truth to it thought the young Berkowitz was "a handful. His mother was taking him to psychiatrists. He did a lot of very strange things. He would push people. He always had a vivid imagination, but what he would say was a little beyond what the average child would say. His mother would laugh and smile." A music teacher, charged with trying to explain the rudiments of the saxophone to Berkowitz, remembered that "he was ter-rible. But the music was the least of it. One time I went into the house and he was throwing a tantrum. Tearing curtains off the wall, throwing pictures, screaming, and kicking. I said I'd come back later. He used to make his mother cry terribly. The tantrums, his arrogance was something else. He was the most erratic kid I've ever known." This is interesting, but all it offers us is one variation of a type of child with which every neighborhood is cursed: here exploiting the early knowledge of his adoption through endless tantrums with his bewildered step-mother.[50]

Super Patriot

The willful child embraced his true *persona* early on—although he would reject it for several years—as he evolved into an arch-conservative patriot. As he emerged into manhood during the dying months of the Vietnam War, and still troubled by the death of his foster-mother and his father's remarriage, it made sense for this pseudo–John Wayne to join the army. "I wanted to serve the country and get an education through the Army," he explained. Moreover, he was suitably enraged when a radical step-sister, who lived in a California commune, sent him an anti-war collage to protest his enlistment. "It really got him mad," his childhood friend Iris Gerhardt recalled. "It was an anti-war type of thing with photographs and her own drawings that said American soldiers were killers and that Dave shouldn't do it too. He really resented that. He showed it to us and said, 'How'd you like to get something like this if you were going into the Army?' "[51]

Explaining his patriotism at a time when such a stance was profoundly out of step with his generation, he admitted: "I sort of lived like behind the times. I wanted to see some action, prove something to myself. It was rebellion then against parents, country and stuff. Kids were hippies and into drugs. I guess, then, I was very patriotic. Nobody else, except a couple of people, were." He was transferred to Korea, not Vietnam, after basic training, and he arrived flaunting his new persona. "I got there in the unit and I was really, you know, just out of training. I was really gung-ho, super straight." Then Berkowitz the super patriot would temporarily disappear, for like everyone else in the army in Korea, he recalled, he changed. "Wow! When we got exposed to everything, everyone changed. Almost everybody went crazy." This persona would resurface through his life (when he took a job as a security guard or served as an auxiliary policeman), but for now he was about to experience his second great transformation.[52]

The Rebel

He was ideologically conservative but, like most of our multiple murderers, his interaction with his social environment produced a fuzzy rebellion. For Berkowitz, this would be expressed as a 1960s-style anti-establishmentarianism which periodically blended with radical religion. Not long after his arrival in Korea, he was writing his friends in the U.S., urging them to "keep the movement moving on the home front and I'll keep it moving here." On January 21, 1972, he wrote his friend Gerhardt, formally announcing what must have been a puzzling ideological shift. "I don't play anymore conservative patriot scenes. I woke up. The world is all fucked up (thanks Nixon). We've got to have some peace. The only thing on my mind is Drugs, Music, Pollution, Poverty, Peace and Love . . . I despise religion, hate prejustice [sic], greed, etc. That's all the world is. A cold mass of hell. It sucks. We're all doomed to the grave."[53]

Despising religion, he changed his mind and converted to evangelical Christianity. In his typically bogus style, he wrote: "One day me and Jesus talked ya know, the usual story. Anyhow, we got to some big thinking. So I decided to do what I wanted to do in this particular situation." Appropriately, he began zealously to proselytize his fellow soldiers on the base. One remembered him "telling the guys they shouldn't be drinking and swearing and running around with women. But as an individual, I didn't think he was bad. He was a little off sometimes, but so were a few other guys who seemed just as strange."[54]

His newfound Christianity would periodically backslide, but his half-baked radicalism would not. Soon he refused to carry his rifle on duty and was placed on court-martial. On

February 2, he wrote to his friend Gerhardt explaining the incident: "I have finally proven that I'm not going to play with there [sic] guns anymore. I made myself promise that I was not to carry any weapons while my unit was on the field. So that day while I was in the chowline, a major and a captain walked up to me and said, 'Private, where is your gun?' And I said, I didn't bring it to the field and I refuse to bring it to the field. Well, all hell broke out after that. They just can't tell me when to carry a gun. I explained to them but they didn't do much good. I also explained it to the chaplain. And guess what? He's with me all the way. He never carried a gun in his life. He is trully [sic] a man of God, and so am I and he knows it. Of course, I'm for a court martial but I'll win. I'll have to prove that I'm a conscientious objector, which I am. It's going to be a ruff [sic] fight but I have one thing going for me. That is God. He's on my side. There is one thing you must admit about me. That is, when have you ever known me to say things about love, Peace, God, etc. I mean, can you ever remember me talking about all this back in the world. . . . These feelings have been deep inside . . . now don't think I'm going insane or anything like that because I'm not . . . yes it's the real me . . . they come out with a little help from my friends. I must truly thank my friends for helping me. Because now I'm an individual again. Free from the war pigs and there [sic] evil ways."[55]

Thus were sown the seeds of the Son of Sam. For all our multiple murderers, the *content* of their ideas matters not at all. This explains how easily they can shift from one extreme to another, since the only important thing is that they take some form of rebellious stance—a Baptist hippie rebelling against the military establishment one day, a super patriot rebelling against his parents and his generation the day before. In this ideological flux too, Berkowitz first caught the scent of how he could establish an identity, and call the world's attention to the affairs of David Berkowitz.

By mid-March, this tentative new identity had been forged, and he wrote to Gerhardt: "Since I got here all I've been doing is fighting the establishment. It gets pretty hard to keep fighting all the time but I and a few others know where [sic] right. I'm just to [sic] anxious to see this great new world develop. But I get down sometimes when I see and think that I'll be dead before I can ever see this change take place. I don't feel like fighting. When I say fighting I don't mean with any violence. When do you think people will see the light. . . . It gets really bad when I get the impression that I have no support from anybody and I'm fighting a losing battle. I often feel this way so I get the urge to escape for awhile. In other words I just take my mind out of the rat race and get into deep meditation. When I do it gives me a chance to think and plan my next move." One can only marvel at the superficiality of motivation that permitted his rebellion to tire within a few weeks: similarly, we should note how his lack of support (for which we should read applause) weakened his commitment. Still, by his standards he held fast. In May of 1972, he would formally announce his refusal "to learn how to kill my fellow man. . . . There ain't nobody gonna get rich over my dead body. Nobody is gonna send me to a war so they can make some money by having me use their products like guns, bullets, bombs, etc." And in June, he saw "the Army as nothing more than a tool of the government to use against another nation. It's just a game of politics. I cannot see why man would wage war on another man. We're all supposed to love each other but we don't . . . I want to promote love and brotherhood. We don't have much love here on earth. . . . War never did a person any good . . . I want to be free . . . I will be pretty soon. There is something I must do first. Give me about 50 days for planning. I sure would like mankind to be free. Hey love, tell me how to be free, tell me how to find peace. I haven't found any answers yet." What was this "next move" that would take "50 days" to plan and might yield him peace?[56]

Soon he would find his peace through killing the representatives of the group he felt oppressed him. For the moment, however, he could only hint at his long-term intentions. "They taught me how to fight. They taught me about many weapons, demolition, riot control and self defense. All of these courses will come in handy one day. I plan to use them and it's not going to be the way the lifers want me to use them. I will use these tactics to destroy them the way they destroyed millions of people through the wars they started. One day there will be a better world. After a few heads from the heads of state are removed . . . the poor man is not lazy like the rich man . . . I am displeased with it and I will try to change it . . . I will make it my resolution to find out what is in the heads of our fearless leaders. I will find out what is in their heads even if I have to crack them wide open . . . I hate rebels but I love revolutionaries." He would soon break open many heads in pursuit of his rebellion but, like all our multiple murderers, he did not have the where-withal to challenge the ruling elite he felt oppressed him: like all his fellow killers, his impotent rebellion would steal the lives of those who were available to him.[57]

The Demons

Still, something was missing before he could put his plans into action, some ideological mediator that would resolve his fear and ambivalence of killing. After he left the army and returned to America, his lot was a succession of dead-end jobs, punctuated by the trauma of his father's move to Florida and the discovery of his complex parent-age. Alone in both his world and his apartment, he found his mediator in the demons who began to visit him. Consciously or otherwise, he constructed a host of spirit forces—arrayed in ranks and hierarchies—who instructed him to do what he wished to do. His demonology has been widely reprinted, but it is central to his homicidal career and must be reviewed briefly here.

He first made his demons public in the letter he wrote to police Captain Joseph Borrelli, one of the senior officers hunting the Son of Sam. "I am deeply hurt by your calling me a wemon [sic] hater," read his four-page letter, left near the bodies of Suriani and Esau. "I am not. But I am a monster. I am the 'Son of Sam.' I am a little brat. When father Sam gets drunk he gets mean. He beats his family. Sometimes he ties me up to the back of the house. Other times he locks me in the garage. Sam loves to drink blood. 'Go out and kill,' commands father Sam. Behind our house some rest. Mostly young—raped and slaughtered—their blood drained—just bones now . . . I feel like an outsider. I am on a different wave-length than everybody else—programmed too [sic] kill." The letter served the dual purpose of announcing the existence of his demons and taunting the police. "Attention all police: Shoot me first—shoot to kill or else keep out of my way or you will die! . . . Police: Let me haunt you with these words; I'll be back! I'll be back! To be interpreted [sic] as bang bang bang, bank [sic], bank—ugh!! Yours in murder Mr Monster."[58]

A few months later, he wrote to the *New York Daily News,* developing the theme that he was under the control of Sam and therefore was not responsible for the killings. "Mr. Breslin, sir," he wrote to a columnist, "I don't think that because you haven't heard from [me] for a while that I went to sleep. No, rather, I am still here. Like a spirit roaming the night. Thirsty, hungry, seldom stopping to rest; anxious to please Sam. I love my work. Now, the void has been filled." To underline this point, he signed himself, "Sam's creation—.44"[59]

During the course of his killings he added new characters to the demonology. One was a neighbor, Craig Glassman, whom Berkowitz claimed was a spirit who had the "power to go into my mind. . . . Someone constantly yelled and howled in that apartment. The noise was deafening. The house, my room, shook, trembling." He began to write messages on his apartment walls, allowing his delusions to take him where they would. "As long as Craig Glassman is in the world, there will never be any peace, but there will be plenty of murders . . . Craig Glassman worships the devil and has power over me. . . . My name is Craig Glassman and I shall never let a soul rest." In mid-June, he sent anonymous threatening letters to Glassman, referring to demons and Satan and "the streets running red with blood at the judgment." In the letters, he described himself as "the slave," while Glassman was "the master" who "drove me into the night to do your bidding." Later, in his prison diary, he developed his demonology still further: but what was the significance of all this literary creativity? What role did the demons play in the formation of his enterprise?[60]

THE SYNTHESIS

> "I love my work. Now the void
> has been filled."
>
> DAVID BERKOWITZ[61]

What was this "void" that had opened in the life of David Berkowitz? What was there in the act of multiple murder that filled this void so completely and left him in such enviable states of ecstasy and fulfillment? To understand the man, we must focus on the enduring social realities in his life and on the social category of his victims; for only then can we decipher the hidden messages in his acts and public communications.

When he began to kill is especially informative. He did not do so during his late adolescence in New York when his imagination was already aflame with violence. He did not do so during his military service in Korea, when he went to great lengths to parade his superficial notions of non-violence before his fellows. He did not do so immediately upon his return to America when, ironically, he found himself guarding the gold of the rich in Fort Knox; or when he went through a series of unstable jobs, passing from one to another in unpredictable bursts. Rather, he did so when he was living in his own apartment and was the holder of a lifetime position in the Post Office. This was no lashing out of the dispossessed.

Abrahamsen was quite correct in pointing to the discovery of his illegitimacy as Berkowitz's primary crisis. "He was unhappy, lonely, obsessed by rejection and neglect," Abrahamsen wrote. "Meeting his biological mother, Betty Falco, proved to be the ultimate frustration." The effect of this discovery that "My birth . . . was either out of spite or accident" was not to provoke some mental disease, but to invalidate his credentials as a social person, to challenge the very basis of his identity and existence. Like Ted Bundy, who was presented with a similar challenge, Berkowitz crumbled. To re-build himself would require an entirely new and powerful re-definition of the world. To reconstruct this view, to allow himself to act (and in doing so, regain his humanity), he drew into himself the month before the killings began. At that time, he wrote to his father and revealed some of the dark thoughts that now obsessed him: "Dad, the world is getting dark now. I can feel it more and more. The people, they are developing a hatred for me. You wouldn't believe how much people hate me. . . . Most of them are young. I walk down the street and they spit and kick at me. The girls call me ugly and they bother me the most. The guys just laugh." The focus of his anger was already clear.[62]

Yet he was tormented by the problem of overcoming his reluctance to kill: "I wanted to take a life, yet I wanted to spare a life. I felt I had to kill someone . . . I wanted to and I didn't want to." He found the solution in the demons. Berkowitz spoke a form of truth when he claimed it was the demons who had turned him into a soldier. In his cramped apartment, alone for twenty-eight days, his mind in neutral, he began to fabricate (a form of lying to oneself with which we are all familiar), and so construct his demonology. Drawing material from somewhere in his consciousness, he scrawled messages with a Magic Marker on his apartment walls: "In this hole lives the Wicked King," "Kill for my Master," and "I turn children into Killers." In the months that were to come, he would flesh out his vision of a spirit order to which he was bound in slavery. It was a simple way of dealing with the ambivalence that, by the third killing, would disappear entirely. His analysts had observed, but failed to explain, the fundamental significance of the fact that "what is common to all of Berkowitz's murders is that his mind raised obstacles to killing." Once he had examined his life and found it unendurable, the demons were the mechanism that could orchestrate his rage. "I believed that I had every moral right to slay a chosen victim," he said, and in his own terms he was right—for the act would fill the void in his life.[63]

The Women of Queens

"The wemon of Queens are prettyist
of all. I must be the water they
drink . . . To the People of Queens,
I love you."

DAVID BERKOWITZ[64]

He began to kill in order to give meaning and excitement to
his life. But *whom* did he kill? He killed the attractive young
women of one borough, Queens. "Queens was special to
me—very special. . . . Shooting someone in Queens was an
obsession." Why Queens? What was there about the borough that distinguished it from other residential areas? Why
did he hunt the streets of Queens, looking for a release of
what he called his "hostile aggression," wanting "to destroy
her because of what she represented"? Queens is the ultimate lower-middle-class family borough. To one who tot-
tered on the edge of the middle class, to one who was utterly
de-stabilized by the complexity of his illegitimacy, Queens
must have been the epitome of everything solid and desirable from which he felt excluded. It was entirely natural
then that, living in industrial blue-collar Yonkers, he would
(as do virtually all serial murderers) prey on one class
segment above him in the social hierarchy. When he wrote
to the public during his killings, he abased himself in a sense
by addressing them "from the cracks in the sidewalks of
New York City and from the ants that dwell in these cracks
and feed on the dried blood of the dead that has settled into
these cracks . . . from the gutters of New York City, which
are filled with dog manure, vomit, stale wine, urine and
blood." Waging his private war, he would raise himself from
the vomit in the gutter by destroying the most vulnerable
and beautiful possessions of those who excluded him.[65]

Late in his killings (as did Starkweather), he tried to raise
his class focus and kill further up the social ladder. He
prowled through middle-class suburban Huntington, but it
was too neat and did not "feel right" for his killings. He
even planned a massive assault upon the stately mansions of

Southampton, and went heavily armed to this "final assignment," in which "I'd have to kill as many as I could, as quickly as possible. That would give the demons meat for a long spell." Yet he called it off, explaining vaguely that it had begun to rain: "They wanted me to kill, but there had to be a nice day for it. Since the day had turned bad, they called the whole thing off." Was it the rain, or was it precisely the same reaction of intimidation that had stopped DeSalvo from preying on the mansions of the upper class? Intimidated by the very social standards his rebellion was protesting, he could only function near his own social niche. The essence of the process was encapsulated in Klausner's description of the killing of Virginia Voskerichian: "Looking into the houses, David thought they were privileged and secure. He remembers thinking he would like to have grown up in this community. . . . Then he saw a slight, attractive young woman walking toward him."[66]

As he had first anticipated, his first kill left him with a profound sense of personal fulfillment. "You just felt very good after you did it. It just happens to be satisfying, to get the source of blood. I felt that 'Sam' was relieved. I came through." Sam had allowed him to overcome his ambivalence and wreak revenge on the society that had nullified him. His only concern was his growing lack of empathy. "I no longer had any sympathy whatsoever for anybody. It's very strange. That's what worried me the most. I said, 'Well, I just shot some girl to death and yet I don't feel.'" Yet his mission was too important for him to quibble so: "The demons were turning me into a soldier. A soldier can't stop every time he shoots someone and weep. He simply shoots the enemy. They were people I had to kill. I can't stop and weep over them. You have to be strong and . . . you have to survive." The rebel was now at war. "You're a soldier in both cases," he explained. "In the United States Army you can't stop to feel grief. You desensitize yourself."[67]

We are a strange species, *Homo sapiens,* for we are often the very things we hate: as Bundy the disguised and illegitimate sex murderer lambasted the FBI as "bastards, fornicators and imposters," so Berkowitz the empty rebel raged that "I hate rebels." He had struggled in former social incarnations to be different persons. He had worn coats of many clashing ideological colors: he had been the super patriot and the spit-and-polish soldier, the anti-violence Bohemian and the peace-loving Christian. Yet none of these persona could address themselves to the yawning chasm in his life. His soul could not rest nor his identity coalesce until the demons helped to unleash his terror upon the people, to "destroy all good and ruin people's lives." He would assault the warmth and security he coveted for himself and "get back on them for all the suffering."[68]

During the killings, much of his spoken and written rage was directed toward the parents—putative and otherwise—of himself ("son of the Evil One, Sam"), the grieving mother of Stacy Moskowitz ("the whore the harlot"), the mother of the bewildered neighbor Glassman ("I curse your mother's grave. I am pissing on her, Craig, urinating on her head"). But it was not mere mother rage that catapulted him into multiple murders: rather mothers stood as symbol and source of his relationship to the social order. In making war upon them and their daughters, he was merely reversing what he saw as their ancient privileges: "Some pretty girls at eighteen lived three times over, with all the attention they got. If a pretty girls dies, what the hell, she had a good time."[69]

Small wonder then that he had a smirk upon his face when he was led to jail. The photographers captured that smirk for all time and distributed it around the world, for he was now a figure of renown. His smirk was not that of one who despised his audience (as many journalists have since charged): rather, it was the smug and self-satisfied response of someone who was very shy, but who has been discovered to have done something marvelous, or to possess something wonderfully rare. Despite his claims of insanity, he was no different from any of our other multiple murderers: he killed for the same reasons as had all the others. The unwanted accident had claimed his identity in the process of taking his revenge. "It was only hostile aggression," he said. Looked at in terms of the central propositions of his culture, it made a certain sense to achieve fame and dignity through violent display. Now he would be a celebrity for all time, propelled by his acts from the suffocating anonymity of an illegitimate and friendless postal clerk living in a small apartment in a working-class neighborhood. "I had a job to do, and I was doing it," he had said manfully. For the price of incarceration—a trifling sum for one who has no social bonds—he had exacted his manhood and achieved a kind of immortality. Such an accomplishment surely buoys his spirits as he lives out his days in prison, holding court with his several biographers.[70]

THE MODERN MASS MURDERER

Part II

THE MODERN MASS
MURDERER

> "I know your character," he said to me. "His name is Erostratus. He wanted to become famous and he couldn't find anything better to do than to burn down the temple of Ephesus, one of the seven wonders of the world."
>
> "And what was the name of the man who built the temple?"
>
> "I don't remember," he confessed. "I don't believe anybody knows his name."
>
> "Really? But you remember the name of Erostratus? You see, he didn't figure things out too badly."
>
> JEAN-PAUL SARTRE, "Erostratus"

In general, mass murderers are similar to serial killers in that their acts are personalized social protest, and in that they are neither revolutionary nor deranged. Yet they are also very *different*. Mass killers are much more likely than serial killers to come from relatively stable lower-middle-class social backgrounds: only rarely, for example, are they adopted, illegitimate, or institutionalized during their childhoods. Moreover, they do not wish to use their killings as a catapult into international celebrity. Rather, they wish to avenge themselves in one sustained burst, and then *die*, knowing that the social statement that is their killings will give them a form of immortality.

During the course of their development, in one manner or another, they become intensely aware of the impossibility of bettering their condition. Starkweather experienced poverty and stigmatization throughout his brief life; Essex did not experience it until he left the warmth of his family and community for the racist embrace of the navy. Regardless, their confrontation with the social abyss renders their lives unbearable. Invariably, they choose to die in an explosion of violence directed at a group they feel oppresses, threatens, or excludes them. Thus, in the McDonald's massacre, Huberty murdered the Hispanics he felt had usurped his social position; Starkweather murdered the middle classes whom he felt despised him as "garbage"; and Essex murdered the whites who oppressed him.

Because Essex was black in a white-dominated and racist world, he touched a sensitive chord in the American psyche, and became a kind of revolutionary hero. Still, his protest was personal and racist, not progressive. When he shot the young woman kneeling at his feet while cradling her young dead husband in her arms, he no more killed whites to help his fellow blacks than Huberty killed Hispanics to help his fellow whites. In fact, it seems likely that Starkweather and Essex made their final commitment to the killings not for lofty ideological reasons at all, but because neither could come to terms with the degraded status in the only careers offered them by society—garbageman, and repairman of vending machines.

Thus, whether mass killers subsequently become "heroes" depends not on the internal motivation or coherence of what they do, but on the possibility that their personal protest is congruent with fashionable themes in the culture. In the two case studies that follow, Essex's anti-white assault was congruent with mainstream liberal thought, and it was therefore lauded, at least in radical circles. Starkweather's anti-middle-class assault, however, was incongruent with fashionable notions of the time, even threatening to the white liberal class: his killings were therefore dismissed as warped and adolescent, even in radical circles.

6.
DEAD PEOPLE ARE ALL ON THE SAME LEVEL

Charles Starkweather*

THE KILLING TIME

> "Shooting people was, I guess, a
> kind of thrill. It brought out
> something."
>
> CHARLES STARKWEATHER[1]

Painfully, he passed through his impoverished childhood, morbidly sensitive to his family's low estate, his entire being acutely attuned to every real or fancied social slight that came his way. By the time he reached adolescence, he was embittered and enraged—emotions which were only exacerbated by his degrading social position as garbageman (in which he felt perpetually imprisoned)—caring for the refuse of the rich, with no hope of escape. A brief but spectacular

---

* Portions of Starkweather's autobiography were printed as a magazine article, "Rebellion," and much more was reproduced in James M. Reinhardt's *The Murderous Trail of Charles Starkweather*. William Allen's thoughtful *Starkweather: the Story of a Mass Murderer* was also most useful, as was *Caril*, by Ninette Beaver, B. K. Ripley and Patrick Trese.

vendetta offered more to his spirit than an eternity of submission.

Starkweather killed first in a robbery. Soon after, he embarked upon his spree: a week-long burst of destruction during which he murdered ten more people. He was nineteen. His personal style mirrored rebellious adolescents' heroes of the day so successfully (especially the cult figure James Dean, who appeared in the film *Rebel Without a Cause*) that it lent his crimes an ominous air of impending insurrection. To neutralize this potential social threat, the media strove to invalidate him, dismissing him as merely "warped" and immature, a kind of meaningless adolescent fantasy. Thus the significance of his homicidal rage remained largely unexamined, as the authorities repudiated his message merely by refusing to decipher it.

His first kill took place during a routine gas station holdup, and it seemed to be an entirely pragmatic operation in which an inconvenient witness was silenced. Starkweather had known most of those who worked at the gas station, and he had memorized their routines. He also guessed that the new attendant would not recognize him with a bandana around his face. At 3 a.m. on December 1, 1957, carrying a twelve-gauge shotgun, he forced twenty-one-year-old Robert Colvert to hand over the money, a total of $108, then shoved him into his car and drove to a remote location outside their city of Lincoln, Nebraska. As they left the car, Colvert tried to grab the gun: "I got into a helluva fight and shooting gallery," Starkweather later recalled. "He shot himself the first time. He had ahold of the gun from the front, and I cocked it and he was messing around and he jerked it and the thing went off." As Colvert tried to stand up, Starkweather pressed the muzzle against the back of Colvert's head and pulled the trigger. "He didn't get up anymore." The killing filled Starkweather with sensations of serenity that he had not experienced since childhood; and left him with the feeling that he was now sufficiently powerful to violate the laws of man.[2]

He did not kill again immediately. He spent the next six weeks with his fourteen-year-old girlfriend, Caril Fugate, practicing knife-throwing and shooting, while the shape of his task crystallized in his mind. On the morning of January 21, 1958, carrying a cheap single-shot .22 bolt-action rifle, he visited Caril's home. An argument ensued, in the course of which Caril's mother, Velda Bartlett, told him she no longer wanted him to see Caril. At the height of the argument, according to Starkweather, "She didn't say nothing. She just got up and slammed the shit out of me . . . in the face." He left the shabby house, but returned a few minutes later to find Caril's step-father, Marion Bartlett, waiting for him in the kitchen: "The old man started chewing me out. I said to hell with him and was going to walk out through the front door, and he helped me out. Kicked me right in the ass. My tail hurt for three days." He returned to the Bartlett home that afternoon to find Caril and her mother "yelling their heads off." Caril's mother turned to him and accused him of impregnating Caril, and then, according to Starkweather, "she got up and slapped the shit out of me again . . . in the head . . . both sides. I hauled off and hit her one back . . . in the head . . . my hand wasn't closed . . . it knocked her back a couple of steps. She let out a cry, a war cry or something, and the old man came flying in. He picked me up . . . by the neck . . . and started carrying me to the front door. I kicked him somewhere and he put me down. We started wrestling around in the front room. . . . Then he took off for the other room. I knew what he was heading for [a weapon] so I thought I'd head for the same thing."[3]

As Starkweather hurriedly slipped a cartridge in the .22, Marion Bartlett ran at him with a claw hammer: the bullet struck him in the head and he collapsed. Verna Bartlett entered the room carrying a large kitchen knife. As Starkweather remembered the events: "The old lady Bartlett said she was going to chop my head off, and I loaded the gun again . . . the old lady started to take a few steps towards me . . . and Caril jerked the gun away and said she'd blow her to hell. . . . The old lady got mad and knocked her down . . . I grabbed the gun from Caril . . . I just turned around and shot her" in the face. "She went on by, heading for the little girl [Caril's two-and-a-half-year-old half-sister, Betty Jean Bartlett] . . . she just stopped, and I thought she was going to pick up the girl, but she never, she just turned around and looked at me again . . . and I hit her with the butt of the gun . . . she fell down, but she wasn't quite all the way down, so I hit her again . . . she just laid there . . . after I hit the old lady, I just came up with the butt of the gun and hit the little girl . . . she fell down against the kind of table . . . stood there screaming . . . Caril was yelling at her to shut up."[4]

According to Starkweather, Caril then informed him that her step-father was still alive in the bedroom. "I picked up the knife that the old lady had . . . and started to walk in there, in the bedroom . . . and the little girl kept yelling, and I told her to shut up, and I started to walk again, and just turned around and threw the kitchen knife I had at her . . . they said it hit her in the throat, but I thought it hit her in the chest. I went on into the bedroom. Mr. Bartlett was moving around quite a bit, so I tried to stab him in the throat, but the knife wouldn't go in [so] I just hit the top part of it with my hand, and it went in." He stabbed Mr. Bartlett several more times in the throat and waited to make sure he was dead. Then he reloaded the gun and sat down to watch television—"I don't even remember what was on. I just wanted some noise," he later told police. "It was too quiet." Later, they wrapped the bodies in rugs and bed-clothes, stuffed Caril's mother down the outhouse seat, left the baby's body on the seat, and then dragged the step-father's body into the chicken coop.[5]

The young couple did a cursory cleaning of the house, removing some of the blood and mess. They then remained in the house as lovers for six days. "To Charlie," his biographer William Allen observed, "the best week in his life was under way. The criminologist James Reinhardt quoted him as saying that they lived like kings, that he had never had a more wonderful time, that at last there was nobody to order them around. He felt no guilt because of what he had done." For six days, they fended off various callers with excuses. Concerned relatives continued to call the police, but the police did not enter the house when they arrived there: they were mollified by the polite reception they received, and by the sign on the door that read, "Stay a way Every Body is sick with the Flue." When it finally appeared to the couple that they might be discovered, they left Lincoln in Starkweather's car: the bodies were found a few hours later, and the police issued an alert.[6]

Charles Starkweather and Caril Fugate drove to the farm of seventy-year-old August Meyer, an old friend of the Starkweather family: they had broken bread together many times, as Starkweather had often hunted on Meyer's property, making a gift to Meyer of half of what he had shot. However, Meyer's lane was mired in mud and melting snow, and the car soon got stuck. Later, Starkweather claimed that was why he had decided to kill Meyer: "Caril got pissed off because we got stuck. She said we ought to go up and blast the shit out of him because he didn't shovel his lane. I said it, too." After several attempts failed to free the car, they walked to the farm. In reconstructing the murder, Starkweather claimed—as he would with all the murders he committed—that it had been "self defense." As he remembered it, he had asked Meyer for a horse to pull the car out of the mud; but, inexplicably, he said, "I got into a helluva argument with Meyer. He couldn't understand why I got stuck there. He thought we should have gotten stuck up closer to his house."[7]

After a heated discussion, according to Starkweather, Meyer said he was going into the house to get his coat, but appeared instead on the porch with a rifle and fired at him. "I felt the bullet go by my head," but Meyer's rifle jammed after the first shot. "Meyer started running back in the house, and I shot him . . . at almost point-blank range with the sawed-off .410 [shotgun]." He dragged Meyer's body to the wash-house and covered it with a blanket. When Meyer's dog approached them, he shot the dog. He then ransacked the house, eating Jell-O and cookies, and stealing what cash he could find (less than $100), along with socks, gloves, a shirt, a straw hat, and a .22 pump-action repeating rifle. They took a brief nap before making another attempt to extricate their car. They soon realized that their frantic digging with a single shovel was in vain. Eventually, they were freed by a passing farmer who tied his truck to the car and pulled it out of the mud. Curiously, Starkweather insisted that the farmer take two dollars for the job, and let him go with profuse thanks. Within moments, the car was mired once more.[8]

Carrying Meyer's .22 rifle and Bartlett's sawed-off .410 shotgun, they abandoned the car and walked down the road until they were offered a lift by two popular and conservative local high-school students, seventeen-year-old Robert Jensen and his fiancée, Carol King. Starkweather later claimed that at this point he had toyed with the idea of telephoning a policeman he knew and turning himself in; but, he said, he did not relish the idea of being "captured" by the chubby young Jensen, thereby making Jensen into a kind of hero. After a few moments' ambivalence, he threatened Jensen with his gun, took his money, and ordered him to drive to a nearby abandoned school. As Jensen walked down the steps of the school's storm cellar, Starkweather shot him from behind. He later claimed that Jensen had tried to grab his gun, but, regardless, Jensen was shot six times in the left ear. He gave several conflicting statements regarding how he had then killed King; but he was alone with her in the cellar for some fifteen minutes. He originally said that he had shot her when she began to scream, but later claimed that Caril had shot her.[9]

Their bodies were not found until the following day. Jensen was fully clothed and was lying on his stomach in a pool of blood at the bottom of the stairs. King was partly nude and was lying on top of Jensen. Her coat had been pulled over her head, her jeans and panties pulled down around her ankles, and her lower body was streaked with blood and mud. Several stab wounds had been directed at her groin, one of them extending through the wall of the cervix into the rectum. An autopsy found internal damage to the vagina, the cervix, and the rectum, caused by an undetermined sharp instrument, but the examiners found no indication of sexual attack and no presence of sperm. Starkweather later admitted that he had been "tempted" to rape King, and that he had "pulled her jeans down," but he was reluctant to admit that he had been involved in her mutilation and insisted that Caril had done it out of jealousy.[10]

He later claimed that after they left the murder scene, he

decided to abandon the spree and turn himself in to the police. "She kept trying to talk me out of it," he insisted. "We was going down shooting on the highway. I told her I was going to give myself up and she said no I wasn't. I said yes I was and she said no I wasn't." Undoubtedly, however, the reality was that he was merely airing his misgivings and anxieties, for there was no one to stop him had he truly wished to quit. Fascinated by their own accomplishments, they continued to argue about whether to go and live with Starkweather's brother in the state of Washington. Then ("incredibly," according to the commentators), after driving for three hours in the direction of Washington, they turned the car around and headed back to Lincoln. Allen wrote that Starkweather tried to explain this decision with facile claims "that he had been too tired to go on, he had to get some rest [and] the car wasn't running well either, and he thought it would be easier to pick up another one in Lincoln," but these claims make no sense: both rest and alternate automobiles would have been obtained more safely elsewhere. The fact of the matter seems to be that they wished to view their exploits and to complete the pillaging of their community. They drove past Caril's house to see if the police had discovered the bodies of her family, and accelerated away quickly when they saw the police gathered around the house. From there, they drove to a section of Lincoln that had special meaning to Starkweather, and would play an important role in the fulfillment of his task—"the wealthy Country Club section of town." It was not yet dawn. They fell asleep in their parked car.[11]

Ostensibly, their plan was to spend the day in one of the mansions, then steal a car, and leave by stealth at nightfall. Starkweather would not be moving in a strange environment, for he knew it well from his job on the garbage route. Although he had not collected garbage from the house they ultimately selected, he had often done so from the same area's estates (or performed odd jobs in them), and he knew the names and occupations of many of the inhabitants. As they drove through the neighborhood, he pointed out several possibilities to Caril before settling on a mansion belonging to forty-seven-year-old industrialist C. Lauer Ward, president of bridge-building and steel companies, and a well-known and highly regarded Lincoln business figure. His wife, Clara, forty-six, was a graduate of the University of Nebraska and, like Ward, was active in community affairs. Lillian Fencl, fifty-one, had been the Wards' maid for twenty-six years.[12]

Mr. Ward was out at work, but Mrs. Ward was upstairs when, brandishing their weapons, Starkweather and Caril forced the maid Fencl to admit them to the house. When Mrs. Ward came downstairs, she was ordered to sit at the table. The women soon asked if they could do housework while they waited, and Starkweather grew bored with watching them. He spent several hours wandering through the mansion's elegant rooms, fascinated by the opulence. Before noon, he ordered Mrs. Ward, *not* the maid, to serve him pancakes in the library, and then petulantly changed his order to waffles. "They was real nice to us," he told Reinhardt. "And I took it while I had it. I knowed it couldn't last long." In the early afternoon, Mrs. Ward asked if she might go upstairs, and when Starkweather went to check on her a few moments later, he said, "she took a shot at me . . . she just stepped out of the boy's room and she took a shot at me with the .22 . . . she started going for the top of the steps . . . I had the knife . . . I threw the knife at her. . . . It stuck to her back . . . she was moaning and groaning . . . I dragged her into her bedroom . . . I laid her on her bed and just left her there." When the Ward's dog began to pester him, he broke its neck with a blow from his rifle butt. He then made certain that Mrs. Ward was secure: "I put the rope around her, or I took a sheet and cut the sheet and put a piece of sheet around her mouth and hands . . . after that I bound her feet and hands and covered her up."[13]

That afternoon, he telephoned his father and, without giving away his location, asked him to deliver a message to his estranged friend, Robert Von Busch, that he (Starkweather) intended to kill him for trying to come between him and Caril. He also wrote a letter, styled as if it had been written from both Caril and himself, addressed to "the law only," and offering a measure of explanation.

"Then ne and chuck live with each other and nonday the day the bodys were found, we were going to kill our selves but BOB VON BRUCK and everybody would not stay a way . . . and [I] hate my older sister and bob for what they are they all ways wanted ne to stop going with chuck snow that sone Kid bob Kwen [knew] would go with ne . . . i feel sorry for Bar, and have a ask [ass] like bob. I and Caril are sorry for what has happen, cause I have hurt every body cause of it and so has caril. but i'n saying one thing every body that cane out there was luckie there not *dead* even caril's sister [sic]."[14]

When Mr. Ward returned to his home at 6 p.m., he was confronted at the door by Starkweather: Ward grabbed the gun and tried to wrest it from him, but Starkweather managed to push him down the basement steps. He raced down behind Ward to retrieve the .22 rifle which had also fallen into the basement, and as he did so, Ward tried to run back up the stairs. Starkweather shot him in the back. Despite his wounds, Ward continued running through the kitchen and living-room, and had opened the front door when Starkweather shot him again. "It probably struck him in the head," he later recalled. "I was standing about five feet from him, maybe less . . . I asked him if he was all right and he didn't answer." After this, he forced the maid Fencl upstairs and tied her up, stealing ten dollars from her and seven dollars from Mrs. Ward. He denied any involvement in killing Fencl, but Caril later insisted that he had tied her legs and hands to the bed and "started stabbing her, and she started screaming and hollering . . . he put a pillow over her face . . . every time he stabbed her she moaned . . . he said he didn't think she was ever going to die . . . and he cut the strips holding her legs and covered her over [with] a blanket that laid on the bed."[15]

The bodies were discovered the following morning when a concerned business associate stopped by the home to ask why Ward had not appeared at the office. He found Lauer Ward inside the front door, with bullet wounds in his temple and back, and a stab wound in the neck. Clara Ward, clad only in a nightgown, was lying on the floor in one of the bedrooms, with multiple stab wounds to her neck, chest, and back. Lillian Fencl's body was tied to a bed in another bedroom, her chest, stomach, hands, arms, and legs covered with many stab wounds.[16]

Now there were nine known dead. The surrounding population responded with fearful alacrity: the governor called out the National Guard, whose members began cruising the streets in jeeps armed with mounted machine guns: "False tips, weird and fantastic rumors added to the situation. People began to fly apart. Work and school ground to a halt. The panic and confusion spread," Allen recorded.[17]

Now piloting Ward's black Packard limousine, Starkweather and Caril turned west once more, heading for the state of Washington. Starkweather later stated that, as they drove, they threw notes out of the car, informing the world of what they had done. They drove through the night, not stopping until they reached a small town near the Wyoming border. There they filled the Packard with gas and themselves with candy bars and nine bottles of Pepsi-Cola before continuing their journey. Worried that the police might be looking for their conspicuous limousine, Starkweather began looking for a replacement. He found it when he saw a Buick parked off the highway, with thirty-seven-year-old salesman, Merle Collison, asleep on the front seat. He awakened Collison and demanded that the two of them trade cars. When Collison refused, Starkweather opened fire with the .22. The results of the autopsy later showed that the salesman had been shot in the nose, cheek, neck, chest, left arm, right wrist, and left leg. Starkweather's own account of the killing was especially contradictory, perhaps because, as Reinhardt suggested, he felt embarrassed by the murder, since its "cold-bloodedness" made it difficult for him to rationalize his usual "self-defense" plea. According to Reinhardt, he thought that he would be considered cowardly because of the way in which the salesman had been murdered; and his solution to the problem was to settle finally on a story that implicated Caril in the killing.[18]

In the meantime, Collison's corpse had slumped forward and jammed in the front seat. As Starkweather tried to shove the body out of the car, another car drove by. "I thought they had had an accident," the driver, a geologist, later testified, "so I turned my car around and came back. . . . Then I asked, 'Can I help you?' He straightened up with a rifle he had behind him and said, 'Raise your hands. Help me release the emergency brake or I'll kill you.' It was then I noticed the dead man behind the wheel. As I approached him, I grabbed at the gun and we fought for it in the middle of the highway. I knew that if he won I would be dead, so I managed to wrestle it from him." As the two of them struggled for the gun, a Wyoming Deputy Sheriff drove past and stopped his car. Caril immediately ran toward his cruiser and jumped in, telling the sheriff, "He's killed a man." Starkweather freed himself from the geologist and, seeing the danger, drove off quickly in the Packard, heading back east toward the town of Douglas, Wyoming. The sheriff called ahead for a roadblock and started off in pursuit: soon he was joined by other cruisers, all pursuing Starkweather into Douglas at a hundred miles per hour. The entire chase clogged in the town's traffic until police began shooting at the Packard's tires and the traffic quickly dispersed. They then cleared the town at speeds rising to 120 miles per hour, and continued until police bullets finally smashed the Packard's rear window. Within seconds of the window's disintegration, Starkweather stopped suddenly in the middle of the highway. He seemed to have thought he had been shot, since he was bleeding copiously from one ear: in fact, he had merely been cut by a piece of flying glass. He left the car and, despite the fact that police were shooting at the ground in front of him, he insisted curiously on carefully adjusting his shirt-tails before he lay face down on the road and surrendered. The arresting officer later told reporters that Starkweather was meek once he was captured: "He thought he was bleeding to death. That's why he stopped. That's the kind of yellow son of a bitch he is." He made no comment on Starkweather's fastidiousness with his shirt.[19]

His murderous spree was over; but his task was only beginning to flower. Allen described his *performance* as the officers escorted this mad-dog killer to Nebraska's State

Penitentiary. The party was met by a "crowd of newsmen, photographers, and movie cameramen. Caril, her head covered by a scarf, smiled tightly into the lenses. Charlie pretended to ignore the attention, but nevertheless was the better subject. Bloodied, in chains, shabby-haired, a cigarette dangling from his lips, wearing his black leather motorcycle jacket, tight black denim pants, blue and white cowboy boots with a butterfly design on the toes—he was a perfect-looking young rebel-killer."[20]

THE KILLER AS AUTOBIOGRAPHER

> "Why did it have to happen to me?
> It is not fair . . . it is not right . . .
> why was the world against me?"
>
> CHARLES STARKWEATHER[21]

It is clear that this embittered and impoverished garbageman thought of his killing spree as an organized retributive task, governed by the rules that regulate warfare. He expressed some regret that he had shot the sleeping salesman, "but I had to shoot quick. It was the end, I guess. People will remember that last shot. I hope they'll read my story. They'll know why then. They'll know that the salesman just happened to be in there. I didn't put him there and he didn't know I was coming. . . . When soldiers have to take a place or do something they don't ask if there's any children and old people, women, or is anybody asleep?" Like a soldier, he was only following the dictates of a higher plan. It made sense then that these "things didn't bother me. . . . How could I be particular about people I had to kill?" What does he mean when he says he *"had"* to kill?

Curiously, his recounting of the killings changed over time, and were issued in radically different versions—so much so that, according to the journalist N. Beaver and her colleagues, "before his trial began, Starkweather had made seven statements of record, all of which conflicted or contradicted each other in at least one respect." Each successive version was more detailed, and seemed to implicate Caril more, but the reader is left wondering whether his motive was accuracy or revenge.[22]

His lengthy autobiography makes it clear that there were only two dimensions of the universe that moved him deeply, his hatred for humanity and his love of nature. Even the house in which he grew up was tainted by its association with humanity, for it was a construction of human beings, designed to illustrate their mean hierarchical motives—"the house was [a] shabby white one story structure," he said. But when he left the works of mankind and tuned in to those of nature, he waxed as poetical as can be expected from a virtually illiterate young man. "I was raised in this house through most of my childhood, the place to me looked like a [sic] enchanted forest, with its large trees surrounding the house, and at times in the evenings when the sun was setting in its tender glory, with its beautiful colors in the western sky, and the birds singing in their melodys that came softly from the trees—everything was nice and pretty, so peaceful, and tranquil—it was as though time itself was standing still. I fell in love with this adventurous land in my earlier days, and the flames still burns [sic] deep down inside of me for the love of that enchanted forest."[23]

My Fighting Reputation

If his entire being is discolored with hatred, if all his memories are filled with the terrible insults that generated his rage, they seem trivial indeed when examined closely. The slights and humiliations he remembered were surely the lot of a major portion of humanity: he was, for example, always the last boy to be picked for teams, but what artist and intellectual in this century has not whined about the same experience? He was always teased about his red hair and bowed legs, but who passes through childhood without having his or her physical peculiarities singled out and giggled over? These are sadnesses, to be sure, for children are as cruel to one another as adults; but they are not what any analyst can easily accept as justification or explanation for mass murder.

Still, there can be no doubt that he hurt intensely, nor any doubt that he reacted to those wounds with sullen rage. "My rebellion against the world started that first day in school," he wrote, "and from that first day I became rebellious. I had stayed in my rebellious mood even to this day. Why had I become rebellious against the World and its human race?—cause that first day in school I was being made fun at, picked on, laughed at. Why were they making fun of me? My speech for one thing and the other was my legs, I was a little bowlegged [sic]. I those younger years of my life I haded builded [sic] up a hate that was as hard as iron and when people tease, make fun of and laugh at a little youngster in hers [sic] or his early childhood, that little youngster is not going to forget it. I wouldn't deny I was like a hound prowling for fights, quarrelling, and doing wild things and placing everyone among my enemies. Kids picking on me and not having a thing to do with me caused me to have black moods, at least that is what I call them, cause most of the time, I would just sit in one place and stay motionless in a gloomy manner and it was obvious that there was no reasoning with me when in one of my black mood [sic] and Boys and girls that I knew didn't bother me while I was in my motionless and gloomy manner, they would just let me and stay in my Black mood and even to this day I still have them melancholy moods."[24]

In his memory, the entire pattern of his life was encapsulated in the first day of school. "School that first morning we didn't go to much, Mrs. Mott let everyone play and do what they wanted, I didn't get along that day in school with the others, they made me a little mad but more upset than anything else, they didn't seem to want to have anothing [sic] to do with me, not let me play with them or anything else and thats the reason I played in the sandbox by myself that first morning, everybody left when I came over to play with them in the sandbox, they'd left went off among some other girls and boys talking about me, because out of corner [sic] of my eye, I glanced at them, the girls giggling and boys giving off their snickers, then they wented [sic] off occupying them selves to some other simple tasks." Was this some form of paranoiac madness? Did he seriously expect us to believe that a sad incident in a sandbox created a multiple murderer? He swore we should. Could a child that young be so class conscious? "I said to myself that some day I'd pay them all back, and a overwhelming sense of outrage grew, it roused itself in my mind for a wild thirsting revenge, I wanted in general revenge upon the world and its human race, my mind and heart became black with hatred as it builded [sic] up in me, a drawn veil of a dilatory cloud seem [sic] to come before my face, the tribute was gratifying, I could not anglyze nor recoqnice [sic] my emotions as I broked [sic] down into tears . . . I had the whole sandbox to myself." Is this ludicrous self-pity, or supersensitivity?[25]

If he overstated the significance of the first day of school, there can be no doubt that he accurately described a growing conviction which formed early enough in life for his rampage to start at the age of nineteen. "The hate that became strong inside of me when I was a youngster by those who were making fun and always teasing me are the ones that started me to fight. I would beat them down and if I had to I would beat them down again until they knew that I wasn't going to take it from them. At times and with the right emphasis my attitude was merely a sporadic outburst, but at other times as I realized now was something thronie [sic], when I was fighting those who picked on me, I fought fast and a little furiously like a mamiac [sic] in rage and fury and as I fought sense of outrage grew to striving, to throw, to bend, to hurt and most of all to beat those who teased me, but as I fought the general opinion of school kids became particularly that I had a reputation for meanness or generosity and that word REPUTATION . . . as many other kids know is a hard thing to stand up to at times, when they say that your [sic] a fighter and have the reputation for doing nothing but fighting and then there's going to be a few kids like yourself that are going to fight and try to take that reputation away from the other fellow."[26]

"My fighting repretation [sic] stayed with me throughout my school years and even after I had stopped going to school that repetation [sic] stayed with me, but my rebellion started against the world and the human race when I was being maded [sic] fun at and that being made fun at is what cause my fights when I was a youngster, but I assure you thats not the reason for fighting when I gew [sic] up but the hatred I had builded up inside of me stayed with me and it made [me] hate everybody other than my family, but with that strong hatred, a person wouldn't look at me cross eye without getting into a fist fight. My speech and bowllegs [sic] were my main cause for being made fun at as I grew older my speech defect was over come and I can now pronounce [sic] words with a defined and correct pronunciation as well as anyone else and for my bowllegs [sic], their [sic] just as crokked [sic] as before, I have never been able to grow out of them and if I have to say so myself, I believe a pig could run between them without touching the sides." In this vein, he described his childhood as a succession of cruel humiliations, as, for example, when a gang of boys took one of his paintings. They "all gathered around the boy that had my painting and right away they started making wise cracks about it. . . . The boy with my picture . . . said, 'this is a piece of junk, besides being a red head, bowlleged [sic], wood pecker—you can't even draw,' and at that, tore it in half and as the laughter and giggling began he glanced around at them and finished ripping it into little pieces . . . then one of the girls yelled searcastily [sic] he's going to cry—hes [sic] a cry baby then they started in the red headed bowlleged [sic] wood pecker is a cry baby."[27]

An important problem here is that while Starkweather remembered a childhood of rage and fighting, no one else remembered him in this way. A neighbor told Reinhardt that "Charles was a pretty quiet sort of boy most of the time"; his parents thought that he was "a normal boy"; and Reinhardt "could find no evidence in Charles' school record that Charles' citizenship was adjudged 'bad' by any teacher. In fact his 'citizenship' record was rather consistently above average. There were no differences of opinion among his former teachers as to whether he could be considered a behavior problem; though I found none who apparently thought that his outward show of pugnacity, his explosive temper, and withdrawal tendencies were signs of deep seated disturbances." The school's psychologist had reported that "many students lack his special insight, but his difficulty was in actually dealing with what he saw, and how to appropriate it. Here he showed inadequacy." Similarly, a school counselor concluded that "he did not have as many fights as he claimed he had," and a teacher suggested: "He is inclined to be timid, doesn't associate too easily but gets along well enough with boys; not so well with girls. Doesn't like to participate in games with other children, either indoors or out." Another thought that "he seems especially fond of two of his brothers and fond of his mother. . . . Often refers to the attention and care that his mother has given him."[28]

What is the significance of the great disparity between Starkweather's autobiography and the memories of those who observed him? It is not necessary, I think, to deduce from this that one or the other lied, or was misled: likely the fights were real enough in Starkweather's tormented imagination. More important, what are we to make of the warmth and pride that characterized his relationship with his family, especially his mother? Should not our killers come from ruthlessly abusive families in order to fit our preconceptions?

Something Worth Killing For

His alienation from the world was intensified by his reaction to the women he pursued. Before he met Caril, he later wrote, "Yes, I went out with girls, some were mild dates with nice Christian girls, but most of the girls I went out with, were either the gibberty-gibbet type, that used too much make-up, and dressed in expensive clothes, or they were the harlot type, that weren't hard to get a date with, and easy to get along with. I had my fights that seem to happen every other day, and like almost everybody, I had my dreams of things I wanted. But of all the dreams, fights, and women to me none of then [sic] ever seen [sic] to fit in this world. I guess that's what I meant when I said, 'I don't know life, or what it was good for,' and the reason I didn't know, I just didn't take time to fine [sic] out. When I was younger, I always said to my self that I was going to have the knowledge of what life was good for in this world, but as I grew older, the more I didn't care to fine [sic] out, and that's the reason why I didn't have time."[29]

His adolescent fantasy-woman was revealed in his response to a drawing Reinhardt showed him of a well-dressed and clearly middle-class woman standing in front of a garden wall and surrounded by modern patio furniture: she was "the kind of girl I used to think I'd like to have . . . [but] that kind a girl would look like hell in my kind a surrounding . . . you got a give the right kind a place to be in," he told Reinhardt. But the reality was that before he met Caril, "nobody could ever ask me how I was getting along with my girl friend. Until I met Caril I never had the kind a kid gets along with. I had a nice girl once, but she got to upsetting my death deal and I had to drop her. . . . Nobody cared about me and my girl friends anyhow. . . . One thing sure I never give nobody much a chance to be dirty to me if I didn't have to." Previous women, then, were either unsuitable in terms of social class, or would interfere with his already rapidly coalescing "death deal."[30]

When he met Caril, everything seemed to slip into place. The liaison spawned no fantasies of conventional marriage and family; and it could not be expected to since its purpose was to provide a romantic and sexual adjunct to his task. Once contracted, the relationship grew obsessive, so much so that he quit his job in order to be free to meet Caril when she walked home from school, perhaps afraid that she might turn to another. Now his identity was fully formed, his task clarifying: "Having Caril with me doing the things we was doing together as the end was coming on was different from anything I'd ever had before. It didn't seem real somehow." He knew that he did not have "much future with Caril," but "whatever it was, was for the both of us." With Caril beside him, his purpose gained in meaning: "One time I was afraid to die, I used to want to shoot up the world for no reason, I used to want to throw garbage in somebody's face, I was mad at the world. Then Caril made things clear; then everything had a reason. I knowed the end was coming, but it had a reason too." Through his relationship with her, it was possible for him to understand why he "hated the world." "I was something to her. She never cared what I looked like. I looked good to her and she liked me because I lived in a shack and she thought whatever I done was good, and if I didn't do no drawing or drive no hot rods that was good too." "She meant something that nothing else had ever meant . . . I knowed that without her it was going right back to the hated world I was trying to leave . . . I started a new kind of thinking after I met her, and it all ended me right here [sic]. It was something to live for, something to live with. How long? It didn't matter. We had to be together," he told Reinhardt. "That's the way it looked then . . . to live with Caril and die with Caril. Anyways I wanted her to see me go down shooting it out and knowing it was for her, for us; I guess for all this hateful world had made us for."[31]

Yet, this great love would not survive trial and imprisonment. If the first words he had blurted out to the arresting officer had been that his beloved had had nothing whatever to do with the murders, his position soon wavered, then reversed itself. Once he was incarcerated, he began to implicate Caril in the killings, and his emotions for her changed rapidly, and without apparent provocation, from love to hate. "My feelings towards Caril are of great regret for ever knowing her," Starkweather wrote, sitting at his table in his cell in the Nebraska State Penitentiary. "Our love in the beginning was very ardent and passionate. But as time went along our love tapered off to emotional passion and then began to fade out. Today my love for Caril is completely dead." If within hours of his capture he had written his parents denying Caril's involvement in the murders—"But dad i'm not real sorry for what i did cause for the first time me and Caril have more fun, she help me a lot, but if she comes back don't hate her she had *not* a thing to do with the killing all we wanted to do is get out of town [sic]"—within days he was insisting that Caril had killed two of the women victims. How appropriate this conclusion was, for the relationship had served its purpose both in hardening his resolve and adding sexual excitement to his task. She no longer played a meaningful role in his life and she now could take her place with the rest of humanity as the enemy. A few months later, he was willing to testify against her in court, and it was this testimony that was one of the prime factors that ensured her conviction.[32]

Death's Pursuit

"The world is lifeless anyhow,
like the people I killed."
CHARLES STARKWEATHER[33]

He looked at life through curiously deadened eyes: little wonder then that all he saw seemed "lifeless." Paradoxically, the only thing that gave meaning to this universe of death-in-life was his adolescent fascination with death. Reinhardt noted that by the time Starkweather was seventeen, two years before the killings erupted, he had become "obsessed with a recurring delusion that Death had him 'marked,'" and he took a "strange bewildering delight" in the thought. This delusion came to him in almost corporeal form when he was seventeen. "She comed [sic] in a dream," Starkweather remembered of Death's first appearance to him. "She tolded [sic] me . . . don't be in no hurry. I won't let you forget. One time Death comed [sic] to me with a coffin and tolded [sic] me to get in . . . then the coffin sailed away with me in it till it comed [sic] to a big fire . . . the coffin sort of melted, I guess, I was down there on a street with great flames of fire on each side of me. But it wasn't hot like I'd always thought hell would be . . . it was more like beautiful flames of gold . . . then I woke up."[34]

Similarly, Reinhardt observed that "Charles had other Death dreams when no word was spoken. These he believed were sent to remind him that 'earth-time' was running out." Starkweather explained this closing tryst with death: "For always after one of those dreams I had a accident just like the one in the dream, only it wasn't so bad. . . . Oh, but it was not just in dreams [that Death came]. She comed [sic] when I was awake, too." Most often, Death came to his bedroom window just before dawn when he was still asleep. "I don't know how it was," he remembered, "but I would

always wake up and see her standing there in the window
. . . and all I could see would be the part from the waist up.
It was a kind of half human and half bear . . . only it didn't
have no neck. It just tapered off from a big chest to a small
pointed head. . . . It didn't have no arms and no ears."
These mystical visitations were sometimes accompanied by
"mournful" whistling sounds: "It was close and loud at first,
but it got further and further away and the sound became
mournful and sad until I couldn't hear it no more. . . . For
about a minute or two, I couldn't move my legs or arms."
Yet Death instilled no fear in him: "The world on the other
side couldn't be as bad as this one. . . . Besides, nobody has
to tell me what a mean world this is . . . I knowed that
Death was coming, but I never thought it would be coming
like this," he told Reinhardt. "Eleven people dead who
wasn't expecting her and me here waiting." This mingled
contempt and fascination for Death explained his love of
fast and dangerous cars, for they assured him that "death
was close by." He had even considered helping Death by
crashing the car: "But, I guess if she had wanted any help
she'd a tolded me.[sic]"[35]

In a fundamental sense, Death became what he pursued,
as it pursued him. He dreamt of "snarling faces, dreams of
wishing death would come soon. Then I got so death was a
friend." With Caril beside him, he would pursue death in
the grand manner, making his mark upon the universe in a
way no garbageman could, leaving messages that "couldn't
rub out, like tracks cut in a rock." With Caril, "something
worth killing for had come. The thought of dying was old to
me. Something to live for, before dying, was new. . . . Why
run away from Caril, why run from death, why go back to
the hate and shame and hiding, when all that I wanted, all
that was left was mine until the clock run down." He
understood that his destiny had become "to live with Caril
and die with Caril. Anyways I wanted her to see me go down
shooting it out and knowing it was for her, for us; I guess for
all this hateful world have [sic] made us for. . . . Sometimes
I thought about murdering the whole human race. I never
thought much about killing individuals."[36]

As he waited for death in his prison cell one night, his
victims came to him "in a dream," he told Reinhardt. They

gazed at him through the bars in the same way that Death had stared at him through his bedroom window. The ghost of the farmer August Meyer spoke to him: "You can't get out this way," Starkweather remembered him saying, "you'll have to go another way." When he recounted the dream, he concluded that "it makes everything even . . . it evens what I done and what everybody is [sic] done. . . . These people were in my way." He even abandoned his fate to God, most forcefully when he was asked if he thought his sentence might be commuted: "Not if the old man upstairs is satisfied with me the way I am. What do I mean? Well, I'll tell you . . . if He thinks I've suffered enough He'll let me go to the chair, [but if He does not] well, the old man wouldn't have nothing else to do but give me life. The old man upstairs wouldn't double-cross Death."[37]

Without regret, he would leave the universe that to his deadened eyes appeared as little more than a barren moonscape. "The world is lifeless anyhow, like the people I killed. It is just a hell of a world. It ain't worthy going back to anyhow." [When] "I go to the chair, I'll be no more dead than the people I killed. They was buried and their relatives grieved. Only my mother would grieve for me. But millions will read about me, I guess, and talk about me, don't you think?" It was satisfaction enough that he would leave this sign of his passage.[38]

Class Consciousness

> "They had me numbered for the bottom."
>
> CHARLES STARKWEATHER[39]

His loathing of the social system and its infinite gradations was matched in intensity only by his romantic and sentimentalized view of nature. As he wrote: "I found the beauty of the country side, in forest and woods of so many times while camping or hunting. At times instead of hunting I would set down against a large tree, and enjoy the scenery that made me delightfully full of satisfaction . . . my neck would be bent back as I gazed above and between the jagged limbs, and branches of greenish, brown, and yellowish foliage, into the sky of miles, and miles, of undiscover, unknown previously [sic] existence, and the more I sat and gaze [sic] into the far miles of the sky a wave of something would come over me, something like directness, and frankness, in a fascinating world away from that of noncommited civilization." Yet if he loved nature for its own qualities, it was clear that its prime attribute for him was as a counterpoint to civilization and humanity. Inevitably, humanity would intrude and spoil his reverie—"Sometimes the dreams . . . would disappear with a quick flash at hearing the snap of a twig, or the sound of a voice," and when the spell was broken, an "irresistible, and irresponsible feeling would sweep over my soul." In the night, occasional horrifying dreams would awaken him with a start, and only the shaft of moonlight across his bed could calm him. "Sometimes," he told Reinhardt, "it took me away from the things I hated . . . it made me forget." The moonlight's glow would help him to forget his poverty temporarily, to forget the worn curtains and the broken furniture, and perhaps even hint at mitigation: "I knowed [sic] better, but that I imagined, I guess, it was what I wanted to imagine."[40]

None of our multiple murderers had quite such an anguished awareness of his position at the bottom of the social hierarchy, and only the killer Mark Essex seemed to have felt such enraged despair. In the midst of this, Starkweather sympathetically recognized the impotence of his own slum-dwelling family. "My dad ain't to blame . . . I just got fed up with having nothing and being nobody. . . . Poverty gives you nothing. People who are poor take what they can get." Marriage and a conventional career were pointless, for "it would be the same thing all over again." One of Caril's prime attractions was that she "never cared what I looked like. . . . When we would go together there would be no 'uppity' kids from big houses whose old man was a doctor or president of a bank. We'd make people the way we wanted to make them." He recognized and felt profoundly the hidden injuries of class: "What did not make this world a good place to live in was that nobody cared about me for what I could do. They hated me because of the way I looked, and because I was poor and had to live in a goddamned shack; it didn't matter what we all loved each other; that my mother worked hard away from home to help support us children, and washed our clothes and cooked and got us off to school. All these goddamn kids cared about was: 'What kind of a job does your old man have? What kind of a house do you live in? What do your legs look like? Are you taller than any girl in school?' "[41]

His flesh crawled when he considered the clothes he wore, for he could afford only to buy them in a second-hand store. As Reinhardt observed, he was forced "to cover his nakedness with the clothes that people who hated him had worn and thrown away." Starkweather felt that "it was like wearing the skin of a dead man" to wear those clothes, "only these people whose clothes covered [me] were not dead." He would have to "see about that." He often wondered what it would be like to "sleep in a big hotel, to eat in a fine restaurant, and ride in a pullman train. I used to stand outside the Cornhusker [an expensive restaurant] and watch the people eating inside. It filled me with hate; not the people in there eating. I just hated the world that made me what I was." "They say this is a wonderful world to live in, but I don't believe I ever did really live in a wonderful world. I haven't ever eaten in a high class restaurant, never seen the New York Yankees play, or been to Los Angeles or New York City, or other places that books and magazines say are wonderful places to be at, there haven't [sic] been a chance for me to have the opportunity, or privilege, for the best things in life." He knew the folk-sayings that "a man makes his own world," and must pay "for his mistakes"; but he knew also that "people who say such things wear nice clothes, eat in fine restaurants and know what to say to the girls." They were the sort who received the credit that was due them. "I got no credit for nothing, I got blamed for everything that somebody don't like." Like many another before him, he decided that "I'll make my own world, I decided, I'll start today. Caril and me will have the kind of world we want."[42]

Searching for a career, he took his first job at the Newspaper Union, but "the people was always watching me. They had me numbered for the bottom . . . I tried to do work good as anybody, even done things by myself that two of us should a done . . . I used to think: now, no more hating, no more fighting . . . I've done what is right . . . then something would happen to take it all out of me. I used to wonder why 'no goods' like some I knowed was getting praised for doing what they done. Guess it's 'cause they talked better'n I did; 'cause they had better places to sleep in at night." It was here, at the bottom of the hierarchy, that the frustrated rebel emerged: "They made me hate. They couldn't a made me like them without their changing and they wasn't going to change." He turned for guidance to his family, but they could not understand his refusal to accept his position: "I am not blaming my old man . . . guess he didn't make me this trouble and I don't remember anything about my home life that wasn't better than what I had away from home. It's just that he was not much for understanding things, I guess. I mean things like a kid thinks about when nothing ain't going right."[43]

To ensure that he would see Caril every day when she came home from school, and perhaps to escape the visible and therefore punishing hierarchy of the Newspaper Union, he left his position and took another that symbolized his detested bottom-feeding role: he joined his brother on a garbage truck. "Throwing garbage" was a job he hated, and he internalized society's contempt for the task. His entrapment in it enraged him further: "A girl deserves better than a garbage hauler [and only] nincompoops . . . would do this dirty work . . . a kid ain't no good without money." At daybreak, his brother's voice calling him to work made him want to "throw garbage in somebody's face." Now reduced to handling the offal of his betters, his sullen rage for his tormentors intensified: "Nobody knowed better than to say nothing to me when is a heaving their goddamn garbage. [sic]" Now it began to dawn on him that only "dead people are all on the same level."[44]

Only the knowledge of his task, and his impending death, sustained him: "I knowed the end was coming, but it had a reason." The price he had had to pay in order to live was too high for his slim emotional pocketbook. "Misery, fear, hate . . . I guess I was frustrated . . . anyhow I got fed up being everybody's nobody . . . being unresponsible

... that's what they was saying. ... Well I got responsible didn't I? Can't anybody be a man if he pays for it? I was paying plenty for being a nobody ... sure I had fun killing squirrels, rabbits and pheasants. They ain't responsible. They don't make their rules as you say. I never hated rabbits. Rabbits ain't never done me no harm. They didn't hate me. Now I said to myself, I guess it's time to be responsible, time to get mixed in something."[45]

Suddenly the task was both defined and imminent. He awoke one morning feeling "like a new man," with a new and strange sense of purpose: "Something like I never felt before. The cost will be payed and nobody can't never say he was cheated," he remembered resolving. The night before his first murder, he thought: "These braggarts and good people are not laughing at a stupid garbage type ... they'll have something real interesting to say after tomorrow ... I am not going to die like a rabbit ... I am going to have something worth dying about ... and I'm not going to be the first one to die neither." Others before him, he thought, had murdered people with infinitely less justification: "They murdered people who never done them no harm. The people I murdered had murdered me. They murdered me slow like. I was better to them. I killed them in a hurry."[46]

In the past, "sometimes the hate was so real I could feel it coming to life like something kind of dead or asleep and beginning to wake up and stir around. Then I always wanted to do something ... maybe go out and rob a bank or throw garbage in some old bitch's face." But now that the tiger had been unleashed, he no longer felt the overwhelming frustrated hatred. "That isn't the way I felt when I killed them people. I killed Caril's parents because they tried to break us up. The kid was crying and there wasn't nothing to do with it. Them others, well, it was each that way out. Dead people don't talk. Besides they can't fight for nothing." What then was his ultimate aim? "I must get her away. I'll let her see that I'll kill for her." It would be a monumental gesture: "Soon, I'll be buried with the dead days. Better to be left to rot on some high hill behind a rock, and be remembered, than to be buried alive in some stinking place, and go to bed smelly like a garbage can every night." Still, the gesture was not to be an empty one, for not only was it a romantic declaration of love and hate, but it would also release him from the "stinking place." "What kind of future do you think I'd have throwing garbage and picking up a whore . . . how long do you think I'd a lived? Forty years? . . . too long . . . ten years? . . . too long . . . better a week with the one who loved me for what I was."[47]

He was that most dangerous of men, the one who has nothing to lose. "The world is lifeless anyhow," he said, "like the people I killed. It is just a hell of a world. It ain't worth going back to anyhow." He had no wish to return to a stigmatizing universe of "rich men's children," "vulgar streetwalkers," and "crazy bosses." "The more I looked at people the more I hated them because I knowed they wasn't any place for me with the kind of people I knowed [sic]. I used to wonder why they was here anyhow? A bunch of goddamn sons of bitches looking for somebody to make fun of . . . some poor fellow who ain't done nothing but feed chickens." It was time to make his move: "Everything was closing in on us fast like a trap-door that starts falling when the animal moves toward it. There was only one way of escape and that was toward the trap-door. The faster we moved the faster it seemed to fall."[48]

Toward the end of his killing spree, when he might have escaped had he headed resolutely west to Washington state, he turned back to Lincoln and drove straight to the upper-class district. Now he would spend his remaining "earth-time" marauding among his betters. But he did more than kill: Reinhardt asked him how he passed the time in the Ward home. "You don't think I just sit around in that mansion on my ass, do you?" He spent the day examining the furniture, lying on the beds and couches, absorbing the texture of upper-class life through its expensive springs and silken slip covers. Perhaps most important, the garbageman savored the sadistic revenge of ordering the mansion-dweller, Mrs. Ward, to serve him pancakes in the library. "Then," he said, "I decided I wanted a waffle." Mrs. Ward brought it to him, her penultimate act in life a servile one. "Ah yes," Starkweather reminisced, "they was nice to us." Later, in the quiet of his prison cell, he wished for nothing more than that his life's story would be read by millions:

"Then I would go with my dreams fulfilled. . . . Only my story will live." Now fulfilled on death row, his headaches disappeared, and he slept deeply.[49]

THE IDEOLOGICAL AUTHORITIES

"Nobody remembers a crazy man."
CHARLES STARKWEATHER[50]

If it was important to Starkweather that he *not* be declared insane (as it was for so many other of our multiple murderers), for such a designation would invalidate both him and his mission, it was equally important to society that he *be* found "insane." Try as they might, however, the authorities could not do so. The press made a sustained attempt to diminish him, singling out in him (as mankind has done since time immemorial) the shared iniquities of the generation they had created. "If Charles Starkweather were a case apart," read an editorial in Omaha's *World-Herald,* "a biological accident, a monstrous freak of nature, then today all Americans could take a deep breath of relief and give thanks that his mad career of murder had been brought to an end. But although his crimes were of a violence beyond precedent, nevertheless there was a certain flavor to the Starkweather story which brought back to mind a thousand others which have been told in recent years to an unbelieving America. The sideburns, the tight blue jeans, the black leather jacket—these have become almost the uniform of juvenile hoodlums. And the snarling contempt for discipline, the blazing hate for restraint, have become a familiar refrain in police stations and juvenile courts throughout the land. To a greater degree than ever before, influences are pulling some youngsters away from the orbit of the home, the school, and the church, and into the asphalt jungle. That is the problem." They were quite right, of course, and it was appropriate that they should single out Starkweather for what they saw as not his insanity, but his terrifying *normality.* The authorities and the public were moved: they correctly sensed the beginning of a fracture line that might shatter traditional structures; and in this process, they saw the rebel Starkweather playing a significant symbolic role that must be crushed. At that late stage, all they could hope to do was to use his impending execution as a warning to all rebellious youth. To underline their point, they circulated his maudlin capitulation—his article, "Rebellion"—in popular magazines, abridging his autobiography to show only its truncated remorse.[51]

The medical and psychiatric examinations were apposite illustrations of the curious tendency for psychiatric diagnosis to accord with the needs of the "side" (prosecution or defense) which has hired the psychiatrist. This revealed itself even in something as relatively "objective" as IQ testing. The prosecution, who wished Starkweather to be found culpable (which required that he be declared "sane") measured his IQ some thirteen points higher than the defense, who wished him to be found insane and not responsible—although Allen suggested here that this disparity may have been less a function of test subjectivity than of Starkweather's own active cooperation with the prosecution: "He simply hadn't tried as hard for the defense." He may have been right, but certainly his lawyer stretched the truth when he insisted that Starkweather's IQ was "only a point or two above an idiot," a remark that Starkweather was profoundly displeased to hear.[52]

The diagnostic differences were even apparent in their analyses of his physical condition. The defense lawyer, Allen, wrote: "made an unsubstantiated claim that he could have a brain tumor or 'pressure on the brain.'" Attempts to "find" some legally useful disorder were frustrated by Starkweather himself, who hindered defense lawyers at every opportunity. He refused to allow the defense's doctors to administer an electroencephalograph to test for brain damage, or to explore his perforated eardrum, which the enthusiastic defense suggested could indicate an infection near the brain, and raise the possibility of organic brain damage. Ultimately, the defense medical team's physical examination could only draw attention to the unremarkable facts that Starkweather was "a short, stocky young fellow with breasts somewhat large but muscularly developed, with tenderness in the spot where we usually expect it to be if a peptic ulcer is present, with a hole in his left eardrum, which apparently has been there quite a long time, with decreased deep tendon reflexes." On the other hand, the prosecution psychiatrists insisted that their examination disclosed no evidence whatever of brain damage or disease.[53]

The prosecution's psychiatric witnesses—two psychiatrists and a psychologist—all testified that they had examined Starkweather and found him to be sane, with no evidence of psychosis: they concluded that he suffered from a minor personality disorder. They agreed that this disorder was insufficiently debilitating to warrant committal to an institution, and reminded the court that if he were committed, he would inevitably be found sane and then released. Their specific diagnosis was "that Charles had a personality disorder characterized by emotional instability, considerable emotional insecurity and impulsiveness, [and] that this would fit into a category under the antisocial personality disorder." One of the psychiatrists felt certain that Starkweather knew the "enormity of his acts" and that he "seemed to recognize the nature and consequences of the acts he had committed." The two state psychiatrists agreed that "Starkweather's comprehension" was "adequate" or "good," and one of them commented on his "very fine memory ability"; concluding that he was "neither medically nor legally insane."[54]

The *defense* psychiatrists agreed that Starkweather was suffering from a diseased mind. One stated that, "my observations lead me to the opinion that Charles Starkweather is suffering from a severe mental disease or illness of such a kind as to influence his acts and has prevented him from using the knowledge of right and wrong at the time of commission of such an act. A number of important facts were found. One of the very important things which I found was that he is suffering from a severe warping of the emotional faculties; that is, he is unable to experience feelings that other people do. People don't mean anything to him. They are no more than a stick or a piece of wood to this boy." He thought that if Starkweather had been examined before the murder spree, his disturbance would certainly have been detected, and concluded that "this person is dangerously sick and has to be put under maximum security because he is dangerous." He thought Starkweather's perceptions were "distorted." "He will pick out things which are not important because of his particular way of looking at things. The act of killing meant to him no more than stepping on a bug. You can take a creature out of a jungle and tame him and maybe develop a surface crust of being domesticated . . . but . . . when such a creature tastes blood it breaks through and a wild rampage occurs in which a primitive impulse comes back." Following this fanciful diagnosis, this psychiatrist refused to give a name to Starkweather's mysterious "disease," saying only that he did not believe in conventional psychological terminology.[55]

A second defense psychiatrist commented on how easy it had been to fluster Starkweather; and found him deficient in his performance under stress, from which he was able to conclude: "If things would come at him one at a time, slowly as in a routine job, he would be able to handle these things, but if things began to flood in on him such as the work not going right, the sprinkler in the ceiling coming on, or somebody yelling and a whistle going all at once, I don't think he could function . . . he would be like a frightened animal." Starkweather was in this confused state during the murder spree, the psychiatrist believed. He concluded that Starkweather had never developed into an adult human being: "Yes, he walks around in the body of a human being, but the thoughts and the feelings are not there like they are in an ordinary person, who has learned by being around others and has feelings for them, and in relation to them. This is the way we learn to be people. I don't think he has ever learned to be a person."[56]

A third defense psychiatrist testified that Starkweather had a kind of stunted emotional repertoire: "I would say that his range of emotions is limited, that he feels perhaps two that we are familiar with: anger and fear, or anxiety. The other shadings of emotions—pity, sympathy, the feeling of attachment for another individual (for the entire person and not just a quality or an attribute of them) is something I think he is striving for but actually only has a dim recognition of. . . . When I asked him what happened and how he felt through this when he committed these acts, he has always come back with the same thing: 'Self-defense.'" He thought that Starkweather's cheerful behavior during and after the murders "would indicate a diseased mind. A person who had committed the act of killing three people including a young child and then returned to friends and family and appeared to be normal and cheerful was not able to feel things the way other people [did]." Still, the defense medical team admitted that his condition could not be regarded as legal insanity, but declined to give a label to Starkweather's condition.[57]

For their part, neither Starkweather nor his family wanted him to be declared insane, although their motives were surely quite different. The family did not wish the "taint" of insanity to stain their family tree; and, on occasion, Starkweather himself pretended that it was to save them embarrassment that he resisted such a categorization. "I have always loved my mother, I am sorry about causing her so much trouble . . . when she cried at the court house . . . she was crying for something already dead. How could she know that I was going [to] the chair for her—for her and my sister and every one of my family . . . I could of give them the 'taunt' of insanity just to save my life. It wouldn't a done no good no how 'cause I was already dead, or same as dead . . . nobody ever gets back hisself again. Wouldn't it be better for me to be dead than having my family 'taunted' with insanity? [sic]" Yet it should be clear that this pseudo-heroic pretense was at best something that reinforced, not caused, his rigid stance on the insanity question. He was terrified that "they might try to prove insane," not because of any altruistic concern for his family, but because "nobody remembers a crazy man." Indeed, he resisted every attempt to thus invalidate him and his mission, ultimately cooperating fully with the prosecution and resisting his own defense team. He sat through the jury selection with a "half-smirk" on his face, "seeming either scornful or bored with the proceedings," but "clutched the corner of the counsel table and glared" when his lawyer placed his IQ near that of an idiot. The jury took less than twenty-four hours to find him guilty of murder in the first degree, and to specify the death penalty.[58]

BURIED ALIVE

"Better to be left to rot on some high
hill behind a rock, and be remembered,
than to be buried alive in some
stinking place."

CHARLES STARKWEATHER[59]

The last months of his life were spent, for the most part, in the elaboration and justification of his rebellious image. In the photographs taken of him at the time, as he was led in chains by heavily armed policemen, an expression of sheer vindictive delight dominated his face. Alone in his cell, the photographs revealed only the distant aloofness of the spy who had come in from the cold, or the soldier who had bravely completed his mission. So consistent was this personal stance, this maintenance of image, that Reinhardt was moved to complain that "in approximately thirty hours of interviewing I never witnessed a sign of genuine remorse in this killer." How could it have been otherwise, when to show remorse would be to capitulate utterly, to render meaningless his sacrifices?[60]

The Killings

What were the origin and meaning of Starkweather's apparently meaningless spree? It is natural to believe—and certainly he himself encouraged that belief—that he had merely gone on a kind of uncoordinated rampage, murdering in "self-defense" anyone who got in his way. But he did not go at random: he chose specific places and types of persons (as did all our multiple murderers) because they were in actual or symbolic relation to the forces that denied him what he wished from life.

His first victim was the gas station attendant, a clean-cut and apparently decent young man with, judging from his photographs, the conservative air of someone who had in

233

fact just been discharged from the armed forces. Allen has told us that "whether Colvert lived or died depended if he recognized Charlie through the disguise," but there is much doubt as to whether this was the case. He had already angered Starkweather the day before when he had refused the latter credit to purchase a stuffed toy dog as a Christmas gift. Further, if there had been no clear intent to kill, there would have been no late-night drive into the countryside (since Colvert had not recognized him, or resisted, until he was shoved from the car on the lonely road). To punish the innocent is the fundamental outrage committed by all our multiple murderers, but from Starkweather's perspective, Colvert's "flaunted" respectability and links to those who controlled wealth were sufficient condemnation. Soon, he would work more closely toward what he thought were his real enemies.[61]

The second set of kills, the three members of the Bartlett family, was central to his mission. They *might* have lived had they not tried so spiritedly to deny him the companion and witness he needed for the proper discharge of his mission, but that is unlikely. They stood in exact relation to what he wanted (Caril) but would be denied for all time. Their verbal and physical assaults upon him did not, as he claimed, require homicide to terminate them: he could in fact have simply taken Caril and left. But he chose not to do so, and for reasons that make perfect sense when viewed from within the logic of the spree. Its purpose was to strike a blow at those "lifeless" ones who denied him his own life: who better then to annihilate than the Bartletts? How better could he express his disdain for his victims than by living in their home close by their rotting bodies, fornicating with their daughter, and eating their food?

The killing of the old family friend, the farmer August Meyer, seems especially cruel and inexplicable, for had they not broken bread together many times before? Having shared his hunting trophies with Meyer, he must have known that the spoils from an attack on Meyer could yield little more than a few dollars, and a gun or two. Certainly his "explanation" that he decided to kill him because he had left his farm's entry lane uncleared makes no sense at all. Neither does his claim of an unprovoked attack by

Meyer. This murder cannot be understood until it is compared to its opposite: to the sparing of the life of the passing farmer who had helped extricate their stranded car from the mud. Rather than killing him, Starkweather insisted on paying him for the service. The answer surely lies then in each one's perceived relationship to treasure he coveted. Meyer, whatever his own slim resources, was a landowner, and one to whom Starkweather had often been forced to pay tribute, as "serf," in the form of shared game; whereas the passing farmer seemed to be a pure proletarian like himself, demanding no tithes and offering only kindness. In this sense, he was slowly killing his way up the social ladder.[62]

Still, Jensen and King, the young couple who were next to die, also offered only kindness—a lift and good will—and they received their own execution as recompense. If to us they must seem the least likely candidates for execution, to Starkweather and Caril Fugate they must have seemed virtually the *most* likely. If Jensen and King were not wealthy, they certainly bore all the marks of happy and conventional middle-class America, which is to say they stood as perfect symbols of that which the spree was designed to assault. They were two unexceptional young people who, according to Allen, "saw nothing wrong with the world, nothing major to rebel against." Every fiber of their being must have radiated the fact that they "had never been alienated from anything," and it was thus entirely appropriate, given the logic of Starkweather's scheme, to strike down these wholesome representatives of the established order. It was not clear if it was he who had mutilated King (for he later claimed that Caril had done so in a fit of jealousy), but it would be in no way inconsistent with his task.[63]

Still, the young couple were merely middle-class. With each killing he had worked his way closer to the apex, up the social hierarchy from gas station attendant to working-class family to small landowner to middle-class persons. Now it was time to go directly to the source. It was for this reason that his otherwise inexplicable decision—to turn away from escape to Washington state and drive back to Lincoln's country club district—can now appear as entirely rational. The mission would not have been properly discharged without a direct assault on those at the top of the social pyramid. Who better to select than a family from the wealthy area in which he had daily humiliated himself, handling their waste and offal, and performing their menial chores? His behavior inside the Ward home is especially revealing: in his savoring of the material culture of the rich and his insistence that the lady of the house, not the maid, wait upon him. The maid was no landed aristocrat, but she was clearly part of the mansion and the established order—reason enough to destroy her too. Starkweather claimed that Caril had dispatched the maid; but it matters not, for either way the mission was clearly defined and responsibly completed.

The only murder which later troubled Starkweather was his last: the salesman Collison—who did not fit the hierarchical climb, and who was killed for purely utilitarian reasons. Reinhardt thought Starkweather's compunctions about this murder must have been because he could not "rationalize self-defense . . . he thought people would think him cowardly because of the way the salesman died." But viewed from our perspective, no such rationalization is necessary: in fact, Collison was killed because he stood in the way, pure and simple. He was only a marginal member, at best, of the oppressive class. In killing him, Starkweather felt the same awkwardness that Edmund Kemper had felt upon killing young Aido Koo, whose middle-class credentials he suspected to be marginal.[64]

The Meaning

Those who perceive themselves to be among the truly dispossessed—including the killers Starkweather, Panzram, and Essex—all share the notion that the bottom of the social order is the only niche they will be allowed to occupy. Too ambitious and self-regarding to accept this position, too cynical to sustain any hope of escape from it (or too acute to be comforted by idle dreams), their lives are rendered hopeless. Only a spectacular adventure, like a killing spree, can give meaning to one whose despair is so extravagant: only in this way can they leave their mark upon the world. It is thus entirely consistent with their perceived position that they formulate their homicidal sprees, and do so with a remarkable sense of class consciousness. Starkweather castigated other murderers who "murdered people who never done them no harm." To him, his own were justified, despite the fact that he had never known half of them, because in terms of their relation to the established order, they were "the people [who] . . . had murdered me . . . slow like."[65]

A rigidly stratified society maintains itself not just through force of arms, but by keeping its lower denizens oblivious to their fate. As the French scholars Peter and Favret observe, "enduring the unlivable, day in and day out," wading through lives "devoid of all future, deprived of all prospects," they become problematic only if they perceive their conundrum and abandon all hope: "should one of them perceive it even for a moment, his whole world falls apart." Such a man was Starkweather: he knew his fate and dismissed it as without value. Such men are dangerous, for they can proceed to carve their mark and exact their revenge with neither scruple nor remorse. Starkweather's biographer, Reinhardt, insisted that "the answer must surely be found in the warped values this boy read into life. His *ego* was empty and defeated; he imagined himself rejected by society, as symbolized by social position and power. These things—position and power—he could not hope to attain and hold by honest toil. Without them, as he had come to believe, life was worthless." But Reinhardt was a simple criminologist, whose unwarped values were formed during his own success in life: surely there was little "warped" about Starkweather's perception of his inevitable fate; and certainly he *was* "rejected," and would continue to be so unless he accepted the lowly position his life offered him. As a guardian of the social order, Reinhardt spoke for many when he demanded that Starkweather adjust to his position, and carry the garbage without complaint.[66]

However, Starkweather saw all too clearly that "a kid ain't no good without money," that only "nincompoops" haul garbage and accept the social stigma that goes with the act. His almost frenzied sensitivity to his low estate turned early to pseudo-radical protest, which took the form of his rebellion. His "sense of outrage grew to striving, to throw, to bend, to hurt and most of all to beat those who teased me," and to turn his boiling hatred on "everybody other than my family," who shared his position and nursed some of his wounds. Killing those who possessed what he wanted, who stood in relation to him as overlord (in reality or as symbol) "makes everything even . . . it evens what I done and what every body is done.[sic]" Without hope of escape, death for him was no obstacle or dilemma, for "the world on the other side couldn't be as bad as this one," could not exceed "the mean world this is." The alternative future he saw so clearly for himself—of "throwing garbage and picking up a whore"—offered insufficient recompense for his humiliation. His relationship with Caril had made him understand fully why he so hated the world: it was because he would not be able to keep her, for "poverty gives you nothing." For a brief time he would create his own world, a world in which he kept what he wanted. Then he would depart in a blaze of snarling glory. "I started a new kind of thinking after I met her. . . . Something worth killing for had come." "It was supposed to be my way out, the last fling before the ending. Guess it's better than just going out like a light with no flicker."[67]

Capitulation

If Starkweather displayed no remorse whatever to Reinhardt, his 200-page autobiography did incorporate a few pages of pseudo-remorse, which were published in a popular magazine under the title "Rebellion," to draw a suitable moral. Those few pages were seized upon by a popular press anxious to suppress the story of his true motivation and to promulgate a kind of morality play in which the consequences of rebellion were clearly outlined. We cannot know if his claims were "sincere" in any sense at all; but even if they were not, it would be by no means inconsistent with the spirit of most multiple murderers finally to acquiesce in this way, to accept the morality of the dominant class. After all, they were never revolutionaries, only rebels angered at their own lowly estate. Having made their radical protest, their anger is dispersed and their headaches and sleepless nights abated. They can now make a separate peace. It should come as small surprise then to see the photograph of the killer with his autobiographer during his last weeks, looking bookish and now smoking a pipe—the 1950s badge of college status.

In his widely distributed capitulation/autobiography, which resurrected all the moralistic clichés of some small-town fundamentalist preacher, Starkweather wrote: "Around eleven o'clock the night Caril Fugate and I were apprehended, it was very quiet in the Douglas, Wyoming, jail. I was lying upon the top bunk and was feeling low and hopeless. Then a clear perception of truth came to me of the villainous and outraging [sic] acts committed, and I thought I would vomit. It all seem like a fantastic dream, but it was no dream, and I knew it. Exhausted as I was, I couldn't sleep. I simply laid there, staring at a couple names that had been scratched into the steel wall, and was lost in my own thoughts. I said to myself, why? Why, why, had everything had to happen to me? . . . I determined then that I would write these thoughts and remembrances down. For I wanted to do something for my parents. I had caused them enough trouble. And I wanted to warn other boys so they wouldn't take the road I took."[68]

"Today," he continued, in what must stand as one of the least convincing documents in the annals of multiple murder, "my feelings are of great sorrow and remorse for the people I killed. And for the heartache and sorrow and grief caused people who lost their loved ones. I pray that God will be forgiving of what has been done . . . today I know that this was wrong. . . . Today, after a year of imprisonment, I can count my life in hours. I have had a great deal of time for thought and to retrace back over my life. I hold no fear for the electric chair, it is the price I am paying for taking the lives of others. . . . Now I feel no rebellion toward anything or anyone, only love and peace. I received this love and peace through the Bible. And if I could talk to young people today I would tell them to go to school, to go to Sunday School, to go to church and receive the Lord Jesus Christ as your own personal Saviour. Our God is a kind God. . . . And I would say to them to obey their parents or guardians, and stay away from bad influences, and never undertake anything that you don't understand, and if in doubt don't do it. And most of all don't ever let your intentions and emotions overpower you. If I had followed these simple little rules, as I was advised to do many times, I would not be where I am today." Whatever his motives may have been in composing this hymn to the republic—and we can only speculate—he was neither the first nor the last rebel to have his mind wonderfully concentrated by his impending execution and the heavenly events that might transpire shortly thereafter.[69]

In any case, by the day he died he had reverted to the *persona* of the swaggering soldier of fortune. Those who watched his execution and what preceded it commented unfavorably on the "stiffness" with which he gave his mother a last embrace, the quick and abstracted handshake he gave his father, and the correct cult-figure style with which he rammed his hands in his pockets and walked boldly ahead of the guard. Reinhardt and the other observers were incensed that he showed neither remorse nor a fear of death, for it invalidated their punishment. No one seemed impressed that he remained in character to the end, striding briskly into the death chamber, and advising his executioners to tighten the straps that bound his arms and chest to the electric chair. When asked if he had any last words, he "pressed his lips together and emphatically said no." The switch which sent 2200 volts coursing through his body was pulled three times: the first shock stunned him, the second rendered him unconscious, and the third "stopped his heart."[70]

7.
HATE WHITE PEOPLE BEAST OF THE EARTH

Mark James Robert Essex*

> "The quest for freedom is death—
> then by death I shall escape to
> freedom."
>
> MARK ESSEX[1]

The mental life of mass murderers is not so difficult to decipher once we have uncovered the social messages which constitute the ciphering key. Many such killers do contrive to leave a kind of enigmatic wake behind them, because the date at which they are stopped is when they are riddled with police bullets (as was the case, for example, with Charles Whitman's shootings from the University of Texas tower in 1966). Yet it is a grievous error to believe that dead men tell no tales, and Essex is perhaps the finest illustration of this point. It is an equally monumental error to dismiss Essex, as so many have done, as a kind of deranged "sniper," and hope to leave it at that. He was much more.

* Essex did not leave us much, but what does remain is reprinted in Peter Hernon's splendid study, *A Terrible Thunder*, a spellbinding account of the case rich in quotations from Essex and recollections of Essex's behavior. Ronald Tobias' *They Shoot To Kill* is very much a secondary, and occasionally inaccurate, source. I am grateful to Harriet and Elliot Liebow who, in introducing me to the slums of Washington D.C., gave me some sense of the black experience in urban America.

During his killing spree, Essex seemed to address himself to some fundamental issues in American life. His "sniping" was an integral part of a coherent campaign. Moreover, he tried to "explain" it in his earlier comments to his friends and family, in his writings on his apartment walls and ceilings, and in his shouted remarks as well as his homicidal actions during the actual assault. His central rebellion, despite the wretched and racist form it ultimately took, was an interesting one, aimed directly at what he perceived to be the racist white establishment in America. Appropriately then, he tried to kill its most visible and powerful representatives, those uniformed, generally white, agents of social control—the police (although he did not shrink from murdering civilians, so long as they were white). He conducted his explosion of radical creativity with considerable style and *finesse:* he challenged the entire police and military forces of the great city of New Orleans. The ensuing gunfight came close to destroying an entire city block, and he escaped to freedom in death, leaving behind him ten dead, twenty-two wounded, and millions of dollars worth of property in ruins. More important to his purpose, he created many admirers for himself in the radical community—and left in his wake an air of imminent insurrection felt so intensely by both the public and the authorities that something might almost have come of it. In his own terms, it was both an exit with *panache* and an achievement of which few young persons dared dream.

KILL PIG DEVIL

His first kill was on New Year's Eve of 1974. He hid across the street from the New Orleans' police department's Central Lockup and opened fire with his Ruger .44 magnum semi-automatic carbine. His first four shots were fired in rapid succession and narrowly missed the head of police cadet Weatherford, blasting cement chips off the wall around him. After the briefest pause during which cadet Weatherford took cover, cadet Al Harrell, one of the few young blacks in the New Orleans police, came into view. Essex unleashed a volley of shots at the nineteen-year-old.

The third shot struck Harrell in the chest, passing through "the anterior thorax causing severe lacerations to the heart," as the death certificate later read. The .44 magnum bullet was not yet spent, and after it passed through Harrell's body, it struck Lieutenant Horace Perez in the ankle. Perez blacked out. Observing the assault, a detective called both for an emergency ambulance and for all available police to rush to the Lockup. Within seconds, they were swarming over the area with shotguns and revolvers ready, fanning out into the area from which the shots had been fired. Their assailant had disappeared.[2]

A few moments later, police officers Edwin Hosli and Harold Blappert were investigating a ringing alarm in a company office a few blocks from the Lockup. Carrying flashlights, and unaware of the recent shooting, they prepared to check out the building. Essex was hiding inside the office. His first shot struck Hosli in the abdomen, ripped through one kidney, collapsed a lung and perforated the bowels, spilling fecal matter through the body cavity. It would take Hosli two months to die. A second shot shattered the squad car's windshield, and a third ricocheted off the hood and penetrated the windshield, while a fourth struck the building behind the officers.[3]

Within minutes, more than thirty police surrounded the office: six men fired shotguns with heavy loads at the door, disintegrating it, and then sent in a dog. A subsequent search of the premises revealed that the assailant had entered the hemp factory by shooting the lock off the door. Blood stains on the window glass through which Essex had left the office indicated that he had been wounded, and bloody handprints on the windowsill suggested that he had tried to dry the blood. Among the items he left behind was a brown leather purse with a black owl painted on its side containing fifty .38-caliber bullets.[4]

Apparently anxious to ensure that police knew where he was going, and to draw them into an ambush, Essex left a trail of bullets—two together always pointing in the same direction—at periodic intervals along his path of retreat from the hemp factory to the front of the First New St. Mark Baptist Church. There he waited. Incredibly, as police arrived in front of the church and found the cartridges, they were pulled out of the neighborhood by a police administrator who was concerned with the high level of tension in this black area. During the "cool-off" period that the administrator wanted, the assailant disappeared from the church.[5]

Although he would not kill for another week, he did not remain inactive. During the afternoon of January 1, 1975, he seems to have set two fires in nearby warehouses in the heart of the city: the fires smoldered for five days, and 200 firefighters were called in to douse the flames. He seems to have returned periodically to the church over several days: on the evening of January 3, police received a complaint that a man was hiding in the church. When they searched the church, one policeman recalled, "the evidence our man had been there was unbelievable. Hidden in the ladies' bathroom, we found a cloth sack filled with .38 caliber rounds. We also found bloodstains on several doors and window sills."[6]

On the morning of January 7, he walked into a grocery store managed by Joseph Perniciaro, who had reported seeing him to the police (it was not determined how Essex had received this information). He entered the store carrying a rifle and called to the manager, "You, you're the one I want," and shot him in the chest. Essex ran for several blocks, then stuck his rifle through the window of an idling car and told the driver, who was black, to get out. "I don't want to kill you," the driver remembered him saying, "but I'll kill you too." Essex drove off, heading toward the downtown Howard Johnson's Hotel, which would be the scene of his ultimate response to the authorities.[7]

He parked his car, and climbed the hotel's outer staircase to the eighth floor—but was refused entry by the hotel staff. On the ninth floor, he rapped on the outer door and asked a maid: "Let me in, sis, I got something to do," she remembered him asking. She refused, and he climbed the outer staircase once more. He finally gained entrance on the eighteenth floor where, carrying his rifle, he brushed past three black employees with the remark, "Don't worry, I'm not going to hurt you black people, I want the whites." A twenty-seven-year-old white doctor of medicine, Robert Steagall, stepped into the corridor as Essex passed his room. They struggled with one another until Essex shot him in the

244

arm and chest. When Steagall's wife, Betty Steagall, rushed at them screaming, and knelt next to her husband, Essex shot her through the head. He then entered the Steagalls' room, set fire to the drapes, and ran down the hall back to the staircase. The fires began to spread, smoke billowing from the rooms.[8]

Frank Schneider, the front-office manager, and Donald Roberts, a bellman, were on their way up to investigate the sounds and smoke. As they stepped out of the elevator on the eleventh floor, they saw Essex standing a few yards away. Schneider and Roberts ran for the nearest exit. "We heard one shot and that was the one that went over my head as I was running low," Roberts said later. "Then the second shot apparently got Frank, who was running behind me; and I kept running." Schneider had been shot in the head and killed.[9]

Walter Collins, the hotel's general manager, and Luciano Llovett, a maintenance man, went up to investigate the reports of a man in the hotel with a rifle. On the tenth floor, Collins saw a youth with a gun and started to run. The bullet hit him in the back and he collapsed to the floor. When he heard Essex leave the corridor, he began crawling on his elbows and knees toward the landing.[10]

Patrolmen Michael Burl and Robert Childress were the first policemen to reach the hotel. As they ascended the hotel's elevator, the first fire engines began to arrive outside the building. Fire Department Lieutenant Tim Ursin was climbing a ladder up the side of the building when Essex appeared on one of the balconies and fired at him: the bullet struck Ursin in the left arm, scouring a wound so severe that his left forearm later required amputation. Essex continued firing when any policemen or firemen showed themselves.[11]

A chaotic scene soon developed (although it was nothing compared to what was to come): explosions from Essex's .44 carbine mingling with sporadic return fire from police, screams from the hotel guests trapped in their rooms, and billowing smoke from the burning floors. The chaos deepened as police began firing at random at the hotel's upper floors—in contravention of all notions of fire control. For his part, Essex continued to prefer uniformed targets; so much so that he even allowed a detective, who appeared to be a civilian, to pass unscathed through the killing ground. By eleven o'clock that morning, one hundred policemen had surrounded the hotel. That number would swell to over 600 policemen from Louisiana, Texas, and Mississippi, as well as FBI, Treasury, and other federal agents (totaling twenty-six state, local, and federal law enforcement agencies), before the affair was finished.

Patrolman Charles Arnold climbed to the tenth floor of an office building across the street from the hotel. When he pushed open the window, Essex fired a shot which shattered on Arnold's shotgun and tore into his jaw, knocking him to the floor. Arnold later told Essex's biographer, Peter Hernon, that as he spat out pieces of jawbone, teeth, and blood, someone had looked at him and said, "Good Christ! He blew your whole face off." As the firing continued, Robert Beamish, a forty-three-year-old broadcasting executive, tried to sneak past the swimming pool out of the hotel, but Essex spotted him and shot him in the stomach, blowing out his belly button. Beamish jumped or fell into the pool, where he remained for two hours. Inexplicably, Essex continued to pass up some targets, whimsically allowing some to pass unscathed.[12]

Now he raced through the upper floors of the hotel, shooting and setting fires in as many rooms as he could manage. Firemen who were trying to fight the fires found themselves exposed to increasingly uncontrolled shooting from the police. The absence of police fire control severely exacerbated the danger to the growing number of tourists who had begun to gather around the hotel to witness the event—some of them, presumably radicalized blacks, shouted "Right on!" each time the sniper fired.[13]

Patrolman Kenneth Solis was using a loudspeaker to direct the tourists to take cover when Essex shot him in the right shoulder under the rib cage, shattering the shoulder and exposing splintered bone. Another bullet hit Sgt. Emanuel Palmisano as he ran across the plaza to help Solis: the bullet fractured Palmisano's left arm, entered his body under the armpit, traveling down his back and grazing his spine. Patrolman Philip Coleman responded to the cries for help from the wounded by driving his squad car across the plaza, sunk low in the driver's seat. Patrolman Paul Persigo died instantly from a shot through the mouth as he stood gazing at the hotel's upper floors. An unidentified man in a civil defense helmet was shot in the right arm as he walked along the street; and when ambulance driver Chris Caton ran out to rescue him, another bullet hit Caton in the back, crushing his shoulder blade, collapsing one lung, and exiting under the armpit. Civilians armed with rifles, some clad in ill-fitting military uniforms, were beginning to show up near the hotel and began to join in the attack on Essex—adding to the air of farce enveloping the scene.[14]

A crowd of several hundred young blacks was now on the street. They acted as a kind of cheering section for Essex: each time he fired, the crowd moved forward a few paces, chanting, "Kill the pigs, kill the pigs," and, as Hernon wrote: "As the tempo of the gunfire increased, these chants became louder, fiercer. Several empty bottles were thrown. . . . Many of the blacks were drinking wine from bottles in brown sacks. 'Hang on, baby,' one of them shouted. 'When it gets dark, we gonna help you.'"[15]

Deputy Supt. Louis Sirgo of the New Orleans police led a small assault team up to the top floors of the hotel. On the stairs above the sixteenth floor landing, a shot from Essex's carbine fractured Sirgo's spinal cord, breaking the vertebral column and perforating his left lung, liver, and right kidney. He died within minutes. Essex continued firing as he ran from floor to floor, lighting more fires (most often by igniting each suite's telephone book and placing it under a curtain or mattress), while nervous and utterly uncoordinated police barely managed to avoid shooting at each other.[16]

When Officer Larry Arthur of the tactical squad smashed through the locked door opening on to the hotel roof, Essex shot him in the abdomen and shouted, "Free Africa! Come on up, pigs!" Essex would not leave the roof alive. For the rest of the siege, he would pop in and out of the concrete cubicles which protected the doorways to the roof, jumping out from them to fire at different angles and then taking shelter again as the torrent of inaccurate and uncoordinated fire from the police bracketed his position. During a lull in the firing, Essex was heard to scream, "Happy New Year's, pigs! I've killed four of you motherfuckers. Come on up and I'll kill four more." At midafternoon, police fired a dozen tear-gas cannisters at the roof. The gas settled on the roof and then dispersed without effect. To taunt them, Essex shouted, "I'm still here, pigs!" Meanwhile, elected officials were beginning to panic. They thought Essex's attack might not be just one individual's idiosyncratic action: "The thing that worried us the most," said one councilman, "was the question, what if this was the beginning of something much bigger? We wondered whether a revolution was coming, whether other blacks would come to the sniper's assistance." Essex would have been pleased.[17]

When a small and unarmored police helicopter circled near the hotel, a volley of shots from Essex drove it off. Soon after, however, a U.S. Marine Air Reserve CH-46 ex-Vietnam armored helicopter, carrying two Marine sharp-shooters armed with M-14 .308s and three policemen with AR-15 .223s, flew to the scene through rain and fog. For what remained of the day, the helicopter would make a total of forty-eight passes over the hotel, and do so in the midst of undisciplined fire from police and civilians. On one swoop, police in the helicopter mistakenly opened fire on a stairwell in which police officers were hiding. "The rounds just poured in on us," one of the policemen later said. "They riddled the door, the hole, everything. Plaster and concrete went flying from the walls and we went tumbling down those stairs. It was amazing no one was killed."[18]

As the gunners on the helicopter poured magazine after magazine into the cubicles, a radio-station announcer broadcasted a "request" from police for citizens with large-caliber rifles to come to their aid. This fabricated request produced a "large number of morons, marginal types, all of them armed to the teeth" at the hotel, all offering to "get the sniper." The police evicted the vigilantes, but the following morning, another group was discovered approaching the hotel by stealth. Incredibly, according to police, one woman telephoned them to offer blankets for the sniper, whom she thought was "probably freezing up on that roof." Their response to the offer has not been recorded. At no point during this operation did any police strategist apparently consider the obvious way to conclude the assault (which would have prevented all police and civilian casualties): to simply clear the area of all human targets, and wait out the sniper.[19]

Meanwhile, Essex continued to address his fire and his abuse at the police. "Come on up, you honky pigs!" he shouted. "You afraid to fight like a black man?" The police responded in kind, shouting, "Fuck you! Fuck you. Fuck you. Fuck you." Once again, the helicopter swooped down on the wrong stairwell and opened fire on the police crouching there. A black policeman briefly tried to talk Essex into surrendering, but Essex merely shouted, "Fuck you. Power to the people!"[20]

The last moments of Mark Essex came at just before nine that night. As the helicopter dove at him once more, he ran out of a cubicle and fired, then ran back inside: at that point he seems to have been hit. As the helicopter pilot remembered it: "I guess the guy figured it was over. They were pouring a lot of lead in there, and he ran out firing." He was met by the full-automatic fire from the helicopter, as well as the heavy rifles (including .375 and .458 "elephant guns") from the hundreds of police on adjoining roofs. One of the gunners in the helicopter, firing on full automatic, said Essex "came out, running toward the helicopter, firing as he came. He was looking straight at us, holding the gun at the waist and firing. He took two or three steps before we opened up. I hit him a whole clip from the thighs to the neck. He was running at full tilt and his momentum carried him another five or ten feet. Then the bullets caught him and held him up, sort of like when you shoot at a pie plate and keep it rolling." Firing his high-velocity Weatherby rifle from the roof of the Bank of New Orleans, another officer said: "The guy came out and turned around to shoot . . . that's when I fired. I hit him in the buttock, and he tumbled forward and dropped his rifle. Then some guys with the big stuff, the .375s and .458 elephant guns, opened up. One of those shells hit his leg. It looked to me like it blew it off." The officers with perhaps the best view of Essex's last stand said: "I think what happened is that some tracers burned up after hitting the walls of the cubicle. Whatever it was, he came out running and screaming and his left arm was up, the fist clenched. It looked like he was running on a charcoal grill. With all that shooting, there was a ring of red fire around him. The bullets actually held him up, twisting him around. Then he went down on his back about twenty feet from the cubicle. Everyone kept shooting."[21]

The heavy fire from the helicopter and the adjoining roofs shattered a water pipe on the roof, unleashing a four-foot wall of water which roared down the stairwell in which the police were watching, and sweeping them off their feet in a wave of weapons, bandoliers, clothing, and police. Moreover, the officers believed there might be a second sniper on the roof, and they continued to "see," "hear," and shoot at the "second sniper." As Hernon described the scene: "Long into the night, police yelled insults from the Rault Center and other buildings as they tried to bait the gunmen into revealing their positions. 'Where does it hurt, Leroy?' they shouted, their voices lost in the darkness. 'Hurts all over, don't it.' No one answered from the roof. 'Power to the people, nigger.'" Reports then came in that another sniper had definitely been spotted on the roof. The police opened fire once more, their spotters observing the flashes of the bullets hitting the building, but interpreting them as muzzle flashes from a second sniper returning their fire. The noise of the police shooting was so intense that it was impossible to tell from whence it came, and thus to disconfirm any notions of a second sniper. In the rising crescendo of police fire, nevertheless, there could still be heard the distinctive sound of a Thompson .45-caliber submachine gun firing on full automatic, and the steady boom of a .375 Holland and Holland big game rifle.[22]

To compound this farce, late that night, the police sent in the K-9 corps. The dogs climbed to the roof, but one of them was so sickened by the tear gas that it simply curled up on its side. A second dog's trainer refused to let it go out alone on the roof, frightened that "they'll kill my dog." A third dog's trainer agreed to send in his dog, but the dog would not oblige. At 5 a.m., the helicopter made another strafing run in the gathering light, pouring fire into the cubicles, but succeeding only in awakening the five policemen who had fallen asleep in the stairwell. Then began the inevitable process in which the police began to shoot at each other. When one officer gingerly stuck his helmet on a stick and climbed slowly out on the roof, police without radios opened fire on him, mistaking him for the sniper. When a police team stormed the roof a little before two in the afternoon, police from City Hall opened fire on them. Soon the assault team was joined by thirty other zealous officers, standing shoulder to shoulder in a semicircle around the boiler room: they opened fire together and the ricochets careered around the roof, wounding nine of them, three seriously. Essex would have loved it.[23]

His body lay twisted on the roof. One leg was virtually severed from his body; the torso was a crushed pulp; the face had been almost shot away; but the left hand was still clenched in a fist. Officers in the morgue later counted at least 200 bullet holes in Essex's body and noted that the gall bladder was the only organ not destroyed by the small arms fire. All that remained in his pockets were two bullets and one firecracker. An inquiry later determined that he had fired between 100 and 150 rounds to kill nine persons and seriously wound another ten during the hotel assault. Police found his stolen car parked within a block of the Central Lockup. In the glove compartment was printed material from the state's Department of Employment on discrimination in hiring practices. In the trunk, police found a duffel bag on which the word WARRIOR had been printed by hand in black ink.[24]

A CURIOUSLY HAPPY CHILDHOOD

The conscious mental life of our civilization, conditioned as it is by notions that it is primarily childhood that produces the man, makes us assume that we will find something bizarre in Essex's family or community to explain his murderous behavior. It would be most satisfactory if we could demonstrate that he had come from a brutalizing family, or a community discolored by ugly racism—and that these experiences had established subconscious drives to manufacture a manhood crushed in childhood. Yet we search in vain for such evidence. Indeed, the evidence from both family and community points resolutely in another direction.

Essex was a young black raised in a thoughtful, progressive, and gentle home, in a community that was insulated from all the vilest excesses of urban or southern racism. We do not know the precise details of the ideological atmosphere in which he was raised, although we can state with little fear of contradiction that it was non-violent. What we can be certain of is that the gentility of his family and community failed to prepare him to accept numbly with suitable meekness the racism he would encounter later on in the navy, or prepare him for the limitations to his chances in life that he would confront in the outside world. What is the process whereby a gentle and non-racist youth is transformed into a violent racist—one who hates with such ferocity that he can kill not only the uniformed white authority figures, but also shoot in the head a young woman kneeling dazed beside her husband's body? To comprehend this transformation, we must follow Essex through his brief and tortured life. To do so, we must examine the artifacts of his life through the prism of the system of social class and race in American life. We will make no progress if we dwell merely on the superficial elements that have engaged some commentators (such as Essex's tiny stature) who have argued that his actions stemmed from his personal inadequacies. It takes more than diminished height, or the reputed sharp tongue of a mother, to finance an explosion of mass murder.

To reach below the surface of Essex's life is to marvel at the uncommon happiness of his childhood. He was a cub scout and well regarded by most, if not all. He spent many hours fishing for perch and catfish in the waters near the town; and a teacher described him as a "crack shot on rabbits and squirrels." He attended a neighborhood primary school and a high school in the downtown business district. As only twenty-nine of the school's one thousand students were black, his minority status constituted no threat to the established white order of Emporia, Kansas. Certainly his relations with other white youngsters were good, for they were his playmates in childhood and his dates during adolescence. The family home was no ghetto slum: it was a detached single story house in a faded suburb, with a large playground across the street.[25]

His family's social-class affiliation is critical. Essex's father was no unemployed slum-dweller conditioned to accept his station in life. His father was a foreman, not a worker, in a small, family-owned firm in Emporia, and they could well afford their lower-middle-class style of living. Ironically and more destructively, he grew up with the deadly misapprehension that his race might not matter very much in the larger scheme of things—or even not at all. His family obviously discussed the racist evils of the society at large; but his own experience of it was once or twice removed. Even when his brothers and sisters left Emporia, they went to other places where the racism was subtle and subdued—a brother found a measure of peace in Cedar Rapids, as did sisters in Los Angeles and Waterloo, Iowa. Most critically, as the son of a foreman who owned his own respectable home, he must have felt that it was possible for him to make a life as a man in his society—a belief that no slum-dwelling urban black could sustain beyond puberty—and even form dangerous ambitions (whether or not they were beyond his personal gifts). Thus the crisis that must hit many blacks in adolescence did not hit Essex until he was an adult and in the navy—a far more difficult time for an individual to absorb the social message that he or she is worthless, especially a young man reared on self-respect. If a class or race is to be easily subordinated, its self-respect must be looted systematically in childhood: in this special sense, the system failed.

Neither was there any agency in the community adequate to decode that social message. Emporia's factories and slaughterhouses did not deny a place to blacks: only one black owned his own business, but many labored in the factories and slaughterhouses. The community's roots in the anti-slavery movement were deep. The town had sent a 144-man regiment to fight the Confederacy during the Civil War, and the ruins of John Brown's log cabin remain as a monument only a few miles to the east. The majority of the community were of Welsh and English stock, shaping a milieu that was deeply religious, prosperous, and puritanical (Emporia was the first "dry" community in the Midwest). Less than 2 per cent of its 28,000 people were black; and if the black and Chicano families lived in the shabbier eastern end of town, the system that kept them there was subtle and without violence. A further safety-valve was that the community exported its most aggressive and ambitious blacks who searched elsewhere for their dreams, for they were not content with Emporia's mediocre horizons. This was not at all the stuff of the destruction of the spirit and the body that Elliot Liebow described in *Tally's Corner,* his classic study of the black slums in Washington, D.C.[26]

Essex was an average student in school—and it was this essential mediocrity, combined with his inappropriate ambition, which would (as much as his soul-destroying encounter with white racism) doom him to his fate. He had a special aptitude for technical subjects, and his teachers and schoolmates remembered him as a "smiling, friendly boy who was always laughing and joking," who dated both black and white girls, and whose ambition was to be a minister. A former girlfriend said: "He really didn't talk about wanting to be anything else. I know his mother was really happy about him wanting to become a minister." He spent one unsatisfactory semester at Kansas State College, after graduating from high school, and then enlisted in the navy in 1969, partly to avoid the draft and certain assignation to Vietnam. He scored in the top 25 per cent in the navy's entrance examination—which emphasized technical matters—and, impressed with the navy's programs, he signed up for four years. Hernon said Essex was "elated" when he discovered he was to be sent to San Diego. That elation would soon disappear, for he was about to be exposed to a hurricane.[27]

THE MANUFACTURE OF DESPAIR

"There is no place in this white man's navy for a self-respecting black man."

MARK ESSEX[28]

The metamorphosis of Essex from a cheerful young Midwestern black into a deeply embittered and increasingly committed young pseudo-revolutionary was accomplished within a few months in the U.S. Navy. He enlisted on January 13, 1969, and arrived in San Diego in early February for three months at the Naval Training Center. By April, Hernon wrote, Essex "had finished boot camp with an outstanding performance rating and was encouraged to take advanced training in a specialty." His superiors encouraged his essentially middle-class aspirations and assumptions, and advised him to enroll in the Naval Dental Center. After completing their three-month course in x-ray procedures and oral surgery, he was rated outstanding and assigned to the Dental Clinic at the Naval Air Station at Imperial Beach in July. There he established a solid working relationship with the young dentist to whom he was assigned, and who would later describe Essex as "a pretty good athlete. . . . He was a good team man, sort of an all-American boy. In those days he was just the nicest person in the world. He was concerned about everybody around him, concerned about learning his job. . . . He was the kind of person I liked to have around, a happy-go-lucky kid who was very hard to get rattled. I'm very demanding, especially when it concerns dentistry. I demanded a lot out of him and he delivered. His folks flew out to visit him early in his tour. They were just fine people. I really liked them. They were nice, down-home people who really enjoyed living and loved their son." A co-worker described Essex in similar terms: "He was an easygoing guy. He would sing to himself and be real friendly with everyone. I remember when I first got to the clinic he took time out and helped me. He showed me how to work with the doctors."[29]

Despite his positive attitudes and sunny personality, an epidemic of racial harassment on the Imperial Beach base began to trouble him. He wrote to his parents to complain that the navy "is not like I thought it would be, not like in Emporia. Blacks have trouble getting along here." When Essex discussed the problem with his black friends on the base, they advised him to adjust to the reality, to work hard enough to receive promotion, and thus be removed from contact with the worst racists. Essex took the advice to heart and was promoted from recruit to seaman in less than a year; but the harassment continued, and as Hernon observed, "it was increasingly clear that blacks were second-class citizens in the Navy, and it was hard for him to understand why no one seemed willing to change things."[30]

Nurtured in the blandness of Emporia, his assumptions about himself as a full citizen and human being were being bombarded, and he had no ready defense for such an assault. When he took an extra job as bartender at the enlisted men's club, he found that while white bartenders could go anywhere without permission, he could not enter certain rooms without first asking a white sailor. The car he bought to celebrate his twenty-first birthday was halted by security guards each time he entered or left the base: invariably he had to produce his license, registration, and insurance as if they did not know him. Frequently, he was ordered out of the car as the guards searched its every seam, elaborately unscrewing even the door panels to make their racist point. When he began to date a Mexican woman and took her to the enlisted men's club, "conversation stopped, heads turned, and it wasn't long before the half-whispered [racist slurs and] comments began to circulate."[31]

The rebellion first surfaced when Essex and his three black bunk mates were put on report for "excessive noise in the barracks." They were accused of playing a stereo late into the night, and forced to face a disciplinary hearing. They were convinced that they were being discriminated against, since whites played their stereos just as loudly and without punishment. Essex and his friends decided to fight the charge and demanded a summary court-martial, which would allow them to argue their case. Essex's patron and boss, the dentist, conducted his own private investigation into the affair and was convinced the matter was a clear case of racial discrimination. The sailor who filed the complaint, he said, "was a guy who was obviously just a prejudiced individual. He didn't like blacks in general. . . . He told me that he walked into Essex's room and here was 'all this nigger shit.'" The dentist told the commanding officer about his findings and the court-martial proceedings were halted. But Essex was not satisfied, for he and his friends were then separated and assigned to different barracks. It was vindication not compromise that he sought.[32]

Essex felt that he and his friends had been "sold out," and

thought that once they had been isolated in their new barracks, "it was really going to hit the fan." As Hernon wrote, "His prediction proved accurate. The riding continued unabated. He was a pariah who lived in virtual silence. No one openly called him 'nigger.' They didn't have to, for he was subjected to every petty indignity imaginable—endless bed checks, extra guard-duty tours, and constant admonitions to turn down his stereo even when the volume was so low he could barely hear it. There were even laughs when he combed his low-riding bush haircut, which he kept well trimmed for fear of being put on report for violating grooming regulations." At the enlisted men's club, the once-muted racial tension escalated into louder and more vicious racial slurs; and the same slurs hounded him into the mess hall or gymnasium until his work at the dental clinic began to suffer and he was forced to take sedatives.[33]

Two black friends of Essex during that period later told the *New York Times* that "all the young blacks around the base were being hassled. Essex felt that he was getting a particularly rough deal and that he wasn't going to take it lying down. White sailors in the enlisted men's club came down hard on Essex, regarding him as a 'cocky nigger'. . . . But what really burned Essex up was the riding he got from petty officers and other officers. They would write him up for the smallest infraction and usually he would get a Captain's Mast while the white got off scot free. We all had that sort of experience." Another friend commented that "Essex came into the Navy expecting to be treated in the same decent way he always had been treated back in Emporia, and he found it wasn't like that at all."[34]

The first explosion of violence from Essex took a remarkably long time to emerge; but in August of 1970, a racial slur triggered a fistfight. As the incident was reconstructed, a white petty officer had remarked to Essex about black "smilin' and shufflin'," and prolonged the taunting until Essex jumped on the man's chest and began flailing at him with his fists. The fight was interrupted by a passing officer, but the chain of thought it had provoked was not. As Hernon noted of this release from the colonial mentality: "For the first time in his life he had struck a white man, a fact so unbelievably startling that its significance was only now beginning to ring in his brain. The blow had seemed as natural as a thunderstorm in summer and as he thought about it, re-creating the fight in his imagination, savoring it, he realized that what he had done was more than justifiable; it was heroic." But Essex paid a heavy price for that blow: everywhere on the base, he was now a marked man, a black who had struck a white NCO. A friend remembered him concluding that "if a black sailor can't get a fair shake when he's in the right, then to hell with the whole United States Navy."[35]

In increasing despair, Essex went absent without leave on the morning of October 19, 1970, one month after the base commander had halted his court-martial. Even with the sleeping pills, he had been unable to sleep, lying awake and dreading another day of racial harassment and denial of self. Sitting in the bus depot waiting for a bus to Emporia, he decided it was necessary for him, purely as a matter of self-preservation, to get out of the navy. He telephoned his parents and told them, "I'm coming home. I've just got to have some time to think." He spent his days in Emporia thinking "about what a black man has to do to survive." According to Hernon, "the intensity of his bitterness at first surprised, then worried his parents, but when they gently tried to caution him about the dangers of hatred, his head would jerk up as if pulled by strings. 'What else is there?' he would say. 'They take everything from you, everything. Your dignity, your pride. What can you do but hate them?' He vowed that he was unwilling to wait any longer to be treated 'like a man.'"[36]

Mrs. Essex later recalled for Hernon that her son "'told us he didn't see how he could go back to the Navy and start it all over again.' While she cautioned moderation, he replied that he was not being treated with 'moderation,' but 'like a nigger.'" The distraught parents asked their minister to intervene: "He told me," the minister recalled, "how badly the Navy had treated him and how fed up he was. We talked a lot about discrimination and I remember him telling me how he had seen 'the whole picture' in the Navy. He was very, very bitter. I'll tell you, I was worried about the boy after we talked. So were his parents." Eventually, however, their counsel prevailed, and Mark returned voluntarily to the navy after a month's absence without leave. "He had had his time to think," Hernon wrote. "He had had his chance, as he would say later at his court-martial, 'to talk to some black people.'" Essex reported to his base's military police and awaited his court-martial.[37]

The Trial

"I have two years left and when I get out I want to become a dentist."

MARK ESSEX[38]

Before the trial, Essex—not yet utterly alienated from white society—explained his dilemma to his patron, the dentist Hatcher. "I just couldn't hack it anymore, and I felt like everybody was out to get me," Hatcher remembered him saying. "I really had to go home to get my head straight, and my mom and dad told me that I had to do it this way. So here I am. You do whatever you have to do and then, that's it. I'm getting out." When Hatcher tried to argue that Essex should not run away from the problem, Essex replied, perhaps with greater wisdom: "Nothing is going to change, doctor. The same old hassles will go on, and me and all the other blacks will keep on coming out on the bottom." Clearly, he had already made his dual decision to leave the navy and to conclude that nothing could be changed—at least not by conventional action.[39]

The trial was appropriately Kafka-esque. Essex's lawyer based his defense on the prejudice issue and used the dentist Hatcher as his primary witness. Hatcher, Essex's superior officer on the base, testified that Essex was "by far . . . the best [assistant] that I have worked with. He is outstanding in his professional performance and duties [and] . . . in my relationship with him he has proven to be a very personable, very warm person. He is sincerely worried about other people, about their needs, about their problems [and] . . . he constantly volunteers his services because he wants to help people." Hatcher further testified that the story behind Essex's absence without leave could be traced to his being put on charge for excessive noise in the barracks: "The men felt that they were being unjustly accused because of their color, and . . . my investigation showed that the man who made the original complaint was a very biased individual, and very obviously racially prejudiced. He had very possibly, to my way of thinking, influenced the other witnesses . . . so that the picture given to the court-martial was a very biased one. The captain, after hearing this, talked to the man who made the original complaint . . . and decided that the whole case was a matter of injustice."[40]

"He [the Captain] at this time ordered that the court-martial be stopped," Hatcher's testimony continued, "and brought the four men before him and made what I think he felt was an honest attempt to get at the problem [but] . . . I think that the feeling from all four of them was that it was just another whitewash of the situation, that, in fact, the Captain was not going to be able to do anything . . . I think that Essex, in this case being the most sensitive and the most responsible of the four, felt that he had been sold out, and he was very despondent over it. Immediately after the initial complaint was lodged and was brought to the XO's mast, they [the four sailors] were separated. . . . They put Essex in a room with totally incompatible people and the harassment started almost immediately, and he was again forced into a situation, this was before the court-martial even came about, that was nothing but a constant hassle, and this in his living spaces, the only place . . . he could go to relax. The harassment occurred in the mess hall lines, recreation areas, and so forth. So all put together, he was a very upset person during this time. . . ." The remarkable Hatcher continued with a denunciation of the harassment that Essex had experienced, and of his own doomed attempts to abridge it.[41]

When it came time for Essex to testify, he essentially concurred with Hatcher. "I am the accused," he said chillingly. "I believe that Dr. Hatcher explained most of everything as to the reason that I went UA. When we asked for a court-martial, the four black people felt that it was a case of discrimination. We had certain things happen to us before we went to trial . . . I went UA because I just needed time to think . . . I had to talk to some black people because I had begun to hate all white people. I was tired of going to white people and telling them my problems and not getting anything done about it. I am twenty-one years old. Almost every time I drove on the base they would search my car. I had a fight in front of the chow hall. Some friends of mine were going back to the barracks, and I was going to chow and they asked me to bring back some chicken for them, and I asked them what color the chicken was to be, and they said that it should be black. Well, someone said to me, 'Why does it have to be black, what is wrong with white?' and I jumped on his chest . . . I have two years left and when I get out I want to become a dentist."[42]

For the crime of fleeing from racist abuse, Essex was sentenced to forfeit ninety dollars of his pay each month for two months, was restricted "to the limits of the Naval Air Station . . . for a period of 30 days," and was "reduced to the pay grade of E-2." The presiding judge could only say that "the prejudice issues that were raised by the defense, while not excusing your offense, do materially explain your actions." Essex left the room with an emotionless expression and the conviction that the system had failed and excluded him. Several weeks later, Essex was asked to sign a document acknowledging that he had been considered "for an administrative discharge for reason of unsuitability due to character behavior disorder." Shortly after this ultimate degradation, the station's commanding officer recommended that Essex be "separated from the naval service . . . [as his] further retention in the service would not be in the best interests of the Navy. Essex continues to display flagrant disregard for Military authority, despite frequent counseling at the departmental and command level. Essex's impulsive behavior, and inability to accept the responsibilities of military service have rendered him a severe liability to this command." Thus the system vindicated itself in this extraordinary document, and "explained" Essex's reaction to intolerable racist abuse as a "behavior disorder." Therein lay the intolerable affront that Essex would redress by carefully planned behavior in which he would accept the responsibilities of quite another form of military service.[43]

THE CREATION OF AN IDEOLOGUE

"It's a revolution!"

MARK ESSEX[44]

The emotional preconditions for his task were created in the profound contradictions embedded in the social order. These were transmitted with the utmost rigor to young Essex. It now remained for him to explore whatever ideological alternatives were available to him in order to reconstruct his damaged sense of self. He appeared to find it in the burgeoning black radicalism of the time. However, like all our multiple murderers, as a true ideological conservative he would not join a revolutionary movement. He would only absorb its rhetoric and style in order to carry out a personal vendetta, an individualized protest against the exclusion of this marginal middle-class black from his own aspirations. It should come as no surprise that his rebellion took such a racist form, for the spirit of the times gave ideological—even divine—sanction to racist excess. All this must have been intoxicating for a maturing martyr and rebel.*

It is not clear exactly what Essex's movements and contacts were during his post-navy career. The journalist Tobias thought that "there was scattered evidence to suggest that Essex had connections with black militant groups," but admitted that "it was not clear." Still, Tobias concluded that since there was an abundance of black revolutionary literature in Essex's apartment, there "seemed little doubt that Essex was intimately connected with black extremist factions." There was insufficient evidence for such a conclusion. Tobias noted that Essex spent "most of the time" between his discharge from the navy in February 1970, and April of 1972, with his parents in Emporia, but added that

---

* For popular accounts of the extreme form these radical black offshoots took, see Clark Howard's *Zebra* and Robert Tannenbaum and Philip Rosenberg's *Badge of the Assassin*.

"he took mysterious trips to New York and New Orleans supposedly to 'visit old Navy friends.'" Whatever the actual contacts with militant groups may have been, "Essex left Emporia somewhat abruptly and went to New Orleans where he joined a militant Black Muslim friend from the Navy." One police report commented that "during this entire investigation into the background of Mark Essex, no firm physical evidence was found which would link him to any of the known subversive or militant groups, although his possible involvement with several such groups was hinted by more than one source interviewed. There can be no doubt that Essex was well trained both in firearms and urban guerrilla tactics . . . and while the investigation failed to develop the sources of and scope of any such training, there is some evidence to indicate that he did undergo a period of training shortly after his release from the Navy." Despite the paucity of the evidence, there was no doubt in the police investigators' minds that Essex's behavior had been a coordinated and well-considered campaign, part of a group's terrorist strategy. As one detective remarked, "this was expert, well planned, well executed, and demonstrated the techniques of urban modern guerrilla warfare."[45]

We will never know the precise details of whether he was involved in personal encounters with revolutionary groups; but it matters not, for the important thing is that in his post-navy maturation, he was exposed to the writings and thoughts of black revolutionary intellectuals, and that his state of mind was such that he was willing to kill and die for such notions. Since no action followed his death, it is unlikely that his terrorism was anything other than an individual *communiqué*. The origin of his ability to make such a social statement lay in the shock of his sudden exposure to white racism. An ugly or lame child may grow accustomed to such stigmatization: it is the beauty whose face is suddenly destroyed or the athlete whose body is crippled by accident who experience the sharpest pain—a shame requiring terrible expiation.

Essex cannot have been exposed to radical thought during his adolescence in Emporia—or if he was, it made no impact upon him. He would only have felt the intense and

Christian sense of injustice which his mother articulated in her no-nonsense way. It was in the navy, Hernon wrote, "that Essex began to read about the black movement, something he had rarely done in Emporia. With interest he followed in the newspapers the legal battles of Huey Newton and Bobby Seale, who had founded the Black Panther Party in 1967 . . . [and of a] five-hour gun battle in Los Angeles between police and eleven Panthers, including three women." At this time too, he formed new associations. What the sociologists call "the significant other," the influential friend, was to be Rodney Frank, a New Orleans black with an extensive arrest record who was in the navy at Imperial Beach with Essex. It was Frank who would interpret Essex's experience for him. According to the police report, "Fellow sailors and superior officers reported that Essex began to have a change of attitude as he became more closely associated with Rodney Frank. Frank, who was described as being militant and antagonistic, later became a Black Muslim, and his attitude towards the white population may have influenced Mark Essex's thinking." A later FBI report noted that Essex, while in the navy, also "associated with and received black militant literature from a member of the Black Panther Party," and Hernon said that Essex "mingled off-base with other tough-talking blacks in the San Diego area. These individuals . . . undoubtedly felt their relationship with Essex was one of student-teacher: the naive black from backwoods America needed to be informed what it was like to be beaten down by the system. What influence they had on Essex is not known; whatever it was, it became increasingly clear to Dr. Hatcher and others that the young sailor had changed."[46]

Hatcher even dated the change to Essex's twenty-first birthday on August 12, 1970. "The change was very sudden," he remembered. "It seemed to come in a matter of weeks . . . I have a feeling that he got in with a group of blacks who really felt they were being put down. . . . Several times he talked about going downtown and meeting with some guys who were putting out an underground newspaper. . . . Once the harassment started, after the fight and after he started getting into trouble, the conversations we had were very terse. He was almost a defeatist at that point. He was really down on the system. And as I said, it really came overnight. It was very quick, and I couldn't understand it. . . . During that first year all our conversations had been happy ones. But then they became very short. He was kind of defensive, belligerent sometimes." Essex's torment was profound: as his sister later put it, he was in the midst of the process in which "the Navy became his own private hell."[47]

Hernon correctly noted that Essex was "a casualty of history," and reminds us of the prevailing mood of protest within the armed forces at the time, in which black sailors also began to rebel. "Fights swept U.S. military bases and naval stations. In Vietnam, black GIs drafted to fight in a war in which they didn't believe were accused of blowing up—fragging—white officers. Morale disintegrated. . . . Resistance organized, and groups with names like 'Black Liberation Front of the Armed Forces' were established. Sabotage increased. In May of 1970, for example, nuts, bolts, and chains were dumped down the main gear shaft of the U.S.S. *Anderson* while she was in San Diego. Other ships were similarly damaged. The revolt of Seaman Essex was the revolt of every black in uniform."[48]

According to the New York City police's Intelligence Division, Essex went to New York in February, shortly after his discharge from the navy, and established contact there with the most militant wing of the Black Panthers. "At that time," the black undercover detective recalled, "that was the headquarters for the Eldridge Cleaver faction of the Panther Party. He must have gotten the revolutionary rhetoric hot and heavy." He spent three months there, at a time when the Panther Party was in such serious financial trouble, due to a severe drop in membership, that Stokely Carmichael, an early hero of the party, had remarked that "the Panthers are practically finished." Out of fashion, the Panthers were divided by the inevitable ideological disputes and had split into two rival factions. The dispute was so divisive that soon after Essex arrived in New York, a shooting war broke out between the two factions and several members were killed.[49]

Still, there was no need to be a member, or a part, of any revolutionary party when the monthly publication of the

Cleaver wing, *Right on,* contained the ideology and instructions for the developing urban guerrilla. "There were, for instance, discussions of revolutionary tactics; 'how-to' techniques for killing 'pigs,' including where to shoot them (in the head) and what kinds of weapons to use ... diversionary tactics, how to manufacture bombs and incendiary devices; first aid; and propaganda." The fashionable revolutionary texts were Chairman Mao's *Red Book,* Che Guevara's *Guerrilla Warfare,* and Carlos Marighella's *Mini-Manual of the Urban Guerrilla.* Marighella stresses that the "perfection of the art of shooting makes him a special type of urban guerrilla—that is, a sniper." Similarly, reference was often made to a "Vanguard Party, capable of leading the black masses into an open, violent revolt to overturn the 'racist capitalistic superstructure,'" and to a "'Black Messiah' who would carry a rifle, not a cross." In this maelstrom, Essex's adult identity was forged. He had little choice by then, for as one undercover officer remarked: "Essex probably peddled the paper, and I'd be surprised if he didn't pick up a lot just by reading it. It's all part of the indoctrination. You read about revolution and killing pigs; you talk about it constantly until it's almost a kind of narcotic."[50]

Hernon speculated quite reasonably that Essex must have become "disillusioned" by his time in New York. "The Panthers were weak, hopelessly divided—instead of shooting 'pigs' they were shooting one another—and for a young, increasingly angry black, polarized by violent rhetoric and conceivably interested in armed revolution, it must have been a serious disappointment to see his heroes in such disarray." He left New York just before militant blacks attacked four city policemen, killing two of them. At home he read and re-read *Black Rage:* "As a sapling bent low stores energy for a violent backswing, blacks bent double by oppression have stored energy which will be released in the form of rage—black rage, apocalyptic and final." Not long after one thousand state troopers opened fire on rioting Attica prisoners, killing twenty-eight prisoners (mostly black), Essex purchased the recommended Ruger .44 magnum carbine and began to practice using the weapon. Late that summer, he decided to move to New Orleans. He left quietly, without telling his parents, for he was certain they would not approve of such a move. With him went his Ruger carbine and his .38-caliber Colt revolver.[51]

In New Orleans, he joined his navy friend, Rodney Frank. While Frank joined the Black Muslim Mosque and sold its newspaper, *Muhammad Speaks,* Essex made one final attempt to grasp a tolerable social status and proscribe his coming suicide. He enrolled in a government training program for underprivileged persons, studying vending-machine repair with pay. This was no easy way of simply obtaining funds, and Essex's instructors reported that he was an enthusiastic and dedicated student. Still, his anxiety reflected itself in his mindless watching of television hour after hour. As well, he was now studying his "heritage," reading books on Africa and learning words from Zulu and Swahili, even dropping them into conversations and adopting the Swahili word for "bow" as his nickname. In late October, he returned to Emporia for a brief visit, and appeared to be in good spirits.[52]

When he returned to New Orleans, his inner contradictions tortured him with headaches and nightsweats. "Thrust up to the edge of an abyss, he could see no way to cross. More and more he stayed to himself, withdrawing to his apartment to watch television or to read." Soon he would grasp fully the insufficiency of his attempt to embrace the identity of a repairer of vending machines. The incident which ultimately committed Essex to his radical course was the police shooting of two black university students at a campus demonstration in Baton Rouge on November 16. With that, Essex committed himself to becoming a god. Late in December, he sent his declaration to a television station: "Africa greets you . . . on Dec 31 1974 appt 11 the Downtown New Orleans Police Dept will be attack . . . Reason—many. But the deaths of two innocent brothers will be avenged. And many others . . . P.S. Tell Pig Gurusso [the police chief] the felony action squad ain't shit." The letter was signed with his Swahili nickname, "Mata" (bow). He attended his final vending-machine repair class, then wrote his parents a letter vowing total war against whites. "Africa, this is it mom," he wrote. "It's even bigger than you and I, even bigger than god. I have now decided that the white man is my enemy. I will fight to gain my manhood or die trying." Having committed the remainder of his destiny, like a Kamikaze warrior, he distributed his most prized possessions among friends—although he did not, apparently, inform them of his intent.[53]

During that period, it would seem, he daubed the walls and ceilings of his apartment with slogans of his hate and rebellion. "The largest wall was practically covered with the word 'AFRICA,' which was painted in wavy letters three feet high and bordered with a black margin. Beneath it, in red, was written, 'My destiny lies in the bloody death of racist pigs.' The words 'destiny' and 'death' were underlined. In some places the paint had run in streaks. Next to the slogan 'Revolutionary justice is black justice' was the word 'blood,' and above that the letters 'KKK.' Also painted in red, 'Blond hair, blue eyes.' The words 'hate' and 'kill' were splashed everywhere, seemingly at random. Next to the word 'Africa' was scrawled, 'Hate white people—beast of the earth.' Inside the giant C of 'Africa' Essex had carefully penciled in, 'The quest for freedom is death—then by death I shall escape to freedom.' Near the ceiling was spelled out, 'The Third World—Kill Pig Nixon and all his running dogs.' No inch of wall space was spared." There were also many words, many of them garbled and misspelled, from Swahili. Essex had left his last will and testament, and done so with an uncharacteristic trace of humor; for when the detectives entered the apartment and looked up at the ceiling, they read his painted insult to them: "Only a pig would read shit on the ceiling."[54]

THE AUTHORITIES RESPOND

"Essex was caught between two worlds
which retarded the maturation of
his self-identity."

RONALD TOBIAS[55]

Hard upon his actions there followed an inevitable deluge of self-serving responses from the authorities, both judicial and intellectual. Leftist ideologues established the legitimacy of his grievance and linked it to the obvious form of society but, typically, ignored the sufferings of his victims. For their part, the rightist ideologues devoted their efforts in equally predictable fashion to exonerate society of all blame and lodge responsibility for the crime in some flaw (such as the retardation of the maturation of his self-identity) in Essex. "He was overwhelmed by the sudden insistence of black survival in a hostile environment where the whites controlling it were less permissive than they had been in Emporia," said Tobias. This unreasonable insistence that blacks should survive, this non-permissive navy attitude toward blacks, seemed to have been at the root of Essex's retarded maturity, thought the spokesmen of the right.

Yet it was not simply journalists who drew such flaccid conclusions. During Essex's first psychiatric examination, when he was in trouble in the navy in early February of 1971, the navy psychiatrist had admitted that there was "no clinical evidence of delusion, hallucinations, inappropriate affect, impaired reality testing, thought disorder, or organic brain disease," but found Essex's judgment to be "poor, impulsive, and immature." The doctor concluded that Essex had an "immature personality" and represented "a liability to himself and to the United States Navy." Then, in a prophetic observation, he wrote: "The patient gives a history of no previous suicidal gestures which were done to manipulate those about him of his environment. At this time, he denies that he wishes to kill himself. However, he alludes to the fact that he 'might do something' if he doesn't get what he wants."[56]

After the shooting, the state's Attorney-General told newsmen that he was "now convinced that there is an underground, national, suicidal group bent on creating terror in America. Their purpose is to cause the people to be dissatisfied, to bring race against race, black against white, young against old, to cause internal national chaos." This sentiment was echoed by the U.S. Attorney-General, who promised that "the full force of the Department of Justice would be behind a national investigation" to uncover the conspiracy. Louisiana Governor Edwin Edwards told reporters that "he would consider state laws to reinstate capital punishment for certain 'heinous crimes.' He also said that he had 'no information whatsoever on a nation-wide conspiracy to kill policemen.'"[57]

More analytically, a black assistant to the Mayor commented: "This event will be what we make of it. There are lessons to be learned. The police will learn tactical lessons. Hopefully, by the same manner, I think people all around this country will learn . . . there are real hard problems to deal with. [Many young blacks] were drawing a link to that man on the roof and blacks pursuing their legitimate grievances." In a similar vein, a black activist told Hernon that "A lot of white people have written Mark Essex off as just a crazy nigger, an extremist. They forget what Malcolm had to say about extremists. He said, 'You show me a black man who isn't an extremist and I'll show you one who needs psychiatric attention.' . . . He was a man who was terribly frustrated and decided to fight. Most blacks deal with frustration in other ways, or if we are violent, we've been brainwashed to the point where we channel our violence against one another. It was different with Essex. And as I watched the shooting at the hotel that Sunday, I kept thinking, why doesn't that happen more often? I don't think Essex believed that he was going to kick off a revolution as some have suggested. I think he just wanted to act. He didn't give a damn any more about what would happen; he wasn't looking at the result. . . . The system had fucked him over. The only thing he thought he could do to the system was to try to destroy it, and if he died trying, he died."[58]

More traditionally, Louisiana psychiatrist Dr. William Bloom de-politicized and diminished Essex's rebellion by analyzing him in terms of a short and impotent person. "He was very short," he told a journalist, "and yet he had a very big gun. . . . There's not a great deal of difference between his drawing of a sword and the image of him striking death with his .44 magnum carbine. The gun probably helped him compensate for feelings of powerlessness. If he saw himself as a crusader, striking back, he would not have to feel disenfranchised. His concept of self-esteem is very important. By acting in the spirit of a black revolutionary, he may well have been acting against injustices which he perceived to have been done against him. The slogans which he sprayed across the walls of his dingy apartment certainly indicated he hated the police as symbols of the white power structure. By killing them, he would assert his manhood and gain esteem from some elements of the black community. And by gaining esteem, he could defend his fragile identity, which probably was the biggest fight. . . . After looking at his apartment and seeing all of those racist slogans painted on the walls, I would say that Essex had no clarity of concept; the slogans from various revolutionaries were mixed together." Bloom admitted that "we can't seem to build any case that Essex was neurologically defective or psychotic. As far as I know, there were no signs of mental illness in his family." Still, he concluded that "I do think, however, that there were indications he was suicidal."[59]

The most important document in the intervention of the state in this case was undoubtedly that prepared by police Superintendent Giarrusso, who moved to exonerate the state. "For his [Essex's] acts," Giarrusso wrote, "he paid with his life and, thus, inflicted pain and suffering on his own family." Drawing attention to the fact that one of Essex's victims had been black, another had been a woman, and that a third one was younger than Essex, he concluded: "They all shared the commonality of membership in a society, a society that Mark Essex had rejected because, in his opinion, it had failed to meet its expectations." Giarrusso cautioned that "an attempt may be made to explain Essex's violent acts against his fellow human beings by the presentation of evidence carefully selected to support the premise that society was the compelling contributor to those acts and, if not responsible therefore, at least to blame." For Giarrusso, this notion seemed easy to refute: "In not accepting that premise, I reject the selected evidence offered in its support. To do otherwise, in my opinion, would fix upon society, instead of individuals, the blame for all criminal acts." Yet where did he find the idea that both cannot be blamed; or that in blaming one, the other was therefore exonerated? It mattered not, for his task was not to understand a phenomenon, but merely to blame the actor. "Mark Essex's footnote in history should state clearly that he murdered and executed, without justifiable cause of purpose; that society did not fail him, but that he failed society; that if society inflicted any indignities upon him, such indignities were minuscule by comparison."[60]

In the final analysis, it was two sociologists who asked the important questions. The social scientist, William Swanson, commented that Essex's apparently suicidal behavior could be linked to other phenomena: "I do think that Essex was suicidal. I think that he was suicidal in the sense that he did think he could start something, that he might begin a revolution . . . start something that was big. I think that he thought that when he went up on the roof of that hotel that he wasn't coming down. He was suicidal in the sense that he was willing to sacrifice himself for the cause. That may not have been realistic but not delusional in that he thought he was a Black Messiah, the chosen one. There are many examples of this kind of suicide through history. It's called altruistic suicide, and one of the best examples is the Kamikaze pilot of the Second World War." More fundamentally, sociologist Daniel Thompson pierced the heart of the issue when he observed: "The problem for society to ponder out of all this is a fundamental one. How is it to deal with such supreme alienation? It doesn't matter whether the individual be black or white, although in Essex's case it's obvious that his blackness precipitated his action. The question is, what do you do with the man who is alone, cut off, willing to die?"[61]

INTERNMENT

> "Man seems to take justice into his own hands when god or secular authorities fail. It is as if in his passion for vengeance he elevates himself to the role of god, and of the angels of vengeance."
>
> ERICH FROMM[62]

If we rely on conventional explanations for such outrageous behavior, we are inevitably left perplexed. Essex was no troubled victim of an abusing family, displacing hatred of father on an innocent society. Neither was he a deranged individual suffering from some mental disease, for even his inquisitors cleared him of any serious charges of this nature. Yet this pleasant young man from a prosperous and loving home killed and wounded several dozens of his fellow human beings—including one of his own race—and came close to obliterating an entire city block. In passing, he exposed the incompetence of the city's security forces (as he had said he would do in his *communiqué* to the media).

Essex shares the self-absorption and simple-mindedness of all our multiple murderers, but he is the only one of their number whose protest *seems* to be more than entirely personal, the only one who appeared to act politically, which is to say on behalf of others besides himself. Indeed, this won him much sympathy in certain circles, for he seemed to represent the needs and aspirations of the disenfranchised black masses. Yet the only difference between Essex's rebellion and that of our other multiple murderers is that many people could identify with, even approve, his outrage at his particular exclusion (in a way they could not, for example, with the failed entrance to the lower-middle classes that haunted DeSalvo). In fact, however, his protest proceeded from precisely the same individual reasons as that of all the others in this book. He had no revolutionary social theory other than a racist hatred, no concept of organized response beyond the .44 magnum.

One is led inexorably to the conclusion that if he had remained in Emporia and achieved his high school ambition of becoming a minister, or even perhaps risen to be a junior executive in a meat-packing plant (instead of venturing into the racist trap of the U.S. Navy) he would have remained forever the gentle and delicate young man he was when he walked through the gates of the San Diego naval yard for the first time. One suspects that if he had been able to fulfill his earlier dream of becoming a dentist, or even if he had been able to come to terms with his considered career in vending-machine repair, he and his victims would have survived. Thus the killing stemmed as much as (or more) from his mundane personal career crisis as from any revolutionary ideas: he could not tolerate the lowly rank that his society and his limited personal talents would make available to him.

His final hours were theatrical and entirely in keeping with the fashionably violent codes of his culture. John Wayne would have understood his explosion into purple ceremony. He had decided that only through monstrous acts could he feel that he addressed himself to what historians of crime Peter and Favret call "the rule of lies and the foul machine at whose whim his fellows, the disinherited of the earth, are and have always been crushed, each day, each life." But the act that was a discourse fell hard on perpetrator and victim alike, along with all their intimates. No repayment, despite the many millions of dollars in law suits against the city, could return what had been stolen. The victims were buried during *days* of funerals: among the first was Patrolman Paul Persigo, at thirty-three, the youngest accredited Rose Show Judge in the United States. He did not deserve to die; and neither did the others who followed him into their graves.[63]

Essex was too proud to face a life he perceived as "devoid of all future, deprived of all prospects," or to thereby endure "the unlivable, day in and day out." In Emporia, his parents gave a hint of the moral rectitude that provided the ideological basis for their son's decision, the means by which a young man described by a lifelong friend as "sort of a soft kid, a delicate sort of man," was transformed into a heartless killer. "Young blacks are not going to accept the white racist society," his mother told a reporter. "It's a clear signal, a clear signal for white America to get off the seat of its pants and do something. I don't want my son to have died in vain. If this terrible thing will awaken white America to the injustices that blacks suffer, then some good will have come of it." His sister added that after "Jimmy went into the Navy, he really saw what life, the world was all about. He saw that white people control the world, and blacks were being oppressed by the white man. He didn't like society the way it is. He wanted to change things. The Navy to Jimmy was his own private hell." Undoubtedly it was, alas, but he changed nothing: however, it mattered not, for his goal had been merely to release his own personal anger, to stage his private rebellion.[64]

The warrior with 200 bullet holes in his body was buried in an unmarked grave in Emporia. A few days after the funerals, one of the policemen who had been in the Marine helicopter which had attacked Essex, shot a slum black who had tried to kill him. As attendants placed the youth in the back of the ambulance, a woman's voice rose over the darkened New Orleans slum: "Sniper comin' back. Sniper comin' back to get you all." As if to confirm this—and to deny the reality that many died for nothing—young blacks sometimes search for Essex's unmarked grave and, finding it, stand beside it in silence.[65]

Part III

AN OVERVIEW

8.
TOWARD A HISTORICAL SOCIOLOGY OF MULTIPLE MURDER

"Other sinnes onley speake;
Murther shreikes out."

THE DUCHESS OF MALFI

This book has explicated the texts left by a half-dozen killers of our time. It has not focused on these murderers because their thoughts or acts are of any merit, but because it is only through a detailed examination of their careers that we can hope to understand the origin and meaning of their activities. We have taken as our starting point the observation of Robert Darnton that it is precisely "when we run into something that seems unthinkable to us [that] we may have hit upon a valid point of entry into an alien mentality." Having done this, we will now try to marry the great historical and anthropological enterprises. In doing so, we will "have puzzled through to the native's point of view" and mounted an explanation of the inexplicable. So far we have tried to reveal the immediate motives behind the killers' acts: now our task is to transcend the immediate, to suggest that these motives are neither insane nor random but buried deeply in the social order, part of a continuously evolving social process.[1]

The murderer of strangers has probably always been among us. However much we may wish to dismiss him as a freak, an aberration, or an accident, his tastes and desires are part of the human repertoire, the human experience, and the human capability. Nor must we dismiss him and his behavior as meaningless, for mankind is a gregarious and social species, and anything its members do has some social meaning. But wherein lies the origin of the social process we have now described, that sequence of events which so deforms a man that he comes to think of himself as a kind of automaton, a "robot" going through the motions of social life without any hope that future events might make his life endurable? The killers customarily explain themselves in conventional ideas borrowed from the wider culture, as did the torturer and multiple murderer, *Joseph Kallinger,* in his autobiographical poem, "The Unicorn in the Garden."[2]

When I was a little boy,
My adoptive parents,
Anna and Stephen,
Killed the unicorn in my garden

Exiled from the street,
Isolated from other children,
I lived among shoes and knives and hammers.
Unknown, unwanted, unloved,
I learned to shape soles, replace heels, drive nails.
My own soul was hidden from me by the shop's
Dead world.
A robot to their will,
I died with the unicorn in my garden.

Yet this self-pitying interpretation leaves unanswered so many questions. If his own adoptive parents were so insensitive to his needs, why was he dramatically more so when he tortured and murdered his own small son? If his childhood was so difficult, was his adulthood (he had a bearable occupation, in which he was very highly regarded, and a loving wife and family, who seemed devoted to him) provocative of anything resembling his gruesome acts? I think not. It is therefore incumbent upon us to look much more deeply into the historical process and its impact upon the lives of individuals, if we are ever to have anything resembling a clear understanding of these men.

Before we do so, let us be clear about the manner of beast we have been discussing, and how he stands in relation to other "criminal" species. He is not quite like the majority, whose thefts of *property* garner a combination of financial profit and "the intoxicating pleasure of intense activity." Such property offenses attract bank robbers, political commissars, and corporate executives, not the men of whom we speak (who reap neither wealth nor security from their crimes). Neither is the multiple murderer quite like those who commit crimes against the *person* (be it rape, assault, or even homicide), for these offenses tend to be little more than a demonstration of individual power and a cathartic release of rage. Our multiple murderers transcend mere catharsis and temporary gratification: their aim is a more ambitious one, a kind of sustained sub-political campaign directed toward "the timelessness of oppression and the order of power." But their protest is not on behalf of others, only themselves; their anguish is trivial, not profound; and they punish the innocent, not the guilty. It is thus only an extreme version of other nihilistic crimes, in which the killer typically reverses all social values as his only way of making "a demonstration to the authorities" in a manner so forceful that they must consider it. Since all he is protesting is his lack of a crisp identity and his refusal to tolerate the position society has allocated him, it is less than tragic— even ironic, but intellectually unacceptable—that what Peter and Favret call a "clumsy psychiatry" tries to declare him insane and suggest that:

> . . . the native's speech had no weight, was not even an effect of monstrosity; such criminals were only disturbed children who played with corpses as they played with words. The resentment they displayed had no reason for its existence; it was merely a product of their imagination.[3]

There is one problem that remains undiscussed and it is central to any biographical enterprise: if we can speak for the mass of humanity in sociological terms, how can we hope to do so for any individual? According to the late historical sociologist Philip Abrams, "The problem of accounting sociologically for the individual in particular is really only a more precise version of the problem of accounting for individuals in general." Analyzed in historical terms, "Lenin and Luther, the Sun King and Shakespeare no more elude or defy sociological explanation than do Russian proletarians in 1900." Abrams insists, and our data force us largely to concur, that "becoming a deviant is not a matter of personal or social pathology, social disorganization, deprivation, broken homes, viciousness, bad company or chance but of *a negotiated passage to a possible identity,*" in which the individual can only be understood as "creatively seizing opportunities for personal self-definition"—as did all our multiple murderers.

> Individuals *are* their biographies. And insofar as a biography is fully and honestly recorded what it reveals is some historically located history of self-construction —a moral career in fact. The setting of the biography is this or that historically given system of probabilities or life chances. The biography realizes some life chances within that system and perforce abandons others.

The point then is that to understand an exceptional individual, we must observe "the meshing of life-history and social history in a singular fate"; which is to say that we must look at the social system's matrix of choices and opportunities, rewards and punishments, in terms of which each individual calculates his future. Later in this chapter, we will suggest that nowhere more than in modern America is an individual likely to negotiate the identity of a multiple murderer.[4]

Yet the problem remains that while many people are subject to the same tainted origins and thwarted ambitions, yet only a tiny minority of them become killers. Why then do most of them refuse to do so? There are no data that would allow us to address the problem in any scientific fashion, no control group of biographies of individuals who have been diverted from the formative process at different stages. Yet it seems most likely that such people (the vast majority) are touched, however superficially, by some person or institution that renders their lives bearable—offering the common life of "quiet desperation" in place of the massive refusal of self and life that characterizes our killers. We can only posit that somewhere in the journey from institutionalized or illegitimate child to lofty but thwarted ambition, some family member, a lover, a job, or group membership (or the hope of any of these) offers most people a taste of fulfillment and interrupts their passage to murderous identities.

THE LITERATURE

> "For crimes against persons (murder, rape, assault) we have no theory as to the value of such offenses, and hence no theory as to what would affect the returns from such crimes."
>
> RALPH ANDREANO AND
> JOHN SIEGFRIED[5]

Homicide

The poverty of conventional explanation is nowhere better represented than in the above quotation from a group of economists who confess to being bewildered by a crime which offers no economic return. The other social sciences have fared rather better in their attempts to deal with homicide, at least in its "normal" manifestations. We have already demonstrated that, at least in theory, single and multiple murder are quite different phenomena, with profoundly different characteristics. The psychiatrist Lunde has made it clear that "the most important single contrast between mass murderers and murderers of a single person is a difference in their relationships to the victims," the former killing strangers, the latter killing intimates. This curious phenomenon of the murder of strangers is extremely rare in so-called "primitive" societies, a fact which social scientist Stuart Palmer corroborates with anthropological data showing that "in the vast majority of non-literate societies analyzed, 41 out of 44, homicidal victims and offenders are rarely if ever strangers." It is in our own tradition, buried both in our historical past and in our industrial present, that stranger-murder has been a major homicidal theme. In criminologist Wolfgang's classic study of 550 homicides in 1958 in Philadelphia, 12.2 per cent of the killings were between strangers; and the FBI report that 15.5 per cent of the 22,516 murders committed in the U.S. in 1981 were between strangers.[6]

The perpetrators of the types of murder are also profoundly different. Virtually all social analysts agree that single murder is primarily the province of the truly disenfranchised. "It is the oppressed who are the homicidal," writes Palmer. "The poor, the uneducated, those without legitimate opportunities, respond to their institutionalized oppression with outward explosions of aggression." This notion of exactly who the oppressed are has been much refined in the current debate on whether it is absolute poverty or relative inequality (or subcultural variation) which actually accounts for homicides. Nevertheless, Williams' tentative conclusion in the sociological journals remains that "racial economic inequality is a major source of criminal violence in the United States," and that "poverty, in addition to racial inequality, also provides 'fertile soil for criminal violence.'" It is obvious that our multiple murderers are drawn from very different social niches, for they are rarely from the ranks of the truly oppressed; they are rarely women, and almost never black. Indeed, they are generally white and gainfully employed, and, sometimes, have reasonable expectations of "brilliant" futures. They are not at all the same men who kill an intimate in a moment of rage or venality; nor are their generally spontaneous acts part of any organized and meaningful campaign. Lunde was quite right then to berate the scholars of homicide for their "tendency to assume that the single fact of having committed a murder is a sufficient basis for identifying a class of people, murderers" who are essentially the same, for nothing could be further from the truth.[7]

There are perspectives on homicide other than the purely sociological, but they tend to be mired in irrelevancy or based on mechanisms that do not exist. Perhaps the most popular of these has been the *pseudo-biological* school, which has held a certain sway since the nineteenth-century criminologist Lombroso began measuring the foreheads of Italian criminals and the twentieth-century criminologists, the Gluecks, assessed the testicles of American delinquents —all searching for the "criminal physical type." This tradition tends to fixate on such unfathomable matters as the purported brain temperatures of murderers, and has long ago been revealed as ideology masquerading as science. The "discovery" of the XYY chromosomes is perhaps the best known example of this nonsense: many unsubstantiated claims have been made that the possession of this chromosome inclines the victim toward violence (including falsely attributing such XYY chromosomes to Richard Speck, the Chicago nurse-murderer). These notions persist in the popular culture despite the fact that later studies have established that only a small proportion of violent offenders actually have XYY chromosomes. Furthermore, the imprisoned offenders who did have the XYY chromosomes were actually *less* likely to have committed violent crimes than those with "normal" chromosomes. Indeed, the only reasonable conclusion that has come out of the biological approach is sociobiologist Edward O. Wilson's observation that there is no evidence whatever for any universal aggressive instinct (as had been posited by ethologists such as Lorenz and Ardrey), and that human "behavior patterns do not conform to any general innate restrictions." Sadly for the scientific enterprise, most "sociobiologists"—even ones as literate as Melvin Konner—simply ignore the reality that human evolution's super-development of the cortex (or thinking, conscious part of the brain) has overridden any instinctive or genetically coded behaviors among humans. Similarly, they ignore the reality that if human behavior were genetically determined, it would be everywhere the same instead of ranging from the gentility of the "primitive" Fore peoples of New Guinea to the violence of South America's Yanomamo.[8]

The *psychological* tradition also looks for the cause of aggression within the individual, but finds it buried in the psyche rather than in the chromosome. Here, the assumption which runs throughout the literature is that anyone who murders must be suffering from some form of psychopathology, a dubious assumption indeed when working-class culture so obviously venerates violent display as an intrinsic manifestation of manhood. The psychologists and psychiatrists differ as to where they find the cause of this disorder. The psychiatrist Abrahamsen points to "persistent internal conflict between the environment around them and the world within them—the world of infantile sexual and life-preserving drives," a conflict which is caused by some traumatic experience in early childhood (before the child is two!). The psychologist Megargee hypothesizes that the violent criminal virtually always "has" one of two types of personalities, either "undercontrolled" or "overcontrolled," which leaves the critic marveling at how many walk the tightrope between the two. Still, two of America's most gifted psychiatrists refute their profession's stance. Lunde notes that "the incidence of psychosis among murderers is no greater than the incidence of psychosis in the total population"; and Willard Gaylin readily admits that psychiatry occupies a "primitive position" regarding "the nature of the cause of the disease." My criticism here is not that psychology and psychiatry have nothing to contribute to the study of murder, for they certainly do; but rather that they, no more than a pseudo-biology, cannot account for variations in homicide rates over time or between societies. Their special gift in fact is not at all to account for cause—for that lies within tensions generated in the social order—but to analyze the process in which the individual psyche accommodates itself to its environment.[9]

Multiple Murder

If the literature on homicide has a certain richness about it, curiously, no such assessment can be made about the subject of our inquiry. Multiple murder has attracted very little specialized attention and should the reader glance through four books, he will have mastered the number which have devoted themselves exclusively to the phenomenon. Even those four are primarily descriptive, not analytic. The first is still the best; but it (criminologist Bolitho's *Murder For Profit*) concerns itself only with the mendacious economic form that we ignore here—killing for profit. However, Bolitho's comments, now over half a century old, repay close examination. He noted then what those who followed him overlooked, that the killers were no "deranged automata" and that they were "the worst men, not madmen."

> If they very commonly construct for themselves a life-romance, a personal myth in which they are the maltreated hero, which secret is the key of their life, in such comforting day-dreams many an honest man has drugged himself against despair.

He observed that many of them thought of themselves as being in a kind of "social war, in which his hand is against society, and all is fair," but he understood that this is a common way of thinking among any "men in an unsheltered corner of this competitive world." He concluded with a remarkably sophisticated recognition of the complicity of the modern nation-state in the creation of these multiple murderers, remarking of the Fritz Haarmann case in Germany between the wars that: "The State had used all its best tools upon him: church, prison, army, school, family, asylum—it can hardly disclaim direct responsibility from the result."[10]

What might have been the beginning of a rich tradition of enquiry soon dissolved. In 1928, two years after the publication of Bolitho's book, criminologist Guy Logan published his *Masters of Crime* which purported to be a study of multiple murder. In fact, however, it was merely unanalyzed case material, and the subject lay unstudied for another thirty years. Then two books appeared in 1958. Criminologist Grierson Dickson's *Murder By Numbers* focused on what today we would call serial murderers, and argued that their motives were either "profit" or "perversion." Regrettably, his work is purely descriptive, and he has no explanation for the phenomenon, merely noting in passing the "unfortunate origins" of the killers and that "parental influence was either absent or hostile." He did however observe one of the striking qualities of the killers, the fact that "lack of economic security does not seem a factor to be considered, as few of our subjects came from really poverty-stricken homes"; and he registered the conclusion that "not one of our perverts could have had that feeling, so comforting to a youngster, that he was a normal boy among other normal boys . . . [for] all of our perverts felt themselves to be set apart from their fellows, mostly by a sense of shame or inferiority." Still, he does not tell us *why* this should be so.[11]

In that same year, crime writer Philip Lindsay published *The Mainspring Of Murder* which again rehashed the classical cases without venturing into much explanation. Yet Lindsay came the closest, despite the fact that he devoted only a few paragraphs in his attempt. "Mass Murder," Lindsay wrote, "is largely a modern phenomenon."

> It begins its great career in the late eighteenth century, growing stronger during the nineteenth century until it arrives in full red horror in the twentieth century. Why? One point which cannot be avoided is its link with industrialism. With the dying of a pastoral England and the growth of industry with wretched communities gathered in towns and cities, the spirit of hatred grew to fury and the lost ones struck at a world they distrusted and feared.

Having glimpsed the key to the puzzle, he passes on, whining evermore about the advance of socialism and the collapse of individuality in modern society. Still, he also noted the strange paradox that it did not seem to be economic insecurity (which had always been with us), but personal and spiritual insecurity that formed the breeding ground for the modern multiple murderer.[12]

The only contemporary authority is Donald Lunde, whose *Murder and Madness* largely concerns itself with multiple murderers who are, in contrast to single murderers, he says, *"almost always insane."* To Lunde, the killers are either victims of a paranoid schizophrenia—"a psychosis characterized by hallucinations ('hearing voices' in most cases), delusions of grandiosity or persecution, bizarre religious ideas (often highly personalized), and a suspicious, hostile, aggressive manner"—or they are victims of sexual sadism, "a deviation characterized by torture and/or killing and mutilation of other persons in order to achieve sexual gratification." Regrettably for this theory, however, none of our multiple murderers in this volume was reliably diagnosed as a victim of *any* serious mental disorder.[13]

Lunde's second point, which also is contradicted by all our data, is that while "we do not *know* the precise causes of these psychotic mentalities," we do know that they "are *not a product of the times.* Other countries and other centuries have produced sex murderers similar to those I have described from recent U.S. history." Lunde takes great pains to lodge the cause of these behaviors in the psyches of the killers, arguing that for "rare individuals, for reasons that are not well understood, sexual and violent aggressive impulses merge early in the child's development, ultimately finding expression in violent sexual assault." Very much in a Freudian vein, he dwells on the sexual pleasure the killer sometimes receives from the murder and mutilation of his victims, reflecting on their rich fantasy lives in which "they imagine sadistic scenes and derive great pleasure from this activity." Lunde's gifts are considerable, but his imprisonment within traditional psychiatry makes it impossible for him to transcend the non-explanation and mere categorization of his art. For an *explanation,* we must turn to the forces that create, shape, and deform individuals in a modern stratified society.*[14]

---

* If there is virtually no social theory of multiple murderers, there is a great deal of purely descriptive case material. See, for example, Hilda Bruch, "Mass Murder: the Wagner Case"; Robert Hazelwood and John Douglas, "The Lust Murderer"; Robert Brittain, "The Sadistic Murderer"; Allen Bartholomew, K.L. Milte and F. Galbally, "Sexual Murder: Psychopathology and Psychiatric Jurisprudential Considerations"; James Calvin and John MacDonald, "Psychiatric Study of a Mass Murderer"; Marvin Kahn, "Psychological Test Study of a Mass Murderer"; as well as M. Foucault, *I, Pierre Rivere . . .* ; and Donald Lunde and Jefferson Morgan, *The Die Song.*

THE HISTORICAL METAMORPHOSES

"We are encountering more and more . . .
(of those who) have turned the life
instinct on its head: Meaning for
them can only come from acts of
destruction."

ROGER KRAMER AND IRA WEINER[15]

Multiple murderers are not "insane" and they are very much products of their time. Far from being a randomly occurring freakish event, the arrival of the multiple murderer is dictated by specific stresses and alterations in the human community. Moreover, far from being deluded, he is in many senses an embodiment of the central themes in his civilization as well as a reflection of that civilization's critical tensions. He is thus a creature and a creation of his age. As such, we would expect him to change his character over time, and all the evidence suggests that that is precisely what he does. In what follows, I shall show that the pre-industrial multiple killer was an aristocrat who preyed on his peasants; that the industrial era produced a new kind of killer, most commonly a new bourgeois who preyed upon prostitutes, homeless boys, and housemaids; and that in the mature industrial era, he is most often a failed bourgeois who stalks university women and other middle-class figures. Thus for each historical epoch, both the social origins of the killers and the social characteristics of their victims are highly predictable: they are thus very much men of their time.

The Pre-Industrial Multiple Murderer

Our evidence is not what we might wish, but we must take what is available, and the overwhelming weight of that suggests that multiple murder for its own sake was very rare in the archaic order of the pre-industrial era. Indeed, the famous multiple murderers of that era killed for profit—as was the case with Sawney Bean in fifteenth-century Scotland who murdered to steal the possessions of passersby and eat their bodies; so too with Madame de Brinvilliers in seventeenth-century France who murdered her family to inherit their wealth; and with Catherine Montvoisin, also in seventeenth-century France, who arranged (for payment) the elimination of hundreds of infants. The only name that emerges from this era as indisputably one of our subjects of enquiry is an aristocrat of great wealth and achievement.[16]

The *Baron Gilles de Rais* was born in 1404 into one of the greatest fortunes of France. During the last eight years of his life, retired to his great estates, he murdered somewhere between 141 and 800 children, mostly boys. He would take the local children to his castle and, after raping them in one manner or another, would torture and kill them. His accomplice Griart told the court in 1440 that "the said Gilles, the accused, exercised his lust once or twice on the children. That done, the said Gilles killed them sometimes with his own hand or had them killed." As to the manner in which the children were killed, Griart remembered that "sometimes they were decapitated, and dismembered; sometimes he [Gilles] cut their throats, leaving the head attached to the body; sometimes he broke their necks with a stick; sometimes he cut a vein in their throats or some other part of their necks, so that the blood of the said children flowed." "As the children were dying," wrote his biographer, Leonard Wolf, "Gilles, the artist of terror, the skilled Latinist who read Saint Augustine; Gilles, the devoted companion of Jeanne d'Arc, squatted on the bellies of the children, studying their languishing faces, breathing in their dying sighs."[17]

When the court interrogators asked him who had induced him to do his crimes and taught him how to do the killings, the Baron replied: "I did and perpetrated them following [the dictates] of my imagination and my thought, without the advice of anyone, and according to my own judgement and entirely for my own pleasure and physical delight, and for no other intention or end." Under threat of being put to the torture, he confessed that "for my ardor and my sensual delectation I took and caused to be taken a great number of children—how many I cannot say precisely, children whom I killed and caused to be killed; with them, I committed the vice and the sin of sodomy . . . and . . . I emitted spermatic semen in the most culpable fashion on the belly of . . . the children, as well before as after their deaths, and also while they were dying. I, alone, or with the help of my accomplices, Gilles de Sillé, Roger de Bricqueville, Henriet [Griart], Etienne Corrilaut [Poitou], Rossignol and Petit Robin, have inflicted various kinds and manners of torture on these children. Sometimes I beheaded them with daggers, with poignards, with knives; sometimes I beat them violently on the head with a stick or with other contusive instruments . . . sometimes I suspended them in my room from a pole or by a hook and cords and strangled them; and when they were languishing, I committed with them the vice of sodomy. . . . When the children were dead, I embraced them, and I gazed at those which had the most beautiful heads and the loveliest members, and I caused their bodies to be cruelly opened and took delight in viewing their interior organs; and very often, as the children were dying, I sat on their bellies and was delighted to see them dying in that fashion and laughed about it with . . . Corrilaut and Henriet, after which I caused [the children] to be burned and converted their cadavres into dust."[18]

In a manner that will be unfamiliar only to those who have not read the other confessions in this book, the Baron interrupted his homicidal memoir to lecture the grieving parents on how to raise children. But first, during the reading in open court of his crimes, surrounded by the families of his victims (peasants all), he allowed himself to express outrage at the lowly estate of those who were acting as his judges. Hearing the bishop and the vicar of the inquisition name his acts in front of the peasant parents, he shouted: "Simoniacs, ribalds, I'd rather be hanged by the neck than reply to the likes of such clerics and such judges. It is not to be borne . . . to appear before such as you." Turning to the Bishop Malestroit, he sneered, "I'll do nothing for you as Bishop of Nantes."[19]

Following threats of excommunication and torture, he

capitulated. "From the time of my youth I have committed many great crimes," he told the court, "against God and the Ten Commandments, crimes still worse than those of which I stand accused. And I have offended our Savior as a consequence of bad upbringing in childhood, when I was left uncontrolled to do whatever I pleased [and especially] to take pleasure in illicit acts." Once more reminiscent of the killers of later centuries, he begged his judges to publish his confessions, and do so in "the vulgar tongue" so that the peasants would know of what he had done. What was the moral he wished to point out to his audience? "When I was a child, I had always a delicate nature, and did for my own pleasure and according to my own will whatever evil I pleased. To all [of you who are] fathers and mothers, friends and relatives of young people and children, lovingly I beg and pray you to train them in good morals, [teach] them to follow good examples and good doctrines; and instruct them and punish them, lest they fall into the same trap in which I myself have fallen." The Baron was hanged and burned on October 26, 1440.[20]

Why should the classic case of pre-industrial multiple murder be a wealthy and powerful aristocrat? And why has this class vanished from participation in modern multiple murder? What was happening in the second quarter of the fifteenth century to put special stress upon the ancient landed aristocracy? The world into which Gilles de Rais was born had existed for centuries: it was essentially a two-class social universe, a vast mass of peasants and a tiny collection of "noble" overlords, who expropriated the surplus of the former. These were hard times for humanity—and especially the peasants—for plague, famine, and war were frequent and devastating. There were, however, some compensations. The peasants' transfer of their surplus to their rulers was balanced by the provision of minimal security for the cultivators, who were given rights of use of the land in perpetuity. A social correlate of this relative economic security was the humanizing personalization of social relationships. The historian Peter Laslett has written that although exploitation was endemic to the system, "everyone belonged to a group, a family group," and "everyone had his or her circle of affection; every relationship could be seen as a love-relationship." This is not to say that "love" was the rule, or even the norm, in human encounters; but rather that human relationships were personalized and on a human scale: whether the relationship was full of warmth or riddled with conflict, it was a relationship between human beings. Institutional relationships and life were virtually unknown; and if groups of men and women occasionally worked together in rural life, they did so as households cooperating with one another for mutual goals. This personal world of the peasant did not encourage the growth of our multiple murderers.[21]

What was happening to the landed aristocracy? It was in a state of *crisis*, assaulted on all sides by peasantry and merchants. For historian Immanuel Wallerstein, the crisis of feudalism began between the thirteenth and fifteenth centuries. What provoked this crisis was that "the optimal degree of productivity has been passed" in the archaic feudal system, and "the economic squeeze was leading to a generalized seignior-peasant class war, as well as ruinous fights within the seigniorial classes." Moreover, the peasantry had begun to protest its condition, and peasant revolts became "widespread in western Europe from the thirteenth century to the fifteenth century"; peasant republics were declared in Frisia in the twelfth and thirteenth centuries and in Switzerland in the thirteenth century; French peasants rebelled in 1358 as they did in Italy and Flanders at the turn of the fourteenth century.[22]

Critical to our purpose, the fifteenth century—the time of the Baron Gilles de Rais—was the era in which the established order strove to re-assert itself, often through the savage repression of political and religious peasant rebellions. This was the century, Wallerstein wrote, that "saw the advent of the great restorers of internal order in western Europe: Louis XI in France, Henry VII in England, and Ferdinand of Aragon and Isabella of Castile in Spain. The major mechanisms at their disposal in this task, as for their less successful predecessors, were financial: by means of the arduous creation of a bureaucracy (civil and armed) strong enough to tax and thus to finance a still stronger bureaucratic structure." It can be no coincidence that the only pre-industrial multiple murderer, who killed purely for its own sake and of whom we have reliable record, was a member of that threatened established order. Neither does it require an impossible stretch of the imagination to comprehend that the manner in which the Baron (accustomed to giving free rein to all his emotional impulses) tortured and killed the children of the peasantry was a personalized expression of the sweeping repressive thrust of his class, and a sexual metaphor in which he tested and enforced his terrible powers. Thus his indulgence of his violent sexual fantasy was an embroidery upon the central political event of his era—the subordination of the rebellious peasantry and the restoration of the absolute powers of the old nobility. What better way to deal with this threatened domination than through the idle torture and murder—as if they were nothing—of the class which dared stake a claim to equality? Three centuries later, with the bourgeoisie ascendant, another noble, the Marquis de Sade, would be relegated to harmless fantasizing and scribbling—for his class was already redundant: de Rais and his *confrères* had lost their struggle.[23]

The Industrial Era

Toward the end of the eighteenth century, there began that profound upheaval of all economic and social relations that we call the industrial revolution. It created entirely new social classes, raising some to prominence and dominance, and displacing others. "The key figure of the eighteenth century," the gifted historian Robert Darnton wrote, was "the owner of the modes of production, a certain variety of Economic man with his own way of life and his own ideology." This new man was the bourgeois: he "acquired class consciousness and revolted [against the old aristocracy], leading a popular front of peasants and artisans." The political culture necessary for the fusion of "this striking force" was designed to allow the bourgeoisie "to saturate the common people with its own ideas of liberty (especially free trade) and equality (especially the destruction of aristocratic privilege)." By the nineteenth century, the series of mechanical inventions made possible a new economic order dominated by machine production. The new bourgeoisie which owned this machinery gained control of the emerging industrial states and relegated the old aristocracy to the sidelines of history (or joined with them through marriage). But it was neither from the ranks of the old aristocracy— nor the triumphant new bourgeoisie—that the leaders of the *homicidal revolution* would be drawn: there are no Wedgwoods or Rockefellers among the multiple murderers of the time. This should not be surprising, for unthreatened classes do not produce them.

Throughout the industrializing world, traditional communal life and activity was snuffed out. In Laslett's terms,

> . . . the removal of the economic functions from the patriarchal family at the point of industrialization created a mass society. It turned the people who worked into a mass of undifferentiated equals, working in a factory or scattered between the factories, the mines and the offices, bereft forever of the feeling that work was a family affair, done within the household.

The new industrial order, Wolf wrote, "cut through the integument of custom, severing people from their accustomed social matrix in order to transform them into economic actors, independent of prior social commitments to kin and neighbors."

> This liberation from accustomed social ties and the separation which it entailed constituted the historical experience which Karl Marx would describe in terms of 'alienation.' The alienation of men . . . from themselves to the extent to which they now had to look upon their own capabilities as marketable commodities; their alienation from their fellow men who had become actual or potential competitors in the market.

The capitalism of the late eighteenth and nineteenth centuries was thus an extraordinarily *radical* force; and its capture of the emerging industrial system left the new worker naked and exposed. At the same time, Europe and America altered its living arrangements in order to supply the workers for the new factory system: vast and anonymous cities were created. Wolf provides British data to illustrate this clustering of populations in urban areas. In 1600, only 1.6 percent of the population in England and Wales lived in cities of 100,000 or more; but the figures through the nineteenth century document the flight from the land. By 1801, one-tenth of the population was living in cities, a proportion which doubled by 1840 and doubled again by the end of the century; by 1900, Britain was an urban society. To this depersonalized new world—in which the worker lost even that tattered blanket of protection of kin and community, and instead toiled in vast factories and took rooms in anonymous boarding houses—was added a further humiliation. The new bourgeois ideology penalized the losers, the unemployed or the under-employed, for the new cultural system transmuted "the distinction between the classes into distinctions of virtue and merit."[24]

Such conditions of poverty and humiliation, insecurity and inequality, entailed many social costs, among the most notable of which was the creation of new types of murderers. Wilson complains that murder in the pre-industrial era had been essentially dull, springing generally "out of poverty and misery": such murders "do not really involve much human choice—much good or evil." The nineteenth and early twentieth centuries would be much more obligating, for "with a few interesting exceptions, all the 'great' murder cases of the nineteenth century—Lizzie Borden, Charles Bravo; Dr. Pritchard, Professor Webster—concerned the socially comfortable classes. Not the extremely rich or the aristocracy . . . but the middle classes." Indeed, one is driven to note the number of professional, especially medical, titles attached to their names—Dr. William Palmer, Dr. Thomas Cream, Dr. Marvel Petiot, and many others.[25]

Of those multiple murderers who were killing apparently for its own sake, two homicidal themes emerged. The major theme was one in which middle-class functionaries—doctors, teachers, professors, civil servants, who belonged to the class created to serve the new triumphant bourgeoisie

—preyed on members of the lower orders, especially prostitutes and housemaids. If the prevailing "need" of the era's economic formations was to discipline the lower orders into accepting the time-table of the machine and industrial employment, then this form of homicide can be usefully seen as the means by which these new members of a new middle class took the prevailing ethos to its logical conclusion. In killing the failures and the unruly renegades from the system, and doing so with such obvious pleasure, they acted as enforcers of the new moral order. We will never know the identity of "Jack the Ripper," who terrorized the prostitutes of London by disemboweling them with surgical precision; but we do know that Dr. Thomas Cream began to poison prostitutes in London in 1891, offering them drinks from his toxic bottle, and sending taunting letters to the police.

By the third quarter of the nineteenth century, they began to appear everywhere in the western world, but most especially in the advanced industrializing nations of England, France, Germany and the United States. By the early twentieth century, it had become a common art form. Few cases have left us with much detail to analyze, although we do have their gory crimes and brief confessions. Between 1920 and 1925, Grossman, Denke, Haarmann and Kurten were all killing in Germany. In Hungary in 1931, *Sylvestre Matuschka* blew up a train, killing twenty-five and maiming 120 others. At first he explained that, "I wrecked trains because I like to see people die. I like to hear them scream. I like to see them suffer"; but later he struck a curiously modern note by blaming his action on a demon spirit named Leo. In France, during the 1860s, *Joseph Philippe* strangled and cut the throats of prostitutes; and many more followed his path. In the 1920s, *Earle Nelson* raped and killed at least twenty boarding-house landladies, strangling in an arc from San Francisco to Winnipeg. In Chicago, *Herman Mudgett* (alias Dr. H. H. Holmes), a medical student who had abandoned his studies when he had run out of funds, killed dozens of young women in his "castle." Among his last words before he was hanged in 1896 was a curious confession: "I have commenced to assume the form and features of the Evil One himself." *Hamilton Fish,* the son of a Potomac River boat captain and a deeply religious man who wished to be a minister, began a serial-murder career that spanned decades, torturing and murdering at least a dozen children, primarily from the working classes. His last child-victim was young Grace Budd: after he killed her, he wrote to her mother: "On Sunday June the 3—1928 I called on you at 406 W 15th St. Brought you pot cheese—strawberries. We had lunch. Grace sat in my lap and kissed me. I made up my mind to eat her. On the pretense of taking her to a party. You said Yes she could go. I took her to an empty house in Westchester I had already picked out. . . . How she did kick—bite and scratch. I choked her to death, then cut her in small pieces so I could take my meat to my rooms, Cook and eat it. How sweet and tender her little ass was roasted in the oven. It took me 9 days to eat her entire body. I did *not* fuck her tho I could of had I wished. She died a *virgin.*"[26]

The Major Theme: Petit Bourgeois Sensibilities

The major homicidal theme of this era was one in which newly middle-class persons (with all the insecurities such *arriviste* status entails) disciplined the lower orders who threatened their morbid sensitivity to their class position, or who behaved without the appropriate "refinement" required by the new era. Perhaps the best illustration of these points was contained in the *Wagner Case* of 1913. He was one of ten children of an alcoholic and braggart peasant father who died when he (Wagner) was two years old, leaving drinking debts of such magnitude that the homestead had to be sold. His mother's second marriage ended in divorce when he was seven, reportedly because of her promiscuity. Even as a child, "he was known in the village as 'the widow's boy,'" the psychiatrist Bruch recorded, "and suffered from depressions, suicidal thoughts, and nightmares." Somehow Wagner obtained an education and qualified as a school teacher; but he never recovered from the hypersensitivity that such a rapid rise in the social hierarchy can create.

During the night of September 4, 1913, the citizens of Muehlhausen . . . were awakened by several large fires. As they ran into the street, they were met by a man, his face covered by a black veil, who was armed with two pistols. He shot with great accuracy and killed eight men and one girl immediately; 12 more were severely injured. Then his two pistols ran out of ammunition, and he was overpowered and beaten down with such violence that he was left for dead; however, he was only unconscious. He had 198 more bullets in his possession. The innkeeper identified the murderer as his 39-year-old brother-in-law, who had been a schoolteacher in this village more than ten years earlier.

Wagner confessed that during the preceding night he had quietly killed his wife and four children. . . . He also confessed that he had come to Muehlhausen to take revenge on the male inhabitants for their scorn and disdain for him. However, even while lying severely wounded and exposed to the hatred of the attacked people, he noticed that no one employed the term of abuse that would refer to his sexual sins, which he felt had been the cause of all the persecution, ridicule, and condemnation.

Wagner's life was spared when it was recognized, during the pretrial examination, that he was mentally ill. He was committed to an insane asylum, where he spent the rest of his life, 25 years.

During the preceding week [before the killings] he had written a series of letters which were not mailed until September 4 . . . one which contained a complete confession of all his crimes. It was addressed to the largest newspaper in Stuttgart and was to be used as an editorial . . . Wagner had planned to return to his brother's house the following night with the intent of killing him and his family and of burning down his house as well as the house in which he had been born. As a final step he had planned to proceed to the royal castle in Ludwigsburg, overpower the guards, set fire to the castle, and die in the flames or jump off its walls, thereby terminating his own life.

He was vituperative in expressing his hatred against Professor Gaupp, in whom he had confided the motives for his deed and who had then expressed the opinion that he was mentally sick and therefore not responsible . . . 'If I am insane, then a madman has been teaching all these years.'

[Former associates] described him as an admirable citizen, dignified, somewhat quiet. . . . Only a few had noted a certain amount of standoffishness and affectation. All commented on the fact that in a region in which a heavy dialect was spoken by educated and uneducated alike, he insisted on using high German, even in his private life.

This fateful chain of events had its beginning, according to his self-accusation, with one or more sodomistic acts in the late summer of 1901, when he was 27 years old. . . . Of decisive importance was the fact that his sexual urges and acts stood in irreconcilable contrast to his high moral standards and ethical concepts. His deep sense of guilt never diminished . . . he soon began to make certain 'observations' and to 'hear' certain slanderous remarks, which led to the unshakable conviction that his 'crime' was known. He felt himself continuously observed, mocked, and ridiculed, and lived in constant dread of arrest. He was determined not to suffer this public shame and humiliation, and therefore he always carried a loaded pistol . . . he began an affair with the innkeeper's daughter. . . . His future wife gave birth to a girl in the summer of 1903 and he married her (with many inner misgivings) in December 1903. He felt that he no longer loved her and that she was intellectually not his equal; he considered her more a servant than a wife. . . . She objected to his spending money and time on his literary interests.

There were five children. . . . He was unhappy about the birth of each child and felt confined by the financial hardship of a large family subsisting on the meager income of a village schoolteacher.

Gradually he began also to make 'observations' in Radelstetten [the village in which he had taken a new position] and felt convinced that the people of Muehlhausen had communicated their 'knowledge' to the people at his new location. He could notice it because of certain insinuations and the occasional arrogance which some allegedly showed against him. He felt caught in the old dilemma: there was never a direct statement, but he 'heard' pointed remarks containing hints. He knew if he reacted he would be publicly humiliated. . . . Gradually the conviction ripened that there was only one way out. He must kill himself and his children, *out of pity* to save them from a future of being the target of contempt and evil slander and *to take revenge* on the people of Muehlhausen who had forced him to this horrible deed. . . . Since the men of Muehlhausen had started and spread the slander, they had to die. In a life that as a whole had been a series of depressing and frustrating disappointments, he was grateful that it had been given to him to avenge his terrible torture and suffering. He was disappointed to learn that he had killed only nine people [plus his own family].

Even in 1938, when he knew that death from advanced tuberculosis was imminent, he still felt that he had been justified in his action—that even if he had killed all of them it would not have balanced the suffering that had been inflicted on him . . . the people of Muehlhausen had made it impossible for him to lead a decent life of work and orderliness and to gain recognition as a literary figure and great dramatist. . . . Since his student days literature had been his great love and avocation. He craved literary success, not only during the frugal days. . . . His profession of schoolteacher was not satisfactory to him. He considered himself in all seriousness as one of the greatest dramatists of his time and spoke with condescension of those whose works were performed.*

I have quoted Bruch at great length because in many important respects the Wagner case can be treated as *the* text for the purple explosion of middle-class multiple murder in the nineteenth and early twentieth centuries. What were the central themes in the memoir of this tormented man? Were his delusions of persecution merely bizarre psychic accident, or did they reflect some of the central fractures in the social order of his time? Let us re-examine his life and his confessions. The son of a drunken peasant and a "promiscuous" mother, his childhood must have been cursed with the demeaning insults of his fellows. Yet he rose from this crushing poverty and abasement to a modest position in the marginal middle classes as the village schoolteacher. But his ambitions were loftier still, for he regarded himself as a literary genius and he hungered for the recognition such status would bring. Being young, he contracted a sexual relationship with the innkeeper's daughter and impregnated her. The rigid demands of his time and his class meant that he had to marry her. This threatened his hard-won status, for an innkeeper's daughter was socially beneath him: moreover, she did not understand his middle-class (which is to say literary) pretensions or the expenses they entailed. Soon he had ceased to "love" her, and began treating her as "more a servant than a wife."[27]

The new industrial order created a host of new "professions," marginal middle-class occupations with a certain status which the clever sons of peasants might fill. Yet few things are so corrosive to the individual than rapid social mobility: he is no longer in the world that he knows; he does not know quite how to behave, nor how much leeway the public will allow him in the performance of his role. All he knows is that the penalty for failure is disgrace and an unceremonious return to the ugly status from which he has escaped: hence the common quality of a defensive status hysteria—which manifests itself as a kind of extreme per-

---

* "Mass Murder: the Wagner Case," by Hilda Bruch, Vol. 124, pp. 693–698, 1967. Copyright 1967, the American Psychiatric Association. Reprinted by permission.

sonal insecurity—that is found so often among those who have risen or fallen dramatically in the social hierarchy. For Wagner, this fearful hysteria focused on the possibility that his brief pre-marital homosexual affair might be discovered: it was not his "high moral standards" that made it impossible for him to cope with this memory, but his high social aspirations which would all collapse if he were unmasked as a sodomist. More and more his fear expressed itself in odd ways—most especially in his strange affectations of speaking and dressing over-formally and inappropriately (inappropriately to whom? To those who understand precisely the demands of middle-class status). Might the neighbors know of his shame? He must watch their every gesture and hear their every word, looking for signs that they would unmask him. His morbid sensibility—only an intense version of the compulsive rigidity of his new class—began to dwell upon, then become obsessed with, this fear of exposure until he was interpreting all the behavior of his fellow villagers in these terms. They knew, they sensed, they felt. Real or fancied insults and slights were converted immediately into "knowledge" of his guilt. Yet he could not react: he could not charge them with tormenting him for if he did so, "he would be publicly humiliated." Therein lay the seed of his terrible crimes: the only way to avoid the impossible abasement of himself and his family, and claim revenge, was to kill them all.

But why burn down his house and that of the royal family? Nothing could have been more appropriate; for in this double and incendiary act he would destroy all evidence of his humble origins and erase his lowly past, while obliterating the seat and symbol of the entire social order—the royal castle—that orchestrated his anguish. This was not so much delusional madness as the response of a sensitive person driven by an unrelenting fear: he knew that its origins lay in the social order, and he sensed that only such a murderous campaign could justify his existence and bury his shame. Small wonder then that he was so affronted when the psychiatrists and court declared him insane, for he knew he was struggling with something that was very real. "If I am insane, then a madman has been teaching all these years," he cried. He knew that he had spared himself any further torment and avenged himself on his oppressors; and ensured that they understood his mission by announcing it to the public in an editorial in the largest newspaper in Stuttgart. No case better represents the timorous nature of the new petite bourgeoisie than Wagner, disciplining the social inferiors who threatened his position.

The Minor Theme: Proletarian Rebellion

The second major homicidal theme that emerged in the burgeoning industrial era was one in which the lower orders engaged in a kind of sub-political rebellion that expressed their rage at their exclusion from the social order. Their confessions remain scanty so we must piece together what we can: still, there is enough to suggest a great deal. If the killer Panzram gives us chapter and verse, his contemporary, *Peter Kurten,* from the Germany of the 1920s, raises many questions. Kurten murdered two boys when he himself was only nine years old; then as an adult, he murdered several dozen men and women, boys and girls, by knifing, by strangling, and by hammering. When he was finally captured, the forty-seven-year-old married factory laborer (whose father had been jailed for abusing him and raping his sister) insisted that, "I derived no sexual satisfaction from what I did. My motives were principally to arouse excitement and indignation in the population. Through setting fire to the body I thought I would increase the rage." But why did he desire to so antagonize his fellows? The authorities rooted through his past and discovered that as a youth he had spent much time in the Chamber of Horrors, a waxwork exhibition in Kölnerstrasse. A childhood friend recalled that he always gravitated toward the wax figures of murderers. Kurten once said to him, "I am going to be somebody famous like those men one of these days." After his arrest, he spoke of his younger days in prison for the murder of the two children: "In prison, I began to think about revenging myself on society. I did myself a great deal of damage through reading blood-and-thunder stories, for instance I read the tale of 'Jack the Ripper' several times. When I came to think over what I had read, when I was in prison, I thought what pleasure it would give me to do things of that kind once I got out again." But why should he need such terrible revenge; and why take it out on the innocent?[28]

For a full explanation of this metaphor we must turn to the American *Carl Panzram*,* one of a small proportion of our murderers who come from anything resembling a truly oppressed segment of society. He was imprisoned first in 1903, when he was eleven, for breaking into a neighbor's home: for that he was subjected to the sexual and physical brutality of a reform-school staff. He did not begin his twenty-year career in multiple murder until he had experienced years of unspeakable torture (which he documented and catalogued in his journal) and sexual assault in the nation's prison system. He raped and murdered sailors, "natives," little boys, whomever he could get his hands on; he destroyed property wherever and whenever he could; and he hatched far more ambitious schemes, which came to naught: poisoning a town, blowing up a passenger train and, he hoped, staging a political incident that might spark a war between Britain and the United States. "In my lifetime," Panzram wrote as he sat in prison *eagerly awaiting his execution,* "I have murdered 21 human beings, I have committed thousands of burglaries, robberies, larcenies, arsons and last but not least I have committed sodomy on more than 1,000 male human beings. For all of these things I am not the least bit sorry. I have no conscience so that does not worry me. I don't believe in man, God nor Devil. I hate the whole damned race including myself." He concluded that, "We do each other as we are done by. I have done as I was taught to do. I am no different from any other. You taught me how to live my life, and I have lived as you taught me. I have no desire whatever to reform myself. My only desire is to reform people who try to reform me. And I believe that the only way to reform people is to kill 'em." He wrote his journal/manifesto, he said, "so that I can explain my side of it even though no one ever hears or reads of it except one man. But one man or a million makes no difference to me. When I am through I am all through, and that settles it with me. . . . If you or anyone else will take the

---

* See Gaddis and Long's *Killer* for Panzram's journal.

trouble and have the intelligence or patience to follow and examine every one of my crimes, you will find that I have consistently followed one idea through all of my life. I preyed upon the weak, the harmless and the unsuspecting. This lesson I was taught by others: might makes right."[29]

Panzram traced the origin of his commitment to revenge against all humanity to the torture sessions he endured in the "reform school." "At that time I was just learning to think for myself. Everything I seemed to do was wrong. I first began to think that I was being unjustly imposed upon. Then I began to hate those who abused me. Then I began to think that I would have my revenge just as soon and as often as I could injure someone else. Anyone at all would do. If I couldn't injure those who injured me, then I would injure someone else." "When I got out of there I knew all about Jesus and the Bible—so much so that I knew it was all a lot of hot air. But that wasn't all I knew. I had been taught by Christians how to be a hypocrite and I had learned more about stealing, lying, hating, burning and killing. I had learned that a boy's penis could be used for something besides to urinate with and that a rectum could be used for other purposes than crepitating. Oh yes, I had learned a hell of a lot from my expert instructors furnished to me free of charge by society in general and the State of Minnesota in particular. From the treatment I received while there and the lessons I learned from it, I had fully decided when I left there just how I would live my life. I made up my mind that I would rob, burn, destroy, and kill everywhere I went and everybody I could as long as I lived. That's the way I was reformed in the Minnesota State Training School. That's the reason why."[30]

Despite his protestations, his resolution did not harden completely until he had been tortured beyond all endurance at the various penitentiaries—for the crime of refusing to bow to authority. Yet once his philosophy had been formed and his life committed to it, there was no turning back until he sickened of life entirely and capitulated to the authorities, demanding his own execution. In his final days in prison, he was well treated: "If in the beginning," he wrote, "I had been treated as I am now, then there wouldn't have been quite so many people in this world that would have been robbed, raped, and killed, and perhaps also very probably I wouldn't be where I am today." "Why am I what I am? I'll tell you why. I did not make myself what I am. Others had the making of me." Still, he rejected all thoughts of "rehabilitation." "I could not reform if I wanted to. It has taken me all my life so far, 38 years of it, for me to reach my present state of mind. . . . My philosophy of life is such that very few people ever get, and it is so deeply ingrained and burned into me that I don't believe I could ever change my beliefs. The things I have had done to me by others and the things I have done to them can never be forgotten or forgiven either by me or others. I can't forget and I won't forgive. I couldn't if I wanted to. The law is in the same fix. . . . If the law won't kill me, I shall kill myself. I fully realize that I am not fit to live among people in a civilized community. I have no desire to do so."³¹

When anti-capital-punishment groups tried to block his execution, Panzram entered into a kind of conspiracy with federal officials to obtain his own death. Musing alone in his cell, he wrote: "Wherever I go, there is sure to be bad luck and hard times for somebody and sometimes for everybody. I am old bad-luck himself . . . I had a lot of different people ask me at different times who I was and what good I was. My answers were all the same. 'I am the fellow who goes around doing people good.' Asked what good I had ever done anyone: Again my answers were the same to all. 'I put people out of their misery.' They didn't know that I was telling them the truth. I have put a lot of people out of their misery and now I am looking for someone to put me out of mine. I am too damned mean to live." "I intend to leave this world as I have lived in it. I expect to be a rebel right up to my last moment on earth. With my last breath I intend to curse the world and all mankind. I intend to spit in the warden's eye or whoever places the rope around my neck when I am standing on the scaffold. . . . That will be all the thanks they'll get from me."³²

The day before his execution, he promised visiting journalists that he would "prance up those thirteen steps like a blooded stallion," and he asked the guard to ensure that the scaffold was "strong enough to hold me." Robert Stroud, later to become famous as the "birdman of Alcatraz," was in an adjoining cell during Panzram's last night of life: "All night long that last night," Stroud remembered, "he walked the floor of his cell, singing a pornographic little song that he had composed himself . . . the principal theme was 'Oh, how I love my roundeye!'" When Panzram's cell door opened just before six a.m. and he saw two men in clerical garb, he roared: "Are there any Bible-backed cocksuckers in here? Get 'em out. I don't mind being hanged, but I don't need any Bible-backed hypocrites around me. Run 'em out, Warden." When Panzram finally emerged from his cell, his biographers Gaddis and Long recorded, he "was almost running ahead, half dragging his taller escorts." Panzram stared straight ahead at the rope, pausing only at the foot of the gallows to notice his audience. He paused for a moment and spat, then returned his gaze to the rope. "Everyone's nostrils inhaled the sweet smell of new oak and hemp. He hurried up the gallows, as toward a gate."[33]

THE MODERN ERA

> "This is the American Dream . . .
> in America, anything is possible if
> you work for it."
>
> VICE-PRESIDENTIAL CANDIDATE,
> 1984

After the Second World War, the industrial economies—both east and west—moved into an era of unprecedented expansion and prosperity. With the growth of the industrial sector came a parallel development of social service agencies—running the gamut from education to medicine to welfare. This remarkable growth in both the corporate and social sectors created two post-war decades in which individuals with even the most marginal of qualifications and abilities could enter occupations which offered a measure of dignity and recompense. As might be expected, these were quiet years for multiple murder as the population scrambled to better itself. The explosion in the rate of production of these most modern of killers began in the late 1960s, and it continued in an almost exponential path for the following twenty years. This directly paralleled, and may well have owed its initial impetus to, the *closure* that was taking place in the American economy. From the late 1960s onward, the myriad of middle-class positions that had been created since the Second World War began to be filled, or reduced in number. Inexorably, more and more socially ambitious, but untalented (or unconnected) young men must have found it difficult to achieve their goals of "successful" careers. A proportion of these men—we can never know how large—began to fantasize about revenge; and a tiny, but ever-increasing, percentage of them began to react to the frustration of their blocked social mobility by transforming their fantasies into a vengeful reality.

All this took place in a *cultural milieu* which for more than a century and a half had glorified violence as an appropriate and manly response to frustration, a cultural motif without parallel in the western industrial world. *The History of Violence In America* documented the public response to a robbery in which a young girl had been shot in the leg: the Kansas City *Times* called the robbery "so diabolically daring and so utterly in contempt of fear that we are bound to admire it and revere its perpetrators." A few days later, the same newspaper commented that,

It was as though three bandits had come to us from storied Odenwald, with the halo of medieval chivalry upon their garments and shown us how the things were done that poets sing of. Nowhere else in the United States or in the civilized world, probably, could this thing have been done.

No single quality of American culture is so distinctive as its continued assertion of the nobility and beauty of violence— a notion and a mythology propagated with excitement and craft in all popular cultural forms, including films, television, and print. This cultural predilection must have been immeasurably enhanced by the television coverage of the Vietnam War, which brought real bloodletting and killing into every American living-room, and rendered death sacred no more. Encouraged thus to act out their fantasies, our killers would come to find that their murderous acts would serve both to validate and to relieve their grievances.[34]

Moreover, the *character* of both killers and victims underwent a further transformation. The social origins of the killers continued to fall: gone were the aristocrats of the fifteenth century, and the doctors and teachers of the nineteenth century. Now the killers were drawn from the ranks of the upper-working and lower-middle classes: they were security guards, computer operators, postal clerks, and construction workers. Conversely, the social origins of the victims continued to pursue an opposite path: where they had been peasants in the fifteenth century, housemaids and prostitutes in the nineteenth century, now they were more likely to be drawn from middle-class neighborhoods: university students, aspiring models, and pedestrians in middle-class shopping malls. Both killer and victim had altered their form because the nature of the homicidal protest had changed most radically: it was no longer the threatened aristocrat testing the limits of his power; no longer the morbidly insecure new bourgeois checking the threat to his hard-won status; now it was an excluded individual wreaking vengeance on the symbol and source of his excommunication. These killers were almost never drawn from the ranks of the truly oppressed: there are few women, blacks, or native Americans in our files. The truly oppressed have no expectations that a bitter-tasting reality might poison.

Table 1 shows the remarkable increase in the frequency of multiple murder in this century. It is still a most useful guide, even if its construction is bedeviled by the statistical problems that overwhelm any student of multiple murder. It may well underestimate the total number of killers in each decade, but it is a revealing indication of the relative frequency of multiple murder. Regardless of any defects the table may have, the pattern is clear. There was essentially no change in the rate of production of multiple murderers until the 1960s, for the decades between the 1920s and the 1950s produced only one or two apiece. In the 1960s, this jumped to six cases during the decade, for an average of one new killer every twenty months. By the 1970s, this had jumped to seventeen new cases, for an average of one new killer appearing every seven months. During the first four years of the 1980s,* the total had leapt to twenty-five, for an average rate of production of one new killer every 1.8 months.

Table 1.

Recorded instances of multiple murderers in the United States, 1920–1984; figure in parentheses is the number of victims with which the alleged killer is implicated.

1920s	Earl Nelson (18–26); Carl Panzram (21)
1930s	Albert Fish (8–15)
1940s	Jarvis Catoe (7); Howard Unruh (13); William Heirens (3)
1950s	Charles Starkweather (11)
1960s	Melvin Rees (9); Albert DeSalvo (13); Richard Speck (8); Charles Whitman (16); Jerome Brudos (4+); Antone Costa (circa 20)
1970s	John Freeman (7); Dean Corll (27+); Edmund Kemper III (10); Herbert Mullin (13); Harvey Carignan (5+); Paul Knowles (18+); Calvin Jackson (9); James Ruppert (11); Vaughn Greenwood (9–11); Edward Allaway (7); John Wayne Gacy (30+); Mark Essex (10); David Berkowitz (6); Theodore Bundy (22+); Kenneth Bianchi and Angelo Buono (10); Juan Corona (25+)
1980–1984	Henry Lee Lucas (150+); James Huberty (21); Arthur Bishop (5+); Randall Woodfield (4+); Gerald Stano (41+); "Green River" killer (20+); Alton Coleman (7); Christopher Wilder (8); Robert Hanse (17); Michael Silka (9); Louis Hastings (6); Charles Meach (4); Robert Diaz (12); Wayne Williams (28+); San Rafael "Trailside Slayer" (8); Douglas Daniel Clark (6); Coral Eugene Watts (22); Randy Steven Kraft (14); Frederick Wyman Hodge (12); Larry Eyler (19); William Bonin

---

* To September 30, 1984.

(10+); Joseph G. Christopher (7); Donald Miller (4); Stephen Morin (4+); Michael Ross (6+)

Source: John Godwin, *Murder USA;* the work of Ann Rule and Andy Stack; and press clippings.

Note: While the figures give a reasonable indication of the relative incidence of multiple murder between decades, it should be assumed that each list is profoundly incomplete.

The number of victims also experienced a parallel increase. During the 1920s, when thirty-nine people were killed, the average number of murders was 0.325 per month. In the 1930s, with only eight killings, the figure dropped to 0.06 per month. During the 1940s, with a minimum of twenty murdered, this average figure rose slightly to 0.16 per month; and in the 1950s, with eleven killings, the average was 0.09 victims per month. The number of victims began to accelerate during the 1960s: the total of seventy represented a rate of 0.58 per month. During the 1970s, 219 were murdered, a trebling of the rate to 1.83 per month; and during the first four years of the 1980s, the 444 victims represent another quadrupling of the rate, to 9.25 per month, a frequency of victimization *one hundred times* that of the 1950s.

Was this a consequence only of the predatory nature of capitalism? The evidence does not warrant such a conclusion. The structures of humiliation and deprivation coalesce around *any* stratified and hierarchical industrial system, whether it be capitalist or communist; and neither system appears to hold any monopoly on alienation and exclusion, dehumanization and depersonalization. We would thus expect the communist bloc states also to produce multiple murderers—but in varying numbers, according to the degree with which their respective cultures glorify and venerate violence. We cannot confirm these speculations with any precision since communist bloc states restrict the flow of information to their citizens. Nevertheless, distinguished emigre writer Valery Chalidze's recent review of Soviet crime makes it clear that multiple murder is by no means unknown in the U.S.S.R. In the early 1960s,

Chalidze wrote, one man "became well known to the Moscow public" for murdering children in their own apartments: curiously, the official explanation given for his behavior was precisely the same as any western psychiatrist or court might offer—"his crimes appeared to be the acts of a maniac, and the general belief was that his motives were sexual." Although the Soviet press did not report the matter, Chalidze suggested that such multiple murders "are fairly common," although nothing like the American rate.[35]

A similar explosion occurred in Poland in 1962, while the communist regime was preparing to celebrate its twentieth anniversary in power. *Lucian Staniak,* a twenty-six-year-old translator for the official Polish publishing house wrote anonymously to the state newspaper: "There is no happiness without tears, no life without death. Beware! I am going to make you cry." With this typically public flourish, he announced a wave of killings that shocked the state. He first killed on the day commemorating the liberation period: a day replete with meaning for the *apparatchik* apprentice killer. His victim was a seventeen-year-old student, her body left naked, raped, and mutilated. The following day he sent another letter to the newspaper, announcing that "I picked a juicy flower in Olsztyn and I shall do it again somewhere else, for there is no holiday without a funeral."[36]

It took him several months, but then he stole a sixteen-year-old girl who had been chosen to lead a parade of students in another rally. Her body was found the day after the parade in a factory basement opposite her home: she had been raped, and a spike had been thrust into her genitals. A third letter to the newspaper told police where to find the body. On All Saints Day, he killed again: a young blond hotel receptionist whom he raped and mutilated with a screw driver. The following day he dispatched a letter: "Only tears of sorrow can wash out the stain of shame; only pangs of suffering can blot out the fires of lust." On May Day of 1966, he took a seventeen-year-old, raping and disemboweling her. Her father, crime writer Colin Wilson recorded, "found her lying in the typical rape position, with her entrails forming an abstract pattern over her thighs, in a tool shed behind the house." As Warsaw's homicide team began assembling data on fourteen other similar murders, police boarded a train on Christmas Eve of 1966 to find the mutilated body of a young woman, her abdomen and thighs slashed. Another letter to the newspaper merely said, "I have done it again."[37]

Staniak was ultimately arrested: he was a member of the liberal Arts Lovers Club, and a painter. One of his paintings, entitled "The Circle of Life," depicted a cow eating a flower, a wolf eating the cow, a hunter shooting the wolf, a woman driving her car over the hunter, and an unspecified force leaving the woman lying in a field with her stomach ripped open, flowers sprouting from her body. After his arrest, Staniak confessed to a total of twenty such murders. He "explained" that he did them because when he was a young man, his parents and sister had been hit by a car driven by a Polish Air Force pilot's wife—who resembled the young blond women he had killed. His explanation is curiously familiar to us, for it possesses that distinctive mixture of bizarre pseudo-rationality and apparent insanity that multiple murderers customarily deliver to us and to authorities. We do not know enough about his life to speak with any certainty about what created him: we can only note how similar in feel and texture the case is to our own.[38]

Regardless of the question of national affiliation—an almost insurmountable one, given the problem of restricted information—is there anything special in the social backgrounds of North American multiple murderers to distinguish them from the remaining mass of humanity (who are of course also subject to the impersonal and depersonalizing forces of the modern industrial state)? Table 2 summarizes the social histories of twenty-three North American multiple murderers for whom such data are available: it shows clearly that they *are* a very distinctive group. Overwhelmingly, they come from that twelve to twenty per cent of the population of a modern nation-state who possess one of four social characteristics indicative of considerable pressure within the natal family: adopted, illegitimate, institutionalized in childhood or adolescence, or with mothers who have married three or more times. What is there about these characteristics that might propel a man toward a career in murder?

Table 2.
North American multiple murderers whose social origins are known.

Joseph Kallinger	Adopted
John Bianchi	Adopted
Earle Nelson	Adopted
David Berkowitz	Adopted, Illegitimate
Theodore Bundy	Illegitimate
Harvey Carignan	Illegitimate, Institutionalized (juvenile home)
Albert Fish	Institutionalized (orphanage)
Edmund Kemper III	Institutionalized (mental hospital)
Jerome Brudos	Institutionalized (mental hospital)
Clifford Olson	Institutionalized (juvenile home)
Albert DeSalvo	Institutionalized (juvenile home)
William Bonin	Institutionalized (juvenile home)
Richard Speck	Institutionalized (juvenile home)
Robert Irwin	Institutionalized (juvenile home)
William Heirens	Institutionalized (juvenile home)
Robert Carr III	Institutionalized (juvenile home)
Carl Panzram	Institutionalized (juvenile home)
Dean Corll	Mother Thrice Married
"Norman Collins"	Mother Thrice Married
Antone Costa	Conventional
Charles Starkweather	Conventional (Mass murderer)
Mark Essex	Conventional (Mass murderer)
Randall Woodfield	Conventional
James Huberty	Conventional (Mass murderer)

Sources: Damore (1981); Klausner (1981); Miller (1978); Olsen (1974); Angelella (1981); Keyes (1976); Stack (1983a, 1983b, 1984); Schreiber (1983); Lunde and Morgan (1980); Tanay (1976); Frank (1967); Allen (1976); Cheney (1976); Rule (1980); Schwarz (1981); Gaddis and Long (1970); Buchanan (1979); Hernon (1978); Freeman (1955); Altman and Ziporyn (1967); and various press clippings. It is of course highly regrettable that so few records of this nature are available on modern multiple murderers.

The simple fact of human social life is that in order for individuals to behave "normally," they must grow up feeling that they have some place in the social order—which is to say a coherent and socially constructed identity. Unfortunately, individuals who bear these social characteristics often come to feel excluded from the social order—a separation I have often heard in "training schools," where juveniles refer to civilians as "humans"—and such exclusion can exact a fearful price. But many people who bear these social characteristics grow into a mature and balanced adulthood: why should some fail to do so? Several other factors are necessary in the biography before a multiple murderer can be produced. He must also be inculcated with an ambition—or a "dream"—which either circumstances rob from him (as when DeSalvo's wife Irmgard refused him admission to the lower-middle class), or which he cannot feel at ease in living (as when Bundy spurned his long-sought socialite fiancée). He is never Durkheim's contented man, who:

> vaguely realizes the extreme limit set to his ambitions and aspires to nothing beyond . . . he feels that it is not well to ask more. Thus, an end and goal are set to the passions. . . . This relative limitation and the moderation it involves, make men contented with their lot while stimulating them moderately to improve it; and this average contentment causes the feeling of calm, active happiness, the pleasure in existing and living which characterizes health for societies as well as for individuals.

It is in this light that we must interpret and understand the fierce social ambition of so many of our multiple murderers —and the feeling of being a robot that torments so many of them as they pursue their goals.[39]

317

Finally, for the production of multiple murderers to reach the unprecedented levels that it has in the America of the 1970s and 1980s, we require the existence of cultural forms that can mediate between killer and victim in a special sense—ridding the potential victims of any humanity, and the potential killer of any responsibility. Both sociologists Christopher Lasch and Barbara Ehrenreich have argued most persuasively that we have developed these forms with no little refinement. Lasch devoted a volume to delineating the nature of this "culture of competitive individualism" which carries "the logic of individualism to the extreme of a war of all against all, the pursuit of happiness to the dead end of a narcissistic preoccupation with the self." Ehrenreich dwelt upon the sources of this ideology which so encouraged the severing of responsibility between people. She saw its roots in the developing post-war male culture of "escape—literal escape from the bondage of breadwinning." Here, men were urged to take part in the superficial excitement of "the nightmare anomie of the pop psychologists' vision: a world where other people are objects of consumption, or the chance encounters of a 'self' propelled by impulse alone."[40]

Thus the freedom for which mankind had struggled over the centuries proved to be a two-edged sword. The freedom from the suffocation of family and community, the freedom from systems of religious thought, the freedom to explore one's self, all entailed heavy penalties to society—not the least of which was the rate of multiple murder. These tendencies are much intensified in America, perhaps the only industrial nation on earth to take the idea of freedom to its bitter logical conclusion. A major by-product of this literal interpretation of freedom is that all systems of value come to be seen as possessing equal legitimacy: therefore, in this ultimate vulgarization of the doctrine of cultural relativity, murder as a response to mundane frustration takes on a culturally programmed and culturally validated appearance.

Moreover, whether the industrial system was socialist or capitalist, its members were forced to look upon themselves and others as marketable commodities. It can hardly be surprising then that some fevered souls, feeling like automatons, might choose to coalesce their fuzzy identity in a series of fearful acts. Their ambitions crushed, some would lash out in protest at objects (most often sexual) which they had been taught to see as essentially insignificant. Now the question asked by the killer Bundy seems less inappropriate: "What's one less person on the face of the earth, anyway?"

Each of our case studies reveals that at a certain point in his life, the future killer experiences a kind of internal *social* crisis, when he realizes that he cannot be what he wishes to be—cannot live his version of the American dream. When these killers reach that existential divide, the seed is planted for a vengeance spree. Sometimes their motives are entirely conscious (as with Essex, Bundy, and Panzram); while with others (like Berkowitz and DeSalvo), they are only dimly understood. In either case, it is unrealizable ambition that motivates them, as they launch a kind of sub-political and personal assault on society, aiming always at the class group they feel oppresses or excludes them. Some require minimal justification for their acts, obtaining temporary relief from their rage through the killings and then "forgetting" or compartmentalizing their memories, as when DeSalvo remarked: "I was there, it was done, and yet if you talked to me an hour later, or half hour later, it didn't mean nothing." Still others construct elaborate intellectual (Panzram) or spiritual (Berkowitz's demons) rationalizations to explain and justify their killings. Only a few (such as Joseph Kallinger, and California's Herbert Mullins, who murdered to "stop earthquakes") detach themselves so much from conventional reality that they construct their own universes, thereby entering that state the psychiatrists call madness.

Yet what they are *all* orchestrating is a kind of social leveling, in which they rewrite the universe to incorporate themselves: no one expressed this more clearly than Starkweather when he said that "dead people are all on the same level." They are all engaged in the same process, punishing the innocent, and in doing so they recreate the dehumanized industrial system in a form that gives themselves a central position. One hundred eyes for an eye: it is by no means the first time in human history that retaliating men have grossly exceeded the degree of the original insult.

Neither do they form their missions in a private vacuum, bereft of all advice, for the larger culture encodes in them a respect for violent display—a central theme in the media messages beamed at the working class—and the ready availability of stimulating materials in books and magazines, films and videotapes, teaches them to link their lust with violence. If we were charged with the responsibility for designing a society in which all structural and cultural mechanisms leaned toward the creation of the killers of strangers, we could do no better than to present the purchaser with the shape of modern America, for the angry and the troubled can reach into the dominant culture to seize a socially validated violent identity. If the negotiation of the identity of a violent culture hero yields the killer little admiration or love, the absence of these qualities will be more than compensated for by the public respect and media attention he will surely receive. In this special sense, the homicidal values and behaviors are in perfect harmony with the dominant culture.

The Negotiation of Murderous Identity

The twilight of the human race on this planet may well have been the thirty or forty thousand years our ancestors dwelt in relatively egalitarian (one assumes) hunting and gathering societies. In such non-stratified societies, there was little specialization of labor, little production of surplus, and few opportunities for aggressive and ambitious individuals to overcome the reluctance of their fellows to submit to any expropriation of the social commodities for which human beings compete—power, prestige, and wealth. However, something like 10,000 years ago all our ancestors began to make the shift from hunting and gathering to agriculture and pastoralism—new forms of economy that captured a larger amount of energy for each hour of work. When eight could thus do the work to feed ten, the stage was set for the production of a surplus and the expropriation of that surplus by an emerging class of elites. And so the form and structure of society was entirely rewritten: now rank and hierarchy, not mutual obligation, began to emerge as *the* organizing principles of human society. That development provided the framework for the growth over the millennia of social classes: clusters of individuals with mutual interests who stood in opposition to individuals of other social classes. Over time, new classes emerged and struggled for ascendancy, as did the bourgeoisie in the nineteenth century. Thus some groups are more threatened than others in different periods of history. It is precisely at the point in time when a single class is most threatened (when its rights are challenged by another class, its legitimacy questioned by a discontented proletariat, or its new-found status imprecisely defined) that we can expect to find some members of that class beginning to fantasize about killing members of another class.

Thus the multiple murderer does not appear at random through history. He appears at special points in social evolution, during periods of particular tension. Durkheim's thoughts on destruction (although he was concerned with self-destruction) are central here. Despite the glories of humanity, it remains a fragile species. Its equilibrium is in such a delicate state of balance that any crisis (financial, industrial, or social) in the larger system disorients the individuals in that system. It matters not whether they are crises of prosperity or of poverty: it merely matters that individuals' expectations are profoundly shaken.

> Every disturbance of equilibrium, even though it achieves greater comfort and a heightening of general vitality, is an impulse to voluntary death. Whenever serious readjustments take place in the social order, whether or not due to a sudden growth or to an unexpected catastrophe, men are more inclined to self-destruction.

In the archaic, pre-industrial period, it was the old and "noble" landed aristocracy which was most threatened by the rebellious peasantry and the rising mercantile classes. It makes a certain terrible sense that it was among this threatened class that fantasies of disordered self-indulgent sexuality might turn to the torture and murder of the lower orders. During the industrial revolution of the late eighteenth and nineteenth centuries, while the aristocracy retired to its estates to lick its wounds and the rising bourgeoisie reveled in its ascendancy, it was the new marginal middle classes—men like Wagner and Dr. Cream—who, insecure in their unaccustomed roles, would grow obsessed with a sense of possible exposure and failure. During that period, it would primarily be doctors, government clerks, and school teachers who might discipline those of the lower orders—who perhaps whispered about past errors exposing class origins or who flaunted their indifference.[41]

In the early twentieth century, a new homicidal theme emerged. Proletarian revolt became a minor expression, in which those (like Panzram then, or Lucas now) who glimpsed their utter exclusion, who felt their torture at the hands of the bourgeois institutions constructed for their "rehabilitation," wreaked a similar havoc. These proletarians would continue into the modern era, but they would always be a minor theme: their class would find alternative forms of protest, either in direct political action, or in smothering their claims in drugs and alcohol, or just as commonly in theft. Murder for its own sake had relatively little appeal to a class with such immediate problems.

The major homicidal form of the modern era is the man who straddles the border between the upper-working class and the lower-middle class. Occasionally, as with Robert Hansen in Alaska or cousins Kenneth Bianchi and Angelo Buono in Los Angeles (The "Hillside Stranglers"), they continue a metaphor from the earlier era and discipline unruly prostitutes and runaways. Much more commonly, however, they punish those above them in the system—preying on unambiguously middle-class figures such as university women.

All stratified industrial nation-states, regardless of their professed ideologies, transform their members into either winners or losers. By the mid-1960s, however, the increasing closure of middle-class positions meant there would be many more losers, many more who were alienated and despairing. Moreover, as these positions were closing, other social forces within society continued their transformation of neighbors into strangers: the constriction of the extended family, the expansion of the anonymous city and suburb, the geographic mobility of individual familial units, and the disintegration of marriage and parenthood, all made it progressively easier for the potential killer to overcome his scruples. The murder and mutilation of such enemy-strangers is but the abuse of a commodity. Thus we find the source of our new multiple murderer primarily among the ambitious who failed—or who believed they would fail—and who seek another form of success in the universal celebrity and attention they will receive through their extravagant homicides. In the performance of this task they are aided immensely by the extraordinary *tolerance* the social system offers their activities, providing only paltry resources for the monitoring and apprehension of potential killers.*

Whether they kill all at once in a bloody hour or day, or whether they kill over an extended period, whether their motives appear to be "sexual" or "psychotic," the objects of our study are all much of a kind. They all decide independently to construct a program of killing many strangers. On the surface of things they appear to be doing it for the thrill of sexual excitement or the intoxication of conquest; but the truth is they do it to relieve a burning grudge engendered by their failed ambition. Some are so finished with life that they wish to die when they have discharged their brief task: they come to be called "mass murderers," and they leave it up to a bewildered public to decipher their message. Others wish to live and tell their stories and bask in their fame: they usually come to be called "serial murderers."

The tragedy and irony is that what has produced this abomination is the achievement of the freedom for which mankind has struggled for centuries—freedom to explore one's self without reference to rigid systems of thought. That freedom exacts a terrible price, for it releases humans too much from their social contract. Under such conditions, those whose ambitions are denied (and there are more of these each year since the 1960s when closure first occurred) in a culture which so glamorizes and rewards violence, find

---

* "Tolerance" may sound merely provocative; but compare the tiny and short-term resources allocated to hunting multiple murderers with the huge sums allocated by the state for the monitoring of political dissidents (the FBI ran 300 major operations in 1983, and its budget for undercover work alone in 1984 was $12.5 million). Nothing comparable is given to the police.[42]

a solution to all their problems in that purple explosion. As many more come to feel excluded in this time of industrial and social crisis, we can expect many more to follow the path of the University of Chicago undergraduate, William Heirens, who searched for something—he knew not what—in the dissected entrails of a kidnapped child, and wrote in lipstick upon the walls of another victim's apartment: "FOR HEAVENS SAKE CATCH ME BEFORE I KILL MORE I CANNOT CONTROL MYSELF."[43]

Notes

N.B. In the interests of readability and the avoidance of notation clutter, the numbering of sources has been limited to one numeral per paragraph within the body text of this book. References to sources noted below beside each numeral are listed in their order of appearance within each respective paragraph of the body text. Ed.

CHAPTER ONE: MULTIPLE MURDERER

1 Lucas, in Rone Tempest, *Los Angeles Times,* Oct. 30, 1983; and Lucas, on ABC Television News *20/20,* July 1984
2 Lucas, ibid
3 *Maclean's* magazine, July 30, 1984
4 Etna Huberty, in ibid
5 Mr. Kembrell, in *Associated Press,* April 16, 1984; *People* magazine, April 30, 1984; and Dennis DeFranceschi, in *Time,* April 16, 1984
6 Peter Wilson 1974: 138
7 Amnesty International 1983: 36
8 Ibid, 34
9 Judge Ronald George, On PBS Television's *Frontline,* May 1984
10 Widely quoted in press reports
11 Nilsen, in Lisners 1983: 178; and Nilsen, ibid, 180
12 Nilsen, ibid, 178; and Olson, unpublished correspondence
13 Cf. Leyton 1983
14 Gaylin 1983: 249
15 Ibid, 156

CHAPTER TWO: KEMPER

1 Kemper, in Cheney 1976: 140
2 Lunde 1979: 54
3 Cheney 1976: 9; and Dr. Joel Fort, in ibid, 183

4 Lunde 1979: 54-55; and West 1974; 187

5 Cheney, 1976: 14, 10

6 Ibid, 15; and Lunde 1979: 54

7 Mrs. Clarnell Kemper, quoted in Cheney 1976: 18, Lunde 1979: 55; Cheney 1976: 21; and Lunde 1979: 55

8 Kemper, in Cheney 1976: 22; quoted in Cheney 1976: 23; and Lunde 1979: 55

9 Cheney 1976: 41-42

10 Kemper, in ibid, 87, 90

11 Kemper, in ibid, 89-91

12 Kemper, in ibid, 95; Cheney 1976: 96-97; and Kemper, in ibid, 97-98

13 Ibid, 53, 104, 105

14 Kemper, in ibid, 105; and Cheney 1976: 108

15 Kemper, in ibid, 113; and Cheney 1976: 113-114

16 Kemper, in ibid, 123, 125

17 Kemper, in ibid, 127; and Cheney 1976: 129

18 Kemper, in ibid, 140

19 Kemper, in ibid, 132

20 Kemper, in ibid, 133; and Cheney 1976: 133

21 Kemper, in ibid, 134

22 Cheney 1976: 135-137, 138-139

23 West 1974: 200; Kemper, in ibid, 200; and Cheney 1976: 148

24 Kemper, in ibid, 169

25 Kemper, in ibid, 154

26 Cheney 1976: 142

27 Ibid, 142

28 Kemper, in West 1974: 196; Kemper, in Cheney 1976: 127, 195

29 Kemper, in ibid, 166

30 Kemper, in ibid, 194, 166

31 Kemper, in ibid, 128

32 Cheney 1976: 167

33 Kemper, in Cheney 1976: 140, 143

34 Kemper, in ibid, 86, 152

35 Kemper, in ibid, 152

36 Kemper, in ibid, 87, 141

37 Kemper, in ibid, 145, 86

38 Kemper, in West 1974: 187, 163; and Kemper, in Lunde 1979: 55

39 Kemper, in Cheney 1976: 88; Kemper, in West 1974: 164; Kemper, in Cheney 1976: 90; and Kemper, in West 1974: 167

40 Kemper, in ibid, 199

41 Kemper, in Cheney 1976: 146, 147

42 Kemper, in ibid, 108

43 Kemper, in ibid, 171; and Kemper, in West 1974: 200

44 Kemper, in Lunde 1979: 55; and Kemper, in West 1974: 193

45 Kemper, in ibid, 199

46 Kemper, in Cheney 1976: 147

47 Cheney 1976: xiii

48 Kemper, in West 1974: 188

49 Mrs. Clarnell Kemper, in Cheney 1976: 8; Mrs. Clarnell Kemper, in West 1974: 194; Kemper's father, in West 1974: 194-195; and West 1974: 195

50 Kemper, in Cheney 1976: 11-12; and Lunde 1979: 54

51 Kemper, in West 1974: 189-190

52 Kemper, in ibid, 186

53 West 1974: 16-17; and Kemper, paraphrased by a neighbor, in West 1974; 17-18

54 Kemper, in ibid, 192

55 Kemper, in ibid, 163-164; West 1974: 83; and Kemper, in ibid, 198

56 Kemper, in Lunde 1979: 198; and Kemper, in Cheney 1976: 69

57 Kemper in West 1974: 192, 160; and Kemper, in Cheney 1976: 153

58 Kemper, in ibid, 32

59 Kemper, in ibid, 144

60 Kemper, in ibid, 140

61 Kemper, in ibid, 147, 148

62 Kemper, in ibid, 151; Kemper, in West 1974: 197, 193-194

63 Kemper, in Cheney 1976: 128; and Kemper, in West 1974: 198

64 Kemper, in Cheney 1976: 39-40, 143

65 Kemper, in ibid, 88

66 Kemper, in ibid, 99; and Kemper, in West 1974: 163

67 Kemper, in Cheney 1976: 106-107, 109

68 Kemper, in ibid, 172

69 Quoted in Cheney 1976: 194

70 Quoted in ibid, 23

71 Quoted in ibid, 23

72 Quoted in ibid, 30

73 Quoted in Lunde 1979: 89-90

74 Quoted in Cheney 1976: 3

75 Dr. Joel Fort, in Cheney 1976: 175

76 Dr. Joel Fort, in ibid, 176-177
77 Dr. Joel Fort, in ibid, 179, 181
78 Lunde 1979: 35, 53
79 Kemper, in Cheney 1976: 152
80 Kemper, in ibid, 152
81 Kemper, in ibid, 129, 151-152, 154
82 Kemper, in ibid, 154
83 Kemper, in ibid, 152, 155
84 Kemper, in Lunde 1979: 89

CHAPTER THREE: BUNDY
 1 Bundy, in Michaud and Aynesworth 1983: 324
 2 Larsen 1980: 100; Kendall, in Larsen 1980: 102; and Michaud
   and Aynesworth 1983: 120, 121
 3 Ibid, 30-31
 4 Ibid, 31-32; and Bundy, in ibid, 127
 5 Ibid, 32-33; quoted in ibid, 34-35; and ibid, 36-37, and 56
 6 Rule 1980: 64; and Bundy, in Michaud and Aynesworth 1983:
   131, 132-133, 136
 7 Bundy, in ibid, 137-138
 8 Rule 1980: 68; and Michaud and Aynesworth 1983: 40
 9 Ibid, 40; Bundy, in ibid, 140-143; and Kendall 1981: 52
10 Michaud and Aynesworth 1983: 54
11 Ibid, 91-92
12 Ibid, 108-110, 104
13 Ibid, 113
14 Ibid, 229
15 Ibid, 260-261
16 Bundy, in Winn and Merrill 1980: 314
17 Quoted in ibid, 110; and quoted in Larsen 1980: 94
18 Winn and Merrill 1980: 28-29
19 Quoted in Michaud and Aynesworth 1983: 319; quoted in Winn
   and Merrill 1980: 154; and Daryl Ondrak, in ibid, 86
20 Quoted in Michaud and Aynesworth 1983: 319, 320
21 Quoted in Winn and Merrill 1980: 163
22 Quoted in ibid, 164; and quoted in Larsen 1980: 159
23 Bundy, in Rule 1980: 203-204, 208
24 Bundy, in ibid, 207
25 Winn and Merrill 1980: 296; and Emanuel Tanay, in Michaud
   and Aynesworth 1983: 264
26 Bundy, in ibid, 313

27 Bundy, in Rule 1980: 218; and Bundy, in Larsen 1980:182

28 Bundy, in Rule 1980: 312, 322

29 Bundy, in Winn and Merrill 1980: 302, 309

30 Bundy, in ibid, 309-310, 311

31 Bundy, in ibid, 313, 314, 315

32 Bundy, in Michaud and Aynesworth 1983: 24; and Bundy, in Winn and Merrill 1980: 358

33 Bundy, in ibid, 119

34 Cathy Swindler, in Larsen 1980: 5-6; and quoted in Larsen 1980: 154

35 Louise Bundy, in Winn and Merrill 1980: 354-355

36 Bundy, in Larsen 1980: 297, 156-157

37 Bundy, in ibid, 232; and Bundy, in Winn and Merrill 1980: 109

38 Rule 1980: 21; Winn and Merrill 1980: 113; and Bundy, in ibid, 110

39 Rule 1980: 31

40 Bundy, in Winn and Merrill 1980: 104, 280

41 Ibid, 22

42 Bundy, in ibid, 116

43 Ibid, 23; and Bundy, in ibid, 116-117

44 Bundy, in ibid, 118

45 Bundy, in ibid, 119-120, 121-122

46 Bundy, in ibid, 123

47 Bundy, in ibid, 123

48 Bundy, in ibid, 130, 141

49 Bundy, in ibid, 219

50 Ibid, 220, 232, 307

51 Bundy, in Rule 1980: 221

52 Michaud and Aynesworth 1983: 59-61

53 Bundy, in Rule 1980: 201; Kendall 1981: 14; and Bundy, in Michaud and Aynesworth 1983: 23

54 Larsen 1980: 96; in Rule 1980: 167; and Bundy, in Larsen 1980: 157

55 Bundy, in Winn and Merrill 1980: 107

56 Bundy, in Larsen 1980: 232

57 Bundy, in Michaud and Aynesworth 1983: 113, 150; and unidentified psychiatrist, in ibid, 152

58 Bundy, in ibid, 163, 180, 181

59 Bundy, in ibid, 265, 267

60 Bundy, in Winn and Merrill 1980: 321, 289

61 Ibid, 257, 104; Terry Storwick, in Michaud and Aynesworth 1983: 65; and Bundy, in Rule 1980: 27

62 Bundy, in Michaud and Aynesworth 1983: 65-7, 68

63 Bundy, in ibid, 69, 70-72

64 Bundy, in ibid, 72-73

65 Bundy, in ibid, 76, 78-79

66 Ibid, 82, 83, 84

67 Bundy, in ibid, 324

68 Bundy, in Kendall 1981: 164

69 Bundy, in Michaud and Aynesworth 1983: 133, 144

70 Bundy, in Kendall 1981: 164; Bundy, in Rule 1980: 207; Bundy, in Winn and Merrill 1980: 172

71 Peter and Favret 1975: 188

72 Bundy, in ibid, 251, 254

73 Bundy, in ibid, 318, 317, 319

74 Bundy, in ibid, 321

75 In ibid, 113, 169

76 Ibid, 107

77 Bundy, in Michaud and Aynesworth 1983: 312, 307

CHAPTER FOUR: DESALVO

1 DeSalvo, in Frank 1967: 352

2 DeSalvo, in ibid, 251

3 DeSalvo, in ibid, 313

4 DeSalvo, in ibid, 288; DeSalvo, in Rae 1967: 9; and Frank 1967: 288-289, 20

5 DeSalvo, in Frank 1967: 351-352

6 DeSalvo, in ibid, 291-293; and Frank 1967: 28

7 DeSalvo, in ibid, 293, 294, 296; and Frank 1967: 25

8 DeSalvo, in ibid, 299-300; and Sgt. James McDonald, in ibid, 39

9 DeSalvo, in ibid, 301, 43

10 DeSalvo, in ibid, 302-303

11 DeSalvo, in ibid, 304-306, 56

12 Ibid, 155, 309-310

13 DeSalvo, in ibid, 312; DeSalvo, in Rae 1967: 123; and Autopsy report, quoted in Rae 1967: 123

14 DeSalvo, in Frank 1967: 355-357, 65

15 DeSalvo, in ibid, 316-317, 83-84

16 DeSalvo, in ibid, 314-315, 85

17 DeSalvo, in ibid, 320-323; and Police Report, in ibid, 87-88

18 DeSalvo, in ibid, 335

19 DeSalvo, in ibid, 325

20 DeSalvo, in ibid, 243-244, 250-251; and quoted by Edward Kearney, in Frank 1967; 252, 253, 254

21 DeSalvo, in ibid, 265

22 Ibid, 273-274

23 DeSalvo, in ibid, 288 and 309

24 DeSalvo, in ibid, 313, 293; DeSalvo, in Rae 1967: 31; and DeSalvo, in Frank 1967: 295-296

25 DeSalvo, in ibid, 296-297, 300-301

26 DeSalvo, in ibid, 303-304, 306, 316

27 DeSalvo, in ibid, 315, 320-321, 330, 352-353

28 DeSalvo, in Brussel 1968: 193

29 DeSalvo, in Frank 1967: 275-276, 326-327; and DeSalvo, in Rae 1967: 97

30 DeSalvo, in Frank 1967: 357

31 DeSalvo, in Rae 1967: 27; and DeSalvo, in Frank 1967: 329

32 DeSalvo, in Rae 1967: 27-28

33 DeSalvo, in ibid, 27-28

34 DeSalvo, in ibid, 39-40, 29

35 DeSalvo, in ibid, 47

36 DeSalvo, in ibid, 48

37 DeSalvo, in ibid, 73-74

38 DeSalvo, in Frank 1967: 334-336

39 DeSalvo, in Rae 1967: 109-110

40 DeSalvo, in ibid, 61-62

41 DeSalvo, in ibid, 97; DeSalvo, in Frank 1967: 296-297; and DeSalvo, in Rae 1967: 108

42 DeSalvo, in Frank 1967: 323, 380

43 DeSalvo, in ibid, 323

44 DeSalvo, in Rae 1967: 82-83; and DeSalvo, in Frank 1967: 240

45 DeSalvo, in Rae 1967: 22

46 DeSalvo, in Frank 1967: 265; and DeSalvo, in Rae 1967: 85

47 DeSalvo, in ibid, 86

48 DeSalvo, in ibid, 130, 133

49 DeSalvo, in ibid, 143-144; and DeSalvo, in Frank 1967: 314, 338-339, 330

50 DeSalvo, in Rae 1967: 40-41

51 DeSalvo, in Frank 1967: 325

52 Dr. Doris Sidwell, quoted in Frank 1967: 342; and DeSalvo, in Rae 1967: 78, 84, 87

53 Dr. Philip Solomon, quoted in Frank 1967: 48; Dr. Ames

Robey, quoted in ibid, 138; and Dr. James A. Brussel, quoted in ibid, 142

54 Quoted in ibid, 165-166, 168; Dr. James A. Brussel, quoted in Rae 1967: 142; and Dr. James A. Brussel, quoted in Frank 1967: 172

55 Ibid, 244; and quoted in ibid, 245

56 Dr. Robert Mezer and Dr. Samuel Tartakoff, quoted in ibid, 371-372; and Dr. Ames Robey, quoted in ibid, 372

57 DeSalvo, in ibid, 331

58 Peter and Favret 1975: 175

59 Ibid, 175

60 DeSalvo, in Frank 1967: 364, 365

61 DeSalvo, in ibid, 366; Rae 1967: 26; Justice John MacLeod, quoted in Frank 1967: 342; and DeSalvo, in ibid, 366

62 DeSalvo, in ibid, 366-367, 321

63 DeSalvo, in Rae 1967: 9

64 DeSalvo, in Frank 1967: 367, 277

65 DeSalvo, in ibid, 331

CHAPTER FIVE: BERKOWITZ

1 Berkowitz, in Willeford 1980: 71

2 Berkowitz 1981: n.p.

3 Berkowitz 1981: n.p.; and Klausner 1981: 265-266

4 Berkowitz, in ibid, 13

5 Berkowitz, in ibid, 15-16

6 There is a discrepancy here between two accounts: Abrahamsen says there was only one knife assault, while Klausner describes two. It is not a significant matter. Berkowitz, in Abrahamsen 1983: 62; Klausner 1981: 17; and Berkowitz, in ibid, 18

7 Berkowitz, in ibid, 56-57

8 Berkowitz, in ibid, 58, 60; and Berkowitz, in Abrahamsen 1983: 63

9 Berkowitz, in Klausner 1981: 62-63; and Berkowitz, in Abrahamsen 1983: 63

10 Berkowitz, in ibid, 190; Berkowitz, in Klausner 1981: 88; Berkowitz, in Abrahamsen 1983: 190; and Klausner 1981: 89

11 Donna DeMasi, in Klausner 1981: 95-96; Berkowitz, in ibid, 98-99; Klausner 1981: 99; and Carpozi 1977: 50

12 Berkowitz, in Abrahamsen 1983: 190

13 Berkowitz, in Klausner 1981: 106-107

14 Klausner 1981: 115-116

15 Berkowitz, in Abrahamsen 1983: 190-192; Berkowitz, in Klausner 1981: 120-121; Carpozi 1977: 83; and Klausner 1981: 126-127

16 Berkowitz, in Abrahamsen 1983: 192; Klausner 1981: 134; and Carpozi 1977: 109

17 Berkowitz, in Klausner 1981: 179, 185; Judy Placido, in Klausner 1981: 185; Berkowitz, in Abrahamsen 1983: 192; and Berkowitz, in Klausner 1981: 187-188

18 Berkowitz, in Abrahamsen 1983: 194; Robert Violante, in Klausner 1981: 226; and Berkowitz, in Klausner 1981: 234

19 Detective John Falotico, in Klausner 1981: 350-351

20 Berkowitz, in Willeford 1980: 272

21 Abrahamsen 1983: 62

22 Berkowitz 1981: n.p. All quotations in this section are from his prison diary, unless otherwise noted; and Berkowitz, in Klausner 1981: 195-196

23 Berkowitz, in Abrahamsen 1983: 63

24 Abrahamsen 1983: 62; and Berkowitz, in ibid, 62

25 Berkowitz, in ibid, 63

26 Berkowitz, in ibid, 63

27 Berkowitz, in ibid, 190, 192

28 Berkowitz, in ibid, 194

29 Berkowitz, in ibid, 193-194

30 Berkowitz, in ibid, 195

31 Berkowitz 1981: n.p.

32 Abrahamsen 1983: 62

33 Klausner 1981: 162; Dr. Edwin Wind in Klausner 1981: 291; and quoted in ibid, 140

34 Police Commissioner Tim Dowd, in ibid, 163

35 Judge R. A. Brown, in ibid, 369; and Dr. Daniel W. Schwartz, in ibid, 373-374

36 Dr. David Abrahamsen, in ibid, 374

37 Klausner 1981: 374-375; and Abrahamsen, in Klausner 1981: 375

38 Abrahamsen 1983: 62

39 Ibid, 62-63

40 Ibid, 192; and Berkowitz, in ibid, 193

41 Ibid, 193, 194

42 Ibid, 194

43 Ibid, 194

44 Ibid, 194

45 Berkowitz, in ibid, 195
46 Ibid, 194
47 Berkowitz, in ibid, 195 (my italics)
48 Berkowitz, letter to Irish Gerhardt, in Carpozi 1977: 281
49 Mrs. Lillian Goldstein, in ibid, 241
50 Goldstein, in ibid, 241; and David Margolies, in ibid, 245-246
51 Gerhardt, in ibid, 257
52 Berkowitz, in Klausner 1981: 69-70
53 Berkowitz, in Carpozi 1977: 259, 268-269
54 Berkowitz, in ibid, 259; and Davi Zammit, in Carpozi 1977: 260
55 Berkowitz, in ibid, 270-271
56 Berkowitz, in ibid, 275, 278-280
57 Berkowitz, in ibid, 280-281
58 Berkowitz, in Klausner 1981: 141-142
59 Berkowitz, in Carpozi 1977: 134
60 Berkowitz, in Klausner 1981: 177-178
61 Berkowitz, in Carpozi 1977: 134
62 Abrahamsen 1983: 62; and Berkowitz, in Klausner 1981: 12
63 Berkowitz, in Abrahamsen 1983: 63; Berkowitz in Klausner 1981: 13; and Abrahamsen 1983: 192, 63
64 Berkowitz, in Klausner 1981: 141-142
65 Berkowitz, in Abrahamsen 1983: 63, 195; and Berkowitz, in Klausner 1981: 168
66 Berkowitz, in ibid, 313, 315; and Klausner 1981: 119
67 Berkowitz, in ibid, 63
68 Berkowitz, in Willeford 1980: 71
69 Berkowitz, in ibid, 68; and Berkowitz, in Klausner 1981: 41
70 Berkowitz, in ibid, 16

CHAPTER SIX: STARKWEATHER

1 Starkweather, in Reinhardt 1960: 78
2 Starkweather, in Allen 1976: 35-36, 40
3 Starkweather, in ibid, 48-49, 50
4 Starkweather, in ibid, 50-51
5 Starkweather, in ibid, 51, 55-56
6 Allen 1976: 59, 65-68
7 Ibid, 73; and Starkweather, in Allen 1976: 77-78
8 Starkweather, in ibid, 78-79; and Allen 1976: 81-82
9 Ibid, 88, 90
10 Ibid, 91-92
11 Starkweather, in Allen 1976: 93; and Allen 1976: 94, 95

12 Ibid, 95-96

13 Starkweather, in Allen 1976: 98, 99, 100

14 Starkweather, in ibid, 102-103

15 Starkweather, in ibid, 108; and Caril Fugate, in Allen 1976:
   111-112

16 Allen 1976: 113

17 Ibid, 118

18 Ibid, 120, 123

19 Joseph Sprinkle, in Allen 1976: 124; Caril Fugate, in ibid, 124;
   Allen 1976: 126; and Sheriff Earl Heflin, in Allen 1976: 127

20 Allen 1976: 135

21 Starkweather, in Reinhardt 1960: 22

22 Starkweather, in ibid, 82-83; and Beaver et al 1974: 91

23 Starkweather, in Reinhardt 1960: 52

24 Starkweather, in ibid, 27-28

25 Starkweather, in ibid, 28-29, 46

26 Starkweather, in ibid, 28

27 Starkweather, in ibid, 95-96

28 Quoted in Reinhardt 1960: 9, 10

29 Starkweather, in Reinhardt 1960: 23

30 Starkweather, in ibid, 14b [sic], 48

31 Starkweather, in ibid, 49, 54, 60, 61, 74, 75, 78

32 Starkweather, in Beaver et al 1974: 198; and Starkweather, in
   Allen 1976: 128

33 Starkweather, in Reinhardt 1960: 90

34 Reinhardt 1960: 32

35 Reinhardt 1960: 32; Starkweather, in Reinhardt 1960: 32-35

36 Starkweather, in ibid, 74-75, 78

37 Starkweather, in ibid, 19, 34

38 Starkweather, in ibid, 90, 94

39 Starkweather, in ibid, 48

40 Starkweather, in ibid, 58-59, 65

41 Starkweather, in ibid, 67, 75, 101. This passage is what Reinhardt calls a "free" or rough quotation.

42 Reinhardt 1960: 81; and Starkweather, in Reinhardt 1960:
   81-82, 77, 22-23, 65

43 Starkweather, in ibid 48-49

44 Starkweather, in ibid, 13, 54, 56

45 Starkweather, in ibid, 60, 104

46 Starkweather, in ibid, 104-105, 49-50

47 Starkweather, in ibid, 50, 51, 53

48 Starkweather, in ibid, 90, 99, 100. A "free" quotation
49 Starkweather, in ibid, 93, 90
50 Starkweather, in ibid, 32
51 Quoted in Allen 1976: 137-138
52 Allen 1976: 153; and quoted in Allen 1976: 144
53 Allen 1976: 148, 139; Dr. John O'Hearne, quoted in ibid, 148; and Reinhardt 1960: 11
54 Dr. Robert Stein, quoted in Allen 1976: 153; and quoted in Reinhardt 1960: 11
55 Dr. Nathan Greenbaum, quoted in Allen 1976: 148-149
56 Dr. John O'Hearne, quoted in ibid, 150
57 Dr. John Steinman, quoted in ibid, 151-152; and Allen 1967: 153
58 Starkweather, in Reinhardt 1960: 98, 32; and Allen 1976: 144
59 Starkweather, in Reinhardt 1960: 51
60 Reinhardt 1960: 16
61 Allen 1976: 33
62 Howard Genuchi, in Allen 1976: 82
63 Allen 1976: 86
64 Quoted in ibid, 123
65 Starkweather, in Reinhardt 1960: 50
66 Peter and Favret 1975: 175-176; and Reinhardt 1960: 3
67 Starkweather, in Reinhardt 1960: 13, 28, 19, 34, 53, 67, 74-75, 99
68 Starkweather 1959: 10
69 Starkweather 1959: 13
70 Allen 1976: 178

CHAPTER SEVEN: ESSEX

1 Essex, in Hernon 1978: 255
2 Hernon 1978: 47, 19-22
3 Ibid, 49
4 Ibid, 55-56
5 Ibid, 68
6 Ibid, 93; and anonymous policeman, in ibid, 95-96
7 Ibid, 110-111
8 Ibid, 112-114
9 Donald Roberts, in ibid, 116
10 Ibid, 117-118
11 Ibid, 123
12 Ibid, 126-129

13 Ibid, 134-138

14 Ibid, 140-154

15 Ibid, 156

16 Ibid, 161-163, 172-174

17 Essex, in Hernon 1978: 176-178, 180-182; and Councilman Peter Beer, in ibid, 184

18 Detective L. J. Delsa, in ibid, 198

19 Councilman Peter Beer in ibid, 203; and Hernon 1978: 200-203

20 Ibid, 204, 210

21 Sgt. Saacks, in ibid, 211; Alex Vega, in ibid, 212; and Officer Thomas Casey, in ibid, 213

22 Hernon 1978: 223, 226-231

23 Ibid, 232-234, 243-244

24 Ibid, 246-253

25 Rev. Mr. Chambers, in ibid, 52

26 Ibid, 50-52

27 Ibid, 52-53; Renee Greene, in ibid, 53; and Hernon 1978: 22-23

28 Essex, in ibid, 66

29 Hernon 1978: 23, 24; Lt. Robert Hatcher, in ibid, 24; and Paul Valdez, in ibid, 24-25

30 Essex, in ibid, 25

31 Hernon 1978: 25

32 Hatcher, in ibid, 38

33 Hernon 1978: 38

34 C. B. Wilson, in ibid, 39-40; and Fred Allen, in ibid, 40

35 Ibid, 18-19; and Essex, in ibid, 19

36 Essex, in ibid, 46, 52, 53

37 Mrs. Essex, in ibid, 53-54; and Rev. Mr. Chambers, in ibid, 54

38 Essex, in ibid, 63

39 Essex, in ibid, 58

40 Hatcher, in ibid, 59-60

41 Hatcher, in ibid, 60

42 Essex, in ibid, 62-63

43 Hernon 1978: 63-64; and Naval Station Commanding Officer, in ibid, 64

44 Essex, in ibid, 146

45 Tobias 1981: 81-82, 87-88; police report, in ibid, 89; and anonymous detective, in ibid, 107

46 Hernon 1978: 25-26; police report, in ibid, 26; FBI, in ibid, 26; and Hernon 1978: 26-27

47 Ibid, 36-37; and Penny Fox, in ibid, 38

48 Hernon 1978: 53-54, 64-65

49 Detective Edwin Cooper, in ibid, 71; and Hernon 1978: 71-72

50 Carlos Marighella, quoted in Hernon 1978: 73; and Detective Edwin Cooper, in ibid, 74

51 Hernon 1978: 74; and Grier and Cobbs 1968, quoted in ibid, 81

52 Hernon 1978: 87, 90-91

53 Ibid, 98-99; and Essex, in ibid, 101-102

54 Hernon 1978: 256

55 Tobias 1981: 112

56 Hernon 1978: 281

57 Louisiana Attorney-General William Guste, in Hernon 1978: 240; U.S. Attorney-General Richard Kleindienst, in Hernon 1978: 240; and Louisiana Governor Edwin Edwards, in Hernon, 239-240

58 New Orleans' Exec. Asst. to the Mayor, Robert Tucker, in Hernon 1978: 260-261; and Larry Jones, St. Bernard Neighborhood Development Center, in Hernon 1978: 277

59 Dr. William Bloom, in Hernon 1978: 279-280

60 New Orleans Police Supt. Clarence Giarrusso, in ibid, 278-279

61 Dr. William Swanson, in ibid, 280-281; and Dr. Daniel Thompson, in ibid, 216

62 Erich Fromm 1975, quoted in ibid, 101

63 Hernon 1978: 177

64 Peter and Favret 1975: Rex Williams, in Hernon 1978: 264; Mrs. Essex, in ibid, 266; and Penny Fox, in ibid, 266-267

65 Quoted in Hernon 1978: 283

CHAPTER EIGHT: TOWARD AN HISTORICAL SOCIOLOGY

1 Darnton 1984: 262

2 Joseph Kallinger, in F. R. Schreiber 1983: 410-411

3 Cusson 1983: 47; and Peter and Favret 1975: 186, 198

4 Abrams 1982; 267, 273-274 (my italics), 280, 297

5 Andreano and Siegfried 1980: 14

6 Lunde 1979: 48; Palmer 1972: 40; Wolfgang 1975: 207; and FBI 1982: 11

7 Palmer 1972: 40; cf. Williams 1984, Blau and Blau 1982, Flango and Sherbenou 1976, Gastil 1971, Loftin and Hill 1974, Messner 1982, 1983, Smith and Parker 1980, who are among the major contributors to the debate; Williams 1984: 288-289; cf. Rule 1980; Stark 1984; and Lunde 1979: 98

8 Cf. Calvert-Boyanowsky and Boyanowsky 1981; for a fascinating discussion of this, see Fox 1971. A solid if polemical critique of sociobiology can be found in Lewontin, Rose and Kamin 1984. Wilson, Edward 1980; Konner 1982; and Montague 1978

9 Abrahamsen 1973: 9-10; Megargee 1966; Lunde 1979: 93; and Gaylin 1983: 274

10 Bolitho 1926: 7, 8, 274, 294

11 Dickson 1958: 203-204

12 Lindsay 1958: 194

13 Lunde 1979: 48

14 Ibid, 49, 59, 53

15 Kramer and Weiner 1983: 73

16 Wilson (Colin) 1969: 29ff. See also Dickson 1958

17 Griart, in Wolf (Leonard) 1980: 145

18 de Rais, in ibid, 202, 205

19 de Rais, in ibid, 194

20 de Rais, in ibid, 204-205

21 Wolf (Eric) 1969: 279; and Laslett 1984: 5, 7ff

22 Ibid, 24

23 Ibid, 29

24 Darnton 1984: 109-110; Laslett 1984: 18; Wolf (Eric) 1969; 279-280; and Wolf (Eric) 1982: 360, 389-390

25 Wilson (Colin) 1969: 89-90

26 Quoted in Lucas 1974: 5-6; Logan 1928: 66ff; quoted in Miller 1978: 156; and Hamilton Fish, quoted in Angelella 1979:150

27 Bruch 1967: 697, 693-697

28 Peter Kurten, in Dickson 1958: 135, 137

29 Carl Panzram, in Gaddis and Long 1970: 11-12

30 Panzram, in ibid, 28, 31-32

31 Panzram, in ibid, 238, 165, 251-252

32 Panzram, in ibid, 213-214, 308-309

33 Panzram, in ibid, 323; quoted in ibid, 325; Panzram, in ibid, 325-326; and Gaddis and Long 1970: 326-327

34 Frantz, in Graham and Gurr (eds) 1969

35 Chalidze 1977: 107

36 Staniak, in Wilson (Colin) 1969: 250, 251

37 Staniak, in ibid, 252; Wilson (Colin) 1969: 252-253; and Staniak, in ibid, 253

38 Ibid, 254-255

39 Durkheim 1961: 919
40 Lasch 1979: 21; and Ehrenreich 1983: 51, 182
41 Durkheim 1961: 918
42 Nat Hentoff, writing in the *Manchester Guardian Weekly*,
   July 8, 1984
43 Heirens, in Freeman 1955

References

ABRAHAMSEN, DAVID
1973 *The Murdering Mind.* New York: Harper & Row
1983 "Confessions of Son of Sam." *Penthouse* 15: 58-194
ABRAMS, PHILIP
1982 *Historical Sociology.* Ithaca: Cornell Univ. Press
ALLEN, WILLIAM
1976 *Starkweather: The Story of a Mass Murderer.* Boston: Houghton Mifflin
ALTMAN, JACK and MARVIN ZIPORYN
1967 *Born to Raise Hell: The Untold Story of Richard Speck.* New York: Grove Press
AMNESTY INTERNATIONAL
1983 *Political Killings by Governments.* London: Amnesty International Publications
ANGELELLA, MICHAEL
1979 *Trail of Blood: A True Story.* New York: New American Library
ANDREANO, RALPH and JOHN J. SIEGFRIED (eds.)
1980 *The Economics of Crime.* New York: John Wiley
BANKS, HAROLD K.
1967 *The Strangler! The Story of the Terror in Boston.* New York: Avon
BARTHOLOMEW, ALLEN A., K. L. MILTE and F. GALBALLY
1975 "Sexual murder: psychopathology and psychiatric jurisprudential considerations." *Australian and New Zealand Journal of Criminology* 8: 143-152
BEAVER, NINETTE, B. K. RIPLEY and PATRICK TRESE
1974 *Caril.* New York: J. B. Lippincott
BERKOWITZ, DAVID
1981 "Prison diary." In Klausner, 1981

BLAU, JUDITH R. and PETER M. BLAU

1982 "The cost of inequality: metropolitan structure and violent crime." *American Sociological Review* 47: 114-129

BOLITHO, WILLIAM

1926 *Murder For Profit.* New York: Garden City

BRITTAIN, ROBERT P.

1970 "The sadistic murderer." *Medicine, Science and the Law* 10: 198-207

BRUCH, HILDE

1967 "Mass murder: the Wagner case." *American Journal of Psychiatry* 124: 693-698

BRUSSEL, JAMES A.

1968 *Casebook of a Crime Psychiatrist.* New York: Dell

BUCHANAN, EDNA

1979 *Carr: Five Years of Rape and Murder.* New York: E. P. Dutton

CALVERT-BOYANOWSKY, JOCELYN, EHOR O. BOY-ANOWSKY, et al.

1981 "Patterns of passion: temperature and human emotion." In D. Krebs (ed.), *Readings in Social Psychology: Contemporary Perspectives.* New York: Harper & Row

CAPOTE, TRUMAN

1965 *In Cold Blood.* New York: New American Library

CARPOZI, GEORGE JR.

1977 *Son of Sam: The .44 Caliber Killer.* New York: Manor Books

CHALIDZE, VALERY

1977 *Criminal Russia: Essays on Crime in the Soviet Union.* New York: Random House

CHENEY, MARGARET

1976 *The Co-Ed Killer.* New York: Walker

CUSSON, MAURICE

1983 *Why Delinquency?* Toronto: Univ. of Toronto Press

DAMORE, LEO

1981 *In His Garden: The Anatomy of a Murderer.* New York: Arbor House

DARNTON, ROBERT

1984 *The Great Cat Massacre: And Other Episodes in French Cultural History.* New York: Basic Books

DURKHEIM, EMILE

1961 "Anomic Suicide," In Talcott Parsons, Edward Shils, Kasper D. Naegele and Jesse R. Pitts (eds.), *Theories of*

Society: Foundations of Modern Sociological Theory. New York: Free Press

EHRENREICH, BARBARA

1983 *The Hearts of Men: American Dreams and the Flight From Commitment.* New York: Anchor

FEDERAL BUREAU OF INVESTIGATION

1982 *Crime in the United States.* Uniform Crime Reports. Washington DC: U.S. Government Printing Office

FLANGO, VICTOR E. and EDGAR L. SHERBENOU

1976 "Poverty, urbanization, and crime." *Criminology* 14: 331-346

FOUCAULT, MICHEL (ed.)

1975 *I, Pierre Rivieré, having slaughtered my mother, my sister, and my brother . . . A Case of Parricide in the 19th Century.* New York: Pantheon

FOX, RICHARD G.

1971 "The XYY offender: a modern myth?" *Journal of Criminal Law, Criminology and Police Science* 62

FRANK, GEROLD

1967 *The Boston Strangler,* New York: New American Library

FREEMAN, LUCY

1955 *"Before I Kill More . . ."* New York: Crown

FROMM, ERICH

1975 *The Anatomy of Human Destructiveness.* New York: Harper & Row

GADDIS, THOMAS E. and JAMES O. LONG

1970 *Killer: A Journal of Murder.* New York: Macmillan

GALVIN, JAMES A. V. and JOHN M. MACDONALD

1959 "Psychiatric study of a mass murderer." *American Journal of Psychiatry* 115: 1057-1061

GARELIK, GLENN and GINA MARANTO

1984 "Multiple murderers." *Discover* 5: 26-29

GASTIL, R. P.

1971 "Homicide and a regional culture of violence." *American Sociological Review* 36: 412-427

GAYLIN, WILLARD

1983 *The Killing of Bonnie Garland: A Question of Justice.* New York: Penguin

GODWIN, JOHN

1979 *Murder U.S.A.: The Ways We Kill Each Other.* New York: Ballantine

GRAHAM, H. D. and GURR, T. R. (eds.)

1969 *The History of Violence in America: Historical and Comparative Perspectives.* A Report submitted to the National Commission on the Causes and Prevention of Violence. New York: Praeger

GRIER, WILLIAM and PRICE COBBS

1968 *Black Rage.* New York: Basic Books

HANDLEMAN, DON and ELLIOTT LEYTON

1978 *Bureaucracy and World View: Studies in the Logic of Official Interpretation.* St. John's, Nfld.: Studies No. 22, Institute of Social and Economic Research, Memorial University

HAZELWOOD, ROBERT R. and JOHN E. DOUGLAS

1980 "The lust murderer." *FBI Law Enforcement Bulletin,* April

HERNON, PETER

1978 *A Terrible Thunder: The Story of the New Orleans Sniper.* New York: Doubleday

HOBSBAWM, E. J.

1969 *Bandits.* Harmondsworth: Penguin

HOWARD, CLARK

1980 *Zebra.* New York: Berkley

KAHAN, MARVIN W.

1960 "Psychological test study of a mass murderer." *Journal of Projective Techniques* 24: 147-160

KENDALL, ELIZABETH

1981 *The Phantom Prince: My Life With Ted Bundy.* Seattle: Madrona

KENNEDY, FOSTER, HARRY R. HOFFMAN and WILLIAM H. HAINES

1947 "A study of William Heirens." *American J. of Psychiatry* 104

KEYES, DANIEL

1981 *The Minds of Billy Milligan.* New York: Random House

KEYES, EDWARD

1976 *The Michigan Murders.* New York: Pocket Books

KLAUSNER, LAWRENCE D.

1981 *Son of Sam.* New York: McGraw-Hill

KRAMER, ROGER and IRA WEINER

1983 "Psychiatry on the borderline." *Psychology Today* 17: 70-73

KONNER, MELVIN

1982 *The Tangled Wing: Biological Constraints on the Human Spirit.* New York: Holt, Rinehart and Winston

LARSEN, RICHARD W.

1980 *Bundy: The Deliberate Stranger.* Englewood Cliffs: Prentice-Hall

LASCH, CHRISTOPHER

1979 *The Culture of Narcissism: American Life in an Age of Diminishing Expectations.* New York: Warner

LASLETT, PETER

1984 *The World We Have Lost: England Before the Industrial Age.* Third edition. New York: Charles Scribner's Sons

LEVINE, RICHARD

1982 *Bad Blood: A Family Murder in Marin County.* New York: Random House

LEWONTIN, R. C., STEVEN ROSE and LEON J. KAMIN

1984 *Not In Our Genes: Biology, Ideology, and Human Nature.* New York: Pantheon

LEYTON, ELLIOTT

1965 "Composite descent groups in Canada." *Man* LXV (98)

1966 "Conscious models and dispute regulation in an Ulster village." *Man (N.S.)* 1: 534-542

1970 "Spheres of inheritance in Aughnaboy." *American Anthropologist* 72: 1378-1388

1974a "Opposition and integration in Ulster." *Man (N.S.)* 9: 185-198

1974b *(ed.) The Compact: Selected Dimensions of Friendship.* St. John's, Nfld.: Papers No. 3, Institute of Social and Economic Research

1975a *The One Blood: Kinship and Class in an Irish Village.* St. John's, Nfld.: Studies No. 15, Institute of Social and Economic Research

1975b *Dying Hard: The Ravages of Industrial Carnage.* Toronto: McClelland and Stewart

1978 "The bureaucratization of anguish: the workmen's compensation board in an industrial disaster." In Don Handelman and Elliott Leyton, 1978

1979 *The Myth of Delinquency: An Anatomy of Juvenile Nihilism.* Toronto: McClelland and Stewart

1983 "A social profile of sexual mass murderers." In Thomas Fleming and L. A. Visano (eds.), *Deviant Designations: Crime, Law and Deviance in Canada.* Toronto: Butterworths

1958 **LINDSAY, PHILIP**
The Mainspring of Murder. London: John Long

LISNERS, JOHN
1983 *House of Horrors.* London: Corgi

LOFTIN, COLIN and ROBERT H. HILL
1974 "Regional subculture and homicide." *American Sociological Review* 39: 714-724

LOGAN, GUY B. H.
1928 *Masters of Crime: Studies of Multiple Murderers.* London: Stanley Paul

LUCAS, NORMAN
1974 *The Sex Killers.* London: W. H. Allen

LUNDE, DONALD T.
1979 *Murder and Madness.* New York: W. W. Norton

LUNDE, DONALD T. and JEFFERSON MORGAN
1980 *The Die Song: A Journey into the Mind of a Mass Murderer.* New York: W. W. Norton

MAILER, NORMAN
1980 *The Executioner's Song.* New York: Warner

MEGARGEE, E. I.
1966 "Undercontrolled and overcontrolled personality types in extreme and social aggression." *Psychological Monographs* 80

MESSNER, STEVEN F.
1982 "Poverty, inequality, and the urban homicide rate." *Criminology* 20: 103-114
1983 "Regional and racial effects on the urban homicide rate: the subculture of violence revisited." *American Journal of Sociology* 88: 997-1007

MICHAUD, STEPHEN C. and HUGH AYNESWORTH
1983 *The Only Living Witness.* New York: Simon and Schuster

MILLER, ORLO
1978 *Twenty Mortal Murders: Bizarre Murder Cases From Canada's Past.* Toronto: Macmillan

MONTAGU, ASHLEY (ed.)
1978 *Learning Non-aggression: The Experience of Non-Literate Societies.* Oxford: Oxford Univ. Press

OLSEN, JACK
1974 *The Man with the Candy: The Story of the Houston Mass Murders.* New York: Simon and Schuster

OLSON, CLIFFORD
1984 *Upublished letters.*
PALMER, STUART
1972 *The Violent Society.* New Haven: College & Univ. Press
PANZRAM, CARL
1970 "Journal." In Gaddis and Long, 1970
PARKIN, FRANK
1979 *Marxism and Class Theory: A Bourgeois Critique.* New York: Columbia Univ. Press
PETER, JEAN-PIERRE and JEANNE FAVRET
1975 "The Animal, The Madman, and Death." In M. Foucault, 1975
RAE, GEORGE W.
1967 *Confessions of the Boston Strangler.* New York: Pyramid
REINHARDT, JAMES M.
1960 *The Murderous Trail of Charles Starkweather.* Springfield, Ill.: C. C. Thomas
RULE, ANN
1980 *The Stranger Beside Me.* New York: New American Library
SCHREIBER, F. R.
1983 *The Shoemaker: The Anatomy of a Psychotic.* New York: Simon and Schuster
SCHWARZ, TED
1981 *The Hillside Strangler: A Murderer's Mind.* New York: Doubleday
SMITH, M. DWAYNE and ROBERT NASH PARKER
1980 "Types of homicide and variation in regional rates." *Social Forces* 59: 136-147
STACK, ANDY
1983a *Lust Killer.* New York: New American Library
1983b *The Want-Ad Killer.* New York: New American Library
1984 *The I-5 Killer.* New York: New American Library
STARKWEATHER, CHARLES
1959 "Rebellion." *Parade* 4: 10-14
TANAY, EMANUEL
1976 *The Murderers.* Indianapolis: Bobbs-Merrill
TANENBAUM, ROBERT and PHILIP ROSENBERG
1979 *Badge of the Assassin.* New York: Fawcett Crest
THOMPSON, THOMAS
1979 *Serpentine.* New York: Dell

TOBIAS, RONALD
1981   *They Shoot to Kill: A Psycho-survey of Criminal Sniping.* Boulder: Paladin

WALLERSTEIN, IMMANUEL
1974   *The Modern World System I: Capitalist Agriculture and the Origins of the European World-Economy in the Sixteenth Century.* New York: Academic Press

WEST, DONALD
1974   *Sacrifice Unto Me.* New York: Pyramid

WILLIAMS, KIRK R.
1984   "Economic sources of homicide: reestimating the effects of poverty and inequality." *American Sociological Review* 49: 283-289

WILSON, COLIN
1969   *A Casebook of Murder.* London: Leslie Frewin

WILSON, EDWARD O.
1980   *Sociobiology.* Abridged edition. Cambridge, Mass.: Harvard Univ. Press

WILSON, PETER J.
1974   *Oscar: An Inquiry into the Nature of Sanity.* New York: Random House

WILLEFORD, CHARLES
1980   *Off the Wall.* Montclair, N.J.: Pegasus Rex Press

WINN, STEVEN and DAVID MERRILL
1980   *Ted Bundy: The Killer Next Door.* New York: Bantam

WOLF, ERIC
1973   *Peasant Wars of the Twentieth Century.* New York: Harper Torchbooks
1982   *Europe and the People Without History.* Berkeley: Univ. of California Press

WOLF, LEONARD
1980   *Bluebeard: The Life and Crimes of Gilles de Rais.* New York: Potter

WOLFGANG, MARVIN E.
1975   *Patterns in Criminal Homicide.* Montclair, N.J.: Patterson Smith

Acknowledgments

I owe the reader a garland of apologies and explanations, all arising from the presumptuousness I display in writing a book about people I have never met, who live in a nation I have hardly ever visited. These deficiencies are not merely a function of the difficulty encountered by any non-police person who wishes to make contact with a large number of prison inmates. Equally important is the fact that I have reached that time of life when an anthropologist may tire of the rigors of fieldwork—of the tacky huts we perch in, the chilblains and amoebic flukes we accumulate, the unctuous smiles we sustain as we make a virtue of the necessity of getting along with our informants, and the manipulative relationships of which we are both perpetrators and victims. I have done my duty during twenty years of the non-judgmental obsequiousness we both dignify and obscure with the phrase "participant-observation." I have completed major field stints among the *nouveau riche* business people of British Columbia; among fishermen in an Irish village nestling in the shadows of the Mountains of Mourne; with dying miners and widows on the foggy south coast of Newfoundland; among the sophisticated bureaucrats of the Workmen's Compensation Board in old St. John's; and most debilitating of all, with the memorably exploitative juvenile delinquents and their families in an Atlantic community.* Thus I have truly had enough; and I see no breach of responsibility in planning a series of books that would save me from the nightmare of enforced sociability.

If the reader feels no sympathy, let me ask what category of person it could possibly be more sensible to avoid than

---

* See references.

multiple murderers? I have never knowingly met a murderer, multiple or otherwise, and I am more than content to keep things as they are. In asserting this, I go no further than did the early anthropologist Sir James Frazer, whose brilliant work, *The Golden Bough,* was one of the very first books to record the study of "primitive" peoples. When Frazer was asked by a suspicious reader if he had ever actually met a primitive, he is reported to have replied with considerable *hauteur:* "Certainly not!" A similar archness would inform my own response to such a query. Still, I had little choice, for it is only the police who have anything resembling free passage in the scattered penal institutions which house my informants. If I have never met any of the persons I study, I have corresponded at length with some of them, although many more refused to answer my letters (for they are celebrities . . . and their thoughts are much in demand), and so many, of course, are now dead. Thus, it should be emphasized that this book contains no new data of any kind: it is simply a revision of the classic texts, from which I have taken for my data the acts and words of the killers as they are recorded in such published literature, and re-interpreted them in terms of modern social analysis. The book is therefore a search for meaning in those acts and words of multiple murderers that hitherto have been dismissed as bizarre or merely "psychotic."

I am also largely a stranger to America, the nation in which the book's events occur. However, I do not feel that this lack of personal exposure damages my analysis beyond repair since in the modern world it is hardly necessary to go to America: if you merely stand still, America will come to you, via its formidable cultural apparatus. America's scholars, films, television, books, magazines, newspapers, records, and videotapes have kept me tolerably well-informed. At any rate, if Carl Sagan can talk about outer space without having been there, then I can venture to discuss the intimate lives of strangers without having met them or lived in their country. My method has been simply to depend on the vast *corpus* that is American scholarship for my understanding of the society. In order to come to "know" the multiple murderers, I have relied upon the splendid, literate, and scholarly accounts of their lives that have been published by gifted journalists and other talented writers. They have provided me with an enormous amount of material, including the diaries and confessions of the killers, as well as the writers' painstaking attempts to reconstruct the sequence of events, the prevailing mood, and the cluster of imponderables that inevitably surround both the killer and the killings. In this manner, a number of eminent authors have been transformed into my personal research assistants; and I must express my gratitude to Norman Mailer, Lawrence Klausner, Gerold Frank, Thomas Gaddis, Leonard Wolf, Richard Levine, Donald Lunde, and Truman Capote who, among many others, have labored so mightily on my behalf. They have been superb and undemanding research assistants indeed. They have interviewed the killers at great length, collected their confessions and their psychiatric interviews, and offered them to me as a gift. Criminologists customarily disregard their work, but they make a grievous error in doing so, for in recording every thought and movement of the modern multiple murderer, the writers have made possible the illumination of many dark corners of the human spirit.

This project has gone on for what seems an interminable time, and a number of good souls have participated in it as my actual assistants. Mr. David Bartlett acted as my official university Research Assistant, thanks to a generous grant from Memorial University, and he did yeoman work on my behalf in hunting sources and negotiating with libraries. He also suggested the title. Ms. Jeannie Kinsella Devereaux acted as my honorary assistant, rooting through magazines and newspapers for long-lost journalistic accounts. A tenured professor should not admit that he knows little of libraries, but I have spent my professional life interviewing the living, not squatting in library carrels interviewing the dead. That era ended with this book, and I am especially grateful to librarians Bernadine Conran, Ronald Crawley, and Joy Tillotson for introducing me to the intricacies of the world's library system. It was also necessary for me to establish relationships with international second-hand book dealers who could provide me with the bloodthirsty titles I sought: Oxford's Blackwell's were, as always, especially helpful, as was New York's Howard Frisch. Finally, I must thank the platoon of friends and relatives who functioned as my honorary clipping service: my mother, Mrs. Lilyan Levson in Los Angeles, my brother, Dr. Bryan Leyton in Seattle, Dr. Richard Nelson in Alaska, Professor Volker Meja in Germany, and Dr. Thomas Nemec in Newfoundland all kept me up to my ears in fresh magazine and newspaper material.

Many of my professional colleagues took me to be quite mad when I set my hand to this task. Still, I must record my debt to those colleagues at the university whose conversations over the past twenty years have immeasurably enriched my understanding of *Homo sapiens:* Douglas Hay, Juan Corradi, Ronald Schwartz, Volker Meja, Victor Zaslavsky, Rex Clark, Judith Adler, Frederick Johnstone, George Story, and the late David Alexander have all been especially provocative.

It is not customary for anthropologists to deal with the police unless, as the British say, they are assisting the police with their inquiries; but my subject has demanded that my contacts with them be frequent. Fortunately, the major police forces around this continent were extraordinarily helpful, and I must acknowledge my debt to a number of individuals for their helpful suggestions and kind encouragement—especially Supt. George Powell, Chief Supt. Dale Henry, Sgt. Robert Lohnes, and Insp. Jack Lavers of the Royal Canadian Mounted Police; Dr. Donald Loree of the Canadian Police College in Ottawa; Special Agents Robert Ressler and John Douglas of the Federal Bureau of Investigation's Academy in Quantico, Virginia; Chief Donald Randell of the Royal Newfoundland Constabulary; Sgt. Gerald McQueen of New York's Homicide Task Force; and Robert Keppel, Chief Criminal Investigator for the Attorney-General's office in the state of Washington.

Writing this book has been a deeply disturbing experience, not just because I was forced to witness such terrible suffering, but also because I was able to glimpse just how powerless police can be in their attempts to find these new murderers in the anonymity of the modern world. During the course of this research, I was lucky enough to stumble upon sets of shared social characteristics of the killers, and find them sufficiently consistent to begin the construction of social profiles, which some police are beginning to see as useful supplements to their conventional investigative techniques. Now when the telephone rings at home, it is less likely to be a dean wondering about some inexpressibly tedious administrative matter, than a police officer from somewhere around the world inquiring if I might run off a social profile of his own troublesome case. Such activities lend a delicious touch of excitement to the dullness of middle age, doubly so since I do not have the moral reservations—which plague so many social scientists—about "helping the power structure," even when it is to stop the massacre of innocents.

I am also indebted, as always, to Bonnie Leyton, my wife and friend for a third of a century; to Professor George Story and the late Professor David Alexander, who always reminded me of scholarly duties when my commitment flagged; to Memorial University and the Social Sciences and Humanities Research Council of Canada for providing me with the wherewithal to purchase eighteen months of quiet in my study; to Ms. Ann Rule, Dr. Willard Gaylin, Dr. Donald Lunde, and Dr. David Abrahamsen, whose path I followed with their encouragement and forebearance; to Professors Gianfranco Poggi, James Stoltzman, and Gordon Inglis, and to Mr. William O'Grady, for helpful criticism and suggestions; and to my Canadian publishers, McClelland and Stewart, especially Marta Kurc and Jan Walter, whose warm ministrations kept this volume alive, and Patrick Crean, whose rigorous editing enriches any manuscript he examines.

I have made something of the fact that I am an anthropologist and that this book is very much a piece of anthropology, or historical sociology if you prefer. Yet the book is not written in a style that will be familiar to many social scientists. I make no apology for this, for if I admire the insights of the social sciences I am able to keep my passion for their style of exposition well under control. In this regard, I merely try to emulate—although I abandon all hope of equaling—the literacy and grace of sociologically inclined historians such as Robert Darnton or Douglas Hay. A union between historians, novelists, historical sociologists, and anthropologists is long overdue; for it is only with the special gifts of all of them that we can hope to join George Eliot's scientists in piercing "the obscurity of those minute processes which prepare human misery and joy, those invisible thoroughfares which are the first lurking places of anguish, mania and crime, that delicate poise and transition which determine the growth of happy or unhappy consciousness." Although I remain scrupulously wedded to empirical fact throughout this book, treating published material as my field notes, I feel free to take my intellectual pleasures where and when I find them—necessarily so, since this is as much an exercise in historical reconstruction as it is anything else.

Finally, I must apologize to the reader for forcing him or her to witness so much human suffering and degradation. We can only bear it if we remind ourselves that the eradication of a disease requires the intensive study of all of the disorder's pus and blood and deformed tissue. So far, the only reliable cure we have discovered is *madame guillotine.* Regrettably, while her use may provide us with some arcane satisfaction, she can do little on her own to staunch the outbreak of this most modern and virulent of social epidemics.

ELLIOTT LEYTON

Torbay, Newfoundland
Lancer, Saskatchewan
September, 1984

About the Author

Dr. Elliott Leyton was born in Leader, Saskatchewan, in 1939, the son of a country doctor. He has taught at the Queen's University of Belfast, University of Toronto and at Memorial University of Newfoundland.

In 1982, Dr. Leyton was elected president of the Canadian Sociology and Anthropology Association. His next book will focus on the mass murderer of "intimates," that is, the phenomenon of middle-class offspring who annihilate their families. His previous books include *Dying Hard: The Ravages of Industrial Carnage* and *The Myth of Delinquency: An Anatomy of Juvenile Nihilism*.